THE HAMMER STORY

MARCUS HEARN & ALAN BARNES

TITAN BOOKS

THE HAMMER STORY

HARDCOVER: ISBN 1 85286 790 6
SOFTCOVER: ISBN 1 85286 876 7

Published by
Titan Books
42-44 Dolben Street
London SE1 0UP

First hardcover edition May 1997
First softcover edition October 1997
10 9 8 7 6 5 4 3 2 1

Copyright © Hammer Film Productions 1997.
Licensed by MTC (UK) Ltd.

Design by Chris Teather.

British Library Cataloguing-in-Publication Data. A
catalogue record for this book is available from
the British Library.

Printed in Italy by Conti Tipocolor.

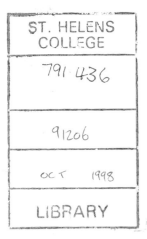
Page 2: Dracula Has Risen From the Grave.
Page 3: The clasp worn by "The most evil man of all time" in Taste the Blood of Dracula.
Page 5 (top): The Satanic Rites of Dracula.
Page 5 (centre): Lust for a Vampire.
Page 5 (bottom): Frankenstein and the Monster From Hell.
Page 6: The Devil Rides Out.

ACKNOWLEDGEMENTS

This book was primarily researched from the files
held by Hammer Film Productions Limited. We are
grateful to Hammer for the opportunity to access
paperwork dating back over sixty years, and further indebted to the following...

Charlie Baker, James Bernard, Tom Chantrell, John
Herron, John Jay, Nigel Kneale, Christopher Lee,
Ingrid Pitt, Michael Ripper, Jimmy Sangster, Ian
Scoones, Roy Skeggs, Gil Taylor, Christopher
Wicking and Aida Young, who gave their time.

Emma Nickolds and Jane Herd, who made light
of our work at Hammer, and David Hanks, who
filled the gaps in our knowledge with crucial
information.

Tony Earnshaw, Tim Greaves, Chris Howarth, Alan
Jeffries, Adam Jezard, Christopher Koetting, Gloria
Lillibridge, Steve Lyons, Denis Meikle, Mark A.
Miller, Eddie Murphy, Joe Nazzaro, Andrew Pixley
and Jonathan Rigby, who provided additional
information.

The British Film Institute, The British Library,
Richard Clarke, John Jay, Stephen Jones, Richard
Klemensen, Denis Meikle, Gary Parfitt, Jens
Reinheimer, Adrian Rigelsford, Adrian Salmon, Ian
Scoones, Roy Skeggs, Jonathan Sothcott, Gary
Wilson and Aida Young, who kindly allowed the
use of items from their collections.

Adrienne Collins and Jonathan Marks, who initiated it all, and Peri Godbold, Paul Neary and Gary
Russell, who played such important roles when it
all began.

Our editor, David Barraclough, designer, Chris
Teather, and Gillian Christie, Vanessa Coleman,
Darryl Curtis, John Freeman, Simon Furman, Bob
Kelly, Adam Newell and Katy Wild, whose support
at Titan was much appreciated.

Finally, our thanks to Hammer's legal and business
affairs director Graham Skeggs, who always found
time to help. His generosity and enthusiasm made
this book possible.

Three books proved indispensable during our
research: *Hammer Films — An Exhaustive
Filmography*, by Tom Johnson and Deborah Del
Vecchio, *The Horror People* by John Brosnan, and
A History of Horrors by Denis Meikle. Our thanks
to Denis for his advice and insight throughout.

Many magazines were used as reference, but the
following were particularly useful:
*Cinefantastique, Daily Cinema, Dark Terrors,
Fangoria, Kinematograph Weekly, Little Shoppe
of Horrors, Time Screen* and *Today's Cinema*.

Our thanks to their editors and writers.

The stills in this book were taken by Albert Clarke,
Tom Edwards, Keith Hamshere, Ray Hearne,
George Higgins, John Jay, Arthur Lee, Pierre Luigi,
Joe Pearce, Robert Penn, Ronnie Pilgrim, Curtis
Reeks, James Swarbrick and George Whitear.

Donald Fearney and Max Décharné helped source
many of the illustrations in this book, and our
special thanks goes to them.

Samantha and Jane, who both showed patience
and understanding beyond the call of duty, can
now have us back. Thanks for putting up with it
for so long.

For my parents, who let me stay up late — MH

For Mum, and thanks for all the buns — AB

AUTHORS' NOTE
Film titles — the titles in this book reflect those
presented on screen in British prints.
Principal photography dates — these
exclude filming conducted before or after major
studio/location work, and pre/post production
work conducted outside major studio/location
photography. Where such extra work is considered
relevant, it has been considered within the text.
Release dates — dates given are those for first
public exhibition in the UK.
Duration — film duration figures are approximate (to the minute) cinema running times of UK
exhibited prints.
Certification — the films in this book are given
the original certification ascribed by the British
Board of Film Censors (now the British Board of
Film Classification) prior to UK exhibition. They
are:

U — Passed for general exhibition.
A — Passed for general exhibition but par-
ents/guardians are advised that the film contains material they might prefer children under
the age of fourteen years not to see.
AA — Passed as suitable only for exhibition to
persons of fourteen years and over. This certificate was introduced on 1 July 1970.
X — Passed as suitable only for exhibition to
persons of sixteen years and over.
This age restriction was raised to persons of
eighteen years and over on 1 July 1970.

C O N T E N T S

The word 'hammer' suggests a blow. And Hammer Film Productions undoubtedly struck a blow for the British film industry — a blow that reverberated throughout the world and is still echoing today. They are probably the most famous independent British production company that ever existed, and undoubtedly the most successful. Hammer continue to inspire many of the genre films made today, and many of the cinema's foremost directors.

Chairman James Carreras and his colleagues knew what the public wanted, and Hammer provided audiences with great entertainment. It's as simple as that. In Jimmy, we had one of the finest showmen and entrepreneurs of any industry. How badly we need someone like him today.

Speaking purely in economic terms, the returns from Hammer's films brought a vast amount of money into the country. All these films were essentially British productions, made at British studios with British technicians and largely British casts.

When everything was starting to fall apart, Hammer kept part of our film industry going. In the United States, Hammer were probably the only British production company with an automatic guarantee of distribution from every major studio. I've never forgotten visiting the president of Universal Films in New York, following their distribution of *Dracula* in 1958. "Gentlemen," he told us, "this film of yours has saved Universal from bankruptcy."

The positive reaction to our films was not always reflected in the newspapers of the day, many of whom seemed appalled by Hammer's earliest colour productions. History has proved such critics wrong — those films were always financially successful, today they are artistically acclaimed as well. Now, we're respectable.

The key to this success was collaboration: everyone who worked at Bray Studios had tremendous dedication and belief, and I believe it shows on screen. Hammer inspired some superb work from a talented group of technicians and actors. Even our canteen, run by Mrs Thompson, was the best in the country! I know this has become a cliché, but, for a while, we really were a family.

Forty years on from *The Curse of Frankenstein*, Hammer films are still being shown in cinemas, on television and on video all over the world. People of all generations are familiar with the name. What other film company has had a comparable impact?

I will always be grateful to Hammer for launching my international career as an actor. Like millions of others, I would welcome the day when the company resumes production.

I wish them all the luck in the world. They deserve it.

Christopher Lee

Christopher Lee
London, February 1997

THE EXCLUSIVE YEARS
1934–1954

PAUL ROBESON
in the British Lion-Hammer Production: "The Song of Freedom"

"Their story is a romance, if ever there was one," claimed trade paper *The Daily Film Renter* in December 1954. Hammer's affair with the cinema had begun twenty years earlier — a further twenty years of even greater success were still to come. To chronicle the romance of Hammer Film Productions is to unfold a drama played out against such diverse backdrops as the music halls of Hammersmith, the smoke-filled clubs of Soho and the executive offices of New York. Yet this heady tale of unparalleled commercial success in British film production is only part of an epic story; a greater romance was played out on screen.

The origins of Hammer are shrouded in the forgotten world of pre-war 'quota quickie' film-making and music hall variety. The inspiration came from William Hinds (1887-1957), an entrepreneur born into the family that established Britain's largest family jewellers in 1856. According to his son Anthony, Hinds was "a successful businessman and a failed comedian." He nevertheless enjoyed a semi-professional career as one half of vaudeville double-act 'Hammer and Smith', so named because he and his partner lived in Hammersmith. Hinds would be more commonly known by his stage name 'Will Hammer' for the rest of his life. Will Hammer's other concerns included a retail interest selling bicycles, the management of numerous theatres and music halls, music publishing, and chairmanship of the Goldhawk Building Society.

As a natural extension of his burgeoning show-business ventures, Hammer diversified into film-making with the formation of Hammer Productions

Limited in November 1934. Under his chairmanship, George A. Gillings, David Gillings (stage name George Mozart), Henry Fraser Passmore and James Elder Wills took offices in Imperial House, Regent Street. The first Hammer film, *The Public Life of Henry the Ninth*, went into production in December that year. A modest sixty minute comedy starring vaudeville comedian Leonard Henry, its title parodied Alexander Korda's *The Private Life of Henry VIII*.

"The film was shot in two weeks," remembers sound camera assistant John Mitchell, "with the Hammer logo filmed during one lunch hour using Bombardier Billy Wells, a famous heavyweight boxer who was later to be the first Rank 'man with a gong'. Editing was completed during the third week, as was the music scoring, and we dubbed the film on the following Saturday and Sunday. My salary was £2 per week — no overtime payment, just one shilling and threepence for supper!" An advertisement in the 13 January 1935 edition of trade paper *Kinematograph Weekly* proclaimed the arrival of Hammer productions with a photograph of Billy Wells standing before an anvil, hammer in hand.

By the time *The Public Life of Henry the Ninth* was released on 17 June 1935, Will Hammer was in formal partnership with entrepreneurial Spanish immigrant Enrique Carreras (1880-1950). Carreras had arrived in Britain with his wife Dolores and brother Alphonse in 1907. Enrique dabbled in a number of generally unsuccessful concerns until, together with

Raymond Lovell

WHO KILLED VAN LOON —
KAY BANNERMAN
ROBERT WYNDHAM
IT'S BRITISH - IT'S "EXCLUSIVE"

Alphonse, he acquired a Hammersmith music hall in 1913. In a pioneering move, the building was converted to accommodate two screens, each showing a different programme. From this foundation, Enrique Carreras established the 'Blue Halls', a nation-wide chain of seven cinemas capitalising on the growing appeal of motion pictures after the First World War.

In the early thirties a disastrous involvement with a new brand of toothpaste left Carreras bankrupt, but he rebounded into the business he knew better than any other. After a fateful meeting with Will Hammer, the two men decided to launch a new distribution business. Exclusive Films Limited was incorporated on 10 May 1935. Companies House documentation of 25 April lists the prospective co-directors as William

Hinds (occupation: Theatre Proprietor) and Enrique Carreras (occupation: Film Renter). From a single office in National House, Wardour Street, Carreras and Hammer, together with Jack Spratling, James Dawson and secretary Mrs Burnham, co-ordinated the new company. Their first distribution programme consisted of the two-reelers *Snowhounds* and *Spilt Salt*. Carreras and Hammer went on to purchase reissue rights to films from British Lion and Korda's London Films.

Will Hammer would continue to head a bewildering array of companies (in 1935, he produced and starred in *Polly's Two Fathers*, a twenty-six minute short produced under the aegis of 'WH Films', and in 1936 he directed *Musical Merrytone No.1* under the same banner), but saved his most lavish project for Hammer Productions.

Hammer's first full-length film featured Bela Lugosi, the star of Universal's *Dracula*, in *The Mystery of the Mary Celeste*. Filmed in summer 1935, the film was the company's most ambitious of the decade. It was followed into production by *The Song of Freedom*, a musical starring Paul Robeson as a dock worker who becomes an opera singer and travels to his ancestral home in Africa. Will Hammer made a brief cameo appearance. Two more films followed in 1936 — a fifty-six minute drama called *The Bank Messenger Mystery*, directed by Will Hammer, and the seventy minute *Sporting Love*, directed by J. Elder Wills — before Hammer's production programme ground to a halt. On 20 July 1937 Exclusive purchased the leasehold on 113/115/117 Wardour Street (the building still bears the title 'Hammer House'), while Hammer Productions was forgotten.

In 1938, Enrique's son James (1909-1990) joined Exclusive, having previously served as the assistant manager of the original Blue Hall in Hammersmith, a manager for the Gaumont-British circuit and a car salesman. His initial term of employment with Exclusive was interrupted by a tour of duty in the Second World War, where he swiftly rose to the rank of Lieutenant-Colonel and was awarded the MBE in 1944. Will Hammer's son, Anthony Hinds (born 1922), briefly served Exclusive as a booking clerk in 1939 before he too joined up.

After the war, James Carreras and Anthony Hinds returned to Wardour Street and the family business. In 1945, James' son, Michael Carreras (1927-1994), became Director of Publicity. "[It] sounded grand," Michael remembered, "but simply meant that I was merely in charge of mailing out stills and posters every week to the cinemas that were showing their films!" Another important post-war recruit was Anthony 'Brian' Lawrence, who joined Exclusive from the Anglo-American Film Corporation. Lawrence was initially employed as a junior salesman/assistant to Jack Spratling (at that time Exclusive's circuit manager), but would graduate to a position of greater influence as the company grew.

The Cinematograph Film Act of 1927 stipulated that a percentage of films screened in the United Kingdom must be of British origin, as a way to safeguard the industry against the overwhelming demand for more popular American product. But even the resulting 'quota quickies' (hastily produced films that were essentially an abuse of that safeguard) could not meet demand. Exclusive began producing films themselves from 1946 onwards. Notable amongst a slew of short subjects were two films released in 1948: *Dick Barton Special Agent*, starring Don Stannard as the daring radio hero, and *Who Killed Van Loon?*, a forty-eight minute thriller featuring Anthony Hinds' first credit as producer.

Licensing the Dick Barton character from the BBC proved particularly successful, and, after some encouragement from Jack Goodlatte of the Associated British Cinemas chain, Exclusive soon decided to pursue this direction through a dedicated production division. Hammer Film Productions Limited — under the directorship of Enrique Carreras (Film Renter), James Carreras (Film Renter), Anthony Hinds (Film Producer) and William Hinds (Theatre Proprietor) —

Previous page (above left): Bela Lugosi as the one-armed Anton Lorenzen, the man behind The Mystery of the Mary Celeste.
Previous page (above right): Acclaimed vocalist Paul Robeson as John Zinga, a London dockworker turned tribal king in The Song of Freedom.
Previous page (below left): Bombardier Billy Wells strikes the anvil in the sequence preceding the films of Hammer Productions Limited.
Previous page (below right): A handbill promoting Who Killed Van Loon?, *the first film from producer Anthony Hinds.*
Below: James Carreras, Hy Hazell, Michael Carreras and Anthony Hinds.
Bottom: Oakley Court, Exclusive/Hammer's second 'house studio', was built in 1859. The building was used as a location in many Hammer films produced during the sixties.

was incorporated on 18 January 1949. The driving force behind the 'new' Hammer was the mercurial managing director James Carreras. "Entrepreneurs are born, they're not made, and Jimmy was an entrepreneur," says Aida Young, an assistant director for Exclusive/Hammer in the fifties. "He was extremely smooth and very handsome. I don't think I can remember a time when he wasn't charming. When he talked to you, you believed him. Tony Hinds was much younger than Jimmy, much quieter, and very much the creative half of the partnership."

Francis Searle, who was one of Exclusive's most prolific directors, working solidly for the company between 1949 and 1952, remembers: "He was a great salesman, was Jim, bit of a villain but I loved him. He very seldom came to the studio — he didn't want to get involved as long as the stuff on the screen looked all right. Tony Hinds didn't interfere either. He was very sympathetic — a clever bloke and very easy to work with. He was particularly good at vetting scripts and so on." Carreras exhibited a remarkable talent for getting his own way, preferring to strike a deal over a brandy and a cigar than through protracted negotiation in the boardroom. He would soon put that talent to profitable use.

The first 'official' picture from Hammer Film Productions was *Dr Morelle — The Case of the Missing Heiress*, released by Exclusive on 27 June 1949. This seventy-four minute film, based on a character devised by Ernest Dudley for the BBC radio programme *Monday Night at Eight*, was the first to be wholly financed by the Labour government's National Film Finance Company. "Jimmy Carreras has set out to make a comedy thriller which can play second feature on the circuit houses and top the bill in industrial halls," reported one trade paper. "He has spent only £14,169.19s 2½d, thanks to careful planning, good teamwork and not paying his executives fancy salaries. Instead, they receive a nominal fee plus a percentage of the profits, while the rank and file get a bonus if the schedule is not exceeded."

The film saw Dr Morelle (Valentine Dyall) solve the mysterious disappearance of a young heiress in a gloomy country house. The location was Dial Close, a private residence in Cookham Dean, Maidenhead, that Hammer used as the first of its 'house studios'.

Anthony Hinds had proposed that, instead of hiring dedicated studio facilities, Exclusive/Hammer should rent large private houses and shoot in the rooms and surrounding locations. Unfortunately, the Cookham Dean locals felt that having second feature film production on their doorstep would lower the tone of the neighbourhood, and planning permission was refused. Anthony Hinds relocated his crew to Oakley Court, a bat-infested Gothic pile in Bray, Windsor. Production recommenced with another BBC radio adaptation, *The Man in Black*, in August 1949. *The Cinema* trade paper sent their reporter, 'Willy', to cover the production. "The house, I was surprised to discover, is still fully furnished," he reported in September. "The owner, too, is still in residence, but keeps himself entirely to his own wing, leaving Exclusive to do as they will in the major part of the building."

The schedule for 1950 featured a taste of things to come with the release of the Jack the Ripper melodrama *Room to Let* and the establishment of another 'house studio' at a former country club in Gilston Park, Harlow, Essex. "[Oakley Court] is ideal for whodunnits," James Carreras told *Kinematograph Weekly*, "but the new place will do for less sombre stories as well."

Exclusive/Hammer would not settle at a house studio until they occupied Down Place, a large private house near Oakley Court. Bray Studios, as the house was later dubbed, would become the company's production base for sixteen years. *Cloudburst*, the first feature produced at the studio, started shooting on 8 January 1957. Director Francis Searle has fond memories of Down Place: "When we first went there it was a store for army kit. The owner was George Davis, a very big name in Aspro and very fond of his ouzo. God, we never left the damned place sober! As a matter of fact, I lived there for two years, which was very convenient. I'd get out of bed, go on the set, give the set-up and then go back for breakfast!"

Most of Hammer Film Productions' earliest features were directed by either Searle or Godfrey Grayson. The subjects were often derived from BBC radio serials, and the stars drawn from a reliable stable of actors: Valentine Dyall, Hy Hazell, Sidney James, Hugh Latimer, Michael Medwin and Don Stannard all became familiar faces.

Chairman Will Hammer's negligible interest in film production left James Carreras free to steer the company in a new direction. While Anthony Hinds supervised the cheap and cheerful second features, Carreras turned his thoughts to enticing American co-production money in Hammer's direction. Short-lived relationships had already been forged with Hollywood financiers Alexander Paal (for *Cloudburst*) and Sol Lesser (for *Whispering Smith Hits London*) before Carreras struck a more rewarding deal with Robert Lippert. Exclusive had been distributing Lippert-produced pictures in Britain since 1948, but James Carreras' new understanding with Lippert and his partner Bill Pizor provided scripts and minor American stars for Exclusive's own films.

"Because of the quota law, a British second feature had to play with the American main feature," explained Michael Carreras. "That meant the American studios had to give away a portion of the box office receipts to the second feature. The studios astutely decided to make these second features themselves, to retain the receipts. But to satisfy the quota law, the films had to actually be made by a British associate. Twentieth Century-Fox released their films on the same circuits which showed the Exclusive/Hammer movies, so they chose us as their British associate. Robert Lippert owned cinemas, and had a small production and distribution company in Hollywood. He was also a close friend of the then-head of Fox, Spyros Skouras. Fox needed a shadow company to produce pictures for them, so Skouras used Lippert as his front."

Anthony Hinds recruited director Terence Fisher

to handle the first film in the Lippert alliance. *The Last Page* was produced in 1951 from a script by Frederick Knott, and starred George Brent. The Lippert/ Exclusive/Hammer partnership continued with such films as *Wings of Danger, Stolen Face, Face the Music* and *Murder by Proxy*, all of which were directed by Fisher. Lippert exported Hollywood stars such as Zachary Scott, Paul Henreid, Alex Nicol and Dane Clark for a string of mundane thrillers. In amongst a steady stream of films concerning American detectives, reporters or gangsters getting into scrapes in London, a handful of pictures suggested that Hammer were prepared to take some risks. Two films directed by Terence Fisher and produced by Michael Carreras in 1952 were especially brave. *Four Sided Triangle*, starring Barbara Payton, Stephen Murray and John Van Eyssen, was a science fiction tale of two scientists who devise a machine that duplicates a human being. *Spaceways*, a BBC radio adaptation that starred Howard Duff and Eva Bartok, was a murder mystery set in a space research facility. While neither can lay claim to being obvious precursors to *The Quatermass Xperiment* or *The Curse of Frankenstein* (Hammer's breakthrough productions), they were early steps towards a more fruitful direction.

By the mid-fifties, most Hammer films were line produced by either Anthony Hinds or Michael Carreras, both of whom oversaw separate units. When Anthony Hinds opted to remain a hands-on producer at Bray, Michael Carreras returned to Wardour Street to become Hammer's executive producer, overseeing all production.

By tracing its history back to the inception of Hammer Productions, Exclusive was able to celebrate its twentieth anniversary in November 1954. "To maintain a company's prosperity over twenty turbulent years calls for effort, imagination, foresight and daring," claimed trade paper *Today's Cinema*. "Exclusive Films have now been a familiar name in the world of entertainment for twenty years, both to the trade

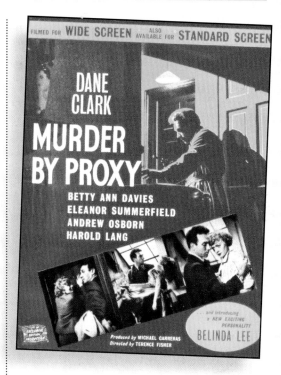

and the great cinema-going public. They have earned for themselves a respected place in this country's fifth largest industry." A celebratory cocktail party was followed by a Savoy luncheon on 2 December, and a ball at the Criterion Hotel the following day. Behind the hyperbole, however, the public's "romance" with Exclusive was waning. While the company continued to distribute American films, diminishing interest from Robert Lippert was adding to the threats that colour, Cinemascope and falling attendance posed to James Carreras' production schedule. Exclusive was facing a crisis: in November, Carreras had openly invited independent producers to fill the vacant Bray Studios. During 1955, only one Exclusive/Hammer feature film (*Women Without Men*) was produced at the facility. For the anniversary celebrations though, Carreras and his fellow executives maintained a contented façade, unaware that the means of their salvation had already been delivered to the Bray cutting rooms.

A film adaptation of a television serial was about to set the company on a new course, and relegate the first twenty years of its history to mere prologue.

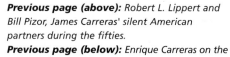

FILMED FOR WIDE SCREEN ALSO AVAILABLE FOR STANDARD SCREEN

DANE CLARK

MURDER BY PROXY

BETTY ANN DAVIES
ELEANOR SUMMERFIELD
ANDREW OSBORN
HAROLD LANG

and introducing a NEW EXCITING PERSONALITY BELINDA LEE

Produced by MICHAEL CARRERAS
Directed by TERENCE FISHER

Previous page (above): Robert L. Lippert and Bill Pizor, James Carreras' silent American partners during the fifties.

Previous page (below): Enrique Carreras on the set of Room to Let at Oakley Court in 1949. Behind him are Vera St John Carreras (wife of James), Constance Smith (who appeared in the film) and Mrs Violet Goodlatte (wife of Jack). Enrique died on 15 October 1950.

Above and top: Murder By Proxy, produced in 1953, was amongst the earliest Exclusive/Hammer films issued in the new 'wide screen' ratio. Face the Music *was the first.*

Left: Michael Carreras, James Carreras, Will Hammer, Anthony Hinds and Brian Lawrence chair an Exclusive sales conference in 1952.

By 1955, the elements that would facilitate Hammer's reinvention were all in place. Managing director James Carreras had become a chief barker for the Variety Club the year before, and would exploit the opportunities the charity offered to make new business contacts and further his influence. Michael Carreras and Tony Hinds, as executive producer and producer respectively, oversaw an efficient production infrastructure at Bray Studios. Brian Lawrence, meanwhile, had become an expert in selling the films his colleagues produced. Together, they made a formidable combination.

"The philosophy was simple," Lawrence asserts, "films cost what James Carreras was able to raise from third parties. The range of Hammer's contacts was anyone interested in providing finance." Up until 1954, James Carreras had come to rely on Robert Lippert's co-finance for Hammer's ongoing production. When that finance began to dry up, Hammer's future was placed in jeopardy. One of the last Lippert co-productions was an adaptation of the BBC serial *The Quatermass Experiment*. "The actual creation process in Hammer was nearly always borrowing something from somewhere else," remembered Michael Carreras. "My father always started a film with a poster — and with a poster, drawing, piece of artwork, the way you did it was that if there was already a public image in some form then you weren't showing a potential backer something they've never seen. The name — the idea — already meant something. He much preferred to sell something that was already familiar..."

The fact that Hammer's *The Quatermass Xperi-*

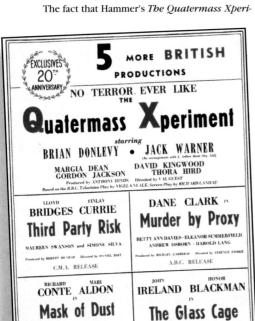

ment (as the original serial was retitled) was a familiar subject was perhaps incidental to the appeal of its lurid content. Here was a British horror film, utterly disassociated in style and intent from the relatively staid television presentation that made the title famous. *The Quatermass Xperiment* was also a huge progression from the undemanding thrillers that

Hammer had been producing since the war. While it would probably be inaccurate to claim that *Quatermass* alone saw Hammer through the difficulties of the mid-fifties, James Carreras' willingness to exploit the 'vulgar' trend of film-making it catalysed was undoubtedly crucial. The launch of commercial television on 22 September 1955 dealt the already struggling British film industry a fresh blow. "I think we were frightened of television," Anthony Hinds claimed, in an interview with Tony Earnshaw. "It was a terrible thing to us. If you owned a restaurant and suddenly the government said it was going to go round door-to-door giving free food away...That's how we felt about television." Propositions such as *Captain Morgan Buccaneer*, *The Cavalier* and *The Deerslayer* were all discarded in Hammer's efforts to win audiences back with X-rated material they wouldn't find on either television channel.

The Quatermass Xperiment gave Hammer a much-needed commercial hit, but was also responsible for bringing the company to the attention of major distributors. In 1956, *Quatermass 2* and *The Steel Bayonet* were co-financed by United Artists, while *The Curse of Frankenstein*, a colour horror film that marked the next major progression for the company, was the first Hammer production co-financed by Eliot Hyman, the most significant of Hammer's silent partners. James Carreras had met Hyman through the Variety Club; Hyman was wealthier, and much better connected, than Robert Lippert, and his influence would underpin much of Hammer's output until the end of the sixties. Hyman brought Hammer the initial script, and a large slice of the budget, for *The Curse of Frankenstein*. Additional funding was found through James Carreras' old friend Jack Goodlatte, the managing director of Associated British Cinemas. Like its supplying distributor Warner Pathé, ABC was a division of the powerful Associated British Picture Corporation. ABPC owned Elstree Studios, and its influence permeated British film production. "Goodlatte's ideas were almost edicts," claimed Michael Carreras.

Before *The Curse of Frankenstein* was completed, Michael accompanied his father and Anthony Hinds to the United States in search of a distributor. "The remarkable thing about American movie moguls is that, no matter how much they may want your picture, they never tell you so. They left us in a cheap hotel, and we thought our phone had been disconnected. We became very despondent, and then suddenly everybody began to make offers. We were asked to go and see the big noises at Warner Bros, and that was a great moment. They bought *Frankenstein* and gave us a wonderful deal. We made more money than we had ever *seen* before." The film was released in May 1957 to phenomenal business. When Will Hammer died on 1 June 1957, he left behind a company with an international audience and a growing reputation with major distributors.

The strictly verbal agreement between Hammer chairman James Carreras and Eliot Hyman continued to bring in supplementary finance for Hammer's budgets (in return for Hyman's share of profits and certain distribution rights) and the remaining cash could now be found with relative ease. For the first time, American distributors welcomed James Carreras with open arms, and he was in a position to pick his partners from the most powerful studios in the world. The follow-up to *The Curse of Frankenstein*, a sequel originally titled *The Blood of Frankenstein*, was sold to the Columbia Pictures International Corporation as part of a package with the thriller *The Snorkel* and

Japanese POW drama *The Camp on Blood Island*. The deal, announced by Columbia's British managing director Mike Frankovich on 6 September 1957, launched Hammer's most important co-production relationship to date. "[This] is the way we anticipate working in the future," Carreras told *Today's Cinema* shortly afterwards. "This is the perfect platform for the independent British producer." The two companies would collaborate on thirty films between 1957 and 1964. The next Gothic horror into production at Bray, however, was *Dracula*. The rights to the subject were tied to Universal-International Films Inc, and the film therefore went to them. When that, too, was an enormous American success, the transformation of Hammer from struggling British production company to major international player was complete.

In Peter Cushing's Frankenstein and Christopher Lee's Dracula, Hammer had found its stars; in Eliot Hyman it had found a wealthy partner; in Columbia and Universal it had found international distribution and in the Gothic horror films of Terence Fisher it had at last found an identity. Audiences flocked to the results of this fortuitous collaboration. Messrs Carreras, Hinds and Lawrence willingly supplied the demand.

Universal opened negotiations with Hammer over its library of classic horror subjects shortly after the release of *Dracula*. The Phantom of the Opera, the Mummy and the Werewolf were all characters offered to James Carreras by enthusiastic Universal president Alfred Daff in 1958. Hammer would, in time, exploit them all.

There was a downside to Hammer's dramatic reversal of fortunes, and it was felt most acutely by Brian Lawrence. "I had a hundred personnel in Wardour Street and our own offices and staff in other major cities. But with the divorce of the Hammer product to the large distributors in return for their investment, Exclusive became starved of films." Hammer's parent company continued to oversee (if not control) distribution of Hammer films, but was gradually wound down throughout the late fifties. Brian Lawrence was retained and promoted to the position of general man-

Previous page (above): *The Warner Theatre, Leicester Square, Thursday 2 May 1957 — James Carreras, Peter Cushing and Will Hammer attend the première of* The Curse of Frankenstein, *Britain's first colour horror film.*
Previous page (below left): *One film stands out in this trade advertisement from Exclusive's twentieth anniversary year.*
Previous page (below right): *Hammer's greatest stars, Peter Cushing and Christopher Lee, off-duty at Bray Studios during production of* The Gorgon. *The film was shot between December 1963 and January 1964.*
Above: *Lieutenant-Colonel James Carreras MBE, pictured in 1962.*
Below: *The world at their feet.* The Phoenix *became* Ten Seconds to Hell, *and* The Man in Half Moon Street *was released as* The Man Who Could Cheat Death.

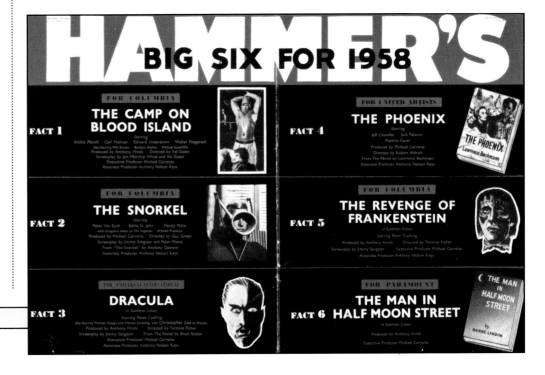

ager of the Hammer group of companies in 1960. Sitting at James Carreras' right hand, he played a more active role in decision-making from then on.

One of the last potential flies in James Carreras' ointment was Bray Studios, now a somewhat incongruous hangover from the days of Exclusive's second feature production. Hammer had purchased the house and much of its surrounding land in 1952 (the Davies family agreed on the condition that they were granted tenancy in a private wing of the house), but keeping the facility and its staff busy (and therefore cost-effective) had caused serious problems during the slump of 1955. As a safeguard against future liability, Carreras pressed Columbia to invest in Bray. Columbia purchased a forty-nine per cent share in the studio, and in January 1959 appointed Mike Frankovich, Kenneth Maidment and L.R. Woolner onto the board of directors of Falcon Films Limited, a Hammer subsidiary created to run the facility. ABPC would later also invest in the studio.

By the end of the fifties, Hammer had produced films for Columbia, Paramount, United Artists and Universal. In addition to receiving funds from such distributors, Hammer benefited from the continued investment of Eliot Hyman, who by 1959 had bought control of Ray Stark's Seven Arts production company. (Eliot Hyman's son, Kenneth, had also become closely involved with Hammer during the late fifties. Taking the first steps in a successful career as a producer, he learned the ropes on *The Hound of the Baskervilles*, *The Stranglers of Bombay* and *The Terror of the Tongs*.) Hammer's commercial reputation ensured that it could easily raise its own shares of budgets from existing resources, or lenders such as banks and the renamed National Film Finance Corporation. The advance submission of all screenplays to the British Board of Film Censors and the Motion Picture Association of America similarly safeguarded Hammer's profit margins — there was little point wasting film on scenes that would not be passed for exhibition.

In the midst of this growing security, Michael Carreras became increasingly disenchanted. Michael had never enjoyed a good relationship with his father, whose dominant personality kept the submissive Anthony Hinds and Brian Lawrence more easily in check. He had found compensation enough in the diversity of film-making Hammer had enjoyed before *The Curse of Frankenstein*, but the unfolding treadmill of Gothic horrors held little appeal. The films Michael Carreras produced in the late fifties, notably *Ten Seconds to Hell*, *Yesterday's Enemy* and *Hell Is a City*, were often indicative of his desire to expand Hammer's identity beyond the horror films that had come to define the company. Under Michael's patronage, *The Strange Case of Dr Jekyll and Mr Hyde* became *The Two Faces of Dr Jekyll*, a profound exposure of bourgeois hypocrisy. At around the same time, at the end of 1959, Anthony Hinds produced *Never Take Sweets From a Stranger*, a sincere drama about the dangers of child abuse. The public's expectations of Hammer's films worked against both pictures, and neither were commercial successes.

Michael suffered the most, however, and it soon became clear that his ambitions to diversify would never be sanctioned by his father. Michael Carreras formed Capricorn Productions in December 1960, soon inviting Hammer writer/producer Jimmy Sangster to join him and his wife Josephine on the board of directors. The company's first film was shot in late 1961. *The Savage Guns* was a Metro-Goldwyn-Mayer backed Western that had started life as *The San Siado Killings*, a screenplay Hammer had commissioned from Peter R. Newman. "It started the whole trend of making Westerns in Spain," Carreras remembered. "This was long before the Italians started making their spaghetti Westerns." With finance from ABPC, Capricorn next made *What a Crazy World* in summer 1963. While *The Savage Guns* was perhaps ahead of its time in its choice of location, *What a Crazy World* was slightly behind them in its choice of Joe Brown, Marty Wilde and 'Bobby's Girl' Susan Maughan as lead players. This breezy teen musical, shot largely on the streets of London, was nevertheless the most engaging film Michael ever directed. (Temporarily free of his father's influence, Michael felt confident enough to acknowledge his past: one scene features Joe Brown proposing to Susan Maughan during a screening of *The Curse of Frankenstein*, while Hammer regular Michael Ripper appears as no less than nine different characters in his credited role as 'The Common Man'.) Michael Carreras, at best an infrequent attendee at Hammer board meetings, resigned from the company in late 1963 to pursue his new career as an independent producer and director. Any hopes he may have had about carving out an identity away from Hammer were soon frustrated, however, and by the time *What a Crazy World* opened in

January 1964 Michael was freelancing for his father.

Anthony Hinds had long-since assumed sole production responsibility at Hammer. From his offices at Wardour Street and Bray Studios, he acted as unaccredited executive producer on many of the Hammer films produced during the sixties. Readily acknowledged by his contemporaries as the chief architect of Hammer's Gothic horror formula, Hinds continued to supervise numerous variations on the themes first established by *The Curse of Frankenstein* and *Dracula*. On 13 November 1963, Hinds' colleagues threw him a surprise party to commemorate his fiftieth film as producer. *The Evil of Frankenstein* was a milestone that, unfortunately, stood as an example of the increasingly homogenous output that had fuelled Michael Carreras' frustration. Trade paper *The Daily Cinema* issued a special supplement to mark the occasion. "Anthony Hinds, in his horn-rimmed glasses and immaculate dark suits, has been described as looking like a divinity student about to sit for his final or like a prosperous author," ran the congratulatory profile. "Prosperous he certainly is with an estate outside Aylesbury, a yacht on the Thames and high-powered cars... He shuns personal publicity, hates cocktail parties and premières, and has no time at all for the asphalt jungle life, but is completely at home in the country, where the only hunting he does is hunting for film stories." Only by reading between the lines could a less than idyllic picture of life as Hammer's executive producer be guessed at. "Tony might say his only mistake was to try his hand at straight comedy instead of the thrills that produce nervous laughter!" claimed the opening editorial, alluding to Hammer's recent abandonment of the comedies that had once shared a more diverse production schedule with horror films. Elsewhere, James Carreras' tribute made mention of the difficulties that were undermining even Hammer's once robust box-office appeal: "Unfortunately, at this moment, things are a bit bumpy on the production side and there are people thinking of pulling out..."

To a degree, Carreras had been able to cushion Hammer from the British film industry's most recent depression. Eliot and Kenneth Hyman continued to finance and initiate a percentage of projects, and the majority of pictures went straight to Columbia. The limited number Columbia permitted Hammer to make outside their deal were usually offered to Universal as outright sales — with careful budgeting, Hammer made a profit on every Universal picture it made, regardless of its box-office performance. By 1964, however, Hammer's relationship with its two most reliable American distributors was becoming strained. Columbia was increasingly dissatisfied with Hammer's delivery of films that deviated from the reliable horror formula that had proved so successful in the fifties. Universal's interest was similarly dampened when falling box-office returns failed to justify its continued support. Columbia ended its regular co-production arrangement with the Indian frontier swashbuckler *The Brigand of Kandahar*, while Universal's final Hammer purchase was *The Secret of Blood Island*, a further instalment of Japanese war atrocities that the distributor found impossible to sell in certain

Far Eastern territories.

Since the mid-fifties, Hammer's product had been largely defined in terms of American distributors' demands. Hammer's most important American customers had taken their custom elsewhere, and James Carreras, Anthony Hinds and Brian Lawrence were faced with a dwindling production schedule that threatened to starve the company.

Had the Hammer story ended with Columbia and Universal's withdrawal in 1964, James Carreras' achievements would surely have been enough to guarantee the company's place in cinema history. Perhaps more admirable than his acumen, however, was the ability of those working under him to craft from the cold mechanics of supply and demand some of the most entrancing British films ever made...

Previous page (above left): Michael Carreras, Hammer's executive producer.
Previous page (above right): Anthony Hinds on location for The Damned in summer 1961.
Previous page (below): Michael Carreras on location in London for the Capricorn film What a Crazy World in summer 1963. Leading man Marty Wilde looks on. "I don't know anybody who wouldn't enjoy directing," said Carreras.
Above: Stars Christopher Lee and Yvonne Monlaur, producers Kenneth Hyman and Michael Carreras, and writer Jimmy Sangster at the press reception for The Terror of the Tongs.
Below: Brian Lawrence (left) and James Carreras (far right) pay tribute to Anthony Hinds at the Café Royal in London.

THE QUATERMASS XPERIMENT

Principal photography 18 October to
December 1954
Released 26 August 1955
Certificate X
Duration 82 mins
Black and white
Director Val Guest

Having travelled 1,500 miles into space, and all radio contact with its three passengers long since lost, experimental rocket ship Quatermass 1 crash lands at Oakley Green. Professor Bernard Quatermass (Brian Donlevy), the British Rocket Group scientist responsible for launching the ship without official sanction, discovers that two members of the crew have disappeared without trace. Sole survivor Victor Carroon (Richard Wordsworth) is desperately ill — his heart rate, pulse and blood pressure are alarmingly low, while his skin and bones appear to be undergoing an horrific transformation. As his condition worsens, Carroon feels compelled to plunge his fist into a cactus. Taken into medical care, he escapes with his arm — which is rapidly mutating to mimic the form of the plant — wrapped in a raincoat. Quatermass hypothesises that Carroon is being consumed by the parasitic alien organism that killed his fellow astronauts. As Carroon's transformation accelerates, Quatermass and his team race to locate and destroy the murderous creature he has become...

*i*n 1953 the outlook seemed bleak for Exclusive/ Hammer: colour and Cinemascope were becoming commonplace and the growing appeal of television offered a new distraction to cinema-goers. The days of modest second feature production were numbered.

BBC Television's *The Quatermass Experiment*, a hugely successful six-part serial which began on 18 July 1953, suggested a fresh direction. "It was something new," remembers its author Nigel Kneale, "and Hammer could smell it." Following transmission of the third episode, an impressed Anthony Hinds and James Carreras offered the BBC a deal. The Corporation was enthusiastic, and signed a contract before producer Sidney Gilliat could launch his own bid. BBC policy excluded staff writer Kneale from negotiations, production and profits.

American distribution was to be handled by Exclusive's long-term co-production partner Robert Lippert. The task of doctoring the script to American audiences' tastes was given to New Yorker Richard Landau, a writer who had worked on Exclusive's science fiction thriller *Spaceways* and five previous

Lippert co-productions. His condensed version of Kneale's teleplay was further streamlined by director Val Guest, who was persuaded to take the project on by Hinds while holidaying in Tangier. Guest had already directed Exclusive's first colour film (*Men of Sherwood Forest*) and would introduce a further innovation in his reworking of Landau's script: "I was going to do it almost factually, as a newsreel or reportage. No science fiction film had been done that way before."

In keeping with a long-established pattern, a Hollywood star was contracted for the benefit of Stateside distribution. Brian Waldo Donlevy, previously notable in such films as *Beau Geste* and *The Glass Key*, was selected. Although Nigel Kneale was appalled by Donlevy's belligerent performance, Guest was pleased with the way his star gave "a very down-to-earth feel to a very off-the-earth subject." The director, however, had to work around problems caused by Donlevy's alcoholism. Rank star Jack Warner took the role of Inspector Lomax, just before his film

EXCLUSIVE *presents* The

QUATERMASS XPERIMENT

BRIAN DONLEVY · JACK WARNER
By arrangement with the J Arthur Rank Organisation

London Pavilion in Piccadilly Circus on 26 August 1955, famously going on to draw queues that almost surrounded the island site. Critical reception varied from the enthusiastic in both *Today's Cinema* ("one of the best essays in science fiction to date") and *News Chronicle* ("the best and nastiest horror film I have seen since the War. How jolly that it is also British!") to the cursory yet prophetic "a poor man's *Frankenstein*" in *The Daily Sketch*.

Aware that the name Quatermass had no pedigree in the United States, Robert Lippert retitled the film *Shock!*, but by the time its distribution rights were sold to United Artists in March 1956 this had become *The Creeping Unknown*. UA cut the running time by four minutes and paired it with the horror film *The Black Sleep*. It was later alleged that the double-bill literally scared one viewer to death — on 6 November 1956 *Variety* reported that nine year-old Stewart Cohan had died of a ruptured artery during a performance in Oak Park, Illinois.

Whether viewed as *The Quatermass Xperiment*, the reissued *The Quatermass Experiment* or the abridged *The Creeping Unknown*, Hammer's first horror film retains much of the pace, atmosphere and sophistication that first fascinated fifties audiences. Richard Wordsworth's heart-rending performance and Val Guest's innovative direction elevated Hammer's film, and the entire horror genre, to bold new ground.

Previous page: *The cast and crew on the Westminster Abbey set at Bray Studios. Brian Donlevy (centre) looks to director Val Guest. Producer Anthony Hinds sits on Donlevy's left.*
Above left: *Quatermass (Brian Donlevy) attempts to make contact with the crew of the crashed rocket.*
Above right: *Lomax (Jack Warner, standing) and the television producer (Gordon Jackson, wearing headphones).*

career was curtailed by his commitment to the role of a lower-ranking officer in television's *Dixon of Dock Green*. Other cast members, including David King-Wood, Thora Hird and Harold Lang, had worked for Guest before, but Margia Dean, the actress playing Judith Carroon, was imposed on the director. According to executive producer Michael Carreras, she was the girlfriend of Twentieth Century-Fox president Spyros Skouras: "Skouras had a girlfriend who was an actress and he wanted her in pictures, but he didn't want her in pictures in America because of the tittle-tattle or whatever, so he set it up through his friend, Bob Lippert. Skouras was the one who said we should have an American partner, so it all came right from the top."

A relatively large amount of location work was required, much of it in or around Windsor. Night-time police dragnet scenes were shot by camera operator Len Harris, the only man to work on all three of Hammer's *Quatermass* films. Chessington Zoo doubled for Regent's Park Zoo on 14 October 1954, while Bray Studios later doubled for Westminster Abbey when producer Anthony Hinds was refused permission to shoot inside the real thing. Les Bowie's matte paintings helped create an impressive illusion of size during these climactic scenes, which also featured another of the effects expert's creations — Carroon's ultimate mutation into a writhing alien organism. Mainly constructed from pieces of tripe and rubber solution, the Carroon creature was operated by wires and strings.

It came as no surprise to Exclusive when they learned, in June 1955, that their latest film had received an X certificate from the British Board of Film Censors. While rival studios were nervous of the new certificate, introduced in 1951, Exclusive gambled on exploiting it in the title of the film. The campaign book clearly spelled out the restriction to those over sixteen: "Send a personal letter to your local editor," cinema managers were advised, "basing it on an appeal to the public regarding the ban on the film being seen by children. Indirectly, it can be worded to form a plug for the film."

The Quatermass Xperiment premièred at the

THE ERIC WINSTONE BANDSHOW

On its original London run, *The Quatermass Xperiment* was preceded by Exclusive's *The Eric Winstone Bandshow*. This twenty-nine minute film, produced in colour and Cinemascope, featured stereo musical turns from The George Mitchell Singers, trumpeter Kenny Baker and singer Alma Cogan, all energetically conducted by bandleader Eric Winstone. The film was shot at the Associated British Picture Corporation (ABPC) studios in Elstree, and was the second of six musical support features produced and directed by Michael Carreras, the others being *Cyril Stapleton and the Show Band, Just For You, Eric Winstone's Stagecoach, Parade of the Bands* and *The Edmundo Ros Half-Hour*. They remain the most intriguing and innovative examples of the company's short films from this period. Michael Carreras was an avid record collector, his enthusiasm for jazz betrayed by his brief cameo as a trumpeter in Exclusive's *Face the Music*.

Principal photography 9 January to February 1956
Released 21 September 1956
Certificate X
Duration 78 mins
Black and white
Director Leslie Norman

An army platoon witnesses the opening of what seems to be a volcanic fissure; the two soldiers nearest to it later develop radiation burns, and one dies from his wounds. Dr Adam Royston (Dean Jagger), chief scientist at Lochmouth's Atomic Energy Establishment, investigates the now dormant chasm. That night, two small boys are exploring nearby marshland when one encounters a mysterious crackling force, and he later dies from first-degree radiation burns similar to those that killed the soldier. At the hospital where he died, the phenomenon reappears in the radiation room and engulfs radiographer (Neil Hallet). The flesh appears to melt away from his bones, while a terrified nurse looks on. Working with McGill (Leo McKern), a representative from the Atomic Energy Commission's Internal Security Division, Royston deduces that the force must adapt its molecular structure to pass through solid barriers in its quest to absorb radiation. Peter Elliot (William Lucas), a scientist from the research establishment, descends into the fissure and barely escapes after confronting the organism it harbours. The creature claims further victims as it grows in size and expands its range. While the army monitors its progress from the air, Royston prepares a lethal radioactive trap...

"X is not an unknown quantity," insisted the campaign book for *The Quatermass Xperiment*. The incredible response to that film convinced Hammer that the new certificate was anything but the box office poison their detractors had expected.

In the months following *The Quatermass Xperi-*

MACHINE GUN BULLETS!
DYNAMITE!
FLAME THROWERS!
Nothing can stop it!
It rises from 2000 miles beneath the earth to melt everything in its path!
IT KILLS... BUT CANNOT BE KILLED!

Sol Lesser Productions, Inc. presents

X ...the Unknown

Starring
DEAN JAGGER with
EDWARD CHAPMAN
Story and Screen Play by
JIMMY SANGSTER
Produced by
ANTHONY HINDS
Directed by
LESLIE NORMAN

ment's release, the company set about trying to repeat its success. Inspiration came from long-term Exclusive staffer Jimmy Sangster, whom producers Michael Carreras and Anthony Hinds turned to in the autumn of 1955. "I came up with the observation that all sci-fi threats and/or monsters seem to come from outer space," recalls Sangster. "How about we do a story about one that comes from inner space, bubbling up from the Earth's core? That way we wouldn't have to build any space ship sets, which were inclined to be large and expensive. After an hour or so we'd talked out the bare bones of a story. 'So go write it,' said Tony Hinds. 'If we use it we'll pay you. If we don't, we won't.' Seeing as they were paying me anyway, as a production manager, I was in a no lose situation."

Sangster's script, written in close collaboration with Anthony Hinds, was once considered as a legit-

imate sequel to *The Quatermass Xperiment*. "I was actually approached by them and asked if they could use the character of Professor Quatermass," remembers Nigel Kneale. "I said, 'No, you can't — it's mine.' They were funny people."

James Carreras finalised a co-production deal for *X the Unknown* with his occasional Exclusive partner Sol Lesser on 9 January 1956. Lesser, who in 1955 concluded a thirteen-year stint producing RKO's successful series of *Tarzan* films, had originally agreed to contribute $30,000 — half the budget — in return for American distribution rights. As negotiations continued, it was agreed that the $30,000 should comprise the salary of American star Dean Jagger, who had won an Academy Award as Best Supporting Actor for his role in the 1949 war film *Twelve O'Clock High*. American Joseph Losey, now resident in Britain after being labelled a

possible Communist sympathiser by Senator Joseph McCarthy's House Un-American Activities Committee, was hired to direct. (Losey was possibly attracted to the script's 'ban the Bomb' ethos, most explicit in the scene where Royston is told: "you meddle with things that kill!") Under the pseudonym Joe Walton, Losey supervised casting and set construction, only to contract pneumonia while location scouting (conveniently, given that his presence riled McCarthyite Dean Jagger and jeopardised American distribution prospects). Days before filming commenced, Anthony Hinds found a last-minute replacement in Leslie Norman, director of *The Night My Number Came Up*. Norman, the father of film critic Barry, was loaned to Hammer while under contract to Ealing Studios. Having reluctantly inherited Losey's production, he made few friends either

in the studio at Bray or on location at Beaconsfield and Gerrards Cross. "Absolutely nothing went right from beginning to end," remembers Sangster. "It rained for the first three days and we spent the next three digging the equipment out."

Make-up supervisor Phil Leakey's 'melting head' effect was achieved by taking a moulding of actor Neil Hallet's head, casting it in two halves of paraffin wax, and placing this over a plaster skull with heating elements inside. This, and the disintegration of the hapless security guard, would prove more impressive than the gelatinous 'Unknown' itself. Much of the film's suspense was generated in anticipation of its anticlimactic unveiling.

X the Unknown received its London première at the Pavilion on 21 September 1956 (*The Times* praised the film as "vastly entertaining" three days later). On 5 November, it was generally released on the ABC circuit, paired with Henri-Georges Clouzot's 1954 shocker *Les Diaboliques*. This classy French suspense thriller made a big impression on Sangster, proving influential to a number of films he'd later make for the company. In America, Sol Lesser's distribution deal with RKO was curtailed when Warner Brothers successfully argued that the title *X the Unknown* bore too close a resemblance to that of their wartime drama *Toward the Unknown*, released the same year. In 1957, American distribution passed from RKO to Warner Brothers, who issued the film as the lower half of a double-bill with *The Curse of Frankenstein*.

X the Unknown seems to have one foot in the relatively staid presentation of Exclusive's earlier thrillers. Dean Jagger's persuasive performance and Jimmy Sangster's laconic humour help redeem a film which, in retrospect, signifies a clear transition between the two most significant pictures in Hammer's history.

JIMMY SANGSTER: SCREENPLAY

Jimmy Sangster joined Exclusive Films in 1949, becoming close friends with producer Michael Carreras and even closer friends with hairdresser Monica Hustler, whom he later married. Under the patronage of chief electrician Jack Curtis and head of props Tommy Money, Sangster worked his way up from a lowly third assistant director's post to become a production manager. In 1955 Michael Carreras encouraged him to adapt the Victor Canning story *Chance at the Wheel* into a short script entitled *A Man on the Beach*. The resulting colour support feature was directed by Joseph Losey and released the same year. Sangster's *X the Unknown* script led him to pen *The Curse of Frankenstein* for the company; the resulting film's immense success made his name as 'Jim the Nasty'. He'd see fifteen further scripts realised by Hammer, later turning his hand to producing and directing.

Previous page: *Peter Elliot (William Lucas) discovers the remains of a soldier inside the fissure.*
Above left: *John Elliot (Edward Chapman), Peter Elliot, McGill (Leo McKern) and Royston (Dean Jagger) face the creature from an inner world.*
Left: *By tracing the creature's progress, Royston concludes that "it's on its way to the biggest meal of its life."*

**Principal photography 28 May to
13 July 1956
Released 24 May 1957
Certificate X
Duration 85 mins
Black and white
Director Val Guest**

While preparing for the launch of new space rocket Quatermass 2, Professor Quatermass (Brian Donlevy) becomes intrigued by a curious phenomenon: the high incidence of meteorite falls over the Winnerden Flats region. However, these are not ordinary meteorites and, at the Flats, Quatermass' assistant Marsh (Bryan Forbes) is injured when one of the objects cracks open, causing him to become somehow infected. The Professor is unable to investigate further, as masked guards seize the stricken Marsh and take him to a highly secret complex nearby. The complex appears to be modelled after Quatermass' own design for a moonbase. The base would have enabled life to thrive in an artificial atmosphere, but was rejected by various Whitehall departments. Quatermass falls in with an MP, Broadhead (Tom Chatto), who is similarly curious about the Winnerden Flats project. They are taken on an official tour of the plant, which they are told manufactures synthetic foodstuffs. To his cost, the MP discovers the 'foodstuff' to be a lethal toxin. Quatermass comes to realise that the plant's domes house a gestalt alien intelligence which has travelled to Earth in the meteorites. Having possessed many senior members of the government, these entities may soon control first Britain, then the world...

For Hammer's sequel to *The Quatermass Xperiment*, James Carreras struck a groundbreaking finance and distribution deal with United Artists. The company that had previously relied on middle men such as Robert Lippert to broker deals with American distributors was clearly growing in stature. United Artists agreed to co-finance *Quatermass 2*'s relatively large budget in return for non-perpetual distribution rights. Hammer was clearly outgrowing its parent company Exclusive and the domestic distribution arm was wound down, entering liquidation ten years later.

This time round, Nigel Kneale was free to take an active role in writing the film version of his original teleplay: "I was leaving the BBC at this point. I'd had enough. Five years of being in that hut was as much as any sane person could stand." Kneale planned his screenplay with producer Anthony Hinds, collaborating with director Val Guest on the second draft. Although it was decided to effectively jettison the spacebound climax of the six-part original, *Quater-*

mass 2 relied heavily on the style dictated by its television predecessor. "There is more of the TV version in that than any of the others," says Kneale, recalling the eerie sequences shot at the Shell Haven oil refinery on the Essex coast. "Rudi [television director Rudolph Cartier] thought up some wonderful circling shots and high camera angles... all of which were reproduced in the second film." Appropriately enough, the fictional new town of Winnerden Flats was found at the real-life new town of Hemel Hempstead, which was still under construction at the time. *Quatermass 2* became the first film to be realised at Danziger Productions' New Elstree Studios when interior scenes were shot on Stages 2 and 5 between 28 May and 18 June. "It literally was a shed," remembers Kneale.

Much to Kneale's dismay, Brian Donlevy resumed his portrayal of Professor Quatermass: "He really was very drunk indeed. He used to take a liquid lunch up in the village, and when he got back he'd sunken half

would have blown off. We did it all very successfully until one take, a very difficult shot, which we had tried a couple of times. Finally I said, 'That's a beauty, cut.' Donlevy said, 'Oh great, now I can have a coffee,' but he turned around and his toupee took off and floated around like a bat. The props men were throwing rakes at it, trying to get it down and save it."

Although Donlevy never worked for Hammer again, his association with horror films continued. In 1965 he returned to Britain to appear in *The Curse of the Fly* (by sometime Hammer director Don Sharp, and produced by Robert Lippert) and the thriller *Five Golden Dragons*, alongside Christopher Lee. Donlevy, who was married to Bela Lugosi's widow Lillian, died in 1972.

Quatermass 2 premièred at the London Pavilion on 24 May 1957. It began its general release, double-billed with *And God Created Woman*, on 17 June. "The 'X' certificate given this film is sheerly for the horror in it," remarked *Picture Show* magazine helpfully on 22 June. "It is sure to satisfy thrill-lovers with strong stomachs."

Nigel Kneale's tale of government conspiracy and alien possession, set against a backdrop of post-war new town paranoia, is economically told by Val Guest. In its stark story and kinetic presentation, *Quatermass 2* was clearly ahead of its time. Genuinely disturbing, it remains one of the most compelling films Hammer ever made.

another dramatic feature shot on ILFORD 35mm cine negative film

"QUATERMASS II" was made on ILFORD FP3

Previous page: Journalist Jimmy Hall (Sidney James) has a sobering discussion with Quatermass (Brian Donlevy) and Lomax (John Longden) about the objects discovered at Winnerden Flats.

Above left: Actor Tom Chatto is prepared for Broadhead's grisly death with the application of smoking chemicals.

Below left: A prototype of the alien creatures seen bursting from the domes at the end of the film. Models of the refinery vehicles and staff suggest the scale of the desired effect.

a bottle of whisky. They had to tell him the name of the film, the scene he was in and then raise the 'idiot board' so he could read off it."

Further problems arose during location filming for the final scenes at the South Downs, near Brighton, as Val Guest explains: "We'd gone to the Downs because they were supposed to be wind-swept, and they weren't." Consequently, aeroplane engines were hired to simulate the required hurri-cane: "I had to arrange it so that in all the scenes Donlevy faced the wind machines, or his toupee

KNEALE VS DONLEVY

In 1995, Nigel Kneale was still vociferous in his low opinion of Brian Donlevy's performance. "I may have picked Quatermass' surname out of a phone book but his first name was carefully chosen: Bernard, after Bernard Lovell, the creator of Jodrell Bank. Pioneer, ultimate questing man. Donlevy played him as a mechanic, a creature with a completely closed mind. He could make nothing of any imaginative lines, and simply barked and bawled his way through the plot. A bully whose emotional range ran from annoyance to fury."

THE CURSE OF FRANKENSTEIN

**Principal photography 19 November 1956 to
3 January 1957**
Released 2 May 1957
Certificate X
Duration 82 mins
Colour
Director Terence Fisher

At a lonely mountain prison, a priest (Alex Gallier) hears the confession of the condemned murderer Baron Victor Frankenstein (Peter Cushing)... At fifteen, the brilliant Victor (Melvyn Hayes) inherits the family fortune. He appoints himself a science tutor, Paul Krempe (Robert Urquhart), and together they research to but one end — the re-animation of the dead. The years pass and, after they succeed in reviving the corpse of a dog with electricity, Victor proposes that they build a perfect human being. Paul reluctantly concurs, and they steal the body of a hanged highwayman. Desiring his Creature possess "a lifetime of knowledge", Victor is driven to murder the distinguished Professor Bernstein (Paul Hardtmuth) for his brain. But Paul turns on Victor; they fight, and the brain is damaged. On a stormy night, a stray bolt of lightning accidentally triggers the process which brings the hideous Creature (Christopher Lee) to life. Deranged, it attempts to strangle Victor before it can be restrained. Come the morning, Victor and Paul discover the monster has escaped. It attacks and kills a blind man and his grandson before being shot and killed by Paul. The Creature is, however, exhumed by Victor and revived...

The irony underlying *The Curse of Frankenstein* — the first of the British Gothic horrors for which Hammer will forever be associated — is that the film was originally conceived by a pair of Americans. Milton Subotsky and Max J. Rosenberg began their prolific partnership with *Junior Science*, an educational series for American television, in 1954. In 1956, they broke into film production with the Subotsky-scripted musical *Rock Rock Rock*. Thinking of ways to diversify within the exploitation market, Subotsky turned his attention to an adaptation of *Frankenstein*, taking his script to financier Eliot Hyman of Associated Artists Productions in New York. Hyman, in turn, sent the screenplay to his Variety Club associate James Carreras.

Hammer were enthused by the idea of pursuing the new direction suggested by *The Quatermass Xperiment*. However, the first British horror film to be made in colour was initially envisaged as a cheap black and white production to feature the ageing Boris Karloff, faded star of Universal's great horror

cycle of the thirties. These plans stalled when Universal, who had been alerted to the company's plans by their registration of the title, raised the prospect of a lawsuit against the company should their picture contain any elements, textual or otherwise, unique to their movies (notably Jack Pierce's distinct and copyrighted Monster make-up).

On 9 May 1956, James Carreras met Subotsky and Rosenberg and asked them to expand the script without adding any new sets or locations — Subotsky's ambitious first draft would only have run to about fifty-five minutes. "They asked us to make some changes and we made some changes," remembered Subotsky, who submitted an expanded script to Michael Carreras in London. "In the end, they decided our script would be too expensive to

NO-ONE WHO SAW IT LIVED TO DESCRIBE IT!

THE CURSE OF FRANKENSTEIN

CERT **X**   COLOUR BY EASTMAN COLOUR

STARRING **PETER CUSHING** WITH **HAZEL COURT** · **ROBERT URQUHART**
AND **CHRISTOPHER LEE** AS THE CREATURE

Produced by ANTHONY HINDS Directed by TERENCE FISHER Screenplay by JIMMY SANGSTER
Based on the classic by MARY SHELLEY Executive Producer MICHAEL CARRERAS

A HAMMER FILM PRODUCTION distributed by WARNER BROS.

make." Subotsky's *Frankenstein* — narrated by Victor from his cell in an insane asylum — would suggest only the broadest of structures for Hammer's eventual film. Subotsky and Rosenberg were placated with a special payment and a percentage of Eliot Hyman's share of the profits. (Subotsky would never forget his unaccredited contribution to Hammer's success and, together with Rosenberg, later founded Amicus, Hammer's chief British competitors throughout the sixties and seventies.)

Having assured themselves of the copyright situation regarding Mary Shelley's original text, from which the film would have to be demonstrably adapted, Anthony Hinds and Jimmy Sangster eagerly wrote a new screenplay, reworking the novel in the style of a gory drawing-room comedy. James Carreras submitted their story outline to Universal in early September 1956, "just so that your boys don't have anything to say after the picture has been completed." Universal's counsel refused to read it, arguing that no script could accurately foretell a motion picture's contents.

Long-time Exclusive director Terence Fisher was entrusted with Hammer's most important film to date. The elegant style he dictated proved highly influential. "I know [Terence Fisher] kept saying that he was only engaged to direct the first one because Hammer owed him a picture, but it is just not true," claims Anthony Hinds. "Terry and I had been good friends for many years before that and I knew he had just the right combination of discretion and let's-give-'em-something-to-make-'em-sit-up that the shows needed."

Eliot Hyman expressed concern that the film's international prospects would suffer from a surfeit of 'Britishness' in its casting, but James Carreras assured him that the cast would "have no trace whatsoever of a British accent"! Hammer were initially open to the idea of casting an American star in the pivotal role of Frankenstein, but Peter Cushing,

"THE CURSE OF FRANKENSTEIN" WILL HAUNT YOU FOREVER!

ALL NEW AND NEVER DARED BEFORE!

in WARNERCOLOR Presented by WARNER BROS.

who had been impressed by a private screening of *X the Unknown*, was contracted to play the Baron on 26 October. At one time, the lumbering Creature might have been played by later *Carry On...* regular Bernard Bresslaw. Instead, Christopher Lee, who fulfilled Hammer's requirement for a very tall man with "some knowledge and experience of movement and mime", was cast in the role. Lee underwent several make-up tests prior to shooting. "We refused to have anything to do with anything mechanical," recalled Terence Fisher. "We wanted the Monster to fit Chris Lee's melancholy personality. We wanted a thing that looked like some wan-

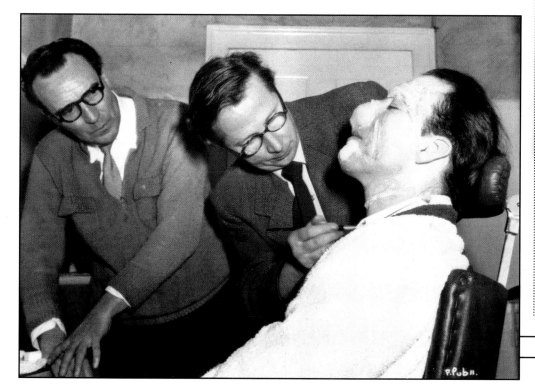

Previous page: Christopher Lee's Creature meets the press in November 1956.
Above: Valerie Gaunt as Frankenstein's doomed mistress Justine.
Left: Phil Leakey (centre) adds layers of make-up to Christopher Lee's face.

Right: A 'minstrel of monstrosity' poses for Hammer photographer John Jay.
Below: Gruesome shots of a head dissolving in acid went unseen in Britain.
Bottom: Shooting the scene in which Victor (Peter Cushing) meets his Creature for the first time. The cramped conditions at Bray are all too evident.

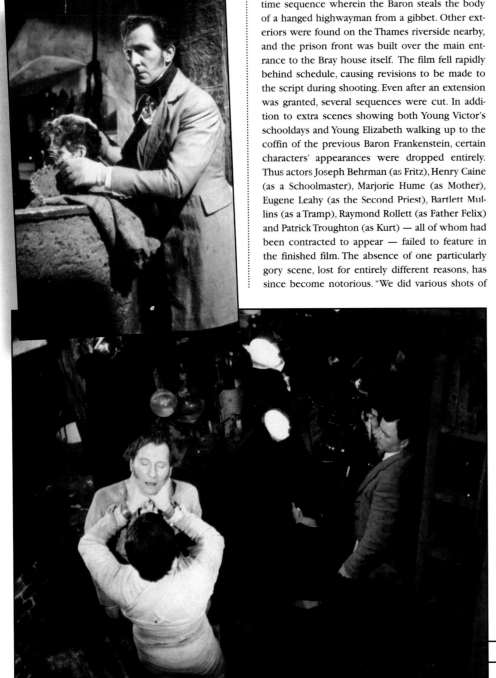

dering, forlorn minstrel of monstrosity." Phil Leakey's early designs, inevitably affected by the need to construct a creature that looked utterly unlike Universal's incarnation, included animalistic interpretations akin to the hybrid Beast Folk of H. G. Wells' *The Island of Doctor Moreau* ("One made me look a bit like the Elephant Man," recalls Lee. "The other was more like some sort of werewolf with the nose tilted up at the end to make you look slightly more pig-like"). The eventual, last-minute design was a collage of mortician's wax, rubber and cotton wool, which took between two-and-a-half to three hours to apply directly to the actor's face. It was unveiled at a press reception at Brooks Wharf, Lower Thames Street, London in late November, where Lee's dramatic entrance as the Creature "made some of the 200 guests reach for their smelling salts."

Shooting at Bray had, by then, commenced. The first scene to go before the cameras was the night-time sequence wherein the Baron steals the body of a hanged highwayman from a gibbet. Other exteriors were found on the Thames riverside nearby, and the prison front was built over the main entrance to the Bray house itself. The film fell rapidly behind schedule, causing revisions to be made to the script during shooting. Even after an extension was granted, several sequences were cut. In addition to extra scenes showing both Young Victor's schooldays and Young Elizabeth walking up to the coffin of the previous Baron Frankenstein, certain characters' appearances were dropped entirely. Thus actors Joseph Behrman (as Fritz), Henry Caine (as a Schoolmaster), Marjorie Hume (as Mother), Eugene Leahy (as the Second Priest), Bartlett Mullins (as a Tramp), Raymond Rollett (as Father Felix) and Patrick Troughton (as Kurt) — all of whom had been contracted to appear — failed to feature in the finished film. The absence of one particularly gory scene, lost for entirely different reasons, has since become notorious. "We did various shots of

the head going into the acid," recalls assistant director Derek Whitehurst. "The close-up of the wax head wasn't shown in the British version."

The Curse of Frankenstein premièred at the Warner Theatre, Leicester Square, on Thursday 2 May 1957, where attendees were treated to an eerie, green-lit display of the Frankenstein laboratory equipment adorned with skeletons and set to a soundtrack of sepulchral music. The conservative British press responded to the film with well-documented distaste: "for Sadists Only," said *The Daily Telegraph*; "among the half-dozen most repulsive films I have encountered," claimed *The Observer*. *Tribune*, meanwhile, asserted that "The logical development of this kind of thing is a peep show of freaks, interspersed with visits to a torture chamber." *The Curse of Frankenstein*'s notoriety led star Robert Urquhart to express in a contemporary interview certain reservations about the film's "salaciousness"; he received a sharp letter from Michael Carreras in reply.

The picture fared extraordinarily well at the box office. After a record-breaking weekend at the Warner, the second weekend topped even that and led to the film running simultaneously in two West End cinemas (the other being the Ritz). Its American receipts, too, were exceptional and the film apparently grossed over seventy times its production costs. A genuine novelty in its day — all that blood, in colour! — *The Curse of Frankenstein* nevertheless redefined the entire horror genre. The performances of both Cushing and Lee — the first utterly cold and utterly convincing as the demented Baron, the second evoking both pity and fear in equal measure as the hopeless Creature — aspire to, and reach, a depth of feeling previously unrealised in the cinema of the strange. A phenomenon in its own right, *The Curse of Frankenstein* breathed life into another: Hammer horror.

eter Wilton Cushing was born on 26 May 1913 in Kenley, Surrey. A long-held ambition to act was temporarily frustrated when Cushing's surveyor father put him to work in the Coulsdon and Purley Urban District Council in 1933. Initial escape attempts were unsuccessful ("I spoke English carelessly and indistinctly," he later recalled), but following evening classes at the Guildhall School of Music and Drama, Cushing found repertory work in June 1936. In January 1939 his father bought him a "one-way ticket to Hollywood." After checking in at a YMCA hostel, the young Cushing began doorstepping major studios, claiming to be a famous actor. He was first contracted to double for Louis Hayward in James Whale's *The Man in the Iron Mask* (he also made a brief on-screen appearance as a messenger) and went on to more substantial roles alongside Laurel and Hardy in *A Chump at Oxford* and Carole Lombard in *Vigil in the Night*. Although turned down for national service on medical grounds, a dutiful Cushing finally succumbed to homesickness in 1941. While acting in *Private Lives* for the Entertainments National Services Association (ENSA) the following year, he met actress Helen Beck and they fell in love, marrying on 10 April 1943.

Laurence Olivier's 1948 adaptation of *Hamlet* gave Cushing the opportunity to resume his film career with an outrageous Osric, but the new medium of television was the first to provide him with any real security as an actor. Beginning in

1951, he braved the rigorous demands of live television to appear in acclaimed productions such as *Pride and Prejudice* and *Beau Brummell*. While much of his work from this period was never Kinescoped, Cushing's moving portrayal of Winston Smith in *Nineteen Eighty-Four* can still be admired. He had, in middle-age, at last found stardom; a brace of prestigious awards won between 1953 and 1956 were evidence of his unrivalled popularity as a television actor. His career would doubtless have continued with the BBC had Hammer not returned him to the big screen and brought him deserved international fame.

While *The Curse of Frankenstein* and then *Dracula* effectively typecast Cushing as a horror star (he was rarely given the opportunity to appear outside the genre thereafter), he and Helen decided the benefits outweighed the disadvantages. The couple moved to the seaside town of Whitstable, Kent, in 1959, soon becoming local celebrities. Visitors to the Cushings' white clapboard house were often regaled with Peter's incredible collection of model aeroplanes and toy soldiers — compensation, perhaps, for a bizarre upbringing that saw him dressed as a little girl. Country life was idyllic: "Mr Cushing has said goodbye to the lean years," wrote Hammer's publicists in May that year. "Today he has a flat in fashionable Kensington, a cottage by the sea, a Jaguar car. And he never stops working." Cushing was undoubtedly greater than some of the roles he was offered throughout the sixties, and he enriched the films of Hammer, Amicus and their contemporaries with dignified and detailed performances. "So often he got me out of trouble," remembers director Freddie Francis. "The luckiest thing that ever happened to Hammer was Peter Cushing."

Peter's happiness was cruelly curtailed when Helen lost her long battle with emphysema on 14 January 1971. He never recovered from the loss. "The only antidote to that devastation was work," he later wrote, "when I could immerse myself in whatever character I was called upon to portray, and thus take refuge from myself." He became sombre, withdrawn and emotionally fragile. He also became extraordinarily prolific in films and on television, shunning the company of all bar his devoted secretary Joyce Broughton and her family.

When Hammer ran out of films for Cushing, George Lucas brought him to a new generation of film-goers by casting him as the callous Grand Moff Tarkin in *Star Wars*. "I've often wondered what a 'Grand Moff' is," Cushing mused, "or in

view of what happened to him, perhaps I should say was."

In May 1982 a diagnosis of cancer began the years of ill-health that blighted the remainder of his old age. He defied a gloomy prognosis to continue working, appearing as an elderly Sherlock Holmes in Tyburn's *The Masks of Death* and in a cameo role in *Biggles*, his final feature film. He received the OBE in 1989, by which time he had earned the mantle "the gentle man of horror." Cushing occupied his final years with radio work, two volumes of autobiography, and reminiscences with old friends and new admirers at Whitstable's Tudor Tea Rooms, where he regularly ate his lunch. The long wait to join his beloved Helen finally ended on 11 August 1994 — the nation mourned one of its best-loved stars, while his friends gave thanks that the years of suffering were over.

Peter Cushing never resisted his close association with Hammer, whose lurid trademarks of sex and horror seemed at such odds with its reserved and courteous star. In 1980, when Brian Lawrence and Roy Skeggs revived the company's fortunes by producing the television anthology *Hammer House of Horror*, Cushing was duly called. "He was very reluctant to take the role we offered him," remembers Skeggs. "But he did it because it was Hammer." This loyalty extended to his final performance: the narration, with Christopher Lee, of *Flesh and Blood*, a two-part television documentary about Hammer. Cushing was too ill to watch the transmitted programme, and died before the final instalment was shown. It is perhaps fitting, however, that he was last heard reminiscing about the films in which his definitive portrayals of Frankenstein and Van Helsing are immortalised.

THE ABOMINABLE SNOWMAN

**Principal photography 28 January to
5 March 1957
Released 26 August 1957
Certificate A
Duration 83 mins
Black and white/Hammerscope
Director Val Guest**

The Himalayas: an expedition in search of the legendary yeti sets off from a Tibetan monastery. Botanist John Rollason (Peter Cushing) has agreed to join the party led by gun-runner Tom Friend (Forrest Tucker), who plans to capture the creature and exploit it commercially. The group soon discover a series of giant footprints in the snow. Shortly afterwards, their camp is attacked by a yeti, which is shot dead by trapper Ed Shelley (Robert Brown). The strain of the expedition has made itself felt — the porters have deserted, one of the party has gone mad, and another will suffer a heart attack while guarding the body of the creature. Rollason comes to believe that the yeti may not be a throwback, but of a greater order of intelligence than Man himself. Have they have hidden themselves away in the mountains, awaiting humanity's inevitable extinction? The explorers move the yeti's corpse to a cave, setting a trap in order to capture a live specimen. The highly-evolved yeti, however, toy with their minds...

*I*n 1954, the *Daily Mail* sponsored a seven-strong party of explorers intent on solving the mystery of the fabled abominable snowman. The scientists and technicians, along with their Sherpa guides, spent sixteen weeks in Tibet, following a trail from Katmandu to Namche Bazaar. Along the way, they found footprints nine inches long and five inches wide in mountain terrain fifteen miles short of Everest. Expedition leader and *Mail* foreign correspondent Ralph Izzard described the discoveries in a book, *The Abominable Snowman Adventure*.

Quatermass creator Nigel Kneale was intrigued by the ensuing wave of interest and wrote *The Creature*, a television play starring Peter Cushing and directed by Rudolph Cartier. To accompany the play's first live transmission by the BBC on Sunday 30 January 1955, Kneale wrote an article about the Snowman for the *Radio Times*: "Is there some prosaic explanation for the footprints?" he asked. "Or does the yeti exist? *The Creature*, in purely fictional terms, is a guess at the answers." On 2 November

DEMON-PROWLER OF MOUNTAIN SHADOWS...DREADED MAN-BEAST OF TIBET...THE TERROR OF ALL THAT IS HUMAN!!

The Abominable Snowman of the Himalayas

WE DARE YOU TO SEE IT ALONE!
Each chilling moment a shock-test for your scare-endurance!!

STARRING **FORREST TUCKER · PETER CUSHING**
A **REGALSCOPE** PICTURE

PRODUCED BY AUBREY BARING · DIRECTED BY VAL GUEST · SCREENPLAY BY NIGEL KNEALE · BASED ON THE PLAY "THE CREATURE" BY NIGEL KNEALE · Released by 20th CENTURY-FOX

1956, Hammer bought the rights to produce a film based on Kneale's story — and soon capitalised on the publicity generated by a follow-up expedition. Pre-production began under the title *The Snow Creature*, although the film was soon retitled *The Abominable Snowman* to distinguish it from an earlier yeti picture.

Greatly enthused, Val Guest needed little persuading to direct the film, recruiting Peter Cushing, Wolfe Morris and Arnold Marle to reprise their television roles. Stanley Baker had played the heartless Tom Friend in the television version; for Hammer's film he was replaced by Forrest Tucker, who'd featured in the company's earlier Guest-directed Lippert production, *Break in the Circle*. *The Abominable Snowman* was Hammer's final co-production with Robert Lippert, whose unaccredited Buzz Productions company contracted Tucker on 6 Dec-

on wonderful special effects, because there wouldn't be any. But it didn't depend on that. It depended far more on conviction. Now, Peter Cushing was a perfectionist. Peter would challenge something, saying 'I don't believe this. Why am I doing this?' And he would want an answer. He would then play to the answer he got and convince you it was possible that he was facing the monster, and there was a monster there to be faced."

The Abominable Snowman made a bizarre pairing with the Mamie Van Doren film *Untamed Youth* on its Warner Brothers-distributed release. In America, where Lippert sold the film to Twentieth Century-Fox, it was retitled *The Abominable Snowman of the Himalayas*. An eerie, H. P. Lovecraft-esque take on the yeti, the film conveys a taut, paranoid atmosphere; set largely in wide open spaces, it's remarkably claustrophobic in feel.

ember 1956. In a customary exchange, Lippert and his partner Bill Pizor received American distribution rights to the film in return.

Between 14 and 24 January 1957, Guest shot establishing footage in the French Pyrenees with a small crew and a handful of actors' doubles. This material was then viewed by production designer Bernard Robinson, who began constructing matching snowscapes at Pinewood Studios. Three weeks of shooting at Bray Studios began on 28 January, Guest centring on the scenes inside the Tibetan monastery (the impressive sets would be recycled for the series of Christopher Lee-starring Fu Manchu films in the mid-sixties). Guest and his crew relocated to Pinewood on 18 February, completing the film with two weeks' shooting on the finished snowscapes.

Nigel Kneale was satisfied with the finished result: "I knew there was no point in me depending

Previous page: *"I'm afraid I was wrong... what I was looking for does not exist."* In the aftermath of his Himalayan ordeal, sole survivor John Rollason (Peter Cushing) agrees to preserve the secret kept by the Lhama (Arnold Marle). Helen Rollason (Maureen Connell) and Peter Fox (Richard Wattis) look on.
Bottom: Trapper Ed Shelley (Robert Brown) studies the corpse of a freshly-bagged yeti — for which Tom Friend (Forrest Tucker) has an ultimately deadly use...

YETI MOVIES

The yeti first entered popular folklore in 1921 after explorer Colonel C. K. Howard Bury's Everest expedition publicised, via the *Calcutta Statesman*, a series of unidentified tracks and Sherpa legends of a beast named *metoh-kangmi* (mistranslated as 'abominable snowman'). After the well-publicised *Daily Mail* expedition of 1954, eccentric Texan millionaire Tom Slick conducted a number of searches between 1956 and 1959. Not surprisingly, exploitation cinema was quick to pick up on this trend. The first known yeti movie was *The Snow Creature*, a 1954 Planet Filmways Inc production. Directed by W. Lee Wilder and starring Paul Langton and Leslie Denison, this piece concerning a Himalayan creature caught up at Los Angeles immigration while officials debate its status as man or animal showed little outside the drive-in circuit. Even less distinguished was the following year's *Man Beast*, a Jerry Warren production which took as its premise a villainous Himalayan Mongol kidnapping women in order to breed them with tame yeti. The film was in production at the same time as *The Abominable Snowman*, so executive producer Michael Carreras ordered a security blackout and ensured that his production was completed first. A 1955 Japanese effort, *Jujin Vukiotoko* ('Monster Snowman'), had new sequences featuring actor John Carradine spliced into it for its 1957 American release as *Half-Human*; and little is known about *Gergasi*, a 1958 yeti film produced in Malayan by Singapore's Shaw Brothers (who would, many years later, collaborate with Hammer on the troubled *The Legend of the 7 Golden Vampires*).

HAMMER GOES TO WAR

"This is not just a story — it is based on the brutal truth", warned an on-screen caption preceding *The Camp on Blood Island*, Hammer's polemical POW shocker of 1958. Rarely seen today, the company's World War Two dramas are among its strongest, most powerful films.

The Steel Bayonet, the first feature directed by Michael Carreras, was set in Tunis, North Africa, in 1943 (the British Army Tank Training Grounds, near Aldershot, stood in). The film centred on a small company of outnumbered British troops who are forced to defend an abandoned farmhouse from an onslaught by the German Afrika Corps. It headlined Leo Genn, a former serviceman in possession of the *Croix de Guerre* (other leading roles were taken by Kieron Moore, Michael Medwin, Robert Brown and Michael Ripper). More well-meaning than accomplished, with its requisite tanks hired from a scrap metal dealer, *The Steel Bayonet* was released early in the summer of 1957.

A sensation in its day, *The Camp on Blood Island* was another matter entirely. At a Japanese prisoner of war camp on an island in Malaya, Allied captives learn that the war has ended via a concealed radio. Their sadistic captors, however, whose radio has failed, are unaware of this. Colonel Lambert (André Morell) fears that cruel camp commandant Yamamitsu (Ronald Radd) will order a massacre if he finds out. Suggested by a former prisoner of war, its narrative was coldly designed to indict Japan for its treatment of wartime hostages. Set-piece scenes such as the one in which a POW is forced, on pain of death, to ignite sackfuls of unseen letters from his fellows' loved ones fully achieve that grim purpose. Its veracity was questioned by Shiro Kido, chairman of the Motion Picture Association of Japan, who requested it be banned

LEO GENN in STEEL BAYONET

KIERON MOORE · MICHAEL MEDWIN with Robert Brown · Michael Ripper · Original story & Screenplay by Howard Clewes · Associate Producer Anthony Nelson-Keys · Produced & Directed by Michael Carreras   **CENTRAFILM N.V.**

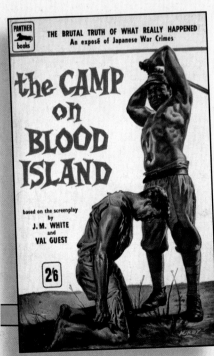

PANTHER books
THE BRUTAL TRUTH OF WHAT REALLY HAPPENED
An exposé of Japanese War Crimes
the CAMP on BLOOD ISLAND
based on the screenplay by J. M. WHITE and VAL GUEST
2'6

from American screens. Today, it's hard to reconcile *The Camp on Blood Island*'s offensive advertising — "Jap War Crimes Exposed!" — with its seriousness of intent. It *is* a very good film, but has to be contextualised as a scab on a sore and open wound. On its release in April 1958, the critical reception was polarised: "sincere", according to *The Times*, but "shameful", "an orgy of atrocities" and "an abomination" elsewhere.

Filmed early in 1959, *Yesterday's Enemy*, set in the Burmese jungle, concerned a group of British troops led by Captain Langford (Stanley Baker), who, when interrogating a captured Burmese (Wolfe Morris), orders two innocent villagers shot in order to loosen the man's tongue. The Padre (Guy Rolfe) expresses the disgust of several of his fellows, but the killings have revealed that a Japanese attack is imminent. The troops are later captured by the Japanese, and their Colonel Yamazaki (Philip Ahn) has Lieutenant Hastings (Gordon Jackson) put in front of a firing squad in order to persuade the Captain to talk.

Writer Peter R. Newman was a former RAF pilot and parachutist who'd spent some time in the intelligence corps. Post-war, he'd written several short radio plays that were broadcast in Australia, Malaysia and Hong Kong. His first television script, *Yesterday's Enemy*, was suggested by a true story told to him by an officer who had first-hand experience of its events. The play was broadcast by BBC TV on 14 October

1958, and caused Newman to receive a flurry of letters. "Some congratulated me," he later recalled, "others were openly abusive. Others accused me of being anti-British or anti-army. I asked some of these letter-writers to come and see me... but they never came... war is not an adventure story from *Boys' Own Paper*. The major point of the play is this: can certain injustices, known for want of a better name as war crimes, be defensible if the means justify the end?"

The film, one of three Hammers to be shot at

VAL GUEST: WRITER/DIRECTOR

Valmond Guest, one of Hammer's premier directors, broke new ground in his no-holds-barred depiction of horrors from recent history in both *The Camp on Blood Island* and *Yesterday's Enemy*, while his documentary-style approach had granted both *The Quatermass Xperiment* and *Quatermass 2* a verisimilitude unprecedented in screen science fiction. Guest had started out his film career co-authoring comedies such as the Will Hay vehicles *Oh, Mr Porter!* and *Ask a Policeman*. He made his directorial début on the Arthur Askey film *Miss London Ltd* in 1943. His association with Hammer began as a result of his friendship with comedian Ben Lyon. He was hired to direct *Life With the Lyons* for the company in 1954, and stayed to guide them through their first two colour features, *Men of Sherwood Forest* and *Break in the Circle*. His other

Hammer credits include *The Abominable Snowman*, *Up the Creek*, *Further Up the Creek*, *Hell is a City* and *When Dinosaurs Ruled the Earth*. He later directed three episodes of eighties TV series *Hammer House of Mystery and Suspense*. "Val Guest was very organised," remembers Gil Taylor, his director of photography on the 1960 thriller *The Full Treatment*. "Every morning he would set up an easel and detail the forthcoming day's work, so everybody on the set knew what they were doing. He would sketch detailed storyboards himself, and nearly always shoot what he outlined. There was 100 per cent co-operation between cameraman and director. He was a good ideas man, very inventive."

The versatile Guest's other works span Cliff Richard's *Expresso Bongo*, *Casino Royale* and *Toomorrow*; he was also responsible for the outstanding *The Day the Earth Caught Fire*, an apocalyptic science fiction thriller since optioned by Hammer.

Shepperton by Val Guest, was so impressively designed by Bernard Robinson that première guest of honour Lord Mountbatten was fooled into believing it had indeed been shot in its native *milieu*. Excellently reviewed and fulsomely endorsed by both British and Japanese military personnel, *Yesterday's Enemy* was banned outright by the Hong Kong censor in June — but, as the company noted, consequent publicity could be exploited to the film's benefit. (A cable of protest was nevertheless despatched to Hong Kong's Governor General by the Burma Star Association.) Japanese audiences received the film, perhaps, with a certain sense of *schadenfreude*; its Tokyo première was apparently an unqualified success.

Not a war film *per se*, 1959 also saw the release of *Ten Seconds to Hell*, a would-be epic melodrama concerning an explosives disposal squad in the ruins of post-war Berlin, directed by Robert Aldrich. Filmed as *The Phoenix*, and utilising genuine German locations, Hammer had the highest of hopes for this much-troubled film, a major co-production with United Artists. It bombed.

I Only Arsked and *Don't Panic Chaps!*, meanwhile, were slight humour-in-uniform escapades. *The Secret of Blood Island*, a squalid 1965 prequel to *The Camp on Blood Island*, featured Barbara Shelley as a British spy whose essential mission is curtailed when

she lands among the camp's prisoners. Unlike its precursor, it doesn't deserve the benefit of the doubt.

In the early seventies, following on from a later revival of interest in the genre prompted by pictures such as *The Dirty Dozen* and *Where Eagles Dare*, Hammer submitted Don Houghton's script *The Savage Jackboot* — "a story of violent resistance set in France in 1945" — to Paramount, who advised that it would be of interest only if stars of the stature of *Ten Seconds to Hell*'s Jack Palance or Yul Brynner could be secured. The project, budgeted at £1.5m, eventually foundered.

Previous page (bottom left): The Camp on Blood Island *novelisation was the most successful paperback adaptation of any Hammer film. Hammer struck a deal with original publishers Hamilton & Co in February 1958. The book based on the screenplay was still being reprinted in the early eighties.*
Previous page (bottom right): Hammer's commitment to realism in Yesterday's Enemy *attracted stringent American censorship.*
Above left: Captain Langford (Stanley Baker) *patrols the Burmese jungle in* Yesterday's Enemy. "I know where that is," *Lord Mountbatten told director Val Guest during the première screening. "I was there!"*
Above right: Val Guest on location in Cornwall for Break in the Circle, *1954.*
Left: Colonel Lambert (André Morell, second from left) and the beleaguered inmates of The Camp on Blood Island. *Imported palm trees helped create the illusion of south east Asia at Bray Studios.*

D R A C U L A

**Principal photography 11 November 1957 to
3 January 1958
Released 22 May 1958
Certificate X
Duration 82 mins
Colour
Director Terence Fisher**

Jonathan Harker (John Van Eyssen) arrives at Castle Dracula where he is to be engaged as librarian to its reclusive, albeit charming, Count (Christopher Lee). However, Harker soon finds himself to be imprisoned within the castle and shortly thereafter encounters a beautiful vampire woman who attempts to drink his blood. Dracula intervenes, taking Harker for himself. It transpires that Harker has been working in tandem with Doctor Van Helsing (Peter Cushing) and together they have plotted to destroy the fiendish vampire Count. Van Helsing follows Harker's route to the castle, where he discovers his vampirised comrade lying in a coffin and stakes him through the heart. Van Helsing then travels to the village of Karlstadt, where Harker's fiancée Lucy (Carol Marsh) is waiting for news of Jonathan in the house of her brother Arthur Holmwood (Michael Gough). But Lucy has fallen ill with an anaemic condition and at night she is being visited by the vengeful Dracula...

elevision cameras covered the London première of Hammer's *Dracula* in May 1958. One cheerful punter, exiting the cinema, was asked for his opinion of the movie. "I love to see the blood spurt," he answered with relish.

By the summer of 1957, *The Curse of Frankenstein* was proving to be a massive success. "I enclose a new batch of figures which are quite fantastic," wrote James Carreras to Eliot Hyman on 7 July. "England is sweltering in a heatwave and NOTHING is taking any money except *The Curse...*" Hammer were already well into pre-production on their retelling of that other Gothic classic, *Dracula*, having brokered a deal between Hyman's Seven Arts production company and Universal-International to do so.

Obtaining the necessary rights to film a new version of Bram Stoker's novel had been no easy business. Universal had drawn up an exclusive contract with Stoker's estate in the thirties, forbidding all others the film rights to the character. At a cost of $40,000, the contract had ensured Universal's noted cycle of pictures originally starring Bela Lugosi. After several months' wrangling a compro-

mise was reached, Hammer granting distribution rights to Universal in exchange for permission to make the picture in the first place. Ironically, *Dracula* entered the public domain — and became, therefore, free for all — in 1962, fifty years after Stoker's death.

Dracula was budgeted, fairly modestly, at £81,412. Jimmy Sangster worked on his adaptation over four weeks in the summer; his screenplay omitted Dracula's journey to England, setting the film entirely in the cod *mittel*-Europe which Hammer would make notorious. Certain characters, such as Renfield, the fly-eating lunatic held in Dracula's thrall, would be likewise excised. Sangster also went to some lengths to avoid the clichés of Universal's vampire. This Dracula, a charming sexual predator, would not be seen to turn into a bat nor scale walls. His powers were left in the realm of supposition; eerily, his footsteps would be eliminated from the soundtrack to underscore the Count's ethereal nature. (And had wardrobe mistress Molly Arbuthnot obeyed Sangster's stage directions to the letter, Dracula would have carried "a black hat" upon his entrance!)

Christopher Lee took the lead role; no one else was auditioned. *Dracula* was shot at Bray over twenty-five days, eventually wrapping on 3 January 1958. Such was the company's desire for secrecy that visiting photographers were told that they might only snap Lee from behind. "We feel it might spoil the fun for millions of film-goers if they see

what Dracula looks like before they take their seats in a cinema," Anthony Hinds explained to *Picture Show* magazine.

Sequences involving the coach were filmed on a local country road. Cushing spurned a double for these, and practised driving the vehicle for two whole days beforehand. The Castle Dracula exterior was constructed on the lot, its appearance bolstered by a matte shot which filled in its turrets and mountain backdrop. As with *The Curse of Frankenstein*, a number of contracted actors never made the finished film when their characters' scenes were eliminated. In this instance, a very early sequence where Harker is seen in a coach travelling to Castle Dracula was omitted; his fellow travellers — a man (Stedwell Fulcher), his wife (Judith Nelmes), a fat merchant (Humphrey Kent) and a priest (William Sherwood) — were to be shown attempting to dissuade him from going. The scene, possibly unfilmed, would ultimately be replaced by Harker's straightforward voiceover. The final day's shooting was devoted to the vampire's climactic disintegration in the dawning sun's rays. Make-up designer Phil Leakey and special effects supervisor Sid Pearson worked closely to achieve this effect, which was shot in three lengthy stages.

The film premièred at the Warner Theater,

Milwaukee, Wisconsin on 8 May as *Horror of Dracula* (Universal having decided to differentiate Hammer's version from their original thus). It took $1,682 on its first day. In Britain, the film opened to the public at London's Gaumont Theatre, Haymarket, on 22 May and hit the circuits soon after. When *Dracula* played Birmingham's Gaumont, a recruitment exhibition posted in the foyer by the Midlands Blood Transfusion Service had to be hurriedly withdrawn after regular donors complained that the display was in "bad taste." Meanwhile, James Carreras — dubbed "King of Nausea" in a *Daily Express* profile on 23 May — was delighted by the response to the film. "This one will clean up," he told reporter Leonard Mosley. "It opens on Broadway next week, and they'll love it..."

Dracula's published detractors were barbed as ever: "I came away revolted and outraged," wrote Nina Hibbin in the *Daily Worker*, "this film disgusts the mind and repels the senses." "One step farther," claimed the *Daily Sketch*'s Harold Conway, "and the licence permitted by the Censor's 'X' certificate will be dangerously abused." Only Paul Dehn in the *Daily Chronicle* stood up in *Dracula*'s defence: "what is an X Certificate *for*," he asked on 23 May, "if we may not see a stake being Hammered into a lady's heart?" But time has been kind to Hammer's *Dracula*. When the film was briefly re-released as part of the Barbican's 1996 Hammer retrospective, the *Evening Standard*'s Neil Norman described it as "romantic cinema that transcends genre. Unimpeachable and unsurpassed." Even veteran critic Derek Malcolm, who once wrote to *Sight and Sound* magazine claiming that "A sane society can-

Page 30: *Mina (Melissa Stribling) succumbs to Count Dracula (Christopher Lee). "Dracula preyed upon the sexual frustrations of his women victims," said Terence Fisher. "The [Holmwood] marriage was one in which she was not sexually satisfied and that was her weakness as far as Dracula's approach to her was concerned."*

Page 31, top right: *The Count defends himself during the climactic struggle with Van Helsing.*

Page 31, middle: *Jonathan Harker (John Van Eyssen) is made welcome by Count Dracula. The actors' freezing breath during this scene illustrates the uncomfortable conditions at Bray Studios.*

Page 31, bottom: *"He is powerful to do much harm and suffers not as we do," wrote Stoker. "This battle is but begun..."*

Right: *Sangster's script described Dracula as "A tall man, his face is thin and saturnine, with deep set eyes, high cheekbones, aquiline nose, high forehead topped by jet black hair. When he speaks we may notice that his two canine teeth are slightly longer than normal..."*

Below left: *Peter Cushing as Van Helsing. "I played the part more or less as myself," he claimed.*

Below right: *Peter Cushing and Terence Fisher celebrate their success.*

not stand the posters, let alone the films!", was moved in *The Guardian* to recant. "It is brilliantly filmed and acted," he wrote on 1 August, complimenting the picture for its "social and poetic connotations".

A lithe, sensuous and near-mesmeric Count, Lee dominates *Dracula* despite his meagre thirteen lines. The film's eroticism, too, is startling: outstand-

ing is the scene where the bedridden Lucy awaits Dracula's coming, like "a bride trembling with anxiety and anticipation on her wedding night", as has been suggested. "It's almost ballet the way she opens the doors, goes back and lies down again, her eyes focused," said director Terence Fisher. "The filming of *Dracula* went like a dream. Everything worked."

*f*or films such as *She*, *Rasputin the Mad Monk* and, of course, *Dracula*, Christopher Lee became as synonymous with Hammer as Peter Cushing. Unlike his co-star, however, Lee would never be comfortable with the typecasting the association brought.

Christopher Frank Carandini Lee was born in Belgravia, London, on 27 May 1922. (Lee's mother's family, the Carandinis, are one of the oldest in Italy.) Following the divorce of his parents in 1928, life became difficult — his mother remarried, only to face further difficulties when her second husband became bankrupt. "He was drunk every night and lost every penny," Lee recalls. His mother divorced his step-father, with far-reaching consequences: "The money went totally. My mother was left at the age of fifty with two teenage children and nothing."

Lee was forced to abandon a promising academic career, leaving Wellington College in 1939, a year before he was due to complete his studies. He took several mundane jobs to help support his struggling family, before joining the RAF in 1941. The remainder of his war was dominated by intelligence work, for which he was mentioned in dispatches. He returned to civilian life in 1946 and, ignoring his mother's advice to avoid the acting profession ("Think of all the appalling people you will meet!"), secured a seven-year contract with Rank. Notable among his earliest films was a gate-crashed role as an extra in Olivier's *Hamlet* and a brief scene in John Huston's *Moulin Rouge*. Although Peter Cushing also appeared in both films, he didn't share a scene with Lee in either.

The early fifties proved difficult for Lee after the Rank charm school 'let him go': "They would send me, and others, to see some of their contract directors and producers. They would say, 'Well, nobody's ever heard of you, you've got no experience, you're too tall, you're too foreign-looking...'" Lee found acting work wherever he could, at one point subsidising his income with a stint as an interpreter in the export department of Simpson's in Piccadilly.

The years of experience eventually paid off: "Between 1947 and 1957, I had learned. And when the time came for me to play a role of consequence, I was ready." Hammer's *The Curse of Frankenstein* and *Dracula* brought him leading parts and global recognition. They also established his personal and professional relationship with Peter Cushing — the two men became close friends and frequent co-stars in subsequent films by Hammer and their contemporaries.

Dracula threatened to sideline Lee's career as soon as it took off. Mindful of the typecasting that had overshadowed Bela Lugosi, he took on diverse roles in films across Europe. One of them, *The Devil's Daffodil*, taxed even his mastery of language: "You tell me, how do you play a Chinese detective in German?"

The man Hammer press releases described as "London's most eligible film bachelor" married Dutch model Birgit Kroencke on 17 March 1961 and the couple spent part of their honeymoon as guests of James Carreras and his wife, Vera. Mr and Mrs Lee emigrated to Vaud in Switzerland in 1962, Christopher taking the opportunity to expand his career and escape Britain's punishing taxation. Their only child, Christina, was born 23 November 1963.

The Lees returned to England in 1965, Christopher's busy career still characterised by the variable quality of the films he was offered. He allowed James Carreras to persuade him into reprising his most famous role again and again, and his initial enthusiasm for Dracula soon turned to resentment. Away from the vampire Count he made memorable contributions to other Hammer films, most notably *The Devil Rides Out* and *To the Devil a Daughter*, while successfully expanding his appeal in major league films such as *The Private Life of Sherlock Holmes* and *The Man With the Golden Gun*. During the early seventies he formed his own production company, Charlemagne, with Hammer producer Anthony Nelson Keys and made *Nothing But the Night* for Rank. *The Wicker Man*, while similarly modest, brought him lasting acclaim for his portrayal of the sinister lord of a Scottish island held in the grip of brutal pagan beliefs. The film is regarded by many, including Lee, as his best.

Keen to escape narrow-minded casting directors for good, Lee took his family to California in 1976. "I guested on *Saturday Night Live*, I made *1941* for Steven Spielberg, I appeared in Westerns, martial arts movies... My whole career changed, which is why, when people ask me 'Don't you ever feel worried about being typecast?' I always reply 'I'm not'. And the evidence is on the screen." Feeling he had "proved a point", Lee returned to London in 1986.

Lee now feels confident enough to dabble in the horror genre in films like *Funny Man*, while affectionately parodying his old image in *Gremlins 2*, directed by admirer Joe Dante. When given quality material, as he was in *A Feast at Midnight*, it is clear why his career as a film star has enjoyed such longevity.

The death of Peter Cushing in 1994 affected Lee deeply: "Without that voice on the telephone I do feel very lonely, very lonely... Real friendship is rare." The last king of horror, a mantle Christopher Lee has reluctantly inherited, continues adding to one of the lengthiest CVs in cinema history. "I don't really know, after all these films, if I have reached my full potential, " he reveals. "Really, to this day I don't know if I have been stretched."

PETER CUSHING
in
"DRACULA"
IN EASTMAN COLOUR
Also starring
MICHAEL GOUGH and MELISSA STRIBLING
with
CHRISTOPHER LEE
as DRACULA
A UNIVERSAL-INTERNATIONAL PRESENTATION
OF A HAMMER FILM PRODUCTION
RANK FILM DISTRIBUTORS LTD.

THE REVENGE OF FRANKENSTEIN

Principal photography 6 January to
4 March 1958
Released 27 August 1958
Certificate X
Duration 89 minutes
Colour
Director Terence Fisher

1860: Baron Frankenstein (Peter Cushing) cheats the guillotine and escapes to Carlsbruck, where he establishes a lucrative medical practise under the pseudonym Doctor Victor Stein. At the nearby poor hospital three years later, he is recognised by visiting doctor Hans Kleve (Francis Matthews) and the two agree to secretly work together. Stein has prepared a 'perfect' body for his hunchbacked assistant Karl (Oscar Quitak), who volunteers his brain to be implanted. While convalescing at the poor hospital, the new Karl (Michael Gwynn) is released by a good-natured nurse (Eunice Gayson) and returns to the Baron's laboratory, where he hauls his old body onto the furnace. Karl is discovered, however, and badly beaten by a sadistic janitor (George Woodbridge). His still-sensitive 'new' brain is damaged, and his corrupted body begins developing cannibalistic tendencies. Before dying, the murderous, slavering Karl reveals Stein's true identity to the denizens of Carlsbruck. The patients of the poor hospital, realising they have been unwitting donors to Frankenstein's experiments, turn on the Baron...

And exactly how, enquired the *Sunday Express*, could James Carreras make a sequel to *The Curse of Frankenstein*, since that film closed with the wicked Baron being condemned to the guillotine? The Colonel replied with typical aplomb: "Oh, we sew the head back on again!"

In fact, Hammer had been considering a sequel as early as January 1957. The title of the follow-up — *The Blood of Frankenstein* — was registered in March and artwork, optimistically portraying Christopher Lee's Creature, prepared soon after. Little is known about Jimmy Sangster's first draft of *The Blood of Frankenstein*, other than it was contracted on 24 July 1957. Sangster was under a lot of pressure to complete a revised version, not just because he was concurrently writing *Intent to Kill* for Twentieth Century-Fox, but also because James Carreras had already struck a deal with American distributors Columbia, partly on the basis of lurid poster artwork bearing the title *The Revenge of Frankenstein*. (This initial package, announced by Columbia's Mike Frank-

ovich on 6 September, also included *The Camp on Blood Island* and *The Snorkel*. It led to the most significant co-production deal in the company's history.) Sangster was given a tight deadline: "Jim Carreras returned to London and presented me with the poster. Please would I write a movie to fit, and hurry it up because he'd promised delivery within an impossibly short space of time." Sangster didn't disappoint him — his final draft was contracted on 15 October. *The Revenge of Frankenstein*, as the script was retitled, was supplemented with 'additional dialogue' by Hurford Janes, while an unaccredited George Baxt notably contributed the light-hearted opening scenes with two drunken grave robbers.

At Bray Studios, a sheep's brain doubled for that transplanted into the 'perfect' body, and was to be used again on the following day's shoot as a double for the Baron's brain. "Someone had forgotten to put

TERROR will seize you!
TENSION will squeeze you!
CHILLS will freeze you!

"THE REVENGE OF FRANKENSTEIN"

If you go alone ...you'll find yourself running all the way home!

IN SUPER-NATURAL TECHNICOLOR

Starring PETER CUSHING · EUNICE GAYSON · FRANCIS MATTHEWS · MICHAEL GWYNN
Written by JIMMY SANGSTER · Produced by ANTHONY HINDS · Directed by TERENCE FISHER · A HAMMER FILM PRODUCTION · A COLUMBIA PICTURE

"In the year eighteen hundred and sixty, I, Baron Frankenstein, was sentenced to death on the guillotine... But I have escaped the guillotine, and I shall avenge the death of my creation." The trailer for *The Revenge of Frankenstein* was distinguished by Peter Cushing's address to the audience, and specially commissioned by Columbia. Footage intended exclusively for promotional use was again prepared at Bray Studios for *Dracula Prince of Darkness*. On 18 December 1965, Christopher Lee starred in a television commercial that gave him more dialogue than the entire film. Such rarities aside, the responsibility for compiling Hammer's trailers fell to National Screen Service Ltd in Perivale, Middlesex. The company was also charged with printing and distributing promotional material, such as front-of-house stills. Working to the approval of each film's producer and director, NSS staff took anything up to four weeks to script, edit and dub trailers of around two minutes' length. The compilation of U certificate trailers, in addition to X certificate versions, was sometimes difficult. "The Hammer situation... seems to present a special problem," NSS's Esther Harris wrote to Brian Lawrence while working on *Taste the Blood of Dracula*. "These are usually horror pictures, and we must have a U certificate trailer, although I think we have got away with some extremely provocative trailers in spite of the U certificate for this country." Hammer's trailers were narrated by such actors as Patrick Allen, Keith Barron, Valentine Dyall and Bill Mitchell, although they were usually re-dubbed in foreign territories.

it into the fridge," remembers Francis Matthews. "They left it out all night in this glass pot thing, and it was alive! It was full of maggots, and the crew were all holding their noses. Instead of the operation, we filmed a few close-ups of Peter and me while they got a new sheep's brain. It took them quite a while before they got one — they had to order it."

The Revenge of Frankenstein received a gala première at midnight on 27 August 1958 at the Plaza in Piccadilly Circus. Francis Matthews remembers some inappropriate reactions to certain lines: "The audience laughed when I had to say, 'Pray Heaven I've got the skill to do this' [before transplanting Frankenstein's brain] and, 'It was a superb operation doctor, I learned a great deal' [after the first brain transplant]. Peter, who was sitting with me, said, 'My dear boy, what have we done?' But it was a big première, and it went very well." In America, Columbia had already double-billed the film with Jacques Tourneur's *Curse of the Demon* to lucrative effect.

Writing in *The Observer*, C.A. Lejeune was less accommodating than many of her Fleet Street colleagues: "The whole thing is, to my taste, a vulgar, stupid, nasty and intolerably tedious business; a crude sort of entertainment for a crude sort of audience; but it leaves me with a sense of nausea rather than horror. I want to gargle it off with a strong disinfectant, to scrub my memory with carbolic soap." Noting the film's climax, where Frankenstein resumes business in London's Harley Street, fellow critic Peter Burnup anticipated a sequel: "The door is open for yet another horror, to be called doubtless *Dr Frankenstein and the National Health Service*."

Cast and crew meet the challenge of this ambitious tragedy with impressive results, making *The Revenge of Frankenstein* a superb all-round accomplishment. Peter Cushing steals every scene, exploiting a sardonic script with an assured performance.

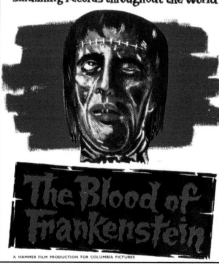

Sensational Sequel to "The Curse of Frankenstein", which is smashing records throughout the world

The Blood of Frankenstein

A HAMMER FILM PRODUCTION FOR COLUMBIA PICTURES

THE REVENGE OF FRANKENSTEIN (EASTMAN COLOR) SOON FROM HAMMER FOR COLUMBIA

Previous page: *The Baron (Peter Cushing) is led to his death. Or is he?*
Above: *Hans Kleve (Francis Matthews) and Baron Frankenstein (Peter Cushing). "The quality of the films came from Jack Asher's lighting and photography and Bernard Robinson's set designs," says Matthews.*
Far left: *An early trade ad under the working title of* The Blood of Frankenstein.

TALES OF FRANKENSTEIN

Early in 1958, a twenty-six minute pilot episode entitled *Tales of Frankenstein* was shot in the United States. It was Hammer's first, abortive, attempt to produce a television series.

he pilot appears to have springboarded from the Hammer/Columbia co-production deal announced on 6 September 1957. Screen Gems, the television production subsidiary of Columbia, would be Hammer's partners. The format for the series was established in early autumn 1957, with twenty-six half-hour instalments proposed, thirteen to be produced in Hollywood and thirteen at Bray. (Surprisingly, only eight were required, at this stage, to feature Baron Frankenstein himself!) Around this time, Jimmy Sangster was approached for story ideas. He came up with eight single-line scenarios — "He has a set to with Zombies"; "He dabbles in some voodoo, and gets himself a big Black assistant"; "his dabblings in time factors turn people into primaeval slime" — all of which appear to have been some way removed from Screen Gems' notions.

Anthony Hinds was originally delegated to go to America to develop the pilot. When he flew home, disenchanted, Michael Carreras took his place at the end of November. Later, he'd call it "one of the unhappiest experiences of my screen career." Screen Gems had employed Curt Siodmak, the German-born writer/director who'd penned much of Universal's forties horror output, including *The Wolf Man* and *House of Frankenstein*, as both associate producer and director. Siodmak provided a story, 'The Face in the Tombstone Mirror', which was developed into a teleplay by husband and wife Catherine and Henry Kuttner, themselves bastions of horror fiction; both had been contributors to legendary anthology magazine *Weird Tales* (Henry, a former writing partner of H. P. Lovecraft's, died shortly after completing the script).

The story begins with the Baron's latest, brain-damaged Monster attacking him in his lab; cut to a local inn, where the terminally-ill Paul Halpert (credited "Max") and his wife Christine are on their way to visit the Baron, whom they believe will be able to alleviate Paul's condition, but he declines to help. Paul dies, is buried — and then exhumed by the Baron, who places Paul's fine brain in his Monster's body. Duly revived, the Monster lumbers after Christine, who's suspicious of the Baron. The Monster comes to some kind of self-awareness and turns on the Baron, pursuing him to the graveyard. Christine begs with Paul/the Monster to spare Frankenstein's life. It hurls itself into Paul's open grave, and is showered with earth.

The aptly European Anton Diffring played the Baron; Christine was played by Helen Westcott, star of *Abbott and Costello Meet Dr Jekyll and Mr Hyde* and *Monster on the Campus*; Don Megowan, a for-

mer Sea Creature (*The Creature Walks Among Us*) and B-movie *Werewolf* played the Monster beneath a Karloff-esque make-up designed by Clay Campbell. Not the most inspiring of half-hours, the pilot was thought effective enough to continue work on the mooted series and the ABC network began searching for a sponsor.

The pilot had cost some $80,000. On 25 March 1958, James Carreras wrote to Screen Gems' Ralph Cohn in New York, informing him that Hammer considered that they could have made a pilot of the same quality at Bray for a mere $45,000 — and under British quota. "Why don't we make more of them in England?" urged Carreras (who hadn't, as yet, seen the pilot). He continued: "I know... we all agreed that only thirteen should be made here and the reason I am making such a bloody nuisance of myself is because I have tremendous faith in this series and I honestly believe that we can make them better than anyone else. Let me know when you are ready to start."

Between March and May 1958, five storylines, broken down scene-by-scene, were prepared in England for the series. In the fairytale *Story No. 1*, by Carreras' friend A. R. Rawlinson, author of Exclusive films *Meet Simon Cherry* and *Celia*, a traveller named Peter, investigating the Baron's castle, finds a lovely girl named Lisa in the grounds. He's sent packing by Frankenstein, but returns to rescue the placid

Lisa from the Baron, who lays down to the lovelorn Peter a challenge: if he can raise but one spark of emotion in the cold Lisa, he may take her away. Lisa is, of course, a creation of the Baron's; she has no emotions, no soul. Berserk and homicidal, the evil Lisa — who's delighted in ensnaring the foolish swain — goes after Peter with a knife...

Producer Hinds' notes were appended to each breakdown and here they suggested Lisa be retained for use in a future tale. (Frankenstein's soulless created woman might be considered an antecedent of a later Hammer *mademoiselle*.) The blackly comic second synopsis, dated 1 April, was by Hugh Woodhouse, later a writer for Gerry Anderson's *Supercar* series. The Baron creates an identical double of himself, Frankenstein-2, which shares all his own "brain impulses." The naive F-2, however, also shares the Baron's "subconscious desires" — including murderous ones, killing a journalist and a priest when sent out to take the Baron's place. Woodhouse's Baron was considered rather childish by the producer. Thought rather better was Cyril Kersh's twenty-eight-scene *Story No. 3*, in which the Baron and a curious colleague concoct a scheme to ascertain what one might experience after death. They drug and murder a local doctor, Ulrich, later revitalising him and quizzing him about his night-time dreams, although Ulrich remains unaware of what's he's been through. (The Baron's accomplice is Zoltan, a name later used in *The Evil of Franken-stein*.)

Story No. 4, from the pen of Edward Dryhurst, a writer/producer/director of thirties films, had the Baron rescuing two frost-bitten travellers from the snow — and using them in his experiments, planning to freeze them and then bring them back to life. Best of all, however, was Peter Bryan's *Story No. 5*. Bryan, a former Exclusive camera operator who was at that time a producer/director of short films for Hammer, went on to pen screenplays for *The Hound of the Baskervilles*, *The Brides of Dracula* and *The Plague of the Zombies*. His prospective *Tales of Frankenstein* episode concerned sideshow mesmerist Khotan, who's asked by the Baron to restore the memory of his latest damaged creation. The Baron's Creature murders the mystic, whose mind is placed in the Creature's body, but Khotan/the Creature then entrances the Baron and returns to the travelling fair whence he came. Eventually exposed, the wretched Khotan/Creature escapes the Baron's clutches only by hypnotising Khotan's own bastard daughter to kill the tortured mystic. Elements of Bryan's tale clearly anticipate portions of both *The Evil of Frankenstein* (the hypnotist, the funfair) and *Frankenstein Must Be Destroyed* (brain transference of an intelligent individual) and as such it most pointedly indicates the potential lost when *Tales of Frankenstein* faltered.

Carreras, keen to make the entire series at Bray, had noted in his earlier letter to Ralph Cohn that "certain subjects made in England have failed on American TV and therefore, sponsors and networks

ANTON DIFFRING: FRANKENSTEIN

PARAMOUNT presents "THE MAN WHO COULD CHEAT DEATH" A HAMMER PRODUCTION TECHNICOLOR

Born in Germany in 1918, Diffring had studied his art at Berlin's Academy of Drama. Post-war, he found stage work in the America, but it was in Britain where he cemented his reputation as the archetypal film Nazi in fifties pictures such as *State Secret* and *Albert RN*. In 1958 he appeared as Baron Frankenstein in the *Tales of Frankenstein* TV pilot and returned to Hammer for *The Man Who Could Cheat Death* and *Shatter*. At the time of *The Man Who Could Cheat Death's* 1959 release, Diffring could be regularly seen as the host of the short-lived TV quiz show *Win a Mink*. His horror career straddled both the lead role of deranged plastic surgeon Doctor Schuler in *Circus of Horrors* and a part opposite Peter Cushing in *The Beast Must Die*. He died in July 1989.

are nervous of these subjects." It may well be that it was the Colonel's keenness to make the entire series at Bray, rather than the quality of the American-produced pilot itself, that scotched *Tales of Frankenstein*. Its moment passed; the proposed series slipped away. Although the pilot has aired sporadically on late-night American TV, it has never been broadcast in the UK.

Hammer attempted twice more to interest Screen Gems in possible TV formats. Early in 1961, Michael Carreras went location scouting in Africa for *Safari*, a mooted thirteen-hour series; in 1967, Screen Gems were sent a proposal for a series based on *Hell is a City*, Hammer's gritty 1959 police drama. Nothing came of either. It wasn't until 1968 that Hammer managed to set up a second TV co-production deal. One that proved markedly more fruitful...

Previous page: Christine (Helen Westcott) and Paul (Richard Bull).
Left: Christine begs the assistance of the reluctant Frankenstein (Anton Diffring) in 'The Face in the Tombstone Mirror'.

THE HOUND OF THE BASKERVILLES

**Principal photography 13 September to
31 October 1958
Released 4 May 1959
Certificate A
Duration 87 mins
Colour
Director Terence Fisher**

According to legend, the wicked eighteenth century landowner Sir Hugo Baskerville (David Oxley) fell victim to a "hound of hell" after murdering a servant girl on Dartmoor. Over a century later, when his ancestor Charles is found dead on the moor, apparently frightened to death, historian Doctor Mortimer (Francis De Wolff) requests the assistance of noted detective Sherlock Holmes (Peter Cushing). Mortimer fears for the well-being of the Baskerville heir, Sir Henry (Christopher Lee); in London Henry discovers a lethal tarantula placed inside his boot. Having travelled to Baskerville Hall, Holmes and colleague Doctor Watson (André Morell) learn that an escaped convict, Seldon (Michael Mulcaster), is at large on the moor. Seldon, however, is slain by some kind of beast; his body is later found mutilated according to a sacrificial rite. Dissolute farmer Stapleton (Ewen Solon) and daughter Cecile (Marla Landi) are behind the killings; also related to the rakish Sir Hugo, they plan to ensure that Sir Henry, too, succumbs to the alleged curse...

Eliot Hyman's son, Kenneth, secured the rights that enabled Hammer to put their version of *The Hound of the Baskervilles* into production. Hyman and Hammer both envisaged a series of movies following on from this, the first Sherlock Holmes adaptation to be filmed in colour. Peter Cushing, an avid collector of *The Strand* magazine — Holmes' original home — was delighted to land the part, albeit slightly concerned when James Carreras presold his incarnation of the Great Detective as a "sexy Sherlock."

Although designed to suit an A certificate, Peter Bryan's otherwise faithful screenplay beefed up the original, adding sensational, horror-tinged aspects to the story. Early on, an attempt is made on Sir Henry's life via a tarantula spider placed in his boot; Stapleton's virtuous sister mutates into blackhearted, half-Spanish daughter Cecile; an attempt is made on Holmes' life in a disused mine; and, most bizarrely, Stapleton's right hand is monstrously webbed.

Surrey's Frensham Ponds doubled as Dartmoor, although brief inserts of both Dartmoor itself and Holyport were spliced into the film. Other parts of the moor were created in the studio at Bray. Cushing had re-read the novel in preparation, and asked for parts of the 221B Baker Street set to be modified: "Holmes had this habit of keeping all his correspondence 'stabbed' on the mantelpiece with his jack-knife. Well, that wasn't in the script, so I said, 'Lets do that.'... As fate would have it, the mantelpiece was made of marble because it was one that they had in stock, so I asked them to put a piece of balsa wood on top of it — little things like that are all-important to a character..."

Arachnophobe Christopher Lee, playing Sir Henry, was dismayed to learn that he'd have to have a tarantula crawl up his arm for the part: "To begin with, it was me and then they cut to the actual spider crawling up the shoulder of the stuntman. Then there was a dummy put on my shoulder. But in point of fact I did have the spider on my sleeve, and I did have it near me, and I hate spiders." The appearance of the Hound in the final reel caused problems. An

SHERLOCK HOLMES' MOST TERRIFYING ADVENTURE!

PETER CUSHING
as SHERLOCK HOLMES

ANDRE MORELL
as Dr. Watson

CHRISTOPHER LEE
as Sir Henry Baskerville

MARLA LANDI

DAVID OXLEY

the Hound of the Baskervilles

TECHNICOLOR

Based on the novel by Sir Arthur Conan Doyle

·A·

A HAMMER FILM PRODUCTION

DER HUND VON BASKERVILLE
nach dem Roman von Sir Arthur Conan Doyle
PETER CUSHING
REGIE: TERENCE FISHER
TECHNICOLOR ®
UNITED ARTISTS

attempt had been made to trick the scale of the beast by having it pounce not on Lee but a small boy called Robert, who was dressed in Lee's costume. The footage was scuppered, and the scene shot with Lee and a Great Dane — named, improbably, Colonel — wearing a mask built by Margaret Carter, wife-to-be of production designer Bernard Robinson.

The BBFC required three minor cuts to be made before *The Hound of the Baskervilles* received an A certificate: in reel one, a shortening of "the scene in which a servant is held against the fire," plus deletion of a shot showing Sir Hugo "smelling girl's garment and his words 'Insolent cow!'"; and in reel nine, a reduction of the number of shots showing the Hound "worrying Stapleton's throat."

No further Hammer Holmeses were made after audiences' lukewarm response to the film's 1959 release. The critics were startled by Cushing's "impish, waspish, Wilde-ian" Holmes (*Films and Filming*), and uninterested by Hammer's souped-up presentation: "Any freshly entertaining possibilities in this much-

filmed story have been lost in a welter of blood, love interest and mood music," moaned the *Monthly Film Bulletin*; "The dialogue is indifferent. The producer, having reasonably cast Peter Cushing to play Holmes, need not have cast two of the tallest men on the English screen, Francis De Wolff and Christopher Lee, to dwarf him," remarked Campbell Dixon snidely in *The Daily Telegraph*. Cushing played Holmes again, both in a 1968 BBC TV series and in Tyburn's *The Masks of Death* in 1984. In 1962, co-star Lee got a crack at Holmes, too, alongside Thorley Walters as Watson: Terence Fisher directed this little-seen German production, *Sherlock Holmes und das Halsband des Todes* ('Sherlock Holmes and the Deadly Necklace'). Almost thirty years later, Lee got a second bite of the cherry as the lead in two nineties TV movies, *Sherlock Holmes and the Leading Lady* and *Incident at Victoria Falls*. Actress Marla Landi later became Lady Francis Dashwood; the Dashwood estate, where Hammer shot the climax of *To the Devil a Daughter*, is now her land.

Unusually, Conan Doyle's *The Hound of the Baskervilles* has a more substantial role for sidekick Doctor Watson than the Great Detective himself, who's absent for much of its middle section. Hammer turned to one of their most reliable leading men to fulfil the role: André Morell. Born André Mesritz in 1909, Morell made his screen début in the long-forgotten six-part film series *On Top of the Underworld* in 1937; the following year, he appeared at the Old Vic for the first time. His career was interrupted by the war, when he served as a Major in the Royal Welsh Fusiliers. He played in *So Long at the Fair*, co-directed by Terence Fisher, in 1949, and was prominent the next year in the Boulting Brothers' *Seven Days to Noon* (which won an Oscar for its storyline by Paul Dehn and Hammer composer James Bernard). Plastic surgery thriller *Stolen Face* took him to Exclusive/Hammer for the first time, and he later impressed as a creased POW in *The Camp on Blood Island*. Post-Watson, he featured in *The Shadow of the Cat*, *Cash on Demand*, *She*, *The Plague of the Zombies*, *The Mummy's Shroud* and *The Vengeance of She*. Married to Joan Greenwood (*Tom Jones*, etc), he was president of actors' union Equity in 1973-1974. Morell's last film was 1978's *The First Great Train Robbery*; he died later that same year.

Previous page: Christopher Lee and Marla Landi are hounded on location in Surrey.
Above left: In a London hotel, Sherlock Holmes (Peter Cushing) greets Sir Henry Baskerville (Christopher Lee); Doctors Mortimer and Watson (Francis De Wolff and André Morell) look on.
Far left and left: "Be like Sherlock Holmes," advised the film's press book, "smoke a pipe."

THE MAN WHO COULD CHEAT DEATH

**Principal photography 17 November to
30 December 1958
Released 30 November 1959
Duration 83 mins
Certificate X
Colour
Director Terence Fisher**

Paris, at the turn of the century: doctor and hobbyist sculptor Georges Bonnet (Anton Diffring) lives in the Rue Noire. Apparently youthful, the charismatic Bonnet has a dark secret: he is 104 years old. His near-immortality has been assured by a gland operation that must be performed every ten years lest accumulated old age and disease strike him down. He is awaiting the arrival of Dr Ludwig Weiss (Arnold Marle), with whom he first pioneered the technique. However, the aged Ludwig has suffered a stroke and is late, forcing Bonnet to murder to obtain a human fluid which delays his body's wasting. When model Margo (Delphi Lawrence) discovers Bonnet's condition, she promptly disappears. Ludwig finally arrives, but the stroke has paralysed the surgeon's right hand and he cannot perform the operation. The only alternative is to persuade fellow surgeon Pierre (Christopher Lee) to stand in for Ludwig. The increasingly deranged Bonnet, meanwhile, has dreadful plans for Janine (Hazel Court), a woman who pursued him from Italy after he broke off their affair — and with whom Pierre is in love...

laywright Barre Lyndon's stage début, *The Amazing Dr Clitterhouse*, had premièred at London's Theatre Royal in 1936, and was shortly thereafter optioned by Warner Bros as a film vehicle for Edward G. Robinson. A second Lyndon play, *The Man in Half Moon Street* — a horror-cum-fantasy

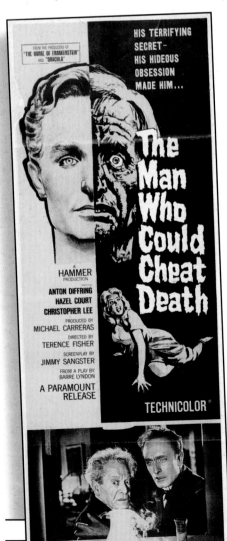

concerning a doctor forced to murder to maintain his artificially-induced youth — was filmed in 1944, headlined Nils Asther. Meanwhile, Lyndon's screenwriting career took an upward turn. Having adapted his own magazine serial *Sundown* for United Artists in 1941, he'd become noted in Hollywood, racking up screenwriting credits for a 1944 remake of *The Lodger*, the influential vaudevillian horror *Night Has a Thousand Eyes*, Cecil B. DeMille's *The Greatest Show on Earth* and *The War of the Worlds*.

Broadcast on the fledgling ITV network at 10.35pm on Saturday 22 June 1957, ABC TV's version of *The Man in Half Moon Street* — the second instalment in suspense anthology series *Hour of Mystery* — starred Anton Diffring as budding Meth-

uselah John Thackeray. Diffring was supported by Arnold Marle as Dr Ludwig Weisz [sic] and Melissa Stribling — later Mina Holmwood in Hammer's *Dracula* — as Betty Ryan, the object of Thackeray's affections. It was preceded in the schedules by the second episode of a whodunit, *Motive for Murder*, authored by Jimmy Sangster...

It was only natural that Hammer should co-produce their own version of Lyndon's play with Paramount, who'd been responsible for the earlier feature. Sangster adapted the original in fine Grand Guignol style; transposing its events to turn-of-the-century Paris was perhaps the least of the changes he wrought upon it (in the contemporaneously-set 1944 feature, Asther's character was undone by his

unchanging fingerprints, a science not yet developed in the era Hammer chose to relocate the story). His character now renamed Georges Bonnet, Anton Diffring reprised his *Hour of Mystery* role. Also joining Diffring from the earlier TV play was Czech-born Arnold Marle, who had previously appeared in Hammer's *Break in the Circle* and *The Abominable Snowman*. Two years on from *The Curse of Frankenstein*, Hazel Court, playing Janine, was reunited with Christopher Lee and director Terence Fisher. Reel three of the film was struck in an alternate 'Continental version', wherein Janine was seen to model for Bonnet topless. "There was a version which they paid me extra for, for Europe," recalls Court, "and it was very beautifully done." Additional footage was also shot for reel nine, which probably comprised more explicit shots of Bonnet's climactic immolation. Make-up artist Roy Ashton

sketched multiple variants of Bonnet's withering; the veins bulging out of Bonnet's features were painted-over strands from one of Ashton's own pullovers. Scenes involving Hammer stalwart Michael Ripper as a mortuary underling are absent from the final print, although his cameo may have not been shot.

The film's title was only settled on after shooting had wrapped; it had been known throughout production as *The Man in the Rue Noire* (a publicity manual for 'Untitled Film, formerly *The Man in the Rue Noire*' had been issued). During the early summer Hammer was horrified to learn that Paramount had been promoting the film in America as a mere second feature; consequently, results from the States had been disappointing. After strong protest, Paramount were dissuaded and attempted to retrieve the position with a large publicity push in selected cities. In Britain, the film premièred at London's Plaza, and went on general release from 30 November. Although beset by distribution problems, a modest cost of almost £84,000 ensured that the picture was not a commercial failure.

Like other critics, *Variety*'s 'Powe' thought the film tame: "*The Man Who Could Cheat Death* is, in a sense, hoist by its own bloody scalpel," he wrote on 19 June. "Aside from a few macabre scenes, there is nothing that will more than ripple the surface sensations of even the most impressionable." Last credited for the unsuccessful 1965 TV pilot *Dark Intruder*, an occult thriller starring Leslie Nielsen, originator Lyndon died in October 1972. The rather static *The Man Who Could Cheat Death* — an odd mish-mash of mad scientist sci-fi flick and Gothic flannel, despite all Sangster's attempts to spice up the tale with a flash of breast and a touch of Jack the Ripper — suffers from an excess of dialogue and a lack of action. Nevertheless, Diffring gives it his all; the climax, wherein Bonnet is consumed both by old age and fire, is realised with gusto enough.

HAZEL COURT: JANINE

Redhead Hazel Court, a former Rank starlet, laid claim to a very particular crown with her role as Elizabeth in *The Curse of Frankenstein*: that given to the first of Hammer's many — for want of a better term — 'scream queens'. She made her film début in 1944, aged seventeen, in Ealing Studios' *Champagne Charlie*, but it was Gainsborough's *Holiday Camp* three years later which made her name; according to publicity notes she'd take delivery of up to 4,000 fan letters per week. In *The Curse of Frankenstein*, Hazel's daughter, Sally Walsh, played her mother's younger self. Hazel made a second Hammer appearance in *The Man Who Could Cheat Death*. In the early sixties she moved to America where, working alongside such genre luminaries as Boris Karloff, Vincent Price and Peter Lorre, she took roles in three of schlock *auteur* Roger Corman's Edgar Allan Poe adaptations (*The Premature Burial*, *The Raven* and *The Masque of the Red Death*). Married to Don Taylor, the Robin Hood of Hammer's first colour feature, *Men of Sherwood Forest*, she is now a sculptor.

Previous page: *In a Parisian vault containing a lifetime's treasures, Janine (Hazel Court) recoils when confronted by the true face of Georges Bonnet (Anton Diffring).*
Above left: *Janine finds the mutilated Margo (Delphi Lawrence) captive in Bonnet's dungeon.*
Left: *An American lobby card: Pierre (Christopher Lee) administers to Georges (Anton Diffring).*

Principal photography 25 February to
16 April 1959
Released 25 September 1959
Certificate X
Duration 88 mins
Colour
Director Terence Fisher

Egypt, 1895: archaeologist Stephen Banning (Felix Aylmer), part-aided by son John (Peter Cushing), discovers and breaks into the lost tomb of the Princess Ananka (Yvonne Furneaux). His transgression releases a hideous presence which drives him insane. Three years pass; now confined to an English asylum, Banning warns his son that the presence — a foetid mummy — will come to kill him. Indeed, Ananka devotee Mehemet Bey (George Pastell) has brought the mummy to England. One night, the creature breaks into Banning's cell and strangles him. John comes to believe that the mummy is the undead incarnation of Ananka's High Priest, Kharis (Christopher Lee), buried alive for attempting to revive the dead Ananka by forbidden magics. Kharis remains utterly devoted to Ananka, to whom Banning's wife bears an uncanny resemblance. The mummy will not rest until it has sought out the remaining members of the expedition which defiled Ananka's sacred tomb — and destroyed them all.

When Hammer next raided Universal's library of classic horror subjects, they enlisted the help of an 'Egyptology advisor'. "A mummy is the body of a human being or animal which has been reduced to a state of desiccation and dehydration by an artificial process," claimed Andrew Low, son of the late Professor A. D. Low. "This process produces what is little more than a hardened or shrunken skeleton." In publicising *The Mummy* for Hammer, Mr Low warned against confusing the mummification process with common or garden embalming: "An embalmed body, on the other hand, undergoes a more complicated process. It involves injection with various media, as well as massage, which gives the body a full and rounded appearance as in real life." Mr Low added that natural mummification was not uncommon; swamps, apparently, act as ideal wombs for "flexible mummies"…

Work began on the film before casting was finalised. Jimmy Sangster amalgamated elements from Universal's *The Mummy*, *The Mummy's Tomb* and *The Mummy's Ghost* to colour his prototype 'stalk-and-slash' screenplay. Sets first used in *Yesterday's Enemy* and *The Man Who Could Cheat Death* were

recycled, while poster artwork bearing scant relation to events in the script was commissioned.

The now famous pairing of Peter Cushing and Christopher Lee made a reappearance, the latter reluctantly concealed behind horror make-up for the last time. The rigours of shooting took their toll on both men. Cushing needed hospital treatment when a prop gun, overstuffed with explosive charge, temporarily deafened him; Lee suffered underneath a mask held rigid with piano wire, and squibs simulating gun shots left him bruised, while his back and shoulders bore the brunt of carrying Furneaux to the swamp over three arduous takes. The unit used the tank facilities at Shepperton Studios for the swamp scenes, which left a disgruntled Furneaux "caked in thick mud from head to foot." Christopher Lee's stunt double, Eddie Powell, took over for the final descent into the murky water.

"Funnily enough, they thought that was going to take a hell of a long time to do," he recalled. "I did it all in one take and [producer] Michael Carreras said, 'Whatever money you're paying him, double it!'" The scene would prove to be a dress rehearsal for Powell's more prominent role as Prem in *The Mummy's Shroud*.

Peter Cushing made a proactive, if discreet, contribution to Terence Fisher's direction of the film, most famously suggesting a new element to his climactic struggle with Christopher Lee: "John Banning (my part) was attacked by Kharis, the

mummy, so I asked Terry [Fisher] if I could grab a harpoon hanging on the wall of Banning's study and during the struggle for survival, drive it clear through my opponent's body. And that's what I did, thus giving some sort of logic to the illuminated gap depicted on the posters."

A Continental version of the film was prepared. Apparently unbeknownst to Terence Fisher, Michael Carreras reshot the actresses playing the Egyptian handmaidens topless. A gorier version of Christopher Lee's tongue-removal also existed, but shots of the detached tongue and a stream of blood from Lee's mouth were cut before the film was submitted for certification.

The British version of *The Mummy* premièred at the London Pavilion on 25 September 1959 (the cinema's lavish display can be glimpsed in location shots for the 1960 film *Gorgo*) and went to general release via the ABC chain on 23 October. At home and overseas business was excellent, Hammer soon recouping its £125,000 outlay. In the States, Universal were especially delighted when receipts outgrossed those of the previous year's *Dracula*. "I've said some hard things about horror films in the past," wrote critic Anthony Carthew, "but I found this one continuously entertaining. It is not intended to be taken seriously, and it has an odd, old-fashioned, Sexton Blake-ish charm about it." Writing in the *News Chronicle*, Paul Dehn tempered an otherwise affectionate review with the observation that: "The skies are painted; the vegetation potted; and surely Hammer has now wallowed in enough mud to appoint a resident designer of plausible bogs."

Structurally little more than a string of picturesque and nicely-lit killings, *The Mummy*'s melancholic presentation and romantic undertow grants it a certain atmosphere which elevates this bandaged brute far beyond its cinematic predecessors.

Previous page: Peter Cushing improvises in his struggle with Christopher Lee.
Left: The original pencil sketch Bernard Robinson used to compile the photo-composite of Ananka seen in Banning's study.
Below left: Kharis (Christopher Lee) has his tongue removed "so that [his] cries... should not offend the ears of the gods."

YVONNE FURNEAUX: ISOBEL/ANANKA

Yvonne Furneaux was cast as Isobel/Ananka, Michael Carreras describing her as "one of the ten most beautiful actresses in Europe." Furneaux was born in Lille, France, and educated at Oxford where she earned a BA in French. Following training at RADA, she appeared alongside Laurence Olivier in *The Beggar's Opera* and Errol Flynn in *The Master of Ballantrae*. She found herself the victim of one of Peter Cushing's practical jokes while at Bray: Cushing tore the perforated lid off a box of tissues and surreptitiously attached the piece of cardboard, which bore the legend 'For Men', to her back. It stayed there for almost a day before she realised. On completing *The Mummy*, she flew to Rome to appear in her fifth Italian picture, *La Dolce Vita*. Director Federico Fellini was dismayed to learn that Furneaux had starred in a Hammer horror. Furneaux also appeared in Roman Polanski's *Repulsion*.

PETER CUSHING
CHRISTOPHER LEE
YVONNE FURNEAUX
in
THE MUMMY
In Technicolor (X)
A HAMMER FILM PRODUCTION
Released by UNIVERSAL-INTERNATIONAL through
RANK FILM DISTRIBUTORS LTD.

Few films better demonstrate the heights scaled by Hammer's behind-the-scenes craftspeople than *The Mummy*, a *tour de force* of sumptuous design, inventive camerawork, grisly effects and soaring music. Hammer had no one *auteur*; the company's genius lay in its harnessing of talents to achieve a harmony of purpose.

BEHIND THE SCENES

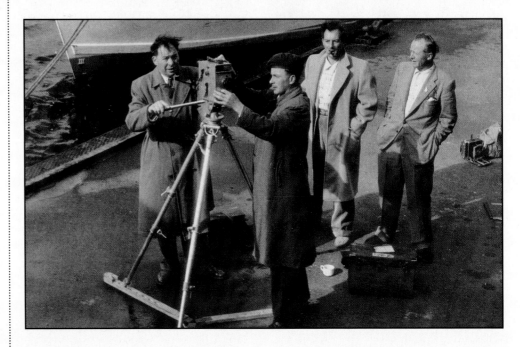

PRODUCTION DESIGN

Over forty Hammer films were enriched by production designer Bernard Robinson, who somehow managed to build huge, rococo palaces at the relatively modest Bray Studios (often incorporating the immovable features of the main house). Born in 1913, Robinson's first Hammer credit appeared on *Quatermass 2*. Soon after, he was called upon to construct the snowy vistas seen in *The Abominable Snowman*. With *Dracula* and *The Mummy*, he came into his own, determining much of what would be retrospectively defined as the Hammer look: glittering ancient tombs, dank and foetid crypts, murky bogs beneath lurid skies, splendidly furnished pseudo-Victorian private houses of the privileged and professional classes. Robinson cemented Hammer's 'neverwhere' with unfailing resourcefulness and style. His other triumphs include the jungles of *Yesterday's Enemy*, the Spanish town seen in *The Curse of the Werewolf*, *The Two Faces of Dr Jekyll*'s voluminous Sphinx club, and the portside in both *Terror of the Tongs* and *Visa to Canton*. Robinson, who met model-making wife Margaret on *The Hound of the Baskervilles*, died shortly after completing 1969's *Frankenstein Must Be Destroyed*. Don Mingaye, a former draftsman who had been Robinson's assistant, designed several pictures solo. (The work put into Hammer's pictures by construction manager Arthur Banks, charged with realising the art directors' conceptions, should also be acknowledged.) Scott MacGregor (1914-1973) assumed the mantle of resident production designer between *Moon Zero Two* and *Frankenstein and the Monster From Hell*. Highlights of his tenure include the glorious church built for *Taste the Blood of Dracula*, itself recycled in later films. "This sort of subject needs special treatment," said MacGregor in 1972. "I try to achieve realism... If you try to 'pretty things up' audiences don't like it and the story, acting and direction is lost against a phoney setting."

CAMERA

Hammer's earliest horror films were emblazoned across cinematographer Jack Asher's celluloid canvas. Asher, formerly a camera operator for Gainsborough, joined Hammer as director of photography on the black and white/Hammerscope production *The Steel Bayonet*, but it was on the Eastmancolour fantasy *The Curse of Frankenstein* that he really made his mark. Asher worked on a string of pictures up to *The Secret of Blood Island* in 1964, and proclaimed camera operator Len Harris his "right hand" (Harris worked regularly for the company between *Mantrap* in 1952 and *The Phantom of the Opera* ten years later, capturing what was in the eye of Hammer's finest directors and cinematographers). Asher's key successor was Arthur Grant, who had been a Hammer DP since *The Abominable Snowman*. Grant fulfilled this role on some thirty films until *Fear in the Night*, shot late in 1971. The equally versatile Moray Grant served as an operator and cinematographer, his association with the company beginning with one of its first films, *The Jack of Diamonds*, and ending with one of its last, *Love Thy Neighbour*.

SPECIAL EFFECTS

Canadian-born Les Bowie devised gruesomes ranging from *The Quatermass Xperiment*'s octopoid monstrosity right up to the obstetric nightmare delivered in *To the Devil a Daughter*. "His days in a prison camp during the war had made him very inventive," remembered Roy Field, one of Bowie's assistants on *The Quatermass Xperiment*. "He had an ability to make do with string when other people used rope." At his workshops at Bray and nearby Slough, Bowie recruited a team of apprentice technicians who earned the nickname 'Bowie's Boy Scouts'. "Les would do most of his designing in the pub, thinking aloud and drawing on the bar with a finger dipped in spilt beer," remembers 'boy scout' Ian Scoones. "I had to make a mental note of all these bar squiggles, translating them onto the back of Players cigarette packets." Bowie inspired genuine loyalty from his staff, many of whom became acclaimed effects experts in their own right. At its peak, Bowie Films Ltd employed over seventy people. Bowie died in January 1979, shortly before he and his colleagues were awarded an Oscar for *Superman*; Scoones took his place for the TV series *Hammer House of Horror*. Hammer's other notable effects supervisors include Sid Pearson, who devised the Count's original disintegration in *Dracula*, and also worked on such films as *The Hound of the Baskervilles*, *The Gorgon* and *Creatures the World Forgot*.

EDITING

Hammer's cutting room floor was littered with more discards than most. Scenes from many films, including *The Curse of the Werewolf*, *Scars of Dracula* and *Twins of Evil* were excised at the behest of various censors. In addition, alternate versions of early Hammer horrors were sometimes prepared for different markets. James Needs, the man most often required to perform such celluloid surgery, joined Exclusive/Hammer in 1949, first splicing Jack the Ripper melodrama *Room to Let*. Later appointed supervising editor, he oversaw the cutting of virtually every film from *The Camp on Blood Island* on. Needs left the company shortly after working on the late sixties TV series *Journey to the Unknown*, but returned to cut several seventies films, culminating in *Holiday on the Buses*. Other noted Hammer editors include Chris Barnes and Spencer Reeve.

MUSIC

James Bernard contributed an eerie score for *The Quatermass Xperiment*, and went on to become Hammer's most prolific composer. "I was given an average of four weeks to compose and orchestrate each film," he remembers. "I was originally given a script, which would suggest certain ideas, and then given the chance see the film itself when it was ready." Scores were generally recorded at Anvil Studios, based originally in Beaconsfield and later at Denham. "Hammer were always very careful about how much they spent," says Bernard. "The biggest orchestra I ever had would have been around thirty-five or thirty-six players, but sometimes it sounded like seventy." Bernard made an enormous contribution to Hammer's greatest successes, creating memorable scores for such films as *The Damned*, *The Kiss of the Vampire* and *The Devil Rides Out*. His best remembered themes, however, are those of the Frankenstein and Dracula films. "The titles suggested a melody, and it seemed to work," he suggests, modestly. The music of Bernard and his contemporaries was conducted by Hammer's musical supervisors. The earliest horror films were supervised by John

Hollingsworth, who died during post-production of *The Evil of Frankenstein*. He was replaced as Hammer's regular musical supervisor by Philip Martell, who stayed loyal to the company until his death in 1993. "Working with John was very easy," remembers James Bernard, "he never interfered at all. He never seemed to want to see the scores until a day or two before the actual recording. Phil was much more hands on, but we got on extremely well." Several albums featuring re-recorded highlights of Hammer music, including one dedicated to the scores composed by James Bernard, have been released on compact disc.

Previous page (above): Camera operator Len Harris (far left) on location with director Val Guest (second from right) for Break in the Circle *in 1954.*
Previous page (below): Les Bowie (with moustache) surrounded by assistants Gordon Gardner, Ian Scoones and Kit West.
Above: James Bernard, Philip Martell and Michael Carreras, during post-production of She.
Below left: Jack Hedley and director Quentin Lawrence on The Secret of Blood Island *in 1964.*
Below right: Scott MacGregor's original design for Simon Helder's private laboratory in Frankenstein and the Monster From Hell.

Principal photography 4 May to 10 June 1959
Released 9 August 1959
Certificate U
Duration 84 mins
Black and white
Director Lance Comfort

At the Palais, a suburban dance-hall managed by part-time jewel thief Dandy 'Sinister' Kingsley (Elwyn Brook-Jones), the Jekyll siblings' Old Time Dancing Team and orchestra, led by Henrietta (Maudie Edwards) and Victor (Jon Pertwee) respectively, are disgraced when the cumbersome steps of hapless youngest Jekyll, Henry (Bernard Bresslaw), wreck their routine. Ridiculed by teenage gang the Rockets, Henry is soundly rebuked when he and his siblings return to their home above the family business — a chemists. Next day, he's visited by tomboyish Rocket Snout (Jean Muir), who apologises for her gang's behaviour. Although patently a 'square', Henry has her propose him for membership of the Rockets, but he's rejected. That night, despairing, and slung out of Henrietta's troupe, Henry discovers an old tin box in the chemical shed, containing a secret formula devised by ancestor Doctor Henry, which claims to transform a man of timid disposition into a 'bold, fearless dragon'. Henry mixes up this pharmaceutical cocktail and drinks it, metamorphosing into slick, designer-clad spiv 'Teddy Hide'. Meanwhile, Dandy is preparing a raid on the Belgravia home of Lady Radcliffe and requires a tightrope-walker and safe-cracker to successfully pull off the job. Hide causes a ruckus at the Palais and when Dandy's gang encounter him, they're sure they've found just the man they need...

*i*n 1958, as gormless buffoon Pte 'Popeye' Popplewell, 6' 5" comic actor Bernard Bresslaw had helped score a sizeable hit for Hammer with his performance in *I Only Arsked*, a big-screen spin-off from the Granada Television comedy *The Army Game*. Bresslaw's special relationship with Exclusive/Hammer had secured him roles in *Men of Sherwood Forest* and *The Glass Cage*; as well as nearly being cast as the Creature in *The Curse of Frankenstein*. His *Army Game* catchphrase had also given Hammer the title of its 1958 feature. That autumn, when Bresslaw reached number six in the hit parade with the ludicrous 'Mad Passionate Love', Hammer had a title for a Bresslaw-headed follow-up.

Sid Colin, doyen of British comedy writing, had co-written *I Only Arsked* and was duly commissioned to pen a story outline for *Mad Pashernate Love* [sic: a phonetic representation of Bresslaw's delivery]. By 14 April 1959, Colin's screenplay, written in collaboration with associate Jack Davies, had become *The Ugly Duckling*, a latter-day burlesque of R. L. Stevenson's *The Strange Case of Dr Jekyll and Mr Hyde*. 'Teddy Hide', their Jekyll *alter ego*, lampooned the then-controversial 'Teddy Boy' phenomenon, while the slow-witted Jekyll was no more or less than 'Popeye' Popplewell reprised, right down to the limp kiss-curl. Hammer was keen to add Bruce Forsyth to the film's cast, and even registered the title *I'm In Charge* (which was inspired by Forsyth's *Sunday Night at the London Palladium* catchphrase) for a sequel, which would have starred the light entertainer as a "crazy courier on a foreign holiday tour." Forsyth proved unavailable for *The Ugly Duckling* and *I'm In Charge* was sold on.

Lance Comfort, an ex-cameraman who'd begun his career making medical research films, was hired to direct. (Comfort later joined the board of Planet Films, one of Hammer's less conspicuous sixties rivals.) *The Ugly Duckling* was shot in the early summer of 1959 at Bray and on location at the Streatham Locarno Ballroom. Lionel Blair choreographed the film's dance sequences.

General release for *The Ugly Duckling* was scheduled for 9 August, just one day after Bresslaw's

wedding to dancer Liz Wright. The film, which producer Michael Carreras had confidently predicted would win Bresslaw "hundreds of thousands of new admirers", was an unmitigated commercial disaster, managing only fair business at children's matinees. By the end of 1959 Hammer was predicting a loss of £20,000 on *The Ugly Duckling* — a film which had cost almost £110,000 to make. Meanwhile, the company was gearing up to produce a 'straight' version of the Jekyll and Hyde story — a project that would prove equally ill-starred...

THE STRANGLERS OF BOMBAY

Asia, 1826: having noted the unaccountable disappearances of thousands of travellers, the British East India Company charges under-qualified military officer Connaught-Smith (Allan Cuthbertson) with overall responsibility for an investigation into the phenomenon, much to the dismay of the older, more experienced Captain Lewis (Guy Rolfe). When Lewis' own servant goes missing, however, the Captain discovers those responsible — a cult of murderous robber Thuggees devoted to the goddess Kali, who strangle their victims and inter them in mass graves. Marked for death by the Thuggees' fanatical High Priest (George Pastell), Lewis finds their secret temple, only narrowly escaping with his life. He learns that the cult's poisonous devotees are to be found not only in the upper echelons of the local administration, but within the heart of the British military establishment itself...

Principal photography 6 July to 27 August 1959
Released 4 December 1959
Certificate A
Duration 80 mins
Black and white/MegaScope
Director Terence Fisher

New Yorker David Zelag Goodman was handsomely paid by Hammer for his pseudo-historical screenplay *The Horror of Thuggee*, receiving just over £7,000 — twice that paid to Jack Davies and Sid Colin for *The Ugly Duckling* — for a script that drew upon Major General Sir William Sleeman's efforts to eliminate the Kali cult from colonial India. (Although substituted by the fictional 'Captain Harry Lewis', Sleeman was referred to in the film's closing captions.) Goodman's original would, apparently, be much bowdlerised prior to its production under the title *The Stranglers of Bengal*, with "stomach slittings", "curse words" and "corpse mutilations" censored.

Briefly planned as a colour production, *The Stranglers of Bengal* was shot in black and white at Bray during the summer of 1959, and was directed by Terence Fisher, who employed the services of 'historical adviser' Michael Edwards. In the lead, as the square-jawed Captain Lewis, was the 6' 4" Guy Rolfe. A supporting actor in fifties productions such as *Ivanhoe* and *King of the Khyber Rifles*, he'd previously appeared as the Padre in Hammer's *Yesterday's Enemy*. George Pastell, noted for his role in *The Mummy*, garnered a further Hammer credit (later followed by roles in *Maniac* and *The Curse of the Mummy's Tomb*).

The film was released as *The Stranglers of Bombay*, and sensationally promoted as a dramatisation of actual events ("This is true! This is real! This actually happened!" ran the poster's strapline, with the *faux* process 'StrangloScope' appended as a particularly ludicrous misnomer). *The Stranglers of Bombay* was, at one time, due to be succeeded by *The Black Hole of Calcutta*; the latter title was registered with the MPAA until 23 February 1962, but ultimately never translated to celluloid, perhaps as a

result of *The Stranglers of Bombay*'s disappointing receipts. The film's London Pavilion results had been very promising but, after general release, takings dropped off sharply.

Bizarrely, the film was granted a lenient A certificate by the BBFC; presumably its catalogue of torture and murder was judged apposite in a semi-factual context. Its excesses, however, were noted by *Monthly Film Bulletin*: "a particularly bestial contribution to the Hammer horror cycle... production is the usual flea-bitten affair, unimaginatively unconvincing, quite without period sense, and relying almost entirely for its appeal on visual outrages — blindings, evisceration, human heads being thrown on to dinner tables, and so forth".

"*The Stranglers of Bombay* went wrong," admitted Terence Fisher in 1964. "It was too crude. The basic idea was the absolutely true story of the Thuggee. The producers felt it was better in black and white because it was a documentary story rather than a myth. But in the written word there was too much Frankenstein and Dracula and I was still with the previous approach."

Cruel, cold-hearted and exploitative, the film — quite rightly — joined the very short roster of pictures whose certificates have been revised upward when released on video, rated 15, in 1996. Despite a number of bloody set-pieces, it is, in essence, a Western: for the East India Company, read railroaders; for the Thuggees, Cheyennes or Sioux.

THE TWO FACES OF DR JEKYLL

Principal photography 23 November 1959 to
22 January 1960
Released 7 October 1960
Certificate X
Duration 88 mins
Colour/Megascope
Director Terence Fisher

Dr Henry Jekyll (Paul Massie) is tirelessly developing a personality-changing drug, despite interruptions from his friend, Paul Allen (Christopher Lee), and his wife, Kitty (Dawn Addams). Allen is dependent on Jekyll for money to pay off his recurrent gambling debts, while the seemingly frigid Kitty is adjusting to her timid husband's reclusive lifestyle. Amid mounting concern from Litauer (David Kossoff), a more genuine friend, Jekyll experiments on himself. He transforms into a younger, more handsome man: Edward Hyde. At the glamorous Sphinx nightclub, Hyde is revealed to be a vicious, swaggering playboy. He discovers that Paul Allen has been taking advantage of more than Jekyll's generosity — he is engaged in an affair with his wife. Hyde begins a passionate affair of his own with Maria (Norma Marla), a snake dancer at the club, and forges a relationship with Allen, who shares with him the decadent pleasures of London's vice dens. Jekyll's transformations into Hyde soon slip beyond his control, and his increasingly dominant alter ego *targets Allen as his first victim...*

"Here is the century old horror classic filmed as it has never been seen before," boasted the trailer for *The Two Faces of Dr Jekyll*. That Hammer should undertake an X-rated version of Robert Louis Stevenson's story was perhaps predictable, but the startling new take on the subject instigated by producer Michael Carreras in February 1959 was anything but.

At the heart of this brave revision was thirty-six year-old Cyril Wolf Mankowitz, whose stage version of his novel *Make Me An Offer* won the *Evening Standard* award for Best British Stage Musical of 1959. In the same year, his successful musical *Expresso Bongo* was filmed by Val Guest, with a cast that included *Room at the Top* star Laurence Harvey and a youthful Cliff Richard. Guest introduced Mankowitz to Michael Carreras in early 1959. Convinced that Mankowitz could provide the fresh

approach he felt the subject demanded, Carreras promised the writer a hefty £5,000 for his story and screenplay, setting him to work over the summer. With Harvey in mind, Mankowitz devised a suave and manipulative Hyde, whose machinations in the sordid underworld of Victorian society ultimately punish Jekyll's faithless wife and parasitic friend. "Evil is attractive to all men," explained Mankowitz, interviewed during production at Bray Studios. "Therefore, it is not illogical that the face of evil should be attractive. That is why I made Mr Hyde handsome instead of repulsive. This is *not* a horror film; it is a comment on the two-facedness of respectable society... My screenplay exposes the evil of the Victorians, tears from the mask of falseness and hypocrisy. It also contains some comment on the evil of scientific pride divorced from both human and ethical considerations."

Harvey proved to be out of Hammer's reach and

the role of Hyde went to twenty-seven year-old Canadian Paul Massie, whose film career had got off to an impressive start in the late fifties with *Orders to Kill* and *Sapphire*. Impressed by his performance in *Libel*, Michael Carreras offered him the role of Hyde, and Massie soon convinced him he could play Jekyll as well. Although upset at not being considered for the film's lead role(s), Christopher Lee gave one of his finest Hammer performances as Paul Allen, Jekyll's traitorous friend and Hyde's debauched partner. "I even accept money from my mistress in the film," he said at the time. "And a man can't sink much lower than that." The role of Kitty — Jekyll's wife, Allen's mistress and Hyde's victim — was loaned a demure sensuality by Dawn Addams, an actress Carreras had pursued since reading the first draft of Mankowitz's script: "I had her constantly in my mind's eye." Toward the other end of the cast list, Oliver Reed made his Hammer début in a brief but memorable

LIKE NOTHING
YOU HAVE
EVER SEEN!
A COMPLETELY
DIFFERENT
VERSION OF
THE CLASSIC
STORY...
A NEW DR. JEKYLL
—A HANDSOME,
EVIL MR. HYDE...

A SHOCK
ENDING THAT
YOU DARE
NOT REVEAL!

AMERICAN INTERNATIONAL presents
ROBERT LOUIS STEVENSON'S
STUDY IN TERRIFYING EVIL!

JEKYLL'S INFERNO

IN COLOR AND MEGASCOPE

PAUL MASSIE · DAWN ADDAMS in COLOR AND MEGASCOPE
CHRISTOPHER LEE   Produced by MICHAEL CARRERAS · Directed by TERENCE FISHER · A HAMMER FILM PRODUCTION

cameo as a troublemaker in the Sphinx nightclub. It was the beginning of a prolific association with the company.

Slated to comprise part of Hammer's ongoing co-production deal with Columbia, *The Two Faces of Dr Jekyll* began shooting at Bray on 23 November. It soon became apparent that director Terence Fisher was out-of-sync with Mankowitz's intentions, as the revisions he made to the shooting script steered it towards the more stereotypical territory of earlier Hollywood versions. Other script changes were imposed for more pragmatic reasons. Whole scenes were lost in an attempt to meet an optimistic completion date of 6 January 1960 — the most significant being the story's climax, which would have seen the executed Hyde transforming into Jekyll on the gallows. The crew shifted to the ABPC studios at Elstree for the final two weeks of production, which ended over schedule and over budget (at a final cost of £146,417) on 22 January 1960. James Carreras was not amused, and on 10 February informed the board of directors that "a picture of world-wide interest and distribution ought not to cost over £120,000." His son wasn't there to hear him.

After a première at the London Pavilion on 7 October, *The Two Faces of Dr Jekyll* began its general release on the ABC circuit (paired with *Green Mare's Nest*) on the 24th. "The direction lacks sensitivity — it's impossible to appreciate fully the spiritual significance of Jekyll's tampering with Nature," lamented *Kinematograph Weekly* on 6 October, who nevertheless conceded that the film was "lewd, lustful, chilling, eye-popping and ornate." On 7 October, *News Chronicle*'s Paul Dehn was less forgiving: "Its horrors are penny dreadful. Its psychology is too shallow to engage our pity. Its dialogue has not a wisp either of moral wisdom or literary distinction." The film's disappointing make-up effects drew further condemnation: "I will stomach many oddities in the cause of science-fiction, but never a potion that substitutes one sort of immaculately brushed coiffure for another and not only removes beards but *puts them back*

again when its effects wear off."

The Two Faces of Dr Jekyll received a similarly cool reception at Columbia who, upon noting the film's salacious content, didn't even apply for the Breen Seal mandatory for American distribution. The rights were initially offloaded to Columbia subsidiary Kingsley, then ultimately sold to American International Productions, who retitled the film *Jekyll's Inferno*. AIP finally released a censored eighty-minute version as *House of Fright* on 3 May 1961. Shortly after, *Variety*'s 'Pit' damned the picture with rather less than faint praise: "Film competently acted, though Terence Fischer's [sic] direction is as tacky as the script."

The Two Faces of Dr Jekyll performed disappointingly in box-offices around the world, and Hammer's returns fell significantly short of its production outlay in the months following its release. While there is much to enjoy in this uncommonly sophisticated Hammer horror, its rich performances fail to surmount an inadequately conveyed central conceit.

Previous page: Paul Allen (Christopher Lee) and Edward Hyde (Paul Massie). "There was not one redeeming character," said Terence Fisher, "it was an exercise, rightly or wrongly, in evil."
Above: Hyde seduces snake-dancer Maria (Norma Marla) at the Sphinx club. Maria's usual partner was a seven-and-a-half foot boa constrictor called 'Fury'.
Below left: The Sphinx club dancing girls.
Below right: The German ad mat for The Two Faces of Dr Jekyll.

Principal photography 26 January to
18 March 1960
Released 7 July 1960
Certificate X
Duration 85 mins
Colour
Director Terence Fisher

Parisian schoolteacher Marianne Danielle (Yvonne Monlaur) is on her way to the Badstein Girls'
Academy when her journey is interrupted. She spends the night with the elderly recluse Baroness
Meinster (Martita Hunt) and her servant Greta (Freda Jackson). During the night, Marianne meets
Baron Meinster (David Peel), a handsome young man kept locked in chains by his mother. The Baron
begs Marianne for help, so she steals the lock's key from the Baroness and gives it to him. Soon after,
a hysterical Greta shows Marianne the body of the Baroness and a terrified Marianne flees into
the night. She is discovered the following morning by Doctor Van Helsing (Peter Cushing), who is
investigating reports of vampirism in the district. Van Helsing takes Marianne to the Girls' Academy;
soon after, he leaves to drive stakes through the hearts of Baron Meinster's undead followers. Van
Helsing tracks Meinster down to a nearby windmill, but is bitten by the vampire in a violent struggle.
He overcomes the vampire's influence in time to see Meinster return, with Marianne his hostage...

*U*niversal had reportedly been saved from bank-ruptcy by Hammer's *Dracula*, so was naturally eager for a sequel. Producer Anthony Hinds commissioned Jimmy Sangster to write *Disciple of Dracula* in early 1959. The villain of the piece, Baron Meinster, was a vampire who terrorised two visiting English girls and preyed on the young ladies attending a nearby academy. At the screenplay's climax, hero Latour summons the spirit of Count Dracula, who appears long enough to curtail his renegade disciple's activities.

Over the summer, Hammer decided to prepare a new vehicle for Christopher Lee, and *Dracula the Damned* appeared on a pre-production schedule in June 1959. Soon after, Peter Bryan was instructed to rewrite *Disciple of Dracula*, removing the vampire Count and relegating Latour to make way for Van Helsing. The resulting *The Brides of Dracula* saw Meinster undone when Van Helsing summoned a swarm of ferocious bats to consume him. ("I indict you, Baron Meinster, by the very code of your own loathsome sect. You have flouted even the evil laws of darkness... I demand the penalty! Creatures of the

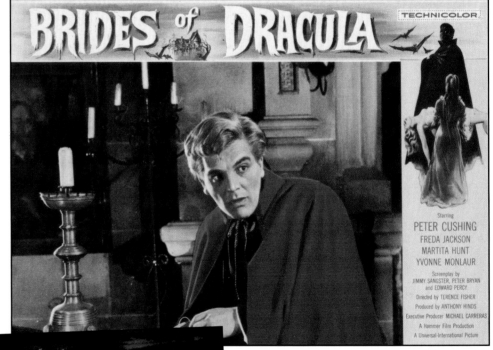

night, I summon you from the grave, from the necropolis of the undead, from the depths of darkness itself. Come, give justice to your code. Destroy this evil being!") In addition, Bryan amalgamated the two female protagonists of Sangster's draft (Margaret and Pauline) into French heroine Marianne Danielle.

Dracula the Damned vanished from Hammer's schedules (why is unclear: Christopher Lee was working steadily for the company at the time and had yet to develop his famous intolerance of reprising "that character"), but *The Brides of Dracula* continued its protracted development. Securing Peter Cushing as Van Helsing was considered crucial, but the actor was unimpressed by the Sangster/Bryan draft of the script. Another cook was duly added to the broth: Edward Percy, a writer whose theatre work was familiar to Cushing, was

cold-called by Anthony Hinds and commissioned to polish Bryan's draft. Percy's rewrite (dated 19 November 1959) was minimal, but enough to appease Cushing. Shortly before the film went before the cameras at Bray, Hinds redrafted the screenplay yet again, diluting its stronger elements in an attempt to second guess the BBFC's inevitable scissor-work. A shooting script, entitled simply *Dracula II*, was completed toward the end of January 1960.

Yvonne Monlaur was cast as Marianne Danielle, with the trailer for *The Brides of Dracula* proclaiming her as "France's latest sex kitten!" The former model came to Hammer's attention when she appeared in the Italian film *Adventure a Capri*. Following a lengthy convalescence to recover from facial burns received shooting in Italy, Monlaur came to Britain with her mother for *The Brides of Dracula*, staying to appear alongside Anton Diffring and Donald Pleasence in *Circus of Horrors* and Christopher Lee in Hammer's *The Terror of the Tongs*. Stacked shoes and a ginger kiss-curl transformed the little-known David Peel into Baron Meinster. Peel (who had appeared alongside Peter Cushing in a BBC adaptation of *Beau Brummell* in 1954) caused quite a stir at Bray Studios when he brought his two pet poodles onto the set. "[He was] an extremely *sweet* actor, if you know what I mean," recalled the film's composer Malcolm Williamson. Peel's matinée idol looks certainly contributed to his accomplished reinvention of the screen bloodsucker, but they barely justified Universal's American promotion of Meinster as a "teenage vampire", particularly as he was forty years old. He retired from acting shortly after this, his most prominent role, to ultimately establish 'David Peel & Co Ltd — Dealers in Fine Art'. He died in 1982.

A superb cast also included Freda Jackson and the fearsome Martita Hunt, who had previously appeared together in David Lean's 1946 version of *Great Expectations*. Andree Melly, the sister of popular jazz musician George, appeared as student teacher Gina, and director Terence Fisher also used her for his little-seen spoof *The Horror of It All* in 1964. At the lower end of the credit roller was

'Village Girl' Marie Devereux, the twenty year-old Hammer publicists described as "the girl with the exuberant statistics." "She had a good figure and particularly large boobs," recalled Andree Melly. "I asked her, 'How did you come to be in the film?' She said, 'Oh, they always want me in these films because I've got such big boobs and they like to put them on the posters.' I thought that was really a sad fate, in a way."

An atmosphere of urgency crept in to the Bray shoot as Universal's delivery date loomed. To save time, Anthony Hinds employed his usual tactic of simply discarding scenes as filming progressed. Shooting wrapped on 18 March, and *The Brides of Dracula* was delivered to its American distributor in April, just two days before a penalty clause would have operated. Supervising editor James Needs was among those congratulated by James Carreras for their swift post-production work.

British distribution was undertaken by Rank, who mounted a lavish première at the Marble Arch Odeon on 7 July before general release commenced on 27 August. *The Brides of Dracula* did excellent business around the world, box-office results in Britain, Japan and the United States being especially impreeive. Hammer's prompt delivery, and the film's impressive quality and performance, significantly strengthened James Carreras' relationship with partners Universal. The American studio was so pleased that in October 1960 it approached Hammer for *Dracula III*. Although *The Kiss of the Vampire* would inherit much from *Dracula II*, it would prove to be an exercise in creative side-stepping.

From Marianne Danielle's beguiling début to Baron Meinster's spectacular demise in a blazing windmill, *The Brides of Dracula* is a beautiful film. The sometimes confused characterisation of an overdone script (which the BBFC dismissed as clearly having been written by "an insane, but very precocious schoolboy") detracts little from a sumptuous, sensual production that highlights the classic Bray line-up of designer Bernard Robinson, cinematographer Jack Asher and director Terence Fisher working together in perfect harmony. This is Hammer horror at its very best.

THE BRIDES OF DRACULA

David Peel and Yvonne Monlaur

PUBLICITY SERVICES

ISSUED BY
RANK FILM DISTRIBUTORS LTD.
127 WARDOUR STREET LONDON W.1

ALSO STARRING...

Hammerland — that strange cod-Europe, part Brothers Grimm, part Victorian colony — was populated by an army of coachmen, gravediggers, priests, doctors and belligerent landlords. They were largely brought to life by a handful of reliable and often brilliant character actors whom the company called upon again and again...

MICHAEL RIPPER

Michael Ripper, by far the most prolific of all Hammer actors, was properly noted by critics — such as *Variety*'s 'Beig' — for his role as Stanley Preston's hapless whipping-boy Longbarrow in *The Mummy's Shroud*. "They said that it didn't usually happen that pathos was brought into a horror film," he recalls. Born in Portsmouth in 1913, Ripper entered drama school at sixteen and made his first film appearance in 1935 in *Twice Branded*. His Exclusive début was *The Dark Road*, in which he was cast by no less than James Carreras. Ripper followed this with roles in more than thirty Exclusive/Hammer pictures. These included a drunken grave robber in *The Revenge of Frankenstein*, the wretched Old Soak in *The Curse of the Werewolf*, and publicans — of varying degrees of hospitality — in *The Reptile*, *Dracula Has Risen From the Grave* and *Scars of Dracula*. His last featured Hammer role was in the comedy *That's Your Funeral*. "I did seem to get cast as the same types of people," says Ripper, "but I always tried to give them

different characters. Tony Hinds was a great friend of mine, and I do miss Hammer." While opening the Barbican's retrospective of Hammer in 1996, Christopher Lee initiated a huge, and richly deserved, ovation for this unassuming actor.

MILES MALLESON

"Dear Miles Malleson," remarked critic Derek Conrad when reviewing *The Hound of the Baskervilles* in May 1959, "[makes] a nice, bumbling Bishop even nicer and more bumbling..." Miles Malleson's four comic relief turns for director Terence Fisher, in *Dracula*, *The Hound of the Baskervilles*, *The Brides of Dracula* and *The Phantom of the Opera*, mark him out as one of the company's most endearing supporting artistes. "I like working with Miles Malleson," said Fisher in 1964. "Give him two lines and he'll work throughout the scene." Born William M. Malleson in 1888, he was a playwright before branching out into acting in 1921. Later a screenwriter (*Nell Gwyn*, *The Thief of Baghdad*, etc), he made several cameo appearances in self-penned films. This industrious actor's other notable films include seminal British horror *Dead of Night* and *Kind Hearts and Coronets*. He died in 1969, failing sight having enforced his retirement four years previously. "It was very difficult not to

laugh when acting with Miles Malleson," remarked Christopher Lee later. "Extraordinary, clever comedian..."

GEORGE WOODBRIDGE

Twice a landlord (in *Dracula* and *Dracula Prince of Darkness*), three times a policeman (in *Cloudburst*, *The Flanagan Boy* and *The Mummy*), Devon man George Woodbridge, born in 1907, was an Exclusive/Hammer regular for fifteen years. Having played Sergeant Ritchie in *Cloudburst*, the company's first Bray Studios feature, Woodbridge turned up as a police sergeant in over ten *Stryker of the Yard* shorts produced elsewhere between 1953 and 1955. He returned to the Exclusive fold for *The Flanagan Boy* and *Third Party Risk* before playing a janitor in *The Revenge of Frankenstein*, his first horror film. Woodbridge moonlighted for Hammer rival Monty Berman in the Jimmy Sangster-scripted *Jack the Ripper*, plus *The Flesh and the Fiends* and *What a Carve Up*, shortly afterwards. As stroppy Spanish shepherd Dominique, he fell victim to lycanthrope Leon in *The Curse of the Werewolf*. Woodbridge's last Hammer role was in *The Reptile*. He died in 1973, his final genre work being in Peter Sasdy's film version of TV's *Doomwatch*.

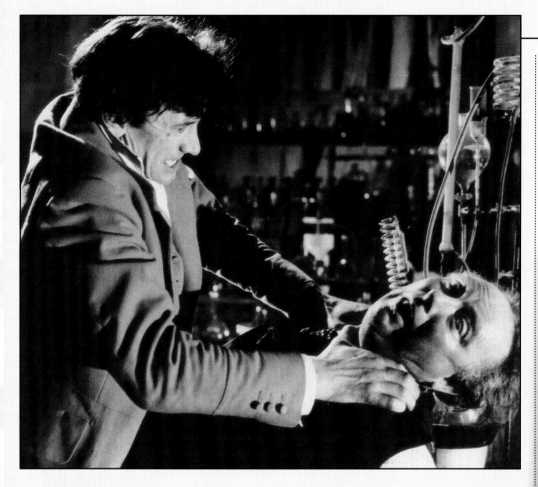

Previous page (above): Dr Hertz (Thorley Walters, left), the Baron's partner in crime in Frankenstein Created Woman.
Previous page (below): Michael Ripper as the feisty landlord in Scars of Dracula.
Left: Karl (Michael Gwynn) exacts a terrible revenge from the sadistic janitor (George Woodbridge) in The Revenge of Frankenstein.
Below: Dr Franklyn (Noel Willman) struggles with his manservant (Marne Maitland) in The Reptile.
Bottom: Van Helsing (Peter Cushing) and Dr Tobler (Miles Malleson) in The Brides of Dracula.

THE REPTILE   TECHNICOLOR

Associated British-Pathe Ltd. Present a Hammer Film Production
Released through Warner-Pathe

MARNE MAITLAND

Swarthy, shifty, black-hearted foreigners were also part of Hammer's stock in trade, and whenever the company's casting directors would require such an artiste, they'd usually call upon one of three possibles: George Pastell, Roger Delgado and Marne Maitland. Anglo-Indian by descent, Maitland made his début for the company in the smuggling melodrama *Break in the Circle*. He cropped up thereafter in *I Only Arsked*, *The Camp on Blood Island*, *The Stranglers of Bombay*, *Sands of the Desert*, *Visa to Canton*, *The Terror of the Tongs*, *The Phantom of the Opera* and finally *The Reptile* — in which, *bien sûr*, he played the inscrutable Malay responsible for Jacqueline Pearce's serpentine affliction.

THORLEY WALTERS

In the touching character of *Frankenstein Created Woman*'s dissolute GP and self-confessed "muddle-head" Dr Hertz, Thorley Walters was granted not only his largest role for the company, but probably his best. Born in 1913, Walters, a stage actor trained at the Old Vic, took his first screen credit in 1934. Much in demand for comedy, he made appearances in such films as *Private's Progress*, *Blue Murder at St Trinian's* and *Two-Way Stretch* before his Hammer début in the 1959 wartime burlesque *Don't Panic Chaps!*. Having played the theatre manager in 1962's *The Phantom of the Opera*, he made a distinct impression as Ludwig, *Dracula Prince of Darkness*' fly-eating Renfield-by-proxy. *Frankenstein Created Woman* was followed by substantial parts in both *Frankenstein Must Be Destroyed* and *Vampire Circus*. A close friend of director Terence Fisher — he played Watson to Christopher Lee's Holmes in Fisher's German-based *Sherlock Holmes und des Halsband des Todes* (*Sherlock Holmes and the Deadly Necklace*) — he was one of but a handful of Hammer alumni to attend Fisher's funeral in 1980.

THE TERROR OF THE TONGS

**Principal photography 19 April to
30 May 1960
Released 29 September 1961
Certificate X
Duration 79 mins
Colour
Director Anthony Bushell**

Hong Kong, 1910: Helena (Barbara Brown), the daughter of British skipper Captain Jackson (Geoffrey Toone), is murdered by members of the Red Dragon Tong, a subversive mafia whose criminal influence permeates Hong Kong society. Jackson vows to bring the Tongs to justice and, after extracting information from a Tong collector, wins the devotion of the collector's "bond slave", Lee (Yvonne Monlaur). His investigations lead him to the headquarters of inscrutable Tong leader, Chung King (Christopher Lee). Captured and tortured, Jackson only escapes through the intervention of an anti-Tong agent. The Captain is now targeted for execution by the Tongs, whose influence spreads as far as Jackson's superior, East India Company official Harcourt (Brian Worth). Dogged by traitors within and without, Jackson's mission will cost the exotic Lee her life...

Often incorrectly nominated as a 'semi-sequel' to *The Stranglers of Bombay*, 1960's colour production *The Terror of the Tongs* is content merely to duplicate the earlier film's storyline. Although rated X, it is less bloody than *The Stranglers of Bombay*, with but a few hand-loppings, syringe attacks and 'bone-scrapings' to its credit (mostly rendered off-screen). Exploitative and hugely patronising to the Chinese, screenwriter Jimmy Sangster now nominates it as "probably the second or third worst piece of writing I ever did."

Sangster was contracted on 1 February 1960. The script was probably commissioned to make optimum use of the expensive, expansive exterior dockside-and-merchant-ship set that would be constructed on the Bray lot for the next project on Hammer's schedule, TV pilot *Visa to Canton*. Director Anthony Bushell, a former actor who'd played Colonel Breen in the original BBC version of *Quatermass and the Pit*, would later work on television series such as *Danger Man*. *The Terror of the Tongs* was produced by Hammer's Seven Arts partner Kenneth Hyman.

Ostensible star Christopher Lee appears only briefly and on just one set, as all of Lee's Tong Room

scenes were shot first, concluding on 29 April. (In addition, Lee's Oriental make-up, devised by Roy Ashton and Colin Garde, was tested, on-camera, at Bray on 13 April.) Leading man, the middle-aged Geoffrey Toone, had appeared as pulp hero Sexton Blake in Francis Searle's 1958 film *Murder at Site Three* (and is still working, his latter-day credits including a part in the BBC's prestigious *Middlemarch*). Roger Delgado, as in *The Stranglers of Bombay*, played the villain's loyal lieutenant. *The Brides of Dracula*'s Yvonne Monlaur, as half-caste concubine Lee, delivered her lines in a bizarre collision of pidgin English and 'ow-you-do' French.

The project was no small undertaking. The wharf scenes, for example, required up to seventy-six extras, most from ethnic minorities; consequently, Hammer hired interpreter S. K. Lam. Attention was

COLUMBIA PICTURES present
A HAMMER FILM PRODUCTION

THEY WERE THE OLDEST SECRET CULT IN THE WORLD — AND THE MOST FIENDISH!

黨的恐怖 黨的恐怖

THE TERROR OF THE TONGS

TECHNICOLOR ®

Starring
CHRISTOPHER LEE · **YVONNE MONLAUR** · **GEOFFREY TOONE**

PRODUCED BY KENNETH HYMAN · DIRECTED BY ANTHONY BUSHELL · SCREENPLAY BY JIMMY SANGSTER · ASSOCIATE PRODUCER ANTHONY NELSON KEYS · EXECUTIVE PRODUCER MICHAEL CARRERAS

even lavished over the various Chinese characters and motifs on set dressings, and a signwriter named Mr Doo was commissioned to paint all of these. *The Terror of the Tongs* (referred to by *Kinematograph Weekly* as *Terror of the Hatchet-Men* during shooting) wrapped on 30 May, one day over schedule.

Hammer was plainly dubious as to the quality of the finished film. Discussions were held during September 1960 as to whether or not to instigate an extensive publicity campaign in the national press: "we ought to be absolutely certain... that it was a film worth backing with this publicity, otherwise our reputation might suffer." Distributed by Columbia, the film did good business when released in America and on the Continent early in 1961; its British release, however, was delayed when its

planned co-feature, *Call Girls of Rome*, was deemed "unsuitable."

The Terror of the Tongs ultimately premièred at the London Pavilion in autumn 1961 alongside the William Castle thriller *Homicidal*, and released to the ABC circuit from 20 November. Despite shocking reviews ("Retrograde blood-bath, stingily staged"), the film performed very well indeed. Business was reportedly sensational throughout its four-week Pavilion run, and it made £21,607 in its first week on general release. Issued with a luridly sensational press book detailing the semi-factual wilder excesses of the real Tong cult ("See... the dreaded Chinese needle torture!"; "See... the throbbing dance of the Manchu maidens!"), *The Terror of the Tongs*, perhaps thankfully a rarely-seen film, remains resolutely undistinguished in all departments, save the chance to see Lee performing in a distinctly Fu Manchu-esque role for the very first time.

Previous page: *A burly Tong torturer (Milton Reid) introduces Captain Jackson (Geoffrey Toone) to the art of 'bone-scraping'.*
Above: *Pages from a lavish promotional brochure.*
Left: *Yvonne Monlaur as chatelaine Lee.*
Below: *Jackson's ultimate confrontation with shadowy Tong leader Chung King (Christopher Lee) and man-at-arms Wang How (Roger Delgado).*

ROGER DELGADO: WANG HOW

A genuine Cockney, albeit of Franco-Hispanic parentage, actor Roger Caesar Marius Bernard de Delgado Torres Castillo Roberto gained the first of his three Hammer horror credits on *The Stranglers of Bombay*. He joined BBC television's Drama Rep in 1950, and seemed everafter to be cast in villainous roles ("When I look at myself in a shaving mirror I am never surprised that I always get these parts," he said. "I'm the nastiest Arab of the lot..."). He appeared in an episode of the original TV *Quatermass II* and followed up *The Stranglers of Bombay* with parts in *The Terror of the Tongs* and, more credibly, *The Mummy's Shroud*. Most renowned for his portrayal of the Master, eternal nemesis to Jon Pertwee's *Doctor Who*, Delgado was killed, aged fifty-five, in a road accident in Turkey in June 1973.

THE CURSE OF THE WEREWOLF

**Principal photography 12 September to
2 November 1960
Released 1 May 1961
Certificate X
Duration 88 mins
Colour
Director Terence Fisher**

Santa Vera, Spain: raped in the dungeon of the wicked Marques Siniestro by a raddled beggar (Richard Wordsworth), a mute servant-girl (Yvonne Romain) escapes her prison and is found by the kindly Don Alfredo (Clifford Evans), who takes her in when he discovers her to be pregnant. The girl dies in labour, but her child, christened Leon, is brought up by Alfredo as his own son. As the boy grows, he is increasingly troubled by dreams of drinking blood and running with the wolves, and a local farmer's flock is found to have been attacked by an unidentified animal. Alfredo consults a priest, who informs him that the cursed Leon's affliction — lycanthropy — might be held at bay with love. Leon (Oliver Reed) reaches manhood, and woos Vintner's daughter Cristina (Catherine Feller). But, after a night in which he is shanghaied into carousing at a bordello, Leon is affected by the light of the full moon and transforms into a murderous werewolf. Arrested for three subsequent killings, and denied access to his beloved Cristina, Leon changes once more. His rampage may only be halted by a bullet cast from silver...

*T*he *Curse of the Werewolf* began with Guy Endore's 1933 novel *The Werewolf of Paris*, an ambitious narrative that spanned the Medieval era, Paris in the mid-nineteenth century and the Franco-Prussian war of 1871. Universal, who owned the film rights, sub-contracted the project to Hammer early in 1960 and *The Werewolf of Paris* was duly slated to begin shooting at Bray on 17 October. The screenplay was attributed to John Elder, actually a pseudonym for producer Anthony Hinds, who'd discovered that the budget simply wouldn't stretch to accommodate a freelance screenwriter. (Hinds had joined the Writers' Guild as Elder, a surname he borrowed from that of Hammer Productions' co-founder John Elder Wills, in an attempt to preclude controversy: "I realised the unions would be up in arms if they found out I'd not only been producing but also writing.")

It was to be preceded in the company's production schedule by *The Inquisitor* (aka *The Rape of Sabena*), a period 'study in fear' wherein the Spanish Inquisition took root in a small town. Scripted by

Peter R. Newman (*Yesterday's Enemy*), *The Inquisitor* was to be directed by John Gilling and feature Philip Latham and Kieron Moore, commencing filming at Bray on 29 August. However, Columbia developed cold feet over the story's content, apparently fearing condemnation by the Catholic Church's then-powerful Legion of Decency. All concerned therefore decided to abandon production. According to Anthony Hinds, "we got a tip that the Catholic Church would ban the picture. So he [producer Michael Carreras] pulled out and I was left with these sets..." By this time, Bernard Robinson's large exterior set — the village of Sabena circa 1560 — had already begun to take shape on the Bray lot. *The Inquisitor* had required the construction of, among others, a church, a main street, the church's interior and a wine cellar. These were worked into the *Werewolf of Paris*

HALF-MAN...HALF-WOLF

The CURSE OF THE WEREWOLF TECHNICOLOR®

CERT X ADULTS ONLY

CLIFFORD EVANS · OLIVER REED · YVONNE ROMAIN · CATHERINE FELLER

Screenplay by JOHN ELDER · *Directed by* TERENCE FISHER · ANTHONY HINDS · MICHAEL CARRERAS   A HAMMER FILM PRODUCTION for UNIVERSAL-INTERNATIONAL

screenplay when Hammer resolved to bring the latter forward to replace the scuppered *Inquisitor*. Now christened *The Curse of the Werewolf*, the story was reworked to take place in *The Inquisitor*'s Spanish milieu, with those sets already built or designed redressed where appropriate. Location sequences were shot at Black Park and Egham, Surrey.

During editing, Hammer became embroiled in their most serious skirmish to date with the British Board of Film Censors. As was now routine, BBFC secretary John Trevelyan had studied the script prior to shooting, and had made no serious objections bar the presentation of one contentious scene: the rape of the servant girl by the beggar, who would have been clearly revealed as half-man, half-wolf ("The censor says no fangs. You can have fangs or relations with the girl, but not both," was how the story was related to actor Richard Wordsworth). To add to this grisly tableau, the Marques

would, had Hinds had his way, have been looking on as the hapless girl was ravished by the beast! In late autumn, the BBFC viewed a complete print — and didn't like what they saw, detailing a very long list of cuts. These included: a shot of the Marques' flaky nose; the rape; the stabbing of the Marques; dialogue about children born on Christmas Day; the baptism; young Leon's hairy palms; all three of the killings committed by the werewolf; Leon's transformation; and shots of the dead Leon's face. After Hinds had written a passionate defence of the film to Trevelyan, the film was re-viewed early in 1961 and the Board relented on certain points (the baptism, for example). However, three key scenes — the murders of the Marques, the prostitute and the Old Soak — would remain extensively cut. Writing to Hinds, the otherwise progressive Trevelyan, perhaps mindful of the furore that had surrounded the 1960 release of Michael Powell's *Peeping Tom*, explained that he was under increasing pressure from special interest groups not to permit horror films to be exhibited: "Frankly, I am reluctant to pass a picture of this kind at all at the present time, even in a heavily censored version..."

The Board would have their way. In the States, only four scenes were trimmed, making the American version of the film three minutes longer. Pointedly, American distributor Universal planned its release (alongside *The Shadow of the Cat*) to coincide with the children's holidays. And whereas the film was well-received in America ("exceptional... a triumph," wrote *Variety*), in Britain its reviews were typified by a notoriously savage attack in the highbrow *Monthly Film Bulletin* ("a singularly repellent job of slaughter-house horror").

In the mid-eighties, the American cuts were restored and, after twenty-five years, *The Curse of the Werewolf* could finally be viewed as Hinds had intended. A fine film it is too; much overlooked is the hopeless and unrelentingly tragic love story at its heart.

OLIVER REED: LEON

Having previously made two bit-part appearances for both Hammer and Terence Fisher — in *The Two Faces of Dr Jekyll* and in *Sword of Sherwood Forest* — twenty-two year-old Oliver Reed was chosen as reluctant werewolf Leon from seventeen other hopefuls. Paid £90 a week for his efforts — "a fortune" — the film effectively launched his star career. Fan clubs reportedly sprang up in Britain, America, France and Italy; he was nicknamed 'Mr Scowl' and was mailed over fifty marriage proposals. ("One of them said, 'Until recently I revered and worshipped the memory of Rudolf Valentino. But after seeing you in *The Werewolf* I have transferred all my allegiance to you.'") The actor featured in six further Hammer productions (*Captain Clegg, The Damned, The Pirates of Blood River, Paranoiac, The Scarlet Blade* and *The Brigand of Kandahar*) before embarking upon more lofty projects (*Oliver!, Women in Love*, etc). In 1990 he narrated the television compilation series *The World of Hammer*.

THE CURSE OF THE WEREWOLF
Technicolor   Cert 'X'
Starring CLIFFORD EVANS   OLIVER REED
YVONNE ROMAIN   CATHERINE FELLER
A Hammer Film Production for UNIVERSAL-INTERNATIONAL
RANK FILM DISTRIBUTORS LTD.

Previous page: *On location, Roy Ashton gives Oliver Reed's Leon that authentic 'morning after' look.*
Above left: *The full wolverine make-up — one of make-up artist Roy Ashton's greatest achievements.*
Above right: *Reed goes over the script with his younger alter ego Justin Walters.*
Left: *A horde of torch-bearing yokels hound Leon (Oliver Reed) to his doom in the Universal-esque climax.*

THE SHADOW OF THE CAT

Principal photography 14 November to
21 December 1960
Released 1 May 1961
Certificate X
Duration 79 mins
Black and white
Director John Gilling

Ella Venable (Catherine Lacey) completes a last will and testament that leaves her house and fortune to her husband, Walter (André Morell). She is then beaten to death by her servant, Andrew (Andrew Crawford), while her pet cat, Tabatha, looks on. Walter joins Andrew and housekeeper Clara (Freda Jackson) in burying the body in nearby woods. Once again, the cat sees everything. Three days later, Walter reports Ella's 'disappearance' to the police, who begin their investigation at the house. In private, Walter, Andrew and Clara agonise over the whereabouts of Tabatha. The previously affectionate and docile cat insidiously observes the conspirators, who decide the only witness to the crime must die. The cat jumps on Walter, weakening his heart and leaving him bed-ridden. Walter sends for other unscrupulous family members, who have already been promised a share of Ella's fortune, and asks them to capture the cat. One by one, the cat exacts a terrible revenge on those who conspired to kill its mistress.

*T*he Shadow of the Cat began life as an outside production offered to Hammer in spring 1960 by BHP Films. Although BHP (a partnership between writer George Baxt, theatrical agent Richard Hatton and producer Jon Penington) was created specifically to produce *The Shadow of the Cat*, its company directors were all experienced filmmakers. Baxt divided his time between London and his native New York, principally writing for television but also scripting such films as *City of the Dead* and *Circus of Horrors*. In 1958 he had made an unaccredited contribution to Hammer's *The Revenge of Frankenstein*. Jon Penington was similarly prolific; in 1959 he had participated in the Val Guest film *Expresso Bongo* and Peter Sellers' breakthrough comedy *The Mouse That Roared*. Richard Hatton was a long-standing acquaintance of Penington's and they had cemented their friendship through casting a number of films together. Hatton would later represent both Michael Carreras and Jimmy Sangster.

After originally rejecting George Baxt's script, Hammer returned to BHP in summer 1960, adding the film to their production schedule. On 17 August

it was confirmed that the picture would be made for Universal, James Carreras anticipating a mere £70,000 for its production. The film went on the floor at Bray Studios immediately after *The Curse of the Werewolf*, but not before director John Gilling carried out an unaccredited rewrite of George Baxt's script. In Baxt's original, the omnipotent menace of Ella's vengeful cat was a powerful suggestion in the minds of the jittery conspirators. Gilling's most significant contribution to the screenplay was to give Tabatha life as a real cat — the feline would be seen to prowl around the protagonists and 'observe' key events through cinematographer Arthur Grant's distorted lens. Gilling's rewrites earned him an extra £150 over his director's fee.

By the time filming began, Hammer had decided to supply *The Shadow of the Cat* to

Universal alongside *The Curse of the Werewolf*. Once informed, BHP increased the film's horrific content to ensure it received an X certificate. "Sequences which could be established by implication, for instance, will be shown in full detail," Penington told *Kinematograph Weekly*. Most of that "detail" relied on a cat borrowed from the landlady of the Duke of Edinburgh pub in Windsor. John Gilling experienced such difficulty with the capricious feline that several stray lookalikes were also roped in. It was one of these lookalikes that was eventually returned to the landlady when filming was completed. Considering the original cat's poor treatment, it was perhaps unsurprising that it had gone AWOL. "One shot involved the cat leaping over the camera to a ledge and looking back with 'fiery eyes'," remembers Ian Scoones, recalling his very first day working under effects supervisor Les Bowie. "Les held the cat above his head and

attempted to throw it towards the plaster rooftop opposite. The poor frightened animal wouldn't let go of Les' duffle-coat sleeve — its claws would hang on each time. Jack Curtis, Bray's chief electrician, attached two metal contacts to a twelve volt car battery. He put the contacts on the tips of broom handles, the idea being to give the cat a mild shock to make it leap. On cue, Les again held the cat above his head. Jack engaged the prongs and the cat disengaged its bowels, completely covering Les with a hot stream of diarrhoea. No one would go near him for at least three weeks afterwards!"

Shooting wrapped just before Christmas at a final cost of almost £81,000 and the film was edited in time to meet a New York delivery date of 13 February 1961. Universal told Hammer it was "delighted" with the package of films, which it decided to double-bill. On 15 February 1961 the BBFC granted *The Shadow of the Cat* the required X certificate on the sole condition that the murder of Aunt Ella be shortened. Hammer received no credit on the finished print (indeed, Jon Penington went to unusual lengths to disassociate BHP from Hammer in the trade press during the film's production). This is perhaps best explained by placing the *Shadow of the Cat*/*Curse of the Werewolf* double-bill in context with Hammer's ongoing co-production/distribution deal with Columbia. Hammer was generally permitted to make only one film a year for other distributors; the delivery of a Hammer-accredited double-bill to Universal may have been too conspicuous at this time.

Released in Britain by Rank as the support feature to *The Curse of the Werewolf*, *The Shadow of the Cat* drew little attention from critics. *Kinematograph Weekly* predicted that the film would "intrigue and grip both sexes... Having clearly proved that 'horrific' melodrama need not be served with 'tomato sauce,' it should have been given an A not an X certificate. Very good British macabre." While praising the cast, the reviewer never-

JOHN GILLING: DIRECTOR

It wasn't until 1947, when this former assistant director was well into his thirties, that John Gilling sold both his first screenplay (*Black Memory*) and directed his first film (*Escape from Broadmoor*). In 1952, he directed Bela Lugosi and Arthur Lucan in *Old Mother Riley Meets the Vampire*, by which time he'd already flirted with Exclusive, scripting or co-scripting horror-tinged melodramas *The Man in Black* and *Room to Let*, an unproduced Dick Barton feature shelved after the tragic death of actor Don Stannard, plus *The Lady Craved Excitement*, *Whispering Smith Hits London* and *Wings of Danger*. Having directed Peter Cushing in the acclaimed Burke and Hare thriller *The Flesh and the Fiends*, he finally made his directorial début for Hammer on *The Shadow of the Cat*, following this with swashbucklers *The Pirates of Blood River* and *The Scarlet Blade*. In 1964 he directed Oliver Reed in the actor's final Hammer film, a cut-price epic called *The Brigand of Kandahar* that integrated discarded footage from Columbia's 1956 film *Zarak*. Gilling scripted *The Gorgon* before directing back-to-back Cornish terrors *The Plague of the Zombies* and *The Reptile* in the summer of 1965. His final Hammer film was *The Mummy's Shroud*. Gilling emigrated to Spain in 1970, making one further picture, *La Cruz del Diablo* ('The Devil's Cross') before his death in 1984. "I never thought that either Anthony Nelson Keys nor John Gilling cared for the genre," reflected Anthony Hinds in 1986, "but seeing some of their shows re-run I'm not sure they weren't among the best."

theless concluded that "it's Tabatha, the cat, who steals the honours." Universal's initial enthusiasm was dampened when the heavily promoted double-bill performed "disappointingly" on its 7 June release Stateside.

Although John Gilling and Arthur Grant succeed in eliciting an evocative atmosphere from some absurd situations, the literal realisation of what really would have been best left imagined renders this film a bizarre curiosity.

Previous page: *Freda Jackson, Jon Penington, John Gilling and André Morell go over the script at Bray Studios.*
Above left: *Barbara Shelley as Beth Venable, in a familiar Hammer publicity pose.*
Above right: *John Gilling on location for* The Scarlet Blade *in 1963.*
Below: *Louise (Vanda Godsell), Inspector Rowles (Alan Wheatley), Michael (Conrad Phillips) and Beth watch as Jacob (William Lucas) meets his doom.*

T A S T E   O F   F E A R

**Principal photography 24 October to
7 December 1960
Released 5 June 1961
Certificate X
Duration 82 mins
Black and white
Director Seth Holt**

Wheelchair-bound heiress and self-confessed neurotic Penny Appleby (Susan Strasberg) arrives at the Côte d'Azur. She has come to live with her estranged father following the death of her nurse Maggie Frensham, whom she claims drowned three weeks earlier in a Swiss lake. However, upon arriving at her father's house, stepmother Jane (Ann Todd) informs her that her ageing father has left suddenly on business. That night, Penny goes to the summer-house where she sees her father's corpse propped up grotesquely in a chair. Alarmed, she falls into a murky swimming pool and is rescued by Bob (Ronald Lewis), the chauffeur. She tells Bob, Jane and a doctor, Pierre Gerrard (Christopher Lee), what she has seen, but there is nothing in the summer-house when they return. The smooth Gerrard speculates that Penny might be going insane. Further bizarre incidents follow, all witnessed solely by Penny. She enlists Bob's assistance, believing that Jane and Gerrard are attempting to have her certified and thus cheated out of her inheritance. However, it is the treacherous Bob who has murdered Penny's father, conspiring with Jane to have Penny propelled over a clifftop in a runaway car. But all is not as it seems...

*O*wing an obvious debt to Henri-Georges Clouzot's 1954 thriller *Les Diaboliques* — in which, likewise, a maybe-or-not dead body may or may not be concealed beneath a leaf-strewn swimming-pool (and which, incidentally, had played with *X the Unknown* on its original release) — Jimmy Sangster's *See No Evil* had originally been written for Rank producer Sydney Box, who would later handle Sangster's Bulldog Drummond picture *Deadlier Than the Male*. Planned to be line produced by sister Betty Box and directed by Ralph Thomas, production was halted when Sydney suffered a heart attack. *See No Evil* consequently transferred to Box's brother-in-law, *Carry On...* producer Peter Rogers. Sangster, however, feared that Rogers, overburdened by his own schedule, would never get around to putting *See No Evil* into production, so the writer showed his script to Michael Carreras, who bought Sangster's screenplay back from

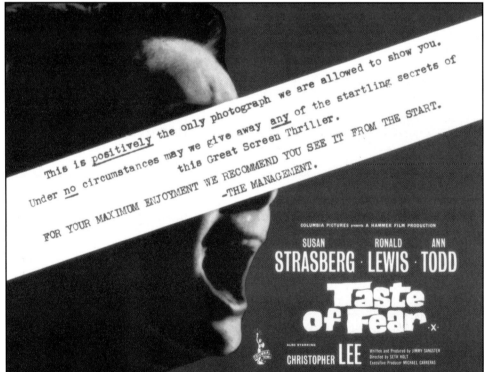

Rogers. It's perhaps fitting that by such shady, roundabout methods Hammer's noted cycle of suspense melodramas began.

See No Evil was retitled *Taste of Fear* when it was noted that MGM had already registered the former title. Shooting would largely take place at the ABPC studios in Elstree, after it was decided that the terraced swimming pool the story demanded could not be satisfactorily realised at Bray. Former assistant director and production manager Sangster persuaded Carreras — above Columbia's wishes — to let him produce his own script, thus gaining his first such credit. The ever-villainous Christopher Lee was purposely cast as a red herring, and the film head-

lined young Susan Strasberg. Strasberg, daughter of American method-acting guru Lee Strasberg, had made her feature début in 1955's *Picnic* and followed this with 1957's *Stage Struck*. For *Taste of Fear* she was accompanied by her mother, Paula, who, according to Sangster, "lurked on the edge of the set putting the fear of God into her daughter... The moment the director called 'cut', the first thing Susan would do would be to look towards her mother, who would either nod or shake her head. If she shook it, Susan would ask to do another take." (Unimpressed by Strasberg's omnipresent Svengali, director Seth Holt eventually demanded that her mother leave the shoot.)

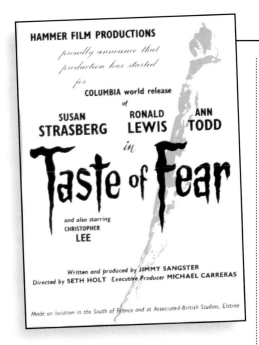

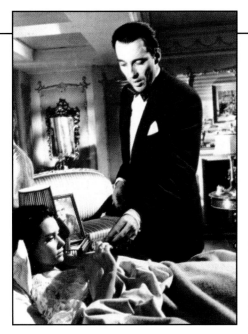

Studio work was preceded by a substantial location shoot at Nice in the south of France. Between Monday 24 October and Thursday 3 November scenes were filmed at the Villa de la Garoupe, Cap d'Antibes and its adjoining cliffs; on roads at Villefranche; outside a local police station; and in and around the runway of Nice airport (the latter using actual passengers and airport staff). Shooting of the airport scenes had to be held over unexpectedly when Sir Winston Churchill and ensuing cortège, returning from a meeting with General de Gaulle, caused the closure of the terminal building (bizarrely, producer Sangster had made a cameo appearance as the young Churchill in the earlier film of his screenplay *The Siege of Sidney Street*). The film's opening scene, wherein the real Penny Appleby's body is dredged up from beneath a Swiss lake, was shot at Black Park; Les Bowie's team were responsible for the elegant glass shot that matted in exotic mountains over the Berkshire trees. At Elstree, underwater sequences were shot by specialist cameramen Egil Woxholt and John Jordan. While shooting interiors, Christopher Lee was astounded to glimpse Hollywood icon Gary Cooper, at Elstree for his final film, *The Naked Edge*. "Can you imagine seeing one of the great stars in the history of cinema looking at you from behind a camera?" says Lee. "I was literally bereft of speech."

The clever promotional campaign, orchestrated by Dennison Thornton and Colin Reid, deliberately obfuscated the film's subject matter. Although *Taste of Fear* (retitled *Scream of Fear* in America) was no spectacular critical or commercial success ("Audiences may be dismayed by [the] barrage of contradictory and doubtful climactic revelations, but at least they will have enjoyed the seventy-one minute buildup to the ten minute letdown," remarked *Variety*), it performed well enough to ensure a string of Hammer horror-thrillers cast from much the same mould, beginning with 1963's *Maniac*. "*Taste of Fear* was the best film that I was in that Hammer ever made," considers Christopher Lee. "It had the best director, the best cast and the best story."

Taste of Fear's impressively effective montage style owes much to the inspired staging of Palestinian-born director Seth Holt. Real name James Holt, and brother-in-law to director Robert Hamer (*Kind Hearts and Coronets*, etc), he had started out as a cutting-room assistant at Strand Films in 1942. In 1944 Holt joined Ealing Studios' editing department and worked his way up to pictures such as *The Lavender Hill Mob* and *The Ladykillers*. In 1958, Holt directed his first feature, *Nowhere to Go*, a taut thriller starring Maggie Smith. An impressed Michael Carreras suggested Holt as eminently suitable for the director's post on *Taste of Fear*. Still much in demand as an editor (most notably on *Saturday Night and Sunday Morning*) Holt's feature career would prove erratic, making *Station Six Sahara*, *Danger Route* and working on two troubled films, *Diabolik* and *Monsieur Lecoq*, during the remainder of the sixties. Holt made only two further features for Hammer: *The Nanny* and *Blood From the Mummy's Tomb*. During completion of the latter in 1971, Holt, whose health had been much compromised by alcoholism, suffered a fatal heart attack elicited — improbably — by a bout of hiccups.

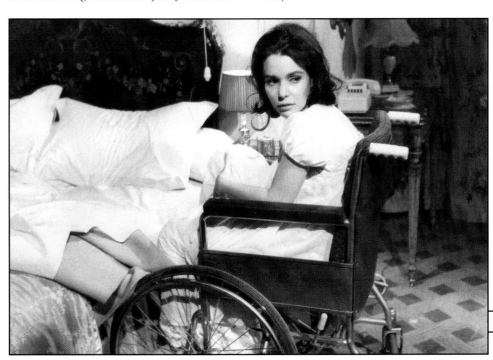

Previous page: Taste of Fear's *entire front of house set consisted of variations on the same image.*
Above centre: *The smooth Pierre Gerrard (Christopher Lee) attends to the neurotic 'Penny' (Susan Strasberg).*
Left: *'Penny Appleby', a mademoiselle* with a past.

Taste of Fear suggested a new genre that Hammer might exploit. The psychological thriller — high on shock, sometimes low on internal logic — formed a staple part of the company's future output.

SUSPENSE THRILLERS

_f_irst off the blocks was _Maniac_, again from a script by Jimmy Sangster — and again set in the south of France. In this complex, 'wicked stepmother' tale, American artist Geoffrey Farrell (Kerwin Mathews) becomes an unwitting stooge to Eve Beynat (Nadia Gray), who wishes to free husband Georges from the asylum where he resides; four years previously, the insane Georges had murdered the rapist of his daughter Annette (Liliane Brousse) with the aid of an oxyacetelene blowtorch. As per _Taste of Fear_, all is not as it seems; Eve and her lover Henri (Donald Houston) plan to frame Geoffrey for their murder of Eve's lunatic husband. _Maniac_ was directed in Megascope by Michael Carreras who, in the early summer of 1962, shot this, his second Hammer feature, partly on location in the Camargue region of France and partly at the Metro-Goldwyn-Mayer studios in Borehamwood (three weeks' studio filming had been planned for Bray, but was hurriedly relocated when _The Old Dark House_ went over schedule).

Maniac's lurid content had been slightly toned down prior to production after reservations were expressed by the American censors and it lacks the intensity and baroque styling of _Taste of Fear_. Much better was the gloriously overblown _Paranoiac_, which was released alongside _The Kiss of the_

Vampire early in 1964. Posing as the eleven-years-missing Tony Ashby, one of three orphaned heirs to the wealthy Ashby estate, an impostor (Alexander Davion) attempts to convince the surviving Ashby children — Eleanor (Janette Scott) and Simon (Oliver Reed) — that he is their long-lost sibling. However, after several attempts are made on his life, the bogus Tony, with Eleanor's assistance, exposes deranged organ-playing paranoid Simon as Tony's killer; the former choirboy's body is bricked up in the family chapel. The first of Hammer's thriller cycle to pointedly swipe from Alfred Hitchcock's _Psycho_ — gruesomely masked, sporting a cassock and wielding a knife, Aunt Harriet (Sheila Burrell) scares off the ersatz Tony by pretending to be the real one — Jimmy Sangster's deft screenplay is replete with markedly Gothic trappings. It is all the more noteworthy considering _Paranoiac_'s true progenitor, novelist Josephine Tey's horse-racing melodrama _Brat Farrar_, a version of which had been on Hammer's roster as far back as 1954. Five years later, the project was scheduled to be produced for Columbia, but shelved. Sangster's _Paranoiac_ screenplay was so far removed from the source material that, on 20 March 1962, Hammer's board of directors had cause to debate whether or not they should actually bother to apply for an extension to their screen rights in the novel! (Ultimately, the company erred on the side of caution.) *Paranoiac* was shot at Bray during July and August 1962 and was the first of several Hammer productions to be directed by award-winning cinematographer Freddie Francis. He returned to the studio just a few months later to helm a further slice of Sangster histrionics, *Nightmare*, over the freezing winter of 1962-1963.

Having been witness to her mother's murder of her father, neurotic schoolgirl Janet (Jennie Linden) suffers visions that she, too, will become a homicidal maniac confined to an asylum. After a succession of disturbing experiences, she is driven to stab to death the wife of her appointed guardian, Henry (David Knight). However, Henry, assisted by lover Grace (Moira Redmond), has cruelly manipulated the girl to commit the crime. Her teacher (Brenda Bruce) helps uncover their scheme. A 'why-dunnit?' rather than a 'who?', *Nightmare*, from an original screenplay ludicrously entitled *Here's the Knife, Dear — Now Use It*, doesn't manage to successfully square its show-stopping central conceit. It remains notable, however, for its atmospheric title sequence — the credits appear throughout a protracted stagger around a dank asylum. The film was released as support to *The Evil of Frankenstein* in 1964.

Francis' third and final Sangster-scripted thriller, *Hysteria*, filmed at Elstree early in 1964 and released in the summer of the following year, proved no more remarkable. In the film, amnesiac 'Mr Smith' (Robert Webber) falls victim to the contrivances of unscrupulous psychiatrist Keller, who attempts to frame his confused patient for the murder of the doctor's wife. Like *Taste of Fear*, *Maniac* and *Nightmare*, a scarlet woman (Denise, played by Lelia Goldoni) turns out to be killer Keller's accomplice.

For their next such excursion — the first of its type to be shot in colour — Hammer turned to stalwart American screenwriter Richard Matheson, with whom the company had been associated ever since its planned adaptation of his sci-fi vampire epic *I Am Legend* had run aground on the rocks of the BBFC seven years earlier. Based, confusingly enough, on an Anne Blaisdell novel entitled *Nightmare*, *Fanatic* concerns Pat (Stefanie Powers), who, upon her engagement to Alan (Maurice Kaufman), goes to inform Mrs

Trefoile (Tallulah Bankhead), mother of now-deceased lover Stephen, of her nuptial plans. Mrs Trefoile, a religous maniac, is less than amused. She regards Pat as Stephen's wife and, with the assistance of her deranged household, imprisons the hapless girl in her rambling mansion, intending to "cleanse her soul." The once-legendary Bankhead, then in her sixties, was in poor shape when she came to Elstree in September/October 1964. "I was told I had to see her and get her to stop drinking so much, so we had a long chat," remembers Roy Skeggs. "When I later visited the set I saw her pouring some tea, so I sent a note to Jimmy Carreras at Hammer House that read: 'Problem over — she's drinking tea.' Later in the afternoon she fell over, so I sent another note to Jimmy that said: 'Sorry — Scotch in the tea!'" Despite this, under the direction of Silvio Narizzano, Bankhead produced a venomous characterisation of terrifying intensity. *Fanatic* was her last film; she died just four years later. A well above

Previous page (top): Geoff (Kerwin Mathews) cowers from the Maniac (Donald Houston).
Previous page (bottom): On location for Maniac in southern France, director Michael Carreras (centre) watches Nadia Gray fix her hair.
Top: Paranoiac gave star Oliver Reed one of his finest Hammer roles.
Above: Jennie Linden (right) as Janet in Nightmare. *The film was based on a screenplay called* Here's the Knife, Dear — Now Use It.
Left: The imposing asylum — the location of Janet's recurring Nightmare.

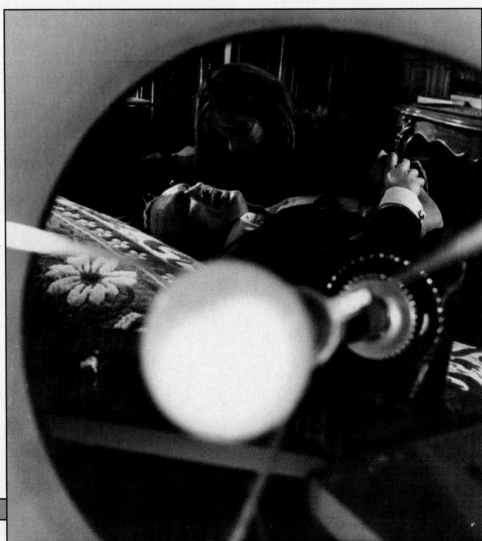

'Jane Brown's Body', an impressive episode of the television series *Journey to the Unknown*, notwithstanding) in *Crescendo*, a thriller once again partly shot in the Camargue region of southern France. *Crescendo* had started out as a screenplay by Alfred Shaughnessy, director of *Cat Girl*. Michael Reeves, who would go on to direct the acclaimed *Matthew Hopkins Witchfinder General*, offered *Crescendo* to Hammer in summer 1966; Bette Davis' old sparring partner Joan Crawford had expressed an interest in appearing. Shaughnessy and Reeves' script was rewritten by John Gilling for Puck Films Ltd, before Hammer hired Jimmy Sangster to redraft Shaughnessy's original work into a final screenplay. The film ultimately went into production in July 1969. Margaretha Scott took the role of matriarchal Danielle Ryman, a widow with an horrific scheme in mind for her crippled son Georges (James Olson) and American music student Susan Roberts (Stefanie Powers). *Crescendo* was directed by Alan Gibson (the director of 'Jane Brown's Body') and released as support to *Taste the Blood of Dracula* in 1970.

After a spell as a freelance producer, Michael Carreras returned to the Hammer fold proper in 1971. Now Hammer's managing director, he soon set about searching for new formats for the company's product. One of his first ideas was to produce a series of themed double-bills. The first pairing, dubbed 'Women in Terror!', was released in the summer of

average thriller, containing an early appearance by a young Donald Sutherland, *Fanatic* was spectacularly retitled *Die! Die! My Darling!* for its American release in the early summer of 1965.

Bar that same year's *The Nanny* which probably more by default than design turned out to be less a stock shock thriller than a psychological drama, Hammer made no further suspense pictures for nearly five years. In 1969, *Fanatic*'s Stefanie Powers made her second Hammer appearance (a leading role in

1972 and comprised the company's final film suspensers: *Straight On Till Morning* and *Fear in the Night*.

Straight On Till Morning derived its elliptical title from a phrase in J. M. Barrie's *Peter Pan*. In this adventurously-edited blend of kitchen-sink drama and psychosexual thriller, Rita Tushingham played a naïve and dowdy fantasist, Brenda, who leaves her native Liverpool for London's Earl's Court, where she becomes entangled with a horribly disturbed gigolo, Peter (played by Shane Briant, the last of Hammer's regular leading men). Every bit as cold and squalid a piece as those other serial killer thrillers set in and around the capital's bedsitterlands, *Peeping Tom* and *Frenzy*, although nowhere nearly so acclaimed, *Straight On Till Morning* was shot at Elstree and on location in London at the latter end of 1971. On 16 March 1972, the completed film, replete with possibly the company's most downbeat ending ever, was viewed by executives from backers Anglo-EMI, who reportedly said that it stood a good chance of taking a lot of money at the box-office. It didn't. The film fell subject to the attentions of the BBFC, who reassessed both the murder of Caroline (Katya Wyeth) and the aurally distressing scenes where Peter plays to his 'Wendy' a tape he'd previously recorded while stabbing both his dog Tinker (ergo, 'Tinkerbell') and the flighty Caroline to death with a Stanley knife.

Its companion piece, *Fear in the Night*, suffered a convoluted evolution, deriving from a Jimmy Sangster script, *Brainstorm*, originally developed for Universal early in 1963. *Brainstorm* had been scheduled to go into production several times: first a six-week shoot in the autumn of 1964, then "tentatively" for 1965. The company "seriously" considered it for 1968, too. By then, it bore an alternative title, *The Claw*. This draft, apparently set on a boat, was to be produced by Anthony Nelson Keys and directed by Freddie Francis for release in 1969, but was postponed early in 1968. In 1971, the script was dusted down and rejigged by Sangster and co-screenwriter Michael Syson. Now set in and around a deserted boarding-school, it required only a few cast members.

The story broke no new ground. Recovering from a nervous breakdown, Peggy (Judy Geeson) marries schoolteacher Robert (Ralph Bates) and goes to set up home at the exclusive school where he resides. Immediately prior to leaving, she is assaulted by a one-armed man. The same happens at the school, where she identifies the culprit as one-armed headmaster Michael (Peter Cushing, who worked a mere four days on the picture) and shoots him point-blank with a shotgun. It is all, of course, part of a conspiracy involving Michael's scheming wife Molly (Joan Collins). Such is the intricacy of the plot, that Molly even remarks upon its deviousness at one point! Mostly shot on location in Hertfordshire at Letchmore Heath's Piggots Manor and on the playing fields of the Haberdasher's Askes public school, the unit transferred to Elstree in December for two weeks interiors, briefly sharing the studios with *Straight on Till Morning*'s production team. Directed by Sangster himself, *Fear in the Night* builds too slowly to a reasonable pay-off, and only one sequence — where

the apparently indestructible Michael stalks Peggy through the school's empty corridors which echo with the rowdy babble of invisible pupils — really hits the right notes.

And there the suspense cycle ended. The notion of the second feature was all but dead, and Hammer had begun to cast its horizons beyond the confines of the cinema screen. In 1973, the company had prepared a format for a television series entitled *The Hammer House of Horror Mystery and Suspense*. That, however, is another story...

**Principal photography 8 May to
22 June 1961
Released 19 May 1963
Certificate X
Duration 87 mins
Black and white/Hammerscope
Director Joseph Losey**

Weymouth: American boat-owner Simon Wells (MacDonald Carey), enticed by the flirtatious Joanie (Shirley Ann Field), is mugged by a gang of leather-clad thugs led by Joanie's vicious and over-protective brother King (Oliver Reed). Recovering, Simon encounters mysterious scientist Bernard (Alexander Knox) and his sculptress girlfriend Freya (Viveca Lindfors). Later, Joanie meets Simon on his boat. They are menaced by King, but escape down the coast and disembark at Freya's clifftop studio, which stands close to an equally remote secret scientific establishment run by Bernard. However, King and his gang find them. In their flight, Simon and Joanie break into the establishment's grounds, but tumble down the cliff, followed by King. They are dredged from the water by a group of eleven year-old children who are kept imprisoned beneath the base; their skin is stone cold to the touch. Cut off from the rest of the world, taught via television screens, the children are radioactive — born of mothers exposed to a nuclear accident. Naturally able to survive atomic fallout, they will be released only if the Bomb is dropped, when they will repopulate the decimated planet. Ignorant of this, Simon and Joanie plot the lethal children's escape, unaware that they have themselves been poisoned by these innocents...

*i*n 1959, Michael Carreras had sent a Jimmy Sangster script, *The Criminal*, to Stanley Baker, anticipating a further Hammer vehicle for the tough-guy actor, to follow on from *Yesterday's Enemy* and the in-development *Hell Is a City*. Baker, who'd been directed by American expat and Hammer acquaintance Joseph Losey in that year's *Blind Date*, had said that he'd only make it if Losey would. However, Losey had ordered Sangster's script to be totally rewritten by Alun Owen and it was eventually shot by Merton Park Studios that December. Soon after, Hammer offered him *The Children of Light*, a science fiction flavoured project adapted from an obscure novel by H. L. Lawrence. Losey, who'd recently seen several plans fall through, accepted the assignment because he saw in its apocalyptic theme a message sympathetic to his political sensibilities — and soon set about altering the script accordingly.

It appears that Anthony Hinds had worked on the script during February 1961. Losey commissioned a screenplay from long-time collaborator

Ben Barzman, visiting the writer's south of France home in April to help see the work through. They fell out, and just two weeks before shooting was scheduled to begin, commissioned a total rewrite from TV scribe Evan Jones. According to Barzman, "Hammer was very unhappy because they said Joe had changed my script completely, and they wanted to go back to the old one."

Losey both staffed and cast his film with a number of regular collaborators. Behind the scenes, he brought to the production editor Reginald Mills, sound editor Malcolm Cooke, continuity girl Pamela Davies and unaccredited storyboard artist Richard

Macdonald. Together, Losey and MacDonald chose the film's two Dorset locations: seaside town Weymouth and the austere, forbidding Portland Bill. Of the key cast members, MacDonald Carey, Alexander Knox and Kenneth Cope had all worked with Losey before. Swedish émigré Viveca Lindfors was an untried product of Lee Strasberg's Actors' Studio, while both Oliver Reed and Shirley Ann Field were imposed on the director by Hammer and its partners Columbia.

Shooting in the early summer of 1961 was by no means smooth. Losey's demands — the helicopter, for example, was an expensive late addition — caused the film's cost to spiral rapidly (an overspend of £25,000 was projected by the time principal photography was complete and its final cost came in at a relatively astronomical £170,155). The director's commitment to the subject matter could not, however, be faulted. Of Losey, Reed recalls, "He used to take the cast out to dinner and preach anti-Bomb stuff to them! He was very left of centre..." The film's climactic stunt, wherein King's car is forced off a bridge and into the sea, nearly went tragically wrong; the car turned over as it hit the water, hit the mud in the bay, and the stunt driver only narrowly avoided drowning when his seatbelt wouldn't release.

The film, now entitled *The Damned* at Hammer's suggestion (Losey had preferred either *The Brink* or *The Abyss*), duly began a tortuous post-production process. By 10 July it appears that differences of opinion had arisen between Losey and producer Anthony Hinds over the treatment of certain episodes. Some additional pick-up shots were deemed necessary, which were completed by 9 August. After some debate between Columbia, Losey and Hammer, it was decided to allow Losey to complete the film according to his own conception. Two versions of the film's final reel had been prepared: one as planned, in which Freya is shot by Bernard, and another in which she is shot by an anonymous figure in a helicopter — a contingency to be used should American censors, in Hinds' words, object to "Bernard's escaping retribution for cold-blooded

murder." (In the event, the original ending would remain.)

Columbia received the film with "mixed feelings", suggesting that it might be coupled on release with William Castle's *Mr Sardonicus*. That didn't happen; *The Damned* hung in limbo until May 1963 when, released direct to the ABC circuit, it made up the latter half of a bill with Hammer's own *Maniac*. The bleak, depressing message of the film seemed to strike a discordant note with both audiences and critics; the *Observer*'s Philip French, however, noted it to be "a disturbing work of real importance." At 1964's International Science Fiction Festival, the film was awarded the *Associazone Stampa Guiliana Trieste Premio della Critica* (top prize). The following year, it received its long-overdue American release, where it was shorn of ten minutes of footage — the cuts were suggested by Losey himself to Columbia's Mike Frankovich — and known as *These Are the Damned*.

Losey claimed to have been asked several times by Michael Carreras to helm another Hammer film, but bemoaned the fact that "he always gives me things that have so much overt violence in them that I just can't bring myself to consider them seriously." He died in 1985, having made such varied pictures as *The Servant*, *Modesty Blaise* and *The Go-Between*. *The Damned* is very nearly a very great film, with Losey's imagery, pacing, and politics struggling against its low-rent sci-fi origins. It has also proved massively influential; the gang, rote learning by screen, King's foppish brolly and, more particularly, his assault on sculptor Freya are motifs all reprised in Kubrick's *A Clockwork Orange* — and Losey's innovative use of a helicopter to personify some terrible, faceless nemesis can be seen in everything from *Apocalypse Now* to *The X Files*. The success of the latter — all state conspiracy and mad science — suggests that *The Damned* might be more timely than ever.

Previous page: On location, producer Anthony Hinds (far left) watches as director Joseph Losey (kneeling, centre) oversees a trick shot whereby Shirley Ann Field (in black leather) might be seen to ride a motorcycle.
Left: The Damned's near-terminal concluding stunt.
Below left: Portland Bill, summer 1961: Losey instructs his juvenile cast; Oliver Reed (kneeling) listens in. Actress Viveca Lindfors (second from far right) is otherwise engaged.

The Damned, despite its science fiction trappings, suggested that Hammer might have worthier pretensions than the manufacture of classy exploitation films. Indeed, the early sixties saw the release of three such loftier pictures, all with a contemporary theme and all resolutely atypical of the company's product.

*i*n its depiction of a community that harbours a known paedophile, *Never Take Sweets From a Stranger* was way ahead of its time — and out of step, too, for its subject matter would be deemed taboo in several countries. It remains the film of which producer Anthony Hinds is most proud.

Based on a Roger Garis play called *The Pony Cart*, the film is set in a prosperous Canadian small town. Ten year-old Jean Carter (Janine Faye), *émigrée* daughter of the town's newly-appointed English school principal, is led by her friend Lucille Demarest (Frances Green) to the mansion of Olderberry Senior (Felix Aylmer), an elderly binocular-carrying voyeur. Later, at home with father Pete (Patrick Allen) and mother Sally (Gwen Watford), Jean lets slip that she danced naked for Olderberry's gratification in exchange for sweets. Pete files a complaint with the local police, but finds the powerful Olderberry family to be above the law. Sally discovers that Olderberry has previously been hospitalised for such activities. The family do succeed in bringing Olderberry before a court, but the prosecution fails; ostracised by their peers, the Carters prepare to leave town. But, in the woods, Olderberry pursues playmates Lucille and Jean, his unchecked proclivities now homicidal...

Hammer purchased rights to the play early in 1959, hoping to persuade Irish-American redhead Maureen O'Hara, then in her late thirties, to star as Sally, but they failed. Joseph Losey, soon to direct *The Damned*, had his hopes to helm the picture dashed by a disapproving Columbia, and one-time British Film Unit documentary-maker Cyril Frankel was hired instead. With Black Park standing in for Canadian woodland, the film went before the Bray cameras between 14 September and 30 October. Columbia were reported to be "immensely pleased" with the finished film, and fulsome endorsements were secured from, among others, magistrate Sir Basil Henriques, former chairman of The East London Juvenile Court ("neither lurid nor sensational but painfully true of what could occur to anyone's child"), the Reverend Arthur Morton, director of The National Society for the Prevention of Cruelty to Children ("the film will perform a service of real value") and Mrs J.C. Gimple of The National Council of Women ("it should be seen by all parents").

Its run at the London Pavilion in March 1960

proved disappointing, however. The manager of the Pavilion was reported to have said that "the usual class of people attracted to his theatre during X certificate runs [have] not been appearing". And whereas the film's British general release was held over until late September, apparently for lack of a suitable support feature — eventually the Brigitte Bardot-starring *Dance With Me* filled the slot — it encountered its greatest resistance overseas. Banned in France and the French colonies, it was rejected outright by the Dublin censor. Most damagingly, its "depiction of sexual perversion" alone ensured that it failed to qualify for the Breen Seal essential for mainstream American distribution, despite Columbia's "vigorous protests" and later attempts to "obtain a special dispensation for the film in view of the enormous support it has received from the various authorities." Under the title *Never Take Candy From a Stranger*, it limped out onto the American arthouse circuit some time later. Its producers were rightly appalled by such treatment. The years have seen this fine film — which masks any naïveté well, despite its drawing a discreet veil over the depiction of Olderberry's actual offences — comprehensively buried.

Conversely, *Hell is a City* appalled professional bodies, but was both widely seen and widely acclaimed. In Manchester, Inspector Martineau (Stanley Baker), whose rocky marriage is failing, learns that criminal Don Starling (John Crawford), whom he had convicted fourteen years previously, has escaped prison. Having returned to the city, Starling

plots a jewel robbery that will enable him to flee the country. Martineau descends into Manchester's underworld in an attempt to track down Starling and his mob, learning a little too much about himself in the process...

Written and directed by Val Guest from a novel by ex-Manchester copper Maurice Procter, *Hell is a City* was as one with Guest's oft-stated documentary style: much of the film, shot between 21 September and 5 November 1959, employed genuine Manchester locations, including the rooftops of the Refuge Assurance Building, where the climactic gunfight takes place. In addition, Guest featured officers from Manchester, Huddersfield and Oldham police as extras; likewise, reporters from *The Huddersfield Daily Examiner* and the regulars of the pub The Fatted Calf (aka The Lacy Arms). What made the film extraordinary was its raw depiction of the flawed and all-too-human Martineau and his fellows, to whom villain Starling is closer than, say, the benevolent PC 49 or the worldly-wise George Dixon. As such, it led to a confrontation with the Chief Constable of Manchester City Police who, after seeing the film early in 1960, took offence to a scene in which the married Martineau and barmaid Lucky (Vanda Sorell) become a little too close for decency (policemen, it seems, didn't do that sort of thing). On 29 January, he wrote to Michael Carreras: "The more I think about it, the more convinced I become that such a scene would give great offence to my Force, to my police authority, to many of the citizens of Manchester and to the police service in general...I must ask you to agree to a retake in such a way

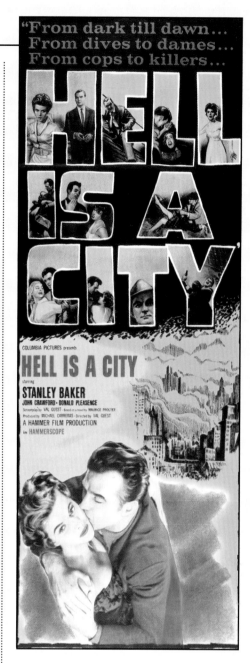

that the offensiveness is removed... Could you also arrange to cut out of the sound track the use of swear words by police officers? The use of such language is not by any means typical of the police service." In America, five minutes of such material was cut or redubbed, including the removal of two uses of "cripes" in a reel two scene and the alteration of the line "You're bitching my luck" to "You're botching my luck".

The film, partly shot on the stages of ABPC Elstree, drew substantive press praise following its gala première at the Apollo Theatre in Manchester's Ardwick Green on 10 April. Despite several attempts to launch a spin-off TV series, even as late as a decade on, Martineau did not appear again. Assessing his film over thirty years later, Guest suggests: "I think *Hell is a City* was one of the first films to tackle the subject of the police with the 'you were there' treatment, with no kid gloves. I think in that respect it may have started a minor wave of films treating the police as human beings."

No less impressive was *Cash on Demand*, a minor co-feature directed by Quentin Lawrence, for which Hammer put up a mere £37,000. From Jacques Gillies' 1960 ATV play *The Gold Inside*, it concerned a petty and vindictive bank manager, Fordyce (Peter Cushing), who, through his unwilling association with suave bank robber 'Colonel Hepburn' (André Morell), learns to become a better man. Essentially a showcase for two of the company's finest performers, its one man's redemption narrative is not so far removed from *It's a Wonderful Life* and *A Christmas Carol*; consequently, it is every bit as endearing. Shot at Bray over a three-week period between 4 and 26 April 1961, it wasn't released in Britain until late in 1963, when it supported Rank's *Bye Bye Birdie*.

As Hammer's reputation as a horror producer continued to grow, distributors became increasingly reluctant to invest in films from the company that didn't match the profile. Bar 1973's *Man at the Top*, from an undistinguished TV sequel to kitchen sink classic *Room at the Top*, Hammer originated no further genre-free contemporary drama films.

Previous page (left): Olderberry (Felix Aylmer) tempts Jean (Janine Faye) and Lucille (Frances Green) in Canadian woodland. The controversial, and disturbing, Never Take Sweets From a Stranger.

Previous page (right): Director Val Guest and John Crawford prepare for the chase sequence in Hell is a City. *Filming took place 200 feet above ground level among the catwalks of Manchester's Refuge Assurance Company building.*

Above: The American poster for Hell is a City.

Left: 'Colonel Hepburn' (André Morell) torments bank manager Fordyce (Peter Cushing) in Cash on Demand.

**Principal photography 25 September to
8 November 1961
Released 7 June 1962
Certificate A
Duration 82 mins
Colour
Director Peter Graham Scott**

1776: a mulatto pirate (Milton Reid) is punished for assaulting the pregnant wife of the ruthless Captain Clegg. The mulatto's ears are severed, his tongue removed, and he is tied up and left to die on a remote island. In 1792, Captain Collier (Patrick Allen) brings a team of revenue men to Dymchurch, determined to prove that the village is harbouring a covert smuggling operation. Collier is intrigued by the legendary 'marsh phantoms' of nearby Romney, and the grave of the executed Captain Clegg in the church cemetery. Beneath Collier's nose, French brandy is indeed being smuggled — in coffins manufactured by local undertaker Mipps (Michael Ripper). The whole campaign is orchestrated by the seemingly benign local vicar, Dr Blyss (Peter Cushing). The marsh phantoms are in reality Blyss and his fellow villagers, disguised as spectral skeletons to frighten strangers away from smuggling activity on the marsh. Collier's suspicions are further aroused when Dr Blyss is recognised and attacked by one of his men — a dumb mulatto rescued from a remote island in 1776...

*i*ndependent producer John Temple-Smith began his career in 1951 with *Home to Danger*, a modest thriller directed by Terence Fisher. Throughout the fifties, he worked extensively for Rank and Sydney Box, ultimately under the auspices of Major Films, a production company he ran with director Peter Graham Scott. In 1961, Major approached Hammer with the idea of filming Arthur Russell Thorndike's 1915 novel *Dr Syn — A Tale of Romney Marsh*. A lengthy legal dispute followed throughout the summer of 1961 after Walt Disney Productions, who were already planning to shoot *Dr Syn, Alias the Scarecrow*, contested Hammer's title rights to the property (Disney had already optioned the title from Thorndike and his publishers Hutchinson in February 1961). Incredibly, two versions of a story last filmed in 1937 were going head-to-head.

Major had purchased remake rights to Gaumont's 1937 version in good faith, but it transpired that these rights were now moot. Keen to safeguard the investment Hammer had already made in the property, James Carreras arrived at a compromise

with Disney in mid-September: Hammer could make their version of Thorndike's story, but they were forbidden to use 'Dr Syn' as either the name of a character in the screenplay or as the title of the film itself. Anthony Hinds reluctantly cancelled an imminent holiday and hastily rewrote Temple-Smith and Scott's first draft, removing all references to Dr Syn and naming Thorndike's undercover pirate Dr Arne. (Peter Cushing was so enthused by the project that he also wrote a screenplay, called simply *Dr Syn*. In 1972, he wrote another on the same subject, entitled *Waiting Revenge*. Both went unrealised.)

Delayed by both legal wrangling and union (in)action, shooting finally commenced on 25 September under the direction of Peter Graham Scott. Hinds entitled the shooting script *The Curse of Captain Clegg*, and finally settled on 'Dr Blyss' as the name of the protagonist. The screenplay was given a

Previous page: Captain Collier (Patrick Allen) exposes the incriminating rope marks around the neck of Captain Clegg (Peter Cushing). The film was released in America as Night Creatures.
Left: The Bosun (David Lodge, left) and Imogene (Yvonne Romain), a girl with a secret past...
Below left: Inside Braywood Church, the Reverend Sidney Doran (left) rehearses Peter Cushing in preparation for the scene where Dr Blyss marries Imogene and Harry (Oliver Reed). Director Peter Graham Scott (right) looks on.
Bottom: Prior to shooting, Cushing sketched his own detailed design for Clegg's costume. Later, Cushing admonished some extras for not taking the film seriously. "Gentlemen," he reportedly said, "if we don't believe in what we're doing, then no one in the audience will. We as actors owe it to them."

last-minute polish by Barbara S. Harper, another of Temple-Smith's long-standing colleagues. Already smarting from the legal costs incurred in the title dispute, Hammer scaled down their original intention to shoot the film on location in Canada. When not using Bray Studios, exterior filming was concentrated around an army training ground in Cobham, Surrey. Scott also used the picturesque Copstone Mill, overlooking Turville Heath in Fingest, Buckinghamshire. For eighteenth-century Dymchurch, he adopted the script's suggestion of nearby Denham. Tinted footage from David Lean's *Great Expectations* helped create the illusion. The most distinctive location, however, was the deconsecrated Braywood Church. The church had been empty since the last vicar of Braywood retired in 1958, after which the parish was reunited with Bray. The church's interior, its graveyard and surrounding woodland were all used, Bray parish priest Reverend Sidney Doran even posing for pictures with Cushing and Scott inside. On the final day of shooting inside the church, engineers arrived to survey the building. Braywood Church, built in 1848, was scheduled for demolition soon after. "I don't think I have

ever felt quite so sad in my life," said Cushing at the time.

The film was lent a supernatural atmosphere by the inclusion of the 'marsh phantoms', which were heavily promoted in the film's publicity. "We painted black body suits for both the horsemen and the horses with codit reflective paint," recalls special effects assistant Ian Scoones. "Two film spotlights were placed either side of the camera lens, giving a bright, luminous effect. For greater mobility, chief electrician Jack Curtis welded the heaviest of film lights — the 'Brutes' — to the backs of two jeeps."

Scoones loaned Hammer 'François', a human skull he discovered in 'Dead Man's Island', unconsecrated Kent marshland where the Admiralty buried French prisoners of war: "It is François, illuminated with codit paint, zooming up to the lens that drives the fleeing Sydney Bromley into the swamp after the 'dance of death' by the marsh phantoms. Unfortunately, Sydney missed the mattress that the props men had covered with bulrushes and injured his back. He was driven off to hospital, still in costume and soaking wet, covered in mud and reeds. The only other shot involving Bromley required him to be a staring corpse in a coffin!"

Premièred on 7 June 1962 at the Leicester Square Odeon by distributors Rank, *Captain Clegg* was the support feature to *The Phantom of the Opera*. The double-bill went on general release from 25 June. For its American release, the film was retitled *Night Creatures*. (The title had been retained from Hammer's version of Richard Matheson's post-apocalyptic novel *I Am Legend*. The project was passed over when Matheson's script was unconditionally dismissed by the BBFC in 1957.)

This macabre *Boys' Own* adventure is an endearing relic. The trappings of Hammer horror spice up the swashbuckling evocatively: graves are exhumed, marsh phantoms scare victims to death and the make-up drips blood red. Peter Cushing is outstanding amongst a fine cast, delivering a performance rich in warmth and versatility.

THE PHANTOM OF THE OPERA

Principal photography 21 November 1961 to
26 January 1962
Released 7 June 1962
Certificate A
Duration 84 mins
Colour
Director Terence Fisher

Monday 27 November 1900: London's Albany Theatre is hosting the première of Saint Joan, *an opera by Lord Ambrose D'Arcy (Michael Gough). The troubled production is curtailed when the scenery rips open to reveal a hanged stagehand. The terrified prima donna resigns, so producer Harry Hunter (Edward de Souza) finds a replacement in Christine Charles (Heather Sears). In her dressing room after the audition, Christine is startled by a mysterious voice warning her that "D'Arcy is a vile and vicious man." When Christine later resists the lecherous Ambrose, she is dismissed. Harry protests, but he too is fired by Ambrose. Harry soon discovers that* Saint Joan *was actually the work of Professor Petrie, who apparently drowned in the Thames after a fire at a nearby printer's shop. That night, Christine is kidnapped by a dwarf and delivered to the secret cellars below the theatre. Following an underground waterway leading from the river, Harry discovers Christine and reveals her masked captor to be Petrie (Herbert Lom). Petrie explains that D'Arcy paid him a pittance to publish his music, then claimed authorship. While trying to burn the sheet music, an accident with the printer's nitric acid left him disfigured. With only the dwarf for company, Petrie has been 'haunting' the theatre while the plagiarist D'Arcy takes credit for his work...*

Early in 1961, Universal suggested *The Phantom of the Opera* as their next Hammer collaboration. James Carreras and Anthony Hinds toyed with the idea in February, mulling over a budget of £150,000. The unexpected arrival of Cary Grant at Hammer House thrust potential greatness on the project. Incredibly, the Hollywood star had dropped in to tell Hammer that he had ambitions to appear in one of the company's celebrated horror films. For a short while he was taken seriously and an adaptation of *The Phantom of the Opera* was written with him in mind, Anthony Hinds tailoring his script to Grant's screen persona. Previous attempts to deviate from characters Grant himself admitted were "a combination of Jack Buchanan, Noel Coward and Rex Harrison" had proved unwise. Therefore, Hinds rewrote Gaston Leroux's story so that the Phantom's victims were despatched by a loyal assassin dwarf, but ultimately there was no need. Grant never contacted Hammer again.

It was hoped a budget of £180,000 would ensure a high quality film, and permission was sought to shoot inside Covent Garden Opera House during its closed season in July and August. Hammer eventually deferred to the more modest confines of Wimbledon Theatre, director Terence Fisher struggling to achieve the required sense of scale when shooting finally commenced in November.

A last-minute Phantom was found in forty-four year-old Herbert Charles Angelo Kuchacevich ze Schluderpacheru, better known as Herbert Lom. "I have never seen Chaney or Rains in the part," he claimed shortly before the film's release. "I had a vague idea the story was just another horror piece about a mad musician who practised some kind of Dracula rites in his cellar." His initial concerns about the role were, he claimed, alleviated by the quality of the script:"I saw this Phantom as a human, pathetic, broken creature, as a hideous outcast and a figure of tragedy in the highest sense. The man's horror was incidental." Famous for such films as *The Ladykillers* and *The Seventh Veil*, Lom had previously appeared in Exclusive/Hammer's *Whispering Smith Hits London*. He would return to Hammer in 1978 for the company's final film, *The Lady Vanishes*. Heather Sears, previously notable in *Room at the Top*, played Christine, with her opera voice dubbed by singer Pat Clark. Anthony Hinds cast the Portugese/Goanese actor Edward de Souza as Harry after seeing him in a television production of *So Long at the Fair*. *The Phantom of the Opera* marked the twenty-nine year-old's first major film role, and he went on to star in *The Kiss of the Vampire*.

The crucial task of crafting the Phantom's mask was given to an outside contractor, none of whose designs were deemed satisfactory. Filming was already underway when make-up artist Roy Ashton was asked to manufacture the piece on the spot from anything that came to hand:"I got a piece of rag, some tape, bits of string and rubber and in about five minutes I had a mask..."

Director Terence Fisher placed a special emphasis on the sentimental themes suggested by the script, perhaps hoping to fulfil a long-held desire to direct a love story. "You can over-emphasise or underemphasise *for a purpose* certain angles of your story," he told *Cinefantastique* magazine. "I emphasised the tragedy of the film which was the important thing to me: this man who had his music stolen, his association with the girl."

An unusually long shoot came to an end on 26 January. During editing in the following weeks, British distributors Rank dropped a bombshell, announcing that *The Phantom of the Opera*, conceived and filmed as an X certificate picture, would have to attain an A certificate for its release. Few shocking scenes remain in the final edit — incredibly, the Phantom's scarred face would only be glimpsed right at the end of the British print. Perhaps as a result, *The Observer* dismissed the film as "a very tame remake of the famous original."

"This third version of Gaston Leroux's melodramatic parade of divas, dwarfs, disfigurement and death, is a well gilded slice of medium guignol," wrote *Films and Filming*'s John Cutts, who mistook Hammer's censorship difficulties to be a new artistic direction. "A little short on genuine thrills perhaps, and more than just a little rushed in pace toward the end (what does happen to Michael Gough?), but nevertheless, a holding piece of lush spookery. It's also good to report that the company at last seem to be learning their trade; have come to appreciate that to *suggest* disquiet is just as effective as to *show* it."

Paired with *Captain Clegg*, another A certificate picture, *The Phantom of the Opera* went on general release on 25 June, failing to excite Hammer's usual box-office business. Universal reported great satisfaction with *The Phantom of the Opera*'s takings in America (where Herbert Lom's Phantom would be seen unmasked), but in Britain the double-bill's performance left Rank and Hammer disappointed.

Although distinguished by some fine acting, sets and music, *The Phantom of the Opera* seems decidedly half-baked. Terence Fisher's misguided approach and Rank's emasculation of the British print sealed its fate. Future Hammer horrors would be less well-mannered.

Previous page: The masked Professor Petrie (Herbert Lom) welcomes the terrified Christine (Heather Sears) to his lair beneath the Albany Theatre.
Above: Two typically inventive gimmicks from the American 'Showman's Manual and Promotion Kit' — a cardboard Phantom mask with press-out nose-piece, and a four-page 'newspaper' carrying details of the film. In a letter to cinema managers, Universal's Philip Gerard urged "Sell it hard! Back it to the hilt! Play it with enthusiasm!" Such aggressive marketing had yet to catch on in England.
Left: Harry (Edward de Souza) struggles with the Dwarf (Ian Wilson) during his journey to rescue the kidnapped Christine.

THE OLD DARK HOUSE

Principal photography 14 May to
22 June 1962
Released 16 September 1966
Certificate A
Duration 76 mins
Colour
Director William Castle

American Tom Penderel (Tom Poston) is asked by daytime flatmate Casper Femm (Peter Bull) to deliver a car to his ancestral home, Dartmoor's Femm Hall. On the way, Tom is caught in a violent thunderstorm. When he finally reaches the Hall, a stone lion tumbles from the gateposts, wrecking the car. Tom goes to pull the house's door-knock, activating a hidden trapdoor which propels him into a cellar containing a number of empty coffins. Released by elderly ark-builder Potiphar Femm (Mervyn Johns), Tom finds Casper to be dead, having 'accidentally' tumbled down the stairs. He meets the remaining Femms: demure cousin Cecily (Janette Scott), matronly Agatha (Joyce Grenfell), vampish Morgana (Fenella Fielding), taciturn Morgan (Danny Green), Casper's twin Jasper (Peter Bull), and gun-collector Roderick (Robert Morley), who believes that Tom may be a distant relative of the family. It transpires that the vast Femm fortune has been left to the house itself and each family member may only take a share if they are present in the Hall at midnight every night. After dinner, Morgana brings Tom a basin brimful of acid. And then the killings start...

"*i* cannot think of anything more loaded with commercial possibilities than a marriage between the chill and chatter schools of Hammer and Bill Castle," wrote James Carreras in 1962, eagerly anticipating the imminent production of *The Old Dark House*. He was wrong.

Playwright and author J. B. Priestley's second novel, 1927's *Benighted*, reputedly written for fun between sessions on a more highbrow effort, had formed the basis of Universal's 1932 suspense melodrama *The Old Dark House*. Directed by James Whale and starring Boris Karloff and Charles Laughton, the Universal version may have taken liberties with Priestley's text but was, and remains, very highly regarded. Hammer's remake had indeed been first proposed as a 1961 production for Universal. Over the Atlantic, however, schlock director William Castle had apparently also been contemplating a new version. The prolific Castle, king of gimmicks, was best-known for devising such promotional japes as wiring up cinema seats to give a low-level shock to viewers of his *The Tingler*. In 1961, he'd made a farcical comic-

horror, *Zotz!*, and was keen to develop this strain with his own *The Old Dark House*. Natural bedfellows anyway — later that year, Hammer's *The Terror of the Tongs* was released in London alongside Castle's *Homicidal* — Hammer joined forces with Castle to make the film, sharing production chores. The film was to be made for Columbia, to whom both parties were contracted.

In March 1962, Anthony Hinds met Castle in New York to discuss script and sets. It had by now been resolved that 'exploitation' would be handled by Castle, and that the film's sets could be revamped for use in forthcoming productions *The Kiss of the Vampire*, *Nightmare* and *Paranoiac*. On 16 April, the BBFC's John Trevelyan sent to associate producer Anthony Nelson Keys his preliminary report on the script, which assumed an A certificate for the finished film ("there is rather too much in it for the U"). The Board asked that care be taken over shots of bodies in

coffins, expressed concern that planned shots of Agatha with knitting needles protruding from her chest might be rather gruesome, but saved their main worries for the soundtrack ("This hyena laughter could be very spooky. It should not be played-up too much") and the dialogue ("I am not sure whether the lines 'Sir! Please! I'm a gentleman' is intended as a homosexual joke. If so, we would not want anything of this kind"). The following morning, Castle arrived at Waterloo Station where he posed for pictures with James Carreras and a skull. Before shooting, Castle and Hinds met with Priestley, who apparently suggested "that the story might perhaps be made this time with as much emphasis on comedy as on thrills."

Studio filming began in May, and was much hampered by an electricians' strike. Brief location inserts were shot on London's Embankment, lanes near Bray and cutaway shots taken of neighbouring Oakley Court, which doubled as flagpoled Femm Hall. An impressive British cast was joined by American light comedian Tom Poston, who'd mugged his way through Castle's *Zotz!*. Grand old man of the theatre Robert Morley was reunited with long-time acting *compadre* Peter Bull on the film. Later, Morley's wife recalled her husband bribing Bull for the latter's dialogue: "'I hate my line,' he would say to Bull over the smoked salmon. 'Give me your line.' As often as not he got it."

Hammer still hoped that the film might be granted a U, but the BBFC's July viewing of an early black and white print minus sound effects scotched this (and cast doubt even on an A). The company intended the film to have a circuit release for the Easter holidays of 1963, but considered an A to be worthless, cutting off both the child audience and their usual horror constituency. In reply, the BBFC outlined cuts that would be needed for both an X and a U — the former would require trims to the shots of Aunt Agatha with knitting needles skewering her neck, and the latter the removal of every single shot in which the face of a corpse could be seen, plus two shots of the (obviously stuffed) hyena "slavering." It was decided to attempt to trim the film for a U, and editor James Needs duly pre-

pared a report on the required cuts. Some new insertions were needed, but in places it would prove impossible to cut around the corpses. Meanwhile, Hammer were preparing a second co-production with Castle entitled *Too Many Ghosts*. Columbia objected to both Castle and his associate Donna Holloway receiving production credits on the American print of *The Old Dark House*, which neither Hinds nor Keys had opposed; Keys, for reasons unknown, gave his credit to brother Basil.

At Easter 1963, as intended, an eighty-six minute black and white version of *The Old Dark House* was released in America without cuts (alongside Michael Carreras' *Maniac*). Having found it impossible to cut the film for a U in Britain, Hammer elected to show the film as an X. Duly delivered, however, the X version failed to find support amongst exhibitors. In 1964, trial dates were given by ABPC for a programme comprising *The Old Dark House* and Castle's later *Strait-Jacket*, but nothing came of this (at various times, the film was due to be paired with *Son of Captain Blood*, *The Man With the X-ray Eyes*, plus Hammer products *The Nanny* and *Slave Girls*). In March 1966, *The Old Dark House* was cut down to seventy-six minutes as an A, and in this form, in colour, it was coupled with the lighthearted Henry Fonda Western *Big Deal at Dodge City* for its ABC circuit release on 16 September. Hammer received just twenty-five per cent of the programme, its film labelled "abysmal" by *Monthly Film Bulletin*. Actress Fenella Fielding had since reprised her *Old Dark House* persona — right down to the red dresses! — in the rather more successful *Carry On Screaming*. Perhaps unsurprisingly, *Too Many Ghosts* never happened. William Castle went on to produce Roman Polanski's seminal Satanic horror *Rosemary's Baby*.

The release on video of the colour, eighty-three minute, X version of *The Old Dark House* in September 1996 enabled British audiences to reappraise this unloved film. It's certainly one of the oddest pictures the company made, but strangely endearing. The cast are uniformly delightful and Janette Scott's final few moments — mad as a snake, and wielding a meat cleaver — are a joy to behold.

Previous page: A cheerful cast and crew at Bray Studios. Director William Castle raises his cup high; star Tom Poston stands to his left. Potiphar's ark is under construction in the background.
Above left: Janette Scott, blanching at the script's (later) X-rated scenes?
Below: Cecily (Janette Scott), Tom Penderel (Tom Poston) and Roderick (Robert Morley) count down to midnight in The Old Dark House.

**Principal shooting 7 September to
25 October 1962
Released 5 January 1964
Certificate X
Duration 88 mins
Colour
Director Don Sharp**

Honeymooning in Bavaria in 1910, Gerald and Marianne Harcourt (Edward de Souza and Jennifer Daniel) are stranded when their car runs out of petrol. While Gerald searches for a fresh supply, Marianne is approached by the elderly Professor Zimmer (Clifford Evans), who warns her not to visit the château on the nearby mountain. The Harcourts eventually find lodging as the only guests in a run-down hotel, and accept a dinner invitation from Dr Ravna (Noel Willman), the owner of the château. That evening, Ravna's son (Barry Wilson) plays a piano rhapsody that has an overwhelming effect on Marianne. The following day, the Harcourts attend a masked ball at the château. Gerald is drugged and Marianne is taken prisoner by a white-robed Ravna. He advances on her, vampire fangs bared. Gerald awakes to find his wife has vanished. He returns to the hotel to discover all her possessions missing; the hotel owners deny she ever existed. Gerald finds an ally in Professor Zimmer, who reveals that he intends to revenge his daughter's abduction by toppling Ravna's vampiric cult. Gerald rescues Marianne from the château, but before Zimmer can put the final part of his plan into place, Ravna telepathically summons the hypnotised Marianne back into his clutches...

T he *Kiss of the Vampire* first appeared on Hammer's schedule as early as 2 January 1961, under the typically economic pre-production title *Dracula III*. Encouraged by *The Brides of Dracula*'s positive reception in the United States, James Carreras sanctioned the film's sale to an enthusiastic Universal, this time anticipating co-production finance from Italian producer Roberto Dandi.

Both Dandi and Dracula had dropped out of the package by the time Anthony Hinds' screenplay was finalised the following year. For *The Kiss of the Vampire*, Hinds pursued young Australian director Don Sharp. "I met with Tony Hinds and told him that I'd never seen a horror picture," remembers Sharp. "He said to me, 'Well, from what I've seen of your work I think you'd be able to handle it, but why don't I run a few for you?' So over the next few days I saw *The Curse of Frankenstein*, *Dracula* and *The Stranglers of Bombay* at Hammer House in Wardour Street. What intrigued me about them was that

after about twenty minutes I was totally hooked despite a totally absurd situation. I thought it was wonderful — here was a genre with its own ground rules and self-contained world, and you could be theatrical but treat it realistically to grab the audience and make them believe something absurd."

Hinds' inventive reinterpretation of the vampire myth was in part composed of ideas and situations discarded from Peter Bryan's draft of *The Brides of Dracula*. Most notably, these included the climactic scene where Zimmer summons a plague of bats to overwhelm Ravna and his disciples. The script would go through further distillation by the BBFC. "Our censors have got very strict and it's got partic-

ularly difficult since Lord Morrison took over," Hinds bemoaned in *Kinematograph Weekly*, 18 October 1962. "We always submit the script to the censors but we invariably get back a three-page letter of things they're not prepared to pass."

Don Sharp had concerns of his own: "What worried me was that, as Hammer progressed, the goal seemed to be for each picture to top the one before it and they were becoming satiated with violence. So I persuaded Tony that it was better to suggest 'is it going to happen?' and give the audience a little touch of it, and then go on and really get your big shock in the end. There could be a good size shock in the middle too, but not all the time. I quoted

Previous page: Professor Zimmer (Clifford Evans) is confronted by the vampire Tania (Isobel Black). "[Clifford Evans] was extremely volatile and Celtic," remembers Edward de Souza. "The thing Don [Sharp] had to do was to make him stand or sit still. I think that's one of the reasons he had so many close-ups. If he didn't have a close-up he'd be all over the place."
Left: Edward de Souza (left) and director Don Sharp in Black Park, with the De Dion Bouton loaned to Hammer by the Montagu Motor Museum.
Below left: Margaret Read and Elizabeth Valentine (two of Ravna's disciples) get a step up at Bray Studios.
Below right: Dr Ravna (Noel Willman) prepares to strike. "I decided straight away he was going to be a creature possessed of bloodlust and great sexual appetite," recalled Willman. "I focused on Ravna's power."

Robert Louis Stevenson: 'To travel hopefully is better than to arrive.' He saw the point immediately and we did a rewrite to reflect this."

The Brides of Dracula had proved Hammer could do without Christopher Lee. In *The Kiss of the Vampire* they tried to do without Peter Cushing as well. A dubious Noel Willman was persuaded to take the role of cult leader Dr Ravna. He told co-star Edward de Souza that "I intend to play this part

without changing my expression once." Edward de Souza had previously appeared in *The Phantom of the Opera*, and Clifford Evans in *The Curse of the Werewolf*, but many of the other cast members were unfamiliar faces. "And that is a good thing in a film of this kind," Sharp claimed at the time. "It allows the public to really lose themselves in the story without associating the actors with another film they may have made. It's often a little distracting when you find yourself thinking, 'Yes, he's very good in the part — but not as good as he was in so-and-so...'"

Distribution difficulties of a unique nature kept *The Kiss of the Vampire* away from American cinemas for nearly a year after its completion. Upon delivery of the film to Universal in New York, the distributor was concerned by the coincidental similarity of the film's ending to that of Alfred Hitchcock's *The Birds*, itself awaiting release by the same company in 1963. Hitch came before Hammer and *The Kiss of the Vampire* was accordingly shelved until September. In Britain it waited its turn until 1964, when it comprised a successful double-bill with *Paranoiac*, ABC outbidding Rank for Universal's British distribution rights.

Films and Filming reserved its most generous praise for the director: "*Kiss of the Vampire* has the appearance of being done tongue in cheek, and fortunately lacks the hefty hands that controlled most of its predecessors from Hammer." Despite the new face behind the camera, and the few in front of it, *The Kiss of the Vampire* is archetypal Hammer horror. The sequences shot in an autumnal Black Park (a location that appears in many of the company's period horror films) embellish the Gothic overtones, but familiarity with the routine blunts the script's innovations. An essentially intelligent and involving film is most seriously diminished, however, by the paucity of the finale's special effects. For the record, the bats were largely purchased from Woolworths.

1954's Robin Hood romp *Men of Sherwood Forest* added more than one string to Hammer's bow. Not only the first of the company's features to be made "In Beautiful Eastman Colour", it instigated a slew of adventure films that packed school holiday matinées for years to come.

SWASHBUCKLERS

According to various sources, swashbuckler means "adventurous, exciting" and "one who clashes a sword on a buckler", although Hammer interpreted it more along the lines of the definition given by film historian Leslie Halliwell: "films of period adventure in which the hero and the villain usually settle the issue by a duel to the death". *Men of Sherwood Forest*, a rousing Val Guest-directed tale of banditry in the reign of Richard the Lionheart, starred Don Taylor as the man in Lincoln green and Douglas Wilmer as the dastardly Sir Nigel Saltire. It was followed six years later by *Sword of Sherwood Forest*, which featured co-producer Richard Greene in the lead. Greene had previously played Robin in 143 episodes of *The Adventures of Robin Hood*, Sapphire Films' successful television series of 1955-1959. Although none of Greene's regular supporting cast joined him, the film was directed by Terence Fisher, who'd previously helmed many of the television instalments. *Sword of Sherwood Forest* was filmed on location in Ireland's County Wicklow between May and July 1960, and featured Peter Cushing as a venomous Sheriff of Nottingham.

A project entitled *Robin Hood and the King's*

Ransom was slated for production during July and August 1964, but it wasn't until 1967 that the company revisited Friar Tuck, Little John and chums in *A Challenge for Robin Hood*, a back-to-basics version of the legend with Barrie Ingham in the title role and John Arnatt playing his nemesis. Barrie Ingham and Gay Hamilton dressed up as Robin and Marian to publicise the film during a tour of ABC 'minors' matinées' in December 1967, and coach-loads of children clamoured to see them. Despite the invention of writer Peter Bryan and director C.M. Pennington-Richards, Hammer's most enjoyable Robin Hood spawned no further sequels.

In 1961, Hammer embarked upon a series of pirate-themed pictures, beginning with *The Pirates of Blood River*. The film featured Kerwin Mathews as an outcast Huguenot who joins a band of swarthy no-goods led by Christopher Lee's LaRoche. This was the first of three adventure features overseen by the fearsome John Gilling, who was impressed enough by the gung-ho attitude of one of its young stars to cast him in the subsequent two. Says Oliver Reed, who played sea wolf Brocaire: "I remember once on *The Pirates of Blood River*, the stunt men wouldn't jump over a bank or something. I went charging over this bank with a sword in my mouth, followed by a medical student, who was one of the crowd — and all the stunt men stopped; they wouldn't do it. John Gilling,

who was the director, fired them all. And from that time on, he thought I was really quite something, because I'd do things that stunt men wouldn't do. It was only because I was stupid!"

Trimmed of a few contentious moments, the U-rated *The Pirates of Blood River* opened at the London Pavilion on 13 July 1962, right in the middle of the school holidays — and cleaned up. Initial results were reportedly "tremendous", and the film was still doing excellent business during the winter half-term of the following year. *Captain Clegg*, the company's second yo-ho-ho outing (albeit with a touch of the supernatural) to go before the cameras had already opened in June 1962 as support to the sadly keelhauled *The Phantom of the Opera*, but *The Pirates of Blood River* had pointed the way to a more *Sturm und Drang* successor. In summer 1963, production got underway on *The Devil-Ship Pirates*. Working around his tax exile, Christopher Lee was top-billed by Hammer for the first time as villainous buccaneer Captain Robeles, whose rotten complement terrorise a Cornish village at the time of the Spanish Armada. Shot on a larger scale than *The Pirates of Blood River*, and this time by *The Kiss of the Vampire*'s Don Sharp, the film opened with a thundering set-piece battle between two galleons. "That was shot in a flooded gravel pit a couple of miles up the road from Bray," remembers Sharp. "One of the reasons there was so much battle smoke was that on the other side of the lake they were starting to build the M4 motorway, and we didn't want all the trucks in the background!" Disaster struck when the massive devil-ship *Diablo* prop proved rather less than seaworthy: "The superstructure was designed to sit on a raft with huge petrol drums making it buoyant. It was so heavy that it took two cranes to put it into the water. On the second or third day of shooting, we had just finished a scene and someone announced that the tea-boat was coming, so everyone rushed to one side of the ship and tipped it over! There were bodies in the water, people swimming for shore — absolute chaos!"

Immediately preceding *The Devil-Ship Pirates* in the company's 1963 production schedule was *The Scarlet Blade*. John Gilling's English Civil War epic starred Lionel Jeffries and Oliver Reed as Roundheads Judd and Sylvester who, having executed a Royalist harbouring King Charles (Robert Rietty), fall foul of the Royalist's son, Edward (Jack Hedley), who has adopted the guise of 'The Scarlet Blade', leader of a rebellious band of gypsies. Released in summer 1963, *The Scarlet Blade* was twinned with *Son of Captain Blood*, an Italian production that featured Sean Flynn, heir to Errol, as the progeny of his father's famous creation. Less successful was Reed and Gilling's final collaboration, *The Brigand of Kandahar*, in which Reed blacked up to play Gilzhai tribesleader Khan, who allies himself with disgraced half-caste Bengal Lancer Ronald Lewis in a tale of insurrection on India's Northwest frontier in the late nineteenth century. The film showcased excess scenes from *Zarak*, a similarly-themed 1956 Columbia/Warwick production led by Victor Mature. Columbia had apparently suggested that Gilling, *Zarak*'s associate director, pen

ASSOCIATED BRITISH
Presents
A HAMMER FILM PRODUCTION
"THE SCARLET BLADE" (U)
Technicolor   Hammerscope
starring
LIONEL JEFFRIES · OLIVER REED
JACK HEDLEY · JUNE THORBURN
Released through Warner-Pathe

a script to incorporate these cut sequences. The film brought both Oliver Reed and Columbia's regular association with Hammer to an end.

The Viking Queen, produced in 1966, adopted the now familiar theme of a plucky band of rebels routing the forces of a formidable oppressor. Intended to be epic in the manner of both *She* and *One Million Years B.C.*, its heroine was clearly inspired by Boudicca, the Iceni warrior queen whose army took the heads of some 70,000 Romans in the first century AD. Salina, Hammer's Boudicca substitute, would foment bloody revolution despite her love for Roman governor general Justinian (Don Murray), whose moderate sensibilities are trampled by harsh lieutenant Octavian (Andrew Keir). The so-called 'Viking queen' (a misnomer; Salina merely has Scandinavian blood on her mother's side) was played by 'Carita' who, despite extensive publicity, failed to be recognised as a new Andress or Welch. First planned as a production "of a spectacular nature" in 1964, it was shot in and around Ireland's Ardmore Studios between June and August 1966 under the auspices of Don Chaffey. The film went £61,000 over its already considerable budget of £350,000 (by comparison, *Frankenstein Created Woman*, shot at Bray in the same period, cost just under £140,000), but failed to make any real impression on its ABC circuit release at Easter the following year.

A footnote: *Mistress of the Seas*, a seafaring odyssey concerning female pirate Anne Bonney — and intended, again, for an Andress/Welch type — was first developed by Hammer in the late sixties. The idea eventually set sail in 1995 as *CutThroat Island*, a troubled vehicle for Hollywood actress Geena Davis.

Previous page (above): *Mac (Michael Ripper, right) and the villainous LaRoche (Christopher Lee) in* The Pirates of Blood River.
Previous page (bottom left): *Barrie Ingham in* A Challenge for Robin Hood.
Previous page (bottom right): *At Pinewood, even archery practice didn't delay a tea break.*
Above: *Edward (Jack Hedley) in* The Scarlet Blade.
Below: *According to* ABC Film Review, *Finnish model Carita (35-23-35) was "every vital inch a Viking Queen."*

Principal photography 14 October to
16 November 1963
Released 1 June 1964
Certificate X
Duration 86 mins
Colour
Director Freddie Francis

Baron Frankenstein's experiments at a watermill are disrupted by a priest. Fearing arrest, the Baron (Peter Cushing) and assistant Hans (Sandor Eles) flee to Karlstaad, site of the Baron's chateau, from whence he was expelled ten years earlier after his Creature ran amok. He finds the chateau looted, but the laboratory intact. In the town, he observes that both the corrupt Burgomaster (David Hutcheson) and Chief of Police (Duncan Lamont) have stolen various of his belongings. Furious, he confronts them, only narrowly evading arrest. Guided by a deaf-mute beggar girl (Katy Wild) to a cave in the mountains, Frankenstein discovers his Creature (Kiwi Kingston) preserved in glacial ice. He thaws out the monster and returns it to the laboratory, but its brain is damaged. The Baron seeks out the dissolute mesmerist Zoltan (Peter Woodthorpe), himself recently expelled from Karlstaad, to aid the Creature's recovery. It lives again, but is now commanded by the vengeful Zoltan, who instructs it first to steal gold — and then to "punish" those responsible for his expulsion...

The second sequel to *The Curse of Frankenstein* was originally developed for Columbia during February 1963, but later packaged for Universal alongside the soon-to-be-dropped thriller *Brainstorm*. Terence Fisher was engaged elsewhere, and therefore unable to direct a further foray into the saga of the Baron and all his ghastly works. Cinematographer-turned-director Freddie Francis stepped in, Francis' only proviso being that he required a very substantive laboratory set to be built (the lab was sketched by designer Frank Humphries). The Baron's Creature was realised according to Francis' hulking vision and a huge New Zealand wrestler called Kiwi Kingston was hired accordingly. Make-up man Roy Ashton was asked to design the Creature as an "assembly of hands and fingers and bits." "To tell you the truth, they did not really know what they wanted," he said later. "I must have done nearly 200 drawings for them to try and narrow down their ideas for something definite..." This time, the company did not need to adopt a design utterly unlike Universal's Boris Karloff make-up as the film was, after all, being made for Universal themselves. The resulting block-

headed Creature reflected this.

The Evil of Frankenstein was shot at Bray in the late autumn of 1963. Peter Cushing reprised his most famous role, and the supporting cast was led by the hypnotic Peter Woodthorpe, who went on to appear in Francis productions *Hysteria* (for Hammer) and *The Skull* (for rivals Amicus). Hungarian Sandor Eles later featured in Hammer's *Countess Dracula*.

Roy Ashton was called upon to build a fake hand so that the Creature might appear to break a pane of glass with its fist, and Cushing took it upon himself to perform a particular stunt during the infernal finale. He recalled: "I said to Freddie Francis, 'Could I jump off the balcony and swing in?' And Freddie said, 'Yes, sir — if you want to kill yourself, I'm willing...' So I did all that myself. It had to be done in two shots, because after I swung in, I swung back again!"

ing away into their Olde German beer mugs seems almost real by comparison." *The Evil of Frankenstein* sits uncomfortably among Hammer's other Frankenstein films. Its plot, structure, settings — not to mention emphasis on ruined castles, sparking laboratory equipment, villagers, burgomasters and all — recall Universal's thirties cycle far more than the bloody tragi-comedies the company had previously produced. Perhaps in consequence, it performed markedly better in America than Britain, where its take was deemed disappointing.

Much-acclaimed Oscar-winning cinematographer Francis, with credits including *Sons and Lovers*, *Saturday Night and Sunday Morning* and *The Innocents*, made his Hammer début with 1959's *Never Take Sweets From a Stranger*. Exercising directorial wings for the first time on the 1961 Bryanston comedy *Two and Two Make Six*, Francis directed thrillers *Paranoiac* and *Nightmare* for Hammer, and followed *The Evil of Frankenstein* with suspenser *Hysteria*. After a spell with Amicus on pictures such as *Dr Terror's House of Horrors* and *Torture Garden*, he returned to Hammer to helm *Dracula Has Risen From the Grave* in 1968. Later responsible for a pair of horrors for Tyburn, the company headed by his son Kevin, and 1985's *The Doctor and the Devils*, Francis was much fêted for his work as director of photography on films such as *The Elephant Man*, *The French Lieutenant's Woman* and *Cape Fear*.

But once I got into that circle of flames, I got third-degree burns; they didn't realise the enormous heat that was building up!" Locations were found at Black Park, Oakley Court and nearby Monkey Island Lane. A young accountant named Roy Skeggs, fresh from the shooting of Cy Endfield's *Zulu*, joined Hammer on an initial three week contract midway through filming. He stayed on to become a hugely significant figure in the company's history — and still retains the Creature's enormous boots as a souvenir of his first Hammer production.

The finished picture wasn't one of Francis' favourites — "more or less 'here is the monster, here is the mad lab and away we go,' so to speak" — and its *mise-en-scène* was singled out by one critic upon its release alongside Francis' own *Nightmare*: "a Bavarian village so stagy that the villagers rhubarb-

Previous page (left): *The Baron (Peter Cushing) rebirths his Creature (Kiwi Kingston).*
Previous page (right): *The huge Creature unwrapped.*
Top left: *Frank Humphries' ambitious plan for the Baron's laboratory...*
Far left and left: *...and the scaled-down, but nonetheless impressive, realisation.*
Top right: *Freddie Francis on location with Katy Wild, who plays the Beggar Girl.*

T H E G O R G O N

**Principal photography 9 December 1963 to
16 January 1964
Released 18 October 1964
Certificate X
Duration 83 mins
Colour
Director Terence Fisher**

The little town of Vandorf, 1910: Sascha Cass (Toni Gilpin), pregnant by rakish bohemian Bruno Heitz (Jeremy Longhurst), is found dead in nearby woodlands, her body turned to stone. Bruno is discovered hanged shortly after. At the inquest, after false testimony regarding Sascha's demise is given by local medico Doctor Namaroff (Peter Cushing), it is decided that the girl was murdered by her lover, who then killed himself in a fit of remorse. The verdict fails to satisfy Bruno's father, Professor Heitz (Michael Goodliffe). It transpires that seven similar deaths have been recorded over the previous five years and Heitz speculates that the killings may be connected to the legend of Megaera, last of the mythic Gorgons. At the ramshackle Castle Borski nearby, Heitz catches the serpentine creature's petrifying gaze. Slowly turning to stone, he leaves a letter to his other son, Paul (Richard Pasco). Soon after, Paul goes to Vandorf himself, closely followed by the eminent Professor Meister (Christopher Lee). Paul falls in love with Namaroff's assistant, Carla Hoffmann (Barbara Shelley), but Meister finds secret records revealing the truth: Carla, who arrived in Vandorf seven years previously, suffers blackouts which coincide with each full moon — when the Gorgon is at large. The truth has been held from her all these years by the lovestruck Namaroff; Carla is possessed by the spirit of Megaera...

*T*he Gorgon started out as a story synopsis submitted to Hammer in 1963 by Canadian writer John Llewellyn Devine. The plot was overhauled by writer/director John Gilling, whose screenplay excised some of Devine's more outlandish notions such as characters sporting "small mask-like periscopes... so that if they meet the Gorgon, they may not look directly upon her." Gilling would be "bitterly disappointed" by Hammer producer Anthony Hinds' later amendments to a script he regarded as one of his best. "In spite of a protest from Bill Graf of Columbia," said Gilling, "he re-wrote the opening, changed much of the dialogue and generally, I suspect, murdered what might have been a very good movie."

Realisation of the picture's ophidian-haired monster also proved contentious. Actress Barbara Shelley sat in Roy Ashton's chair for cosmetic tests, the intention being that Shelley herself would play both Carla and her snake-like *alter ego*. She was all for the head-

piece comprising live grass snakes — "we would have had *the* classic Gothic horror film of all time" — but was eventually substituted by Prudence Hyman, who played Megaera when shooting commenced at Bray at the end of 1963. (Producer Anthony Nelson Keys, wishing to keep the revelation of Carla's shadow-self a surprise, feared that audiences might identify her as the Gorgon too early — and consequently vetoed Shelley's mooted dual casting.) Effects supervisor Sid Pearson built the Gorgon's headpiece, moulding twelve latex rubber snakes which he hoped, with cables inserted, would give the impression of movement. Stop frame photography was used on two model severed heads, one covered in wax, to achieve the effect of the Gorgon's features peeling away to reveal Carla's face.

The Motion Picture Association of America did not receive the script for approval until 3 January 1964, more than three weeks into the film's shooting schedule. The only particular criticism voiced by reader Geoffrey M. Shurlock concerned the early scene between Sascha Cass and artist lover Bruno, where Sascha poses "half naked" on a chair. "We could not approve... any complete exposure of this girl's body," he noted. "Her breasts and other more intimate parts should be properly severed [sic]." In Britain, the BBFC, having expressed concern over several shots in the black and white rough cut (including Bruno's hanging, the removal of a brain and the Gorgon's ultimate decapitation), required Hammer to resubmit the finished colour print. In the event, all of the picture was passed intact. "We

were impressed by the standard of acting in this film," remarked John Trevelyan on 5 March, "and we think that it should turn out well."

Anthony Hinds' input extended beyond his unaccredited rewrite. On 14 February 1964, he wrote to Anthony Nelson Keys: "I saw the picture today and, except for the very sticky, second-feature beginning, thought it first-class... I would strongly recommend you do the following," he continued, detailing a list of suggested amendments. They included "a two-line written prologue... identifying the village with the castle" (Hinds felt that Castle Borski was not properly referred to until too late in the picture otherwise. His suggestion was duly adopted); "replace the present establishing shot of the mill-house (which does not look like anything at all) with a library shot. You can use my mill/matte from *Evil of Frankenstein* if you like" (again, this would be amended). He went on, suggesting that the initial scene between Sascha and Bruno be cut "right down to the bone" (it would remain extant), that Keys "build up the running through the woods" and that the attack on Sascha would be better presented if double-printed to appear "retarded and flickery." (This latter suggestion, too, was passed over.) "Once Peter Cushing appears, the picture comes to life... Congratulations!" he concluded.

A cold and depressing film, *The Gorgon* does achieve a certain grim serenity, particularly in its final moments where the dying Paul weeps, horror-struck, over the severed head of his sometimes-monstrous paramour, now free of Megaera's curse. Its bleak text contrasts horribly with its American marketing. When released alongside *The Curse of the Mummy's Tomb*, blacked-out gimmick eyemasks were distributed, which voyeurs could don to protect themselves from the creature's petrifying aspect.

Previous page (left): Doctor Namaroff (Peter Cushing) and Paul Heitz (Richard Pasco) — both besotted by Carla — duel in the ruins of Castle Borski.
Previous page (right): Carla's serpentine form (Prudence Hyman).
Above left: Producer Anthony Nelson Keys and Peter Cushing compare notes at Bray Studios.
Above right: Patrick Troughton as the Bodysnatcher in Frankenstein and the Monster From Hell.
Left: Line up at the inquest — bereaved father Janus Cass (Alister Williamson), Inspector Kanof (Patrick Troughton), Carla (Barbara Shelley), Doctor Namaroff and the grief stricken Heitz (Michael Goodliffe). A German front of house still from 'The Burning Eyes of Castle Bartimore'.

Columbia-Bavaria zeigt einen Farbfilm der Hammer Film Produktion
Die brennenden Augen von Schloss Bartimore
mit **Peter Cushing · Christopher Lee**

THE CURSE OF THE MUMMY'S TOMB

Principal photography 24 February to
27 March 1964
Released 18 October 1964
Certificate X
Duration 80 mins
Colour/Techniscope
Director Michael Carreras

Egypt, 1900: eminent archaeologist Professor Dubois (Bernard Rebel) is horribly murdered in the desert. The expedition to which he was attached, having recently disinterred the sarcophagus of the legendary Ra-Antef, prepares to decamp to London, as the expedition's vulgar American sponsor, Alexander King (Fred Clark), wishes to roadshow Ra-Antef's treasures around the world. This runs contrary to the wishes of both Sir Giles Dalrymple (Jack Gwillim), the expedition's head, and Egyptian civil servant Hashmi Bey (George Pastell), who warns that such sacrilege will bring disaster to all those present at Ra's unearthing. Already, a nightwatchman, plus, of course, the Professor, have been killed. On the voyage home, the Professor's daughter, Annette (Jeanne Roland), falls in with Adam Beauchamp (Terence Morgan), a stranger who holds a particular interest in the legend of Ra-Antef. At the London press night, King opens the sarcophagus. It is empty. The mummy lives again; as does his brother, Be, cursed to eternal life for murdering Ra. Only the mummy might release his brother — actually Adam — from the curse. The mummy, however, has yet to fulfil its legendary promise, and murder all those who disturbed its rest...

A follow-up to Hammer's 1959 *The Mummy* was long overdue, especially bearing in mind the outstanding business it had done. First story-lined for Universal in mid-1963, *The Curse of the Mummy's Tomb* soon transferred to Columbia. Late in the autumn, a résumé of Hammer's over ambitious plans for a *Mummy* successor saw print in *Daily Cinema*: "a group of archaeologists on a routine expedition into the Sahara Desert... discover an ancient tomb containing the mummy of a Pharaoh. Dabbling in things they don't understand, they bring to life a monstrous twenty-foot giant which goes on a murder rampage in Cairo. When the gigantic Creature escapes into the desert, aircraft and parachute troops go in pursuit." Perhaps unsurprisingly, this contemporaneous epic was deemed unfeasible (or perhaps technical adviser Andrew Low, retained from Hammer's 1959 original, questioned the likelihood of discovering a pharaoh's tomb in the Sahara, hundreds of miles to the east of the Nile). Regardless, the pre-production imagery

accompanying this synopsis — depicting a gargantuan mummy with a helpless girl in its grasp — would be retained for the finished film's poster!

At the outset, the film was scheduled to be shot at Bray over six weeks between July and September 1964, which was later amended to January/ February. By early December 1963, it was established that *The Curse of the Mummy's Tomb* might be coupled with *The Gorgon*, then entering production. A scaled-down and much-rethought script, by the now freelance Michael Carreras under the pseudonym 'Henry Younger', was delivered late in January.

The BBFC's comments of 10 February queried the treatment of the many dismemberments contained in the screenplay, the costume of a belly-dancer ("This should not be censorable") and a specified shot of a beetle on the side of a roast pig ("a bit dis-

COLUMBIA PICTURES presents A HAMMER FILMS Production

THE CURSE OF THE MUMMY'S TOMB

TERENCE MORGAN · FRED CLARK
RONALD HOWARD And Introducing **JEANNE ROLAND**

Screenplay by **HENRY YOUNGER** · Associate Producer **BILL HILL** · Produced & Directed by **MICHAEL CARRERAS** **TECHNISCOPE and TECHNICOLOR** A BLC RELEASE

gusting"). More substantially, the Board suggested that King's scripted throttling be altered to a scene where the Mummy murders the hapless showman by hurling him down a flight of steps, placed a question mark over shots where bulletholes placed in the Mummy's flank by Sir Giles seal themselves up "as if... oozing mud", but saved their greatest objections for the manner of the dismembered Adam's demise in the sewer: "We would not want any shots of the torn arm waving about during the drowning. Surely the wretched man could be tipped in and left... script direction suggests that we are to see the corpse floating about among a lot of filthy debris. I would think that most cinema audiences would object to this, but would accept the sort of sewer we had in *Les Miserables* [the fifties version of the Victor Hugo novel]."

Shooting took place at ABPC's Elstree studios in two blocks: on the 150-feet square stage three between 24 and 28 February, and on a smaller stage between 9 and 27 March. The film headlined smooth British leading men Terence Morgan and Ronald Howard (the latter the son of renowned actor Leslie), plus industrious American comedy actor Fred Clark and twenty-one year-old Anglo-Burmese

model Jeanne Roland. George Pastell all but reprised his *Mummy* role, and playing the lumbering revenant itself was Dickie Owen. Roy Ashton applied prosthetic temples and cheeks to Owen's gaunt features after an early screen test of the make-up was thought unsatisfactory. While shooting the film's sewer-bound climax, Owen stumbled and fell into the water, and Ashton had to cut him free of the bindings restricting his breathing.

Delivery of the film to backers Columbia was slightly delayed after a hold-up at the Technicolor laboratories. Released in October, the double-bill did good business both at the British and American box-office. Across the Atlantic, black stamps — of no redeemable value — were given free to the first 10,000 paying punters willing to sample Hammer's latest wares.

The Curse of the Mummy's Tomb, an efficient if underinvolving exercise, contains more than a few well-staged scenes, but the whole is rather lost in a muddled storyline (and its effect is massively diminished when viewed in anything other than its original Techniscope format). In its narrative sweep and sense of scale, however, it does betray the sometimes frustrated ambitions of prodigal son Michael Carreras.

Like most of the features Michael Carreras directed, *The Curse of the Mummy's Tomb* used an elongated, so-called 'widescreen' panorama. This anamorphic effect came into prominence in the fifties, when film studios sought to give cinemagoers a greater viewing vista than the feared television screen, which remains fixed at an aspect ratio of 1.33:1 (ie, a rectangular shape slightly wider than tall). The vast majority of Hammer's films were shot in either 1.37:1, 1.66:1 or 1.85:1, all standard film ratios which lose relatively little on a television screen, and are thus not noted throughout this book. Most wide 'scope' variants bore identical specifications to Twentieth Century-Fox's Cinemascope process — 2.35:1. *The Curse of the Mummy's Tomb* employed Techniscope; other ratios occasionally used by Hammer included Megascope (on *The Stranglers of Bombay* and *The Two Faces of Dr Jekyll*, for example), and even their own patented variant, Hammerscope (see *The Abominable Snowman*). Exclusive director Francis Searle remembers the process well: "What they laughably called Hammerscope... had been cobbled together by George Hill, the king of camera gear in Wardour Street, but oh dear oh dear, talk about string and elastic!" Sadly, scope films are often 'panned-and-scanned' for either broadcast or video release, select portions being cropped to fit the television screen.

Previous page: Scotland Yard net the mummy (Dickie Owen).
Above left: *Director Michael Carreras goes over Henry Younger's script with Jeanne Roland.*
Above centre: *Transgressive archaeologist Dubois (Bernard Rebel) is gored in the (studio) desert.*
Above right: *Michael Carreras shooting* Maniac *— a MegaScope production.*
Left: *Under the spotlights, Alexander King (Fred Clark) hosts a London press show to unveil the mummy of Ra-Antef.*

FRESH BLOOD
1965 – 1969

"The other night I toured the Hammer Script Crypt," wrote Raymond Durgnat in *Films and Filming*, in November 1964. "There was Major Carreras, cracking his whip over the sweating backs of the writers as they groaned at their tasks, with an Associate Producer beating out the time on his kettle-drums. As the light of the full moon poured in through the open windows, Anthony Hinds stared in horror at his hands which grew hairy and claw-like — another script was taking him over, he was turning into John Elder once again. Baron Sangster-stein was there, cackling hideously as with fiendish cunning he sewed together bits of scenarios from the old Universal book. The dialogue was inserted by an old man entirely wrapped in dirty bandages; he was looking it up in a stack of stone tablets the topmost of which bore hieroglyphics which only a trained Hammerologist like myself could decipher. It said, 'The Best-Tried Bits of Screen Dialogue,' by Amen-Ra..."

By 1965, Hammer had largely eschewed suspense thrillers, comedies and swashbucklers. Falling cinema attendance and the withdrawal of production partners/distributors Columbia and Universal prompted James Carreras to play it safe; film distributors and cinema managers were all looking for a low-risk route out of the doldrums and Hammer horror was just the ticket.

After a brief flirtation with Metro-Goldwyn-Mayer, Hammer struck a deal with the Twentieth Century-Fox Film Corporation that ensured American distribution and co-finance from *The Nanny* onwards. The film was the first to be produced by Hammer in association with its long-term partners Seven Arts (who were granted American television rights in return for their support), ABPC (who were granted British and Commonwealth distribution rights) and Twentieth Century-Fox (who were granted world theatrical distribution rights excluding Britain and the Common-wealth). Between 1965 and 1968, the financing of

eleven, and then six pictures was carved up between the four partners. Kenneth Hyman, who had cut his producer's teeth on such films as *The Hound of the Baskervilles* and *The Terror of the Tongs*, would remain an influential, if shadowy, presence at Hammer in his capacity as Seven Arts' executive vice-president in charge of world-wide production. His father, Seven Arts' president Eliot, continued to be a powerful ally.

Hammer's new-found stability coincided with a shift away from the production qualities that exemplified the films produced in the late fifties and early sixties. Award-winning director of photography Jack Asher had already been replaced, apparently because the complex set-ups that contributed towards the rich atmosphere of his films took too long. "In view of our future production policy, I do not think we can afford Jack Asher," Anthony Hinds wrote to Michael

Carreras in 1963. "It was very sad to think that the old time-and-cost studies would triumph in the end," said Asher. "It was not my salary to which he objected but [at having to make] repeated requests that my photographic excellence be repeatedly speeded up and expedited until a pint of pre-eminent photography be squeezed into a half pint pot. As we were always shooting at breakneck speed, particularly toward my final days, it was just not humanly possible."

A series of horror films produced 'back-to-back', beginning with *Dracula Prince of Darkness* in 1965, similarly indicated that an air of economy had begun to take precedence. The staff at Bray struggled to meet the demands from Hammer House. Bray Studios itself would be the next casualty of the new regime.

The ongoing arrangement with ABPC had been struck partly on the condition that Hammer played its part in keeping the distributor's own studio occupied. Hammer was obliged to concentrate production at Elstree from 1964 onwards, only using Bray when the larger studio proved unavailable. Hammer vacated Bray altogether in 1966, returning only to conduct special effects photography for *When Dinosaurs Ruled the Earth* and *Moon Zero Two*.

The new influx of money from American distributors had its own effect on Hammer. Subjects were geared to international consumption (*One Million Years B.C.* reaped astonishing rewards from the new approach) and, perhaps as a result, became less sophisticated. *Dracula Prince of Darkness*' set-piece throat-slitting and *The Plague of the Zombies*' walking corpses seemed indicative of a shift towards a more sensational style of film-making. Hammer's attempts to move with the times had significantly altered the flavour of its films, even if the recipe remained essentially unchanged.

"The overall thing that always bothered me with Hammer was their literalness," says Nigel Kneale, whose *Quatermass and the Pit* was an eloquent reminder that genre films could function on more than one level. "There was this thing, particularly in the Draculas and so on, about making your stomach turn over — blood, guts and the squeam factor. They would adopt this instead of implying, which is much stronger because it's much more worrying if you don't know what may be coming."

Hammer's reputation nevertheless did it no harm at the British Board of Film Censors. "John Trevelyan was very sympathetic toward Hammer," remembers producer Aida Young. "He liked Hammer because there was no pretension — I mean, if a film was called *Taste the Blood of Dracula* then you couldn't really pretend... How many times I used to sit watching our films with John. He used to hold my hand and

Previous page (left): *Suzan Farmer and Christopher Lee shoot* Dracula Prince of Darkness.
Previous page (right): *Christopher Lee and Ursula Andress meet at the gala première of* The Blue Max *on 30 June 1966.*
Above left: *Veronica Carlson, Christopher Lee, director Freddie Francis and producer Aida Young at Pinewood Studios in 1968.*
Above right: *Michael and James Carreras at Elstree during production of* She *in 1964.*
Below: *Hammer executives, staff and guests celebrate receiving the Queen's Award to Industry outside the Green Room at Pinewood Studios.*

also disappointed with *The Viking Queen* and *Quatermass and the Pit*, and took a dim view when neither *The Devil Rides Out* or *The Lost Continent* performed well in America.

Although Hammer's relationship with Fox continued with the television series *Journey to the Unknown*, by the beginning of 1968 the company was left without an American distributor for its film product. Salvation once again came in the form of Seven Arts. In November 1966, Eliot Hyman had instigated a process that culminated in a merger between Seven Arts and Warner Bros. By the time negotiations concluded in late June 1967, Hyman had purchased Jack Warner's controlling interest in the studio and all its assets. By February 1968, Hyman's new company, Warner Bros-Seven Arts, had stepped into the breach left by Fox. The Hymans' loyalty to James Carreras had thrown Hammer a timely lifeline.

The new partnership, between Hammer and Warner Bros-Seven Arts, kicked off with the latest instalment of Hammer's premium product — *Dracula Has Risen From the Grave*. On 10 April 1968, days before filming began, Hammer learned that its application for a Queen's Award to Industry had been approved. The company claimed to have generated £2,742,797 in export earnings between October 1964 and September 1967, an impressive amount that nevertheless became greatly exaggerated in the pages of newspapers such as *The Daily Telegraph* and *The News of the World*. Hammer's profile hit its highest point since the release of *The Curse of Frankenstein* and *Dracula*. "Dracula and co. win Queen's Award", ran the front page of the *Daily Sketch* on Saturday 20 April. "Now the exporters' accolade is going to the dollar-spinning horror-film makers."

As was traditional, the Queen's Award itself was bestowed at the company in question's factory. In Hammer's case, factory of the month was Pinewood Studios. "You are the first British film production

squeeze it every time he saw something he didn't like. 'Darling,' he used to say, 'I can't have that!' I have good memories of him."

Aida Young had returned to Hammer under the wing of Michael Carreras, who continued to produce films for the company on a freelance basis. *She* and *One Million Years B.C.* were huge successes, but Michael's relationship with his father remained poor. Then-production accountant Roy Skeggs remembers one especially traumatic confrontation: "Michael was directing *The Lost Continent* at Elstree and the film had gone over budget and behind schedule. Jimmy arrived on the set one day, with his lawyers in tow, and stopped production there and then. It was a very difficult situation."

The Lost Continent, an ambitious fantasy adventure based on Dennis Wheatley's novel *Uncharted Seas*, was the last film produced under the Seven Arts/ABPC/Fox alliance. Throughout 1967, Hammer's relationship with the American distributor had suffered for a combination of reasons: Fox were unhappy at Seven Arts' cut of the deal, and wanted television rights to the films for themselves; Fox were

company to receive the Queen's Award, and that is a distinction of which you can all be proud," claimed Brigadier Sir Henry Floyd, Lord Lieutenant of the County of Buckingham, during the ceremony on Wednesday 29 May. "Your company has made over 100 films. These films have been played with much success in all parts of the world, which shows that the work produced by your company is of the highest quality and technical achievement."

"One cannot help finding something bizarre in the idea of this ceremony," wrote Kingsley Amis in *The Observer Magazine*. "But perhaps one ought to try a bit harder not to. There is nothing very bizarre about an export contribution worth millions of dollars last year, unless its rarity makes it so."

Of course, the award was in recognition for revenue that largely went into the pockets of funding American distributors — not Treasury coffers — but Hammer's five-year entitlement to the accolade served as a symbolic high point at the very least.

Dracula Has Risen From the Grave was delivered to Warner Bros-Seven Arts on Friday 11 October 1968. That day, James Carreras threw a party at the Savoy Hotel for Kenneth Hyman, who was in town for the British launch of the ill-fated musical *Finian's Rainbow*. "The tribute luncheon given by Jim Carreras for Ken Hyman was characteristic of Jim's open-handed hospitality and his flair for showmanship," wrote Bill Altria, editor of *Kinematograph Weekly*. "The Savoy's silver room was bedecked with eye-catching, eye-popping posters and grotesque masks, in the distinctive style of Hammer's highly imaginative merchandising and brand image."

Carreras took the opportunity to announce the programme of forthcoming pictures in Hammer's ongoing deal with Kenneth Hyman and his father: a further Frankenstein picture (*Frankenstein Must Be Destroyed*) and a science fiction epic, *Moon Zero Two*, were on the cards. That weekend, two charter planes flew the unit and crew of *When Dinosaurs Ruled the Earth* to the Canary Islands.

In 1968 Hammer was occupied by *Journey to the Unknown*, and the first two films in the Warner Bros-Seven Arts pact. While the Hymans' patronage continued, Hammer thrived. Around it, the British film industry continued what would prove to be a near-terminal decline. The rising prominence of independent American film-makers, and a dramatic change in film-going habits (best illustrated by the box-office failure of traditional money-makers such as *Finian's Rainbow*) had caused a significant restructuring in Hollywood's working methods. The escalating cost of the Vietnam war had also indirectly led to a cutback in American investment overseas — when traditional tax benefits were diminished, America's traditional interest in British film production diminished accordingly.

On 10 February 1969, BBC television transmitted a documentary profiling the previous year's Queen's Award winners. "We're very grateful to the Americans who do have the courage to put their money up to back British pictures," said James Carreras. "As far as I'm concerned, we'd bring back three or four times as much into the country if we had 100 per cent British backing."

Whether Carreras meant it or not, 100 per cent British backing would soon be all that was on offer. In June 1969, Eliot Hyman, James Carreras' most reliable co-production partner since *The Curse of Frankenstein*, retired when Warner Bros-Seven Arts changed hands. New owners, the Kinney National Service Corporation, appointed Ted Ashley to head the company, which ultimately reverted to the title Warner Bros. When Eliot Hyman failed to persuade Ashley to strike a new deal with Hammer, Carreras approached him direct, eventually convincing him to honour Warner Bros-Seven Arts' commitment to *Taste the Blood of Dracula*. On 3 September, Carreras broke some bad news to the executives at Hammer House: "The new deal with Warner Bros-Seven Arts will be on a picture to picture basis with each subject being treated on its merits... the new Warner Bros-Seven Arts Board have decided not to produce or finance any production costing over one million dollars outside their own studio."

Of similar magnitude was the dissolution of Hammer itself. Anthony Nelson Keys' regular association with the company ended on *Frankenstein Must Be Destroyed* in 1969. The same film also featured the final contribution from talented designer Bernard Robinson. By 1969, company secretary James Dawson (whose association with Hammer began with the establishment of Exclusive Films Limited in 1935) had retired. The arduous production of *Journey to the Unknown* had already caused supervising editor James Needs to quit, and seriously disenchanted producer Anthony Hinds.

Hinds finally threw in the towel after a dispute over *Taste the Blood of Dracula*. He attended his last board meeting on 6 August 1969, and resigned his directorship the following year. "He was never happy in the film business," claims Roy Skeggs. "He fell into it and he was happy to fall out."

Hammer entered the new decade with its future once more in jeopardy. Fourteen years of major American finance was finally petering out, and the creative head of the company was gone. There were troubled times ahead.

Previous page (above): *Peter Cushing and Veronica Carlson are joined by James Carreras, making a rare studio visit during production of* Frankenstein Must Be Destroyed *in 1969.*
Previous page (below): *EMI/ABPC executives Bernard Delfont, J.R. Wallis and John Read visit producer Michael Carreras at Elstree in March 1969. Principal photography on Moon Zero Two would begin on the 31st.*
Above: *James Carreras at Hammer House in 1968.*
Below: *Hammer announce production of "the greatest Dracula of them all" in the trade press. This pre-production artwork was prepared when the company confidently expected to replace Christopher Lee in the title role.*

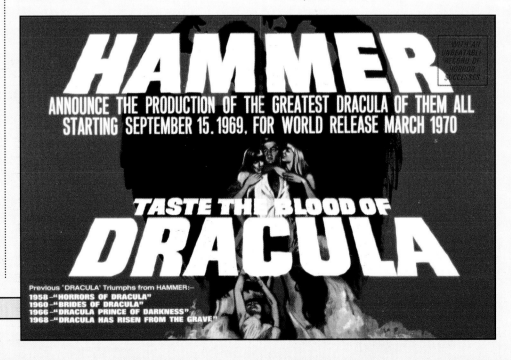

S H E

Principal photography 24 August to
17 October 1964
Released 18 April 1965
Certificate A
Duration 105 mins
Colour/Hammerscope
Director Robert Day

Reluctant to return to Cambridge after the end of hostilities in 1918, Major Holly (Peter Cushing) samples the hedonistic pleasures of Palestine with his valet Job (Bernard Cribbins) and colleague Leo Vincey (John Richardson). Leo's attraction to local girl Ustane (Rosenda Monteros) leads him to a romantic encounter with the beautiful Ayesha (Ursula Andress). She gives Leo a map, and urges him to follow the route it outlines. Intrigued by the promise of discovering a lost civilisation, Holly joins the expedition with Job in tow. During the long journey to the 'Mountains of the Moon', the men have their camels stolen in a skirmish with marauding Arabs, and Leo is wounded. When their water supplies are exhausted, the men collapse and are rescued by Ustane, who takes them to the village of slaves ruled by her father Haumeid (André Morell). Close to death, Leo is delivered to Ayesha by her loyal High Priest Billali (Christopher Lee). Leo learns that Ayesha, She Who Must Be Obeyed, has waited over 2,000 years for the reincarnation of her dead lover, Killikrates. Leo's resemblance to Killikrates, and his survival of the arduous journey, convinces her that they are reunited. She offers him the chance to share in her immortality, but the jealousy of Billali and Ustane's love for Leo threaten her long-awaited happiness...

"There's no doubt the future lies with bigger productions," an optimistic Michael Carreras told *Kinematograph Weekly* during production of *She*. At a colossal £323,778, *She* was Hammer's most expensive film to date, and the perfect vehicle for "the World's most beautiful woman!", Ursula Andress.

Kenneth Hyman, Seven Arts' Vice-President in Charge of European Production, had first suggested *She* to Anthony Hinds as an ideal subject. In late 1962, Hinds commissioned an adaptation of Sir Henry Rider Haggard's 1887 novel from John Temple-Smith, planning a sale to Universal. Temple-Smith's second draft, written in February 1963, set out his stall: "This script is derived from Rider Haggard's classic story... whilst it retains the theme of suspense and mystique in the searching for *She*, it highlights many moments of physical danger and violence which are box office today." Temple-Smith went on to list some of the most exciting, which included run-ins with cobras, vultures and crocodiles, plus such adult selling points as "Ustane, half-naked, flogged by the guards."

By 20 March 1963, a budget of £225,000 had been prepared with the co-operation of Seven Arts, who suggested that Bond girl Ursula Andress would be a suitable star. Andress was obliged to make herself available to Seven Arts because of an existing deal between the company and her then husband John Derek. "I did *She* because John wanted to make some films," she claimed. "Seven Arts financed them. I had to guarantee that I would work in case those films did not make back the money. So I guaranteed two films. The first one they put me in was *She*."

By summer, Universal were still reluctant to commit to the film, even with Andress attached. Temple-Smith's script was discarded and Hinds commissioned Berkely Mather, an American crime writer whose most conspicuous credit was on Andress' big break, *Dr. No*. Mather's more sedate retelling of the story was written over the summer and redrafted by

8 September. By 1964, the project was still languishing on Hammer's 'for imminent production' schedules. After a fruitless attempt to sell *She* to American independents Joe Levine and AIP in January, Michael Carreras was invited back to Hammer to take the project over. Michael commissioned David T. Chantler (who had co-written *Cash on Demand* for Hammer in 1961) to rework Mather's script with the emphasis on action. Chantler's rewrite accordingly jettisoned such elements as the book's Cambridge opening, which had been retained in all previous drafts. By June 1964, Seven Arts had found a buyer in Metro-Goldwyn-Mayer.

Backed with an increased budget, and Michael Carreras' long-held determination to broaden Hammer's appeal, location shooting began in southern Israel on 24 August 1964. Director Robert Day (who had previously handled similar fare such as *Tarzan's Three Challenges* for MGM in 1963) was forced to briefly postpone filming when John Richardson contracted dysentery. Other problems included Peter Cushing's uncooperative camel, Daisy, and some unpredictable explosive charges. Bernard Cribbins was hospitalised when one detonated beneath his bottom, while another errant charge cost a special effects man his finger. The political climate was almost as delicate. "While we were in the Danagao desert the Arab sector was quite near. They just sat there with machine guns in their laps," remembered Peter Cushing. "In the meantime, we were popping off our prop guns hoping we would not be attacked." Peter and his wife, Helen, relaxed by scuba diving in the seaport of Eilat, where the crew were based.

In the studio at Elstree, Robert Day was presented with further challenges. The schedule fell behind and scenes were dropped in an attempt to wrap on time. One scene, in which Christopher Lee was to sing a religious chant he co-wrote with the film's composer James Bernard, would never be filmed. The relatively inexperienced Ursula Andress also proved taxing: during post-production in late November, Andress' lines were dubbed by Monica Van der Syl, the same actress

that had revoiced *Dr. No*. André Morell suffered the same indignity, dubbed by George Pastell throughout.

Massive publicity campaigns launched *She* in Britain (on 18 April 1965) and the United States (on 1 September). Triple-page advertisements in the American trade press over the summer fuelled the hype: "*She* is the biggest box-office news in England since *Goldfinger*!" boasted MGM. In April, *Variety*'s 'Murf' gave the thumbs up: "Production values save the day, with crowd scenes and palace pomp worthy of far more expensive films."

She successfully blends the sanitised eroticism and violence of Hammer with a colourful slice of sixties matinee mayhem. Such endearing 'epics' would become rare in a schedule increasingly dominated by X rated pictures. A sequel was nevertheless commissioned from *Modesty Blaise* creator Peter O'Donnell — *The Vengeance of She* saw John Richardson return as Killikrates, this time with Czechoslovakian beauty Olinka Berova as his co-star. The film was released in 1968, but failed to make the same impact as its predecessor.

Previous page: Ursula Andress and producer Michael Carreras on location in southern Israel.
Above left: "Aren't these girls athletic sir!" remarks Job. Off-duty, Bernard Cribbins enjoys their company at Elstree.
Above centre: Peter Cushing as explorer Major Holly.
Above right: Pre-production artwork, prepared when Hammer were hoping to sell the subject to Universal.
Below: "People tend to be slightly apprehensive on first meeting me," said Christopher Lee, publicising *She* in 1964. Director Robert Day does his best not to look intimidated.

**Principal photography 5 April to
3 June 1965
Released 7 October 1965
Certificate X
Duration 93 mins
Black and white
Director Seth Holt**

Ten year-old Joey Fane (William Dix) returns home after two years in a school for disturbed and diffi-cult children, where he'd been sent after being held responsible for the accidental drowning of his younger sister Susy (Angharad Aubrey) in the bathtub. His institutionalisation appears to have done him little good, however, and he remains paranoid and belligerent. Joey delights in tormenting Nanny (Bette Davis), a benevolent spinster who has been in the family since Joey's mother, the neurotic Virginia (Wendy Craig), and aunt, the ailing Penelope (Jill Bennett), were themselves children. He befriends Bobby (Pamela Franklin), the laid-back fourteen year-old daughter of upstairs neighbour Dr Medman (Jack Watling), and tells her that Nanny murdered Susy and wants to do the same to him. Meanwhile, Bill (James Villiers), the distant head of the household, has gone away on business. That evening, Nanny's home-cooked steak and kidney pie is found to have been poisoned and Virginia falls ill. Nanny and Dr Medman discover the medicine responsible concealed in Joey's room. Medman takes Virginia to hospital, leaving Joey in the care of Nanny and Aunt Penelope, who suffers from a chronic heart condition. Later, a wringing wet Joey wakes Penelope, telling her that Nanny has tried to drown him in the bath. Later still, Penelope sees Nanny hovering outside Joey's room, a smothering pillow in her hands. What if, all along, Joey has been telling the truth?

for their latest Seven Arts co-production (and the first film in a four-way pact with distributors Twentieth Century-Fox in America and ABPC in Britain), Hammer signed up the then fifty-seven year-old Bette Davis to play the title role in *The Nanny*, a psychological thriller from a novel by Evelyn Piper. (Seven Arts' Kenneth Hyman had been the executive producer of Davis' Oscar-nominated comeback, the 1962 film *Whatever Happened to Baby Jane?*) Despite Davis' formidable Hollywood track record, she was only screenwriter/producer Jimmy Sangster's second choice. Sangster had originally offered the role to Greer Garson, star of *Goodbye Mr Chips* and *Mrs Miniver*, but she'd declined.

Davis' involvement rested upon her approval of director Seth Holt: "He sat with her in the Beverly Wilshire and she said yes," recalls James Villiers, who

WOULD YOU TRUST THE NANNY... OR THE BOY?

BETTE DAVIS

THE NANNY 'x'

Also starring WENDY CRAIG · JILL BENNETT · JAMES VILLIERS and WILLIAM DIX and PAMELA FRANKLIN as the children

featured in the film as uptight diplomat Bill Fane. In the spring of 1965, Davis arrived in England with Violla Rubber, the vice-president of BD Productions Inc. Before filming commenced, Roy Skeggs was instructed to lay on some special hospitality: "There's a pub in Elstree village that I got to open at 6.30 in the morning," he remembers. "Before she went into make-up Bette would have two large Scotches, and her manager Violla would have two large gins. 'I need my kickstart!' Bette told me."

The film's seven-week production schedule included several days' work on location in Regent's

Park and at a school near Radlett, with studio photography commencing on 5 April at Elstree. Holt's patience was much tried by his fearsome star, who even purchased her own starchy Nanny outfit for the part. "She got the 'flu' during shooting," he said later, "and sometimes she'd stay away altogether, holding up shooting while she sent in day-to-day reports on her condition — 'It's worse!' — 'It's better!' — 'Oh God, I've relapsed!' — and so forth... oh it was hell! Then she was always telling me how to direct. When I did it her way, she was scornful; when I stood up to her, she was hysterical..." Much to Holt's chagrin, Davis refused to watch the daily rushes. "I might have made her realise that she was pouring it on too much!" he later moaned. Davis held firm. "You'll get depressed about how you look and you won't be able to do a thing about it," she told co-star Jill Bennett. Indeed, Davis and Bennett struck up a certain friendship during shooting. They went to see drag artiste Danny La Rue perform at a London nightclub, lunched at Grosvenor House and even went to the dogs together. "Always make love to your props. To the furniture," Davis would implore the younger actress over vodkas in her dressing-room.

Regardless of the friction between director and star, producer Sangster, like many others, got on famously with Davis. "On *The Nanny*, we had an end-of-picture party at a restaurant near Elstree," remembers script supervisor Renée Glynne, "and Bette Davis stood up and said, 'I know I have a reputation as a hard cow, and I do usually fire the director and hairdresser and the costume designer, but this has been the happiest picture of my career.' And, of course, on Hammer's *The Anniversary* a few years later, she *did* fire the director!"

The Nanny gave Hammer a sizeable hit, both critically and commercially, on both sides of the

Atlantic, making *Kinematograph Weekly*'s year end list of 1965's top money-makers, and taking $263,000 in twenty New York cinemas, apparently one of the best runs of the year. Subtly directed, redolent less of suspense than near-tangible dread, *The Nanny* keeps the viewer guessing right up until its final few minutes, where Nanny's reasoning becomes horribly clear. Its uniformly excellent adult cast, however, are knocked off the screen by juvenile lead Dix, who is never anything less than utterly compelling as disturbed Fane son Joey.

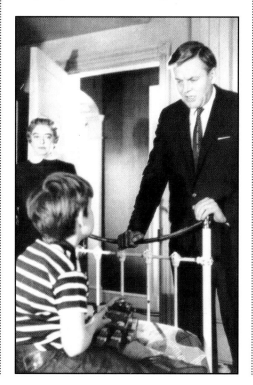

Previous page: Nanny (Bette Davis) watches impassively as Penelope (Jill Bennett) clings to life.
Above: Davis on location at Regent's Park.
Far left: Nanny and the precocious Joey (William Dix).
Left: Dr Medman (Jack Watling) quizzes the dysfunctional Fane son.

BRAY STUDIOS

At the end of a secluded track leading off from the A4 near Windsor is Down Place, a seventeenth century mansion by the banks of the Thames. Between 1951 and 1966 Hammer made the mansion its own, shooting some of its greatest films in and around the house. Down Place was renamed Bray Studios, but is perhaps now best known as the original house of horror...

a new era began on 8 January 1951 when the cameras rolled on *Cloudburst*, the first Exclusive/ Hammer feature shot at Down Place. Director Francis Searle recalls that visiting American star Robert Preston was unimpressed. "It was left to me to take him over to Down Place," says Searle. "We arrived at the studio and he seemed a bit subdued, so I said, 'Well Bob, here we are — this is it.' He said, 'Erm, this is the prop department,' and I said, 'No mate, this is the studio!'"

Picturegoer magazine later reported that Preston was "tickled by the studio out Windsor way. 'Why build phoney interiors in a studio when you can film the real thing?' he asks." The reason was economy. Down Place was simply the latest 'house studio' that Exclusive/Hammer hoped would prove cheaper than hiring dedicated facilities elsewhere. Managing director James Carreras committed to Down Place by purchasing the house and much of its surrounding land in 1952. The company was now free to develop the property as Bray Studios, and customisation began in earnest.

In October 1953, *Kinematograph Weekly* reported that "Exclusive's craftsmen have so altered and adapted the historic mansion that it has the equivalent facilities to those of a medium size conventional studio." Bray's expansion ground to a halt, however, when Robert Lippert's investment in Exclusive/ Hammer pictures began to dry up. By 1955, Bray employed just sixty staff, and relied on outside productions.

James Carreras considered selling the studios to cut his losses, but Bray was safeguarded by the boom in horror pictures effectively instigated by *The Curse of Frankenstein*. Peter Cushing, the film's star, grew fond of the studio. "When I used to live in Kensington it took only forty-five minutes to get there and we had the road to ourselves," he remembered. "No one at all used the road at 7am, there were no motorways, and you used to arrive at what was a large country house by the river and this was Bray Studios. In the very first picture we did there, there was a bedroom scene and we literally went up to the bedroom of the house and used the bedroom. For dining-room scenes we went down to the dining-room..."

Hammer's co-production deal with Columbia introduced a staggered programme of American investment into Bray, the most obvious benefit being the acquisition of a third stage in 1957. Bray's latest, and biggest, sound stage was first used for *The Snorkel* in autumn 1957. *Dracula* followed soon after, before Columbia saw a further return on its outlay when *The Revenge of Frankenstein* went into production on 'stage three'.

Hammer continued to make a virtue of the main house, which production designer Bernard Robinson inventively redressed from film to film. Elsewhere at Bray Studios, business continued as usual. Special effects assistant Ian Scoones started working for Hammer in 1961: "Our office-cum-workshop was a blue wooden shed with a leaking roof, sandwiched between the waste bins from the canteen and kitchens on one side and the compost heap from the garden on the other. This isolation was mainly due to the fact that we held pyrotechnics and explosives and it was thought that as we were an insurance risk it was better for us to be away from the production offices, the editing suite, the props and wood store and the studios themselves."

By 1963, Bray employed over 130 people, all overseen by executive producer Anthony Hinds and general manager Anthony Nelson Keys. Hinds kept in

touch with the "floor spaces" by means of an intercom system that allowed him to monitor shooting progress from his office in the main house. The sound of unrest amongst the technicians would have a dramatic effect. "Any problems and he'd be off," remembers his production accountant Roy Skeggs. "Unfortunately, some of the floor staff realised that every time there was a row they'd see his car pull out. I later found out that they'd pretend to have arguments knowing that Tony would hear them through his intercom and leave!"

Francis Matthews, who appeared in *I Only Arsked, The Revenge of Frankenstein, Dracula Prince of Darkness* and *Rasputin the Mad Monk* —

all shot at Bray — enjoyed the studio's team spirit: "There was none of that class thing that you got in the commissaries of the big studios, where the directors, the executives and the money men would sit in one area, the stars in another and the supporting players in another. At Bray, everybody ate and worked together. You knew everybody. It was a lovely time."

Sadly, the executives at Hammer House were less well-disposed towards the studio. It was efficient while busy, but union difficulties, and a devastating fire in early 1961, all caused headaches. James Carreras began sounding out potential purchasers in 1962, the BBC and the Rodwell Group soon expressing an interest. In 1963, ABPC offered to purchase a slice of Bray Studios, and an agreement effective from 1 January 1964 made them co-owners alongside Hammer and Columbia. The new deal guaranteed that the studio stayed under Hammer's control — at a price. From thereon, Hammer was obliged to consider ABPC's Elstree studios over and above its own, using Bray only when Elstree proved too busy.

Bray, which had been mothballed since the expiry of Hammer's co-production deal with Columbia in 1964, re-opened on 29 March 1965. *Dracula Prince of Darkness*, the first of four films shot back-to-back at the facility, began production on 26 April. Bray's new lease of life proved short-lived, however, and Hammer's obligation to use ABPC Elstree meant that it could no longer afford to maintain a permanent production base at Bray after *The Mummy's Shroud* wrapped on 21 October 1966. The studio was closed on 18 November.

For the next four years, Hammer only used Bray as an overflow facility for the demanding effects photography conducted for *When Dinosaurs Ruled the Earth* and *Moon Zero Two*. "Nobody is there," James Carreras later told *Today's Cinema*, "and it costs us a fortune." In 1969, ABPC proposed that Bray be sold, and Brian Lawrence broke the news to the board. A number of offers were considered in the latter half of 1969 and throughout 1970, before Roy Skeggs finalised the sale of the freehold to Redspring Ltd on 19 November 1970. The £65,000 price was divided between Columbia, EMI (ABPC's new owners) and Hammer.

Redspring had initially intended to build a housing estate on the land, but the studio survived as the Bray International Film Centre. Such films as *The Music Lovers*, *Sunday, Bloody Sunday*, *Pope Joan* and *The Rocky Horror Picture Show* were shot there during the seventies. Bray was sold to the Samuelson Group for £700,000 in 1984, and changed hands once again in 1990 when Bray Management Ltd took over. The studios are still much in demand for commercials, pop videos and television series. In the reception of the house, framed photographs of Peter Cushing and Christopher Lee stand as testimony to an illustrious past.

"I look back with enormous nostalgia upon what I call our 'Bray period'," said Michael Carreras. "There is no question that having a permanent unit in a permanent home gave our films a uniquely personal quality... It was a great atmosphere which will never be recreated."

Previous page (above): *Bray Studios, during production of* Dracula Prince of Darkness *in summer 1965. Behind, and slightly to the right, of 'Castle Dracula' is the Down Place house itself.*

Previous page (below): *The cover of a four-page leaflet outlining Bray's facilities, issued by general manager Anthony Nelson Keys.*

Above: *The struggle between Baron Meinster (David Peel) and Van Helsing (Peter Cushing) in* The Brides of Dracula *affords the chance to admire Bernard Robinson's sumptuous sets.*

Left (top): *Anthony Nelson Keys (centre) and Barbara Shelley (right) are interviewed during the production of* Rasputin the Mad Monk.

Left (centre and bottom): *More contact sheet pictures, showing André Morrell and Diane Clare filming* The Plague of the Zombies.

**Principal photography 26 April to
4 June 1965
Released 9 January 1966
Certificate X
Duration 90 mins
Colour/Techniscope
Director Terence Fisher**

At an inn in the Carpathian mountains, four English tourists — Charles Kent (Francis Matthews), his wife Diana (Suzan Farmer), Charles' older brother Alan (Charles Tingwell) and shrewish wife Helen (Barbara Shelley) — encounter Father Sandor (Andrew Keir), the Abbot of Kleinberg, who wages a campaign against those locals who still adhere to the rituals necessary in the days when dreaded vampire Count Dracula stalked the region prior to his destruction. Nevertheless, he warns them not to go near a certain castle on the Carlsbad road — a castle which appears on no map. Helen, however, insists they press on. Late the next day, the tourists are abandoned en route *by their coachman, who refuses to continue down the Carlsbad road after dark. Fortuitously, a driverless carriage draws to a halt beside the stranded group. They board and are taken to the castle Sandor had spoken of, where they find a table set for four and rooms prepared. A gaunt figure introduces himself as Klove (Philip Latham), retainer to "an old and distinguished family": the Draculas. Later that night, Alan investigates Klove's covert manoeuvrings. He discovers a vault containing Dracula's stone sarcophagus, but is murdered by Klove, who strings up his body over the sepulchre, into which he empties an urn full of ashes. He slits Alan's throat, and watches, rapt, as the traveller's blood coagulates with the Count's remains. A sinister shape begins to form — that of Dracula (Christopher Lee), alive once more...*

"*i* hope people will not be disappointed by a greying Dracula," remarked Christopher Lee in a self-deprecating letter to his fan club dated 9 May 1965. His comments concerned *Dracula Prince of Darkness*, then shooting at Bray, in which he reprised the role which had catapulted him to notoriety seven years before. "And, incidentally," he continued, "as Dracula I never say a word. As I am already a vampire from the word go there is nothing I can say — not even a courteous, 'Well, here we are again...'"

Part of the ongoing deal with Seven Arts, Twentieth Century-Fox and ABPC, the film was shot back-to-back with *Rasputin the Mad Monk*. Both he and Barbara Shelley signed one contract each to appear in both films. In the summer of 1964, these, plus two other "horror subjects" (*The Plague of the Zombies* and *The Reptile*) had been put into production after producer Anthony Nelson Keys was mandated to bring in

CHRISTOPHER LEE · BARBARA SHELLEY · ANDREW KEIR · FRANCIS MATTHEWS · SUZAN FARMER · CHARLES TINGWELL · THORLEY WALTERS

all four at around £100,000 apiece. The films would be made in immediate succession and sets recycled to further spread costs. (While the exercise would ultimately prove relatively economical, all bar *The Reptile* overshot their budgets. The final certified costs for the four amounted to £429,648.)

Derived from *The Revenge of Dracula*, a late fifties treatment written to follow on from Hammer's original, the script was accredited to John Sansom, a pseudonym hiding both Jimmy Sangster and Anthony Hinds. Sansom's intentions fell foul of the BBFC, who advised against several grisly scenes, including the script's cheeky stage direction: "This is a quick cut, as long as we can manage. It shows what is left of Alan. The decapitated body is jammed into the trunk, drained of all blood, and the head has been put on the top, from where it grins towards camera, the lips pulled back over the teeth."(The only other major loss was a scene lifted directly from Bram Stoker, wherein Dracula was to bare his chest to Diana, draw blood and compel her to lap at it.)

Dracula Prince of Darkness was the first film to be shot at Bray since its closure for refitting following production of 1964's *The Brigand of Kandahar*. The façade of Dracula's castle, constructed on the lot, was surrounded by a 'frozen moat', in which the vampire was seen to drown on screen. Alarmingly, the sequence nearly curtailed stuntman Eddie Powell's career. Doubling for Lee, he'd failed to realise that when the 'lid' of the fake ice closed above him he'd be unable to see his way underwater to find the oxygen cylinders placed there for his use. Shooting wrapped on location at Black Park on Friday 4 June.

Dracula's resurrection was screened at a trade and press show on 17 December, and went directly to a successful ABC circuit release, double-billed with *The Plague of the Zombies*. The press show had been followed by a star-studded luncheon thrown to celebrate 'Ten Years of Hammer Horror'. Attending was *The Daily Worker*'s Nina Hibbin, who, distinctly unmoved by her free lunch, described it as "a sad occasion. It was sad to look around at the bright and intelligent faces of present and former horror players — like Peter Cushing, Andre Morell, Charles Tingwell, Heather Sears and Oliver Reed — and to dwell upon that prodigious waste of talent. Saddest of all was the contemplation of the Hammer Company's spectacular rise to power and prosperity through ten years of trading in morbidity, putrefaction and pain..."

The Christopher Lee Club, however, awarded the film a rapturous reception. Wrote member Stanley Nicholls: "The way in which the count returns is ingenius [sic]...The suspense is consistent throughout the film's duration and sometimes reaches unbearable heights... Christopher need have no worries about his new portrayal of the part. He's come a long way since 1958 but he still remains the best Count Dracula ever..."

Cut-out 'Dracula Fangs' were supplied as give-away gimmicks to American audiences. By 15 January 1968,

the film had made $364,937 in America and Canada, an astonishing $24,584 in the tiny Philippine Islands — and a meagre £19 in India. The adventures of its ecclesiastical hero, Father Sandor, would continue, when *Dracula Prince of Darkness* was adapted as a comic strip in the pages of *The House of Hammer* magazine in the mid-seventies. Sandor was named "Shandor", as per the script and, under that name, he made a number of solo appearances commencing in issue sixteen (Hammer's then chairman, Michael Carreras, apparently took that first strip's pencil artwork to America where, unsuccessfully, he attempted to excite interest in a solo Sandor film). *Father Shandor, Demon Stalker* concluded in the pages of the influential eighties comic, *Warrior*.

Previous page: At Bray, James Carreras holds on tight to one of his most valuable assets.
Top: Diana (Suzan Farmer) in Dracula's thrall – the filmed scene was less explicit than that originally scripted.
Above: The vampirised Helen (Barbara Shelley) ensnared by Kleinberg's monks.
Left: Charles (Francis Matthews), about to stumble across the dormant denizen of a below-stairs vault.

RASPUTIN THE MAD MONK

Principal photography 7 June to 20 July 1965
Released 6 March 1966
Certificate X
Duration 91 mins
Colour/Cinemascope
Director Don Sharp

Russia, the early twentieth century: expelled from a monastery after a fracas at a local inn, Grigori Yefimovitch Rasputin (Christopher Lee), who is possessed of seemingly unnatural powers of healing, travels to St Petersburg. At the Café Tzigane, he takes part in a drinking competition versus struck-off alcoholic doctor Boris Zargo (Richard Pasco). Rasputin is performing a victory dance when four well-to-do young thrill-seekers enter the bar: Sonia and Vanessa (Barbara Shelley and Suzan Farmer), ladies-in-waiting to the Tsarina, and their brothers, Peter and Ivan (Dinsdale Landen and Francis Matthews). Rasputin is insulted when the drunken Sonia apparently slights him and he demands an apology. After a night disturbed by visions of the entrancing stranger, Sonia traces him to Zargo's filthy tenement, where she is seduced and given a sequence of mesmeric instructions. Covertly, Sonia causes harm to come to the young Tsarevitch (Robert Duncan). With the royal heir gravely ill, Sonia tells the Tsarina (Renée Asherson) that she knows of only one man who may cure her son — Rasputin. He does so, and is rewarded with a villa where he sets up practice as a faith healer. His malign influence has now extended to the peak of Russia's high society...

"This is an entertainment, not a documentary," read the first page of John Elder's shooting script for *The Mad Monk*, unequivocally. "No attempt has been made at historical accuracy... all the characters and incidents may be regarded as fictitious." The life and sudden death of Grigori Yefimovitch Rasputin, a self-styled 'holy man' who'd held Russia's last Tsar, Nicholas II, in his thrall, had proved fertile ground for many film-makers since he'd been murdered on the night of 16 December 1916; numerous early European shorts had chronicled the so-called Holy Sinner's rise and fall. More famously, in 1932 MGM released *Rasputin and the Empress*, featuring members of the fabled Barrymore acting clan. A lawsuit was brought against the studio by Princess Irina Yousoupoff, wife to one of Rasputin's real-life assassins, the still living Prince Felix Yousoupoff. She took exception to a scene in which a character corresponding to her, Natasha, was apparently raped by Rasputin. After a long and much-publicised trial in 1934, the jury

ASSOCIATED BRITISH-PATHÉ LTD. PRESENTS

A HAMMER FILM PRODUCTION

"RASPUTIN—THE MAD MONK" (X)

starring

CHRISTOPHER LEE

BARBARA SHELLEY   RICHARD PASCO

CINEMASCOPE   TECHNICOLOR®

RELEASED THROUGH WARNER-PATHE DISTRIBUTORS LTD.

found in the Princess' favour, awarding her £25,000 in damages.

Hammer had dropped a project entitled *The Sins of Rasputin* from a provisional production schedule for 1961; concern that Yousoupoff (or any fictional *alter ego*) should not be misrepresented became of paramount importance to the company when the notion was revived over four years later. The screenplay was entrusted to Anthony Hinds, who drew extensively upon two of Yousoupoff's literary endeavours, *Rasputin* (1927) and *Lost Splendour* (1953), in preparing it. Nevertheless, the script was revised several times prior to shooting, legal consid-

FROM HAMMER, THE HOUSE OF HORROR!

RASPUTIN THE MAD MONK

THE REPTILE

ALL COLOUR!

RASPUTIN-THE MAD MONK
starring
CHRISTOPHER LEE
BARBARA SHELLEY · RICHARD PASCO
FRANCIS MATTHEWS · SUZAN FARMER
DINSDALE LANDEN *and* RENEE ASHERSON

THE REPTILE *starring* NOEL WILLMAN · RAY BARRETT
with JENNIFER DANIEL · JACQUELINE PEARCE

"We were cutting as we went along," he claims. Lost were extra scenes in both the monastery and the Tzigane, and a significant dialogue between Vanessa and the Tsarina. Also absent from the finished print was Sonia's suicide (a scene was filmed in which she slashed her wrist with a shard of glass) and much of the climactic struggle between Ivan and Rasputin — the cutting of this punch-up, apparently for timing reasons, is all-too-obvious on screen.

Even after the conclusion of principal photography, Yousoupoff still managed to give Hammer a fright when, late in 1965, the Prince attempted to sue American TV corporation CBS over a half-hour play, *If I Should Die*, which had been broadcast in 1963. Day-to-day *New York Times* clippings from the ensuing court case were forwarded to executive producer Anthony Hinds by representatives of Seven Arts. (Hinds' scrapbook cuttings remain: "Very frightening!" he scribbled on one.)

The Prince lost his case on 9 November. He'd objected to CBS' "sexual" portrayal of his using Irina as a lure to ensnare Rasputin (which is why Hammer's surrogate Yousoupoff, Ivan, has a sister, Vanessa, for this purpose, not a wife — and why Vanessa and Rasputin do not meet in the all-important climax).

Double-billed with *The Reptile*, *Rasputin the Mad Monk* was released to only fair reviews early in 1966. Free "Rasputin beards" were distributed among certain picturegoers when the film subsequently played the American circuits. Whereas the film contains an arresting performance from Lee, only Barbara Shelley comes close to equalling him, and its shock moments — a dismemberment, an acid attack — are contrived concessions to Hammer's horror constituency. *Rasputin the Mad Monk* never achieves the greatness to which it clearly aspires.

erations overriding factual accuracy. (Yousoupoff himself signed every page of a copy of the script as an indemnity against a lawsuit.)

The film went before the Bray cameras in the summer of 1965; Hammer redressed and reused many of the sets for *Dracula Prince of Darkness*, which had been shot immediately beforehand. The 'castle' on the lot became the exteriors of palatial Russian apartments, parts of Dracula's subterranean vault became the Café Tzigane, and so on. Four days of woodland exteriors were shot at Black Park and the St Petersburg street market was constructed immediately outside the doors to Bray's stage two.

Christopher Lee became passionately involved in researching the role of Rasputin, partly because as a young boy he'd been introduced to Yousoupoff and fellow conspirator the Grand Duke Dimitry Pavlovich. Actor Francis Matthews — who, like Lee, Barbara Shelley and Suzan Farmer, had been retained from *Dracula Prince of Darkness* — recalls the star sharing bundles of relevant history books among the cast. Lee even sought advice on how to play a medically accurate death by cyanide poisoning.

Due to overspends on *Dracula Prince of Darkness*, however, *Rasputin Mad Monk* director Don Sharp was forced to foreshorten the script in places.

Previous page: Rasputin (Christopher Lee) terrorises the besotted Sonia (Barbara Shelley).
Top left: Contractual tie? Christopher Lee and producer Anthony Nelson Keys at Bray.
Middle: Sonia's suicide by wrist-cutting would not survive in the finished print.
Above: Shooting Rasputin's death throes.
Left: Rasputin seduces Sonia in Zargo's flat.

**Principal photography 28 July to
8 September 1965
Released 9 January 1966
Certificate X
Duration 90 mins
Colour
Director John Gilling**

The folk of a small Cornish village are falling victim to a fatal malady with previously unidentified symptoms. Distraught GP Peter Tompson (Brook Williams) calls on his former tutor Sir James Forbes (André Morell) for help. Sir James arrives with his daughter Sylvia (Diane Clare) and the two are greeted by Peter's sick wife Alice (Jacqueline Pearce), an old school friend of Sylvia's. At night, Sylvia passes a disused mine and sees a corpse-like figure toss aside the body of Alice. Under cover of darkness, Sir James and Peter attempt to exhume a body from the local cemetery in order to conduct a post mortem. They discover the coffin to be empty, but are soon interrupted by police Sergeant Swift (Michael Ripper) who grants them forty-eight hours breathing space to investigate. Sir James' post mortem on Alice reveals no rigor mortis, and that her blood is no longer human. Sir James, Peter and Sergeant Swift visit the tin mine, and the policeman speculates as to how the powerful local squire earns his money since the mine was closed following an accident. It soon transpires that Squire Hamilton (John Carson) is using the power of voodoo to raise the dead 'plague' victims. In the graveyard, a horrified Peter looks on while Sir James is forced to decapitate the zombie Alice. Reality blurs and the surrounding graves spew forth an advancing army of rotting corpses...

y the early sixties, Hammer had run out of classic Universal films to remake and were forced to seek fresh inspiration. They found it in the voodoo ceremonies of Haiti, and resurrected a subgenre that dates back to the 1932 Bela Lugosi vehicle *White Zombie*.

Peter Bryan originally storylined *The Zombie* in 1962, colouring it with elements recalled from his screenplay for Hammer's *The Hound of the Baskervilles*. By November, Anthony Hinds had begun developing Bryan's ideas and the two men collaborated on a gruesome synopsis delivered in September 1963: "Taking a spade that has been left, Sheldon hacks repeatedly at the neck of the dead girl as she walks... until the head falls. There is no blood, just an oozing whiteness and a stink of putrefaction

Z 29

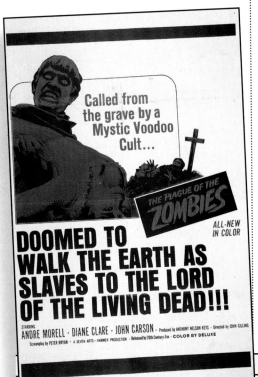

that makes even the Doctor retch. It was the only way, Sheldon tells him. Someone had breathed the air of life into its nostrils. If he had not destroyed it... it would have become a slave for ever. One of the Walking Dead!"

It was all a bit too much for the faint hearts at Universal and the undead were left in their graves. *The Zombie* was dusted off in June 1964 and nominated for inclusion in Anthony Nelson Keys' four-film Seven Arts/Fox/ABPC package. With its Haiti opening sequence discarded, Keys felt confident it could be economically produced (back-to-back with John Elder's *The Reptile*) and presented as the

support feature for *Dracula Prince of Darkness*. Peter Bryan's shooting script accommodated the economies involved and changed the characters' names. On 7 July 1965, the MPPA advised on the cuts necessary to bring the anticipated film in line with the American Production Code. Amongst Geoffrey Shurlock's recommendations was an amendment to one of Bryan's original highlights: "In the action where Sir James decapitates Alice, the business of bringing the spade down on her must be done out of frame... Sir James is described as striking a second and third blow with the spade and starting to strike a fourth. Peter is described as 'stumbling, gagging' at this as a result, and we urge that you omit the second and third blows less the audience likewise gag." Writing on 14 July, the BBFC's John Trevelyan stressed that "we would not want to see anything really unpleasant" during the coffin examinations, and expressed concern over the burning zombies scripted in the tin mine climax. He would save his strongest condemnation for the controversial 'spade incident': "We would certainly not accept this if shot in anything like the way it is described. Nor would we want to see the severed head of Alice in the trick sequence that follows. We get nasty shots of the dead rising from their graves and the headless torso with severed head smiling. This is horror-comic material which simply would not do; it must be rewritten." Anthony Hinds replied on 23 July, reassuring Trevelyan that the severed head and flaming zombies would present nothing stronger than sequences already passed for exhibition in *The Gorgon* and *The Curse of Frankenstein* respectively. And as for the spade — "we will handle this with great delicacy," he promised.

Anthony Nelson Keys' favoured director, John Gilling, began shooting at Bray a mere one week after *Rasputin The Mad Monk* wrapped. Four days location work (which took in nearby Oakley Court) in hot weather caused much discomfort for the fifteen actors underneath Roy Ashton's zombie make-up. Even the economically-minded Keys found space in the tight budget for a large consignment of ice lollies for the cast and crew. One year after his criminal misuse in *She*, André Morell was top-billed as Sir James Forbes. Morell would lace a convincing performance with delicately balanced humour, evoking the memory of Hammer's old sophistication in the midst of its new-found crudity.

Processing difficulties at Technicolor delayed the film's delivery to distributors, as did some last-minute revoicing instigated by executive producer Anthony Hinds. "I think that has paid off," he explained in a letter of 3 December, "and the picture is now not at all bad." In Britain, ABC released *The Plague of the Zombies* alongside *Dracula*

Prince of Darkness on 9 January, a huge publicity campaign helping to ensure outstanding box-office results. The double-bill made its début in the United States three days later, distributors Twentieth Century-Fox promoting *The Plague of the Zombies* with a television trailer compiled from the most striking sequences. Promotional gimmick of the week was a pair of free cut-out zombie eyes.

Much has been said of *The Plague of the Zombies'* influence on genre landmark *Night of the Living Dead*, made in 1968. A unique and shocking experiment in pushing the parameters of Hammer horror, *The Plague of the Zombies* perhaps deserves greater recognition in its own right.

FROM HAMMER "THE KINGS OF HORROR" — A SHOCKER ABOUT THE 'WALKING DEAD'!

The Horror of the Zombie

Previous page: The body of Alice (Jacqueline Pearce) is dumped outside the tin mine.
Top right: The nightmare begins – John Gilling (far right) supervises Tompson's encounter with the walking dead.
Above: Pre-production artwork.
Left: André Morell and Brook Williams cool down at Bray Studios.

Principal photography 13 September to 22 October 1965
Released 6 March 1966
Certificate X
Duration 91 mins
Colour
Director John Gilling

Upon the death of his brother Charles, Harry Spalding (Ray Barrett) inherits a cottage in the village of Clagmoor Heath, Cornwall. Harry is regarded with suspicion by the locals, and pub landlord Tom Bailey (Michael Ripper) advises him to sell up immediately. Harry and his wife Valerie (Jennifer Daniel) are disturbed by local eccentric Mad Peter (John Laurie), who falls victim to the village's 'Black Death'; he dies in agony, his skin discoloured and his mouth choked with foam. Valerie is visited by her distant neighbour, the beautiful Anna Franklyn (Jacqueline Pearce). Before they can talk for long, Anna is collected by her abrupt father Dr Franklyn (Noel Willman) and his Malay manservant (Marne Maitland). At Franklyn's mansion, the Doctor explains that his "fascinating, horrifying" researches into primitive religions of the Far East have had a profound effect on his life. After Harry and Valerie are asked to leave, the Malay torments Anna, and tells Franklyn that he and his daughter will never be free. Together with Tom, Harry examines the corpses of Mad Peter and Charles Spalding, finding that both bear neck incisions. Returning to Franklyn's mansion, Harry is seized by a grotesquely transformed Anna. He is unable to resist, and the creature sinks her fangs in deep...

following rejection by Universal in 1963, John Elder's *The Curse of the Reptiles* was resurrected as last in line for Anthony Nelson Keys' back-to-back Bray Studios shoot. Anthony Hinds completed his shooting script, entitled *The Reptiles*, on 18 August 1965. Director John Gilling retained Jacqueline Pearce and Michael Ripper from *The Plague of the Zombies*, although their fees were substantially increased to reflect their expanded roles. Noel Willman and Jennifer Daniel were reunited from *The Kiss of the Vampire*, while lower down the cast John Laurie delivered a wild-eyed performance as Mad Peter Crockford that anticipated his role as Pte Frazer in the television sit-com *Dad's Army*.

On 27 August, the MPAA completed their report on John Elder's screenplay. One of the script's earliest scenes was the first to be singled out as inadvisable: "Please eliminate the action of Dr Franklyn removing the whip from its place on the wall, and the subsequent scream of pain from off-stage. This would seem to imply the practice of sadism which is in no way connected to the plot of the story." Geoffrey Shurlock also objected to the scene where Franklyn briefly

mistakes his reptilian daughter's shed skin for her naked body. "She should be adequately clothed." The BBFC's report of 1 September followed similar lines, adding that "the victims of cobra bites do not in fact turn black or suffer convulsions, and these shots may easily be too strong, even for an X."

John Gilling's objections to John Elder's script were of an altogether different nature. He took John Elder's "very bad" screenplay and "rewrote [it] more or less as I went along." When rushes of the reptilian Anna failed to find favour, Anthony Nelson Keys instructed Gilling and his crew to shoot new sequences. Not all of them survived in the released print. The additional material outlined in a memo of 18 October featured Jacqueline Pearce in snake make-up, and began with a new close-up of her underneath

THE REPTILE Starring **NOEL WILLMAN** · **RAY BARRETT** also starring **JENNIFER DANIEL**
JACQUELINE PEARCE Screenplay by JOHN ELDER · Produced by ANTHONY NELSON KEYS · Directed by JOHN GILLING

FROM HAMMER "THE KINGS OF HORROR"
THE STORY OF A HIDEOUS EVIL...!

THE CURSE OF THE REPTILES

ROY ASHTON: MAKE-UP ARTIST

The eponymous creature in *The Reptile* was the creation of Roy Ashton, in his final regular engagement as Hammer's make-up artist. Howard Roy Ashton was born in Perth, Australia, in 1909 and emigrated to Britain in 1932. A 1954 meeting with fellow make-up man Phil Leakey, chief designer for Hammer, encouraged him to lend a hand at Bray Studios. Ashton assisted Leakey on a number of projects, including *The Curse of Frankenstein* and *Dracula*, before becoming head of department two years later. In an article written for *The Christopher Lee Club Bulletin*, Ashton described his special relationship with the Hammer star: "He has a rich bass voice and I myself sang in opera for some twelve years. The early hours in the studio are often enlivened by operatic duets — tenor and bass in rivalry. Challenges are frequently made — an aria is commenced and left for the other to finish — to the considerable amusement or consternation of other studio personnel." *The Reptile* was typical of Ashton's attention to detail: the fangs worn by Jacqueline Pearce were specially grooved so drops of glycerine would seem to salivate from her mouth. "They convey a real feeling of pathos," he said, summing up the appeal of his creations. "I don't think anybody really dislikes them. I look on these stories as fairy tales. This is one of the reasons I have no conscience about frightening people." In later years, Ashton worked for Amicus, Tyburn and Walt Disney. He died in January 1995, having long since gained a reputation as a genuine pioneer in his field.

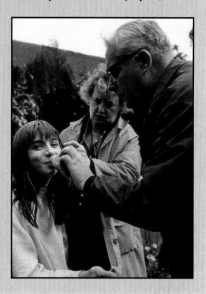

the rug in the cavern. Notable amongst Keys' other requests was a new take on "the first time we see [Anna] as the snake woman at the green baize door." Keys asked for two new "big shock close-ups" of the scene, the first "just filling the screen with mouth open and fangs dripping", the second "just below the nose and above head filling screen. Anna raises head revealing mouth open. Fangs and teeth dripping." Keys concluded his instructions by stressing "these shots to be as menacing as possible." *The Reptile* was given the thin end of a four-film wedge. Anthony Nelson Keys had found it impossible to bring *Dracula Prince of Darkness*, *Rasputin The Mad Monk* and *The Plague of the Zombies* in on budget, and he was determined that the final picture would hit the mark. *The Reptile* wrapped slightly *under* budget, at a final cost of just £100,599.

"Jacqueline Pearce is an attractive Anna and a quite horrible cobra," said *Kinematograph Weekly* in February 1966. "Reviewed in the cold light of reason this is utter nonsense but it is directed with intelligence and very well acted, and should please most audi-

ences. Excellent shocker." *The Reptile* later joined *Rasputin the Mad Monk* on its 6 March ABC release, following on a month later in America.

John Gilling invests this lycanthropic spin with a rich atmosphere and carefully orchestrated tension that belie its support feature status. *The Reptile* is quintessential sixties Hammer, the relaxed pace and subdued lighting adding extra *frisson* to the sharply edited shock sequences.

Previous page: *Anna's transformation.*
Above left: *Pre-production artwork.*
Above right: *Roy Ashton with Jacqueline Pearce on The Plague of the Zombies.*
Below left: *Mad Peter (John Laurie) returns to the Spaldings' cottage.*
Below right: *Valerie (Jennifer Daniel), Harry (Ray Barrett) and Tom (Michael Ripper) watch the Franklyn mansion burn.*

Principal photography 18 October 1965 to
6 January 1966
Released 30 December 1966
Certificate A
Duration 100 mins
Colour/Panamation
Director Don Chaffey

Long, long ago, when the world was just beginning...Tumak (John Richardson), the son of head man Akhoba (Robert Brown), is exiled from the dark-haired Rock tribe and his mate Nupondi (Martine Beswick) is claimed by Tumak's wicked brother Sakana (Percy Herbert). In the wilderness, Tumak encounters many strange creatures. Eventually, exhausted, he reaches a strange ocean, where he is saved from falling victim to a gargantuan turtle by Loana (Raquel Welch) and other members of her tribe, the blond-haired and more civilised Shell clan. Tumak saves a Shell child from the attentions of a rampaging allosaurus, but later offends their leader, Ahot (Jean Wladon), and is again banished. Accompanied by Loana, Tumak embarks upon a hazardous journey home, narrowly evading man-eating gorillas — and worse. Upon his return, however, he finds that the evil Sakana, having attempted patricide, has installed himself as the tribe's leader...

"This is the most important film that the company has ever produced," stressed Brian Lawrence in a memo inviting all Hammer's staff to a special screening of *One Million Years B.C.* on 14 November 1966. He was not exaggerating. *One Million Years B.C.* would become the company's biggest ever commercial success.

It appears that the film was designed to recreate the formula that had made *She* a smash, reuniting Seven Arts contract artistes Ursula Andress and John Richardson in a remake of the 1940 Hal Roach-produced epic, *One Million B.C.*, which had featured Victor Mature and Carole Landis. And whereas Mature and Landis shrank only from magnified reptiles in cutaways, Hammer and Seven Arts would have their characters menaced by you-can't-see-the-join stop-motion monstrosities concocted by Ray Harryhausen, a mould-breaking animator whose labours on films had brought to life the seemingly impossible. The project was instigated by Kenneth Hyman, and was being prepared for production by Hammer by the latter end of 1964. Come 1965, the film comprised part of the ever-swelling deal with

ASSOCIATED BRITISH-PATHE PRESENTS
A HAMMER FILM PRODUCTION
"ONE MILLION YEARS B.C." (A)
starring
RAQUEL WELCH · JOHN RICHARDSON
with
PERCY HERBERT · ROBERT BROWN
MARTINE BESWICK
TECHNICOLOR ®
RELEASED THROUGH WARNER-PATHE DISTRIBUTORS LTD.

RAQUEL WELCH · JOHN RICHARDSON
PERCY HERBERT · ROBERT BROWN · MARTINE BESWICK

distributors Twentieth Century-Fox and ABPC.

When Andress passed on the project, Fox put forward the name of their newest starlet, a former TV weather girl fresh from playing a miniaturised submariner in Richard Fleischer's *Fantastic Voyage*. Raquel Welch learned of the film via a telephone call from Richard Zanuck, by then Fox's vice-president in charge of production. Underenthused, Welch took the role believing that "nobody will remember this thing. I can shove it under the carpet." Far from it. Photographer Pierre Luigi's notorious still of Welch on the barren plains of Lanzarote, sporting costumier Monty Berman's doeskin-and-fur bikini, established her as a totem of pop cinema.

Logically enough, *Jason and the Argonauts* director Don Chaffey was hired, as was *Jason*'s director of photography, Wilkie Cooper. Cast and crew flew to the Canary Islands, where principal

A HAMMER-SEVEN ARTS PRODUCTION
in GIANT PanaMation
and TECHNICOLOR®
For TWENTIETH CENTURY-FOX RELEASE

ONE MILLION YEARS B.C.

photography on its blasted, volcanic terrain commenced on 18 October. Much of the actors' time was spent shadow-boxing with as yet invisible dinosaurs, although Harryhausen was on hand to help choreograph the action. "They told us exact eyelines," remembers Welch. "When you were doing it, it just seemed so ridiculously silly." The Lanzarote shoot was followed by several weeks' work at ABPC Elstree between 20 November and 6 January 1966. Meanwhile, Harryhausen began to matte his creations into the available footage, work that would take nearly nine months to complete. (The lizard sequence was shot between 14 and 16 March, the pterodactyl scenes between 17 March and 7 April, the turtle sequence between 12 and 30 April, the allosaurus scenes between 2 May and 3 June, the triceratops/ceratosaurus scenes between 6 June and 15 July, and the brontosaurus, plus various others, between 18 and 29 July.)

Meanwhile, Bowie Films Ltd were contracted to supply a special effects prologue for the film. "We will produce at least four minutes of the creation of the Earth," confirmed Les Bowie, deadpan, in a letter dated 12 May. In the event, much of the completed work, featuring "cosmic dusts", "spiral nebulae" and volcanic eruptions, was deemed unsatisfactory, and partly substituted by stock footage from the MGM, Rayant and Elmer Dyer film libraries. In mid-1966, it was decided that an explanatory voice-over might be needed to guide the viewer through the film's events, all of which were related without anything approaching conventional dialogue. David Kossoff was employed as the film's narrator, but his spiel was much reduced from that planned, which bore something of the tone of a junior wildlife documentary. "Very primitive people... They knew nothing of traffic jams or rush hours or queues or hire purchase or overdrafts or television commercials or tranquillisers or income tax. They weren't like us." Or, as the survivors of the volcanic eruption emerge in the film's finale: "How lucky we are. We can create such destructions and disasters without any help from Nature at all. Goodnight children... everywhere."

The film had been budgeted at £367,415, but by 31 October its costs had risen to £422,816. *One Million Years B.C.* was released on 30 December. Extensively promoted and pre-sold, its results exceeded the wildest hopes of all concerned, breaking ABC circuit records and grossing something in the region of $8,000,000 worldwide. Not surprisingly, by May 1967, plans were in place to produce both a sequel and a spin-off television series...

Beautifully filmed but hopelessly naïve, rambling and sometimes barely comprehensible, *One Million Years B.C.* might so easily have been the company's greatest folly. However, there's much to enjoy: dinosaur effects to satisfy the most demanding of schoolboys (and which would not be substantially improved upon for twenty-five years), a cast who grunt through their bestial roles sometimes horribly well. Without recourse to language, it's unsurprising that it should translate on an international scale. For all that, *One Million Years B.C.* seems so dated today as to feel near-prehistoric in itself.

Previous page: "Akeeta!" A pterodactyl swoops.
Above left: Shell girl Loana (Raquel Welch).
Above right: Pre-production artwork, clearly prepared before the casting of Raquel Welch.
Below: Don Chaffey starred in his own storyboards, compiled from photographs taken on location reconnaissance.

The sensational response to *One Million Years B.C.* inspired Hammer to produce a number of Stone Age successors, in which nubile Neolithic nymphets would do battle with rampaging reptiles galore…

b izarrely, the first Hammer film to follow on in the style of *One Million Years B.C.* was actually completed while the Raquel Welch dino-epic was still in post-production! *Slave Girls*, filmed as *Prehistoric Women*, was hastily devised by Michael Carreras to make optimum use of the Elstree sets constructed for *One Million Years B.C.* — and, indeed, the talents of Amazonian supporting actress Martine Beswick, a Jamaican-born model/actress hitherto most notable for her role as a catfighting gypsy girl in the second James Bond feature, *From Russia With Love*. In the film, big game hunter David Marchant (Michael Latimer), lost in the African bush, is mysteriously transported back to a strange era whence the region's legends concerning a fabled white rhinoceros apparently originate. He encounters a blonde girl, Saria (Edina Ronay), one of a number of fair-haired tribeswomen oppressed by a rival group of dark-haired vixens led by the evil Kari (Beswick). Kari's clan regard all men as their inferiors — and Kari soon marks out Marchant for her own…

Directed by Carreras in his beloved Cinemascope between 10 January and 22 February 1966, *Slave Girls* was a quite cynical slice of exploitation more akin to the company's later sensation-seeking Carmilla sequence than its output of the time. It was over two years before it was finally released as the support feature to *The Devil Rides Out*, and then shorn of nearly

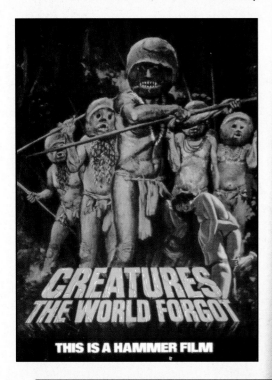

twenty minutes worth of footage. The terrible reputation this admittedly ludicrous B-movie has since acquired is perhaps undeserved; although fatuous, it's hugely entertaining, and performed, especially by Beswick, with a certain lewd splendour. (Apologists will find succour, too, in the presence of two notables on the cast list: Carol White, renowned for her role at the heart of Ken Loach's agenda-setting TV play *Cathy Come Home*, and Steven Berkoff, now a *bête noire* of the British theatre establishment.)

Michael Carreras would also be responsible for *The Lost Continent*, based on novelist Dennis Wheatley's fantasy *Uncharted Seas* — wherein the SS Corta, running both passengers and an illegal cargo of Phosphor B, crosses unmarked territory and, having become entangled in sentient seaweed, is dragged to a forgotten island. Ringed by scuppered galleons, the island is inhabited by the feuding descendants of their crews — plus a host of terrifying monsters. Shot at Elstree late in 1967, its cast including Eric Porter, Suzanna Leigh and the remarkable Dana Gillespie, this would-be epic — although not dinosaur adventure *per se* — could certainly be said to pre-empt later 'lost world' sagas such as Amicus productions *The Land That Time Forgot* (1974) and *At the Earth's Core* (1976).

The company's follow-up to *One Million Years B.C.* proper didn't appear until 1970. *When Dinosaurs Ruled the Earth* would not feature the effects work of Ray Harryhausen, who was otherwise engaged; the commission went instead to Jim Danforth, whose team's innovative labours would eventually be rewarded with an Academy Award nomination. Novelist J. G. Ballard wrote the film's treatment, which was developed into a full screenplay by Val Guest ("I'm very proud that my first screen credit was for what is, without doubt, the worst film ever made," Ballard later claimed). A rather more literate piece than *One Million Years B.C.*, the story concerned a

story concerned a girl, Sanna (Victoria Vetri) who escapes the ritual sacrifice ordained upon her by tribal chief Kingsor (Patrick Allen), and her subsequent adventures against a backdrop of turbulent climate change and upheaval — during which she is accepted by a mother dinosaur as one of her own hatchlings. Vetri, a one-time *Playboy* centrefold, was as extensively publicised as the film, which was shot by Guest on location in the Canaries and in studio at Shepperton between 14 October 1968 and 9 January 1969.

When Dinosaurs Ruled the Earth performed well at the box-office upon its release in October 1970, but couldn't scale the heights of its direct predecessor, the spectre of which still loomed large over the company; alongside *She*, *One Million Years B.C.* had made £190,000 when briefly re-released at the turn of the decade, and repeated attempts had been made to find backers for a TV series based upon it (as late as 1969, studies were prepared on the feasibility of shooting in Antigua). Hammer would re-employ Don Chaffey to direct their last such effort, *Creatures the World Forgot*. Filmed entirely on location in South Africa in July and August 1970, *Creatures* took for its narrative thrust the wanderings of the nomadic Rock Tribe, but forsook animated dinosaurs for barbarism and acres of naked flesh, earning Hammer's dino-series its first ever X rating; Julie Ege, a former Miss Norway, headlined. "See pre-historic love rites! See primitive chieftains duel in naked fury! See the young lovers sacrificed! See staked girl menaced by giant python!" the posters promised.

Creatures the World Forgot was released in March 1971 to only moderate returns — it had already proved impossible to raise the finance for *Zeppelin vs Pterodactyls*. Virtually overnight, Hammer's prehistoric sagas became extinct.

Above left: *African queen Kari (Martine Beswick) looks daggers in* Slave Girls.
Above right: *Sarah (Dana Gillespie) on* The Lost Continent.
Below: *Sanna (Victoria Vetri) gets tactile with Tara (Robin Hawdon) in* When Dinosaurs Ruled the Earth.

Principal photography 18 April to
10 June 1966
Released 21 November 1966
Certificate X
Duration 91 mins
Colour
Director Cyril Frankel

Schoolteacher Gwen Mayfield (Joan Fontaine) suffers a breakdown in Africa after falling victim to a rebellion led by witch-doctors. The Reverend Alan Bax (Alec McCowen) offers Gwen the post of head mistress at the school he owns in the peaceful village of Heddaby. In the ruins of the local church, Alan reveals that he merely assumes the identity of a priest, but refuses to fully explain why. Alan's sister, Stephanie Bax (Kay Walsh), is a successful journalist who frowns upon the rumours of witchcraft in the village — even after the sudden illness of one of Gwen's pupils coincides with the discovery of a headless doll, impaled with pins. Prior to his illness, schoolboy Ronnie (Martin Stephens) had been developing a close relationship with another of Gwen's pupils, fourteen year-old Linda (Ingrid Brett). Could Linda's protective grandmother, Granny Rigg (Gwen Ffrangcon-Davies), have induced Ronnie's coma with witchcraft? Stephanie seems keen to help investigate, and suggests that she and Gwen collaborate on an article. However, as Gwen's suspicions grow, a flashback to the horrors of African voodoo induce another breakdown. On Gwen's return to Heddaby, she discovers the extent of the conspiracy against her, and the terrible secret it has hidden. Linda is to be sacrificed so that someone may live again...

oan de Beauvoir de Havilland's career peaked when, under her stage name of Joan Fontaine, she won a Best Actress Oscar for her role in Alfred Hitchcock's *Suspicion*. By the early sixties, however, she was being offered little of consequence and decided to develop a suitable subject herself. Impressed by *The Devil's Own*, a novel written by Nora Lofts under the pseudonym Peter Curtis, Fontaine bought the screen rights in September 1962.

By June 1964, Seven Arts had brought *The Devil's Own* to Wardour Street. In March the following year, Hammer considered offering the film to Universal with John Temple-Smith as producer. It was later added to the roster of films produced in association with Twentieth Century-Fox and ABPC. After completing *Quatermass and the Pit*, Nigel Kneale adapted *The Devil's Own*, delivering his screenplay on 19 August 1965. "Tony Hinds asked me back," he remembers. "I read the book and thought it was all right, up to a point. The interesting part for me was the very ordinary-seeming country setting, with all its double meanings and sinister things popping through occasionally."

Director Cyril Frankel had most recently worked on the filmed television series *The Baron* when Anthony Hinds renewed their acquaintance. "Joan Fontaine had director approval," recalls Frankel, "and it was arranged from the [critical] success of *Never Take Sweets From a Stranger* that when Hammer had a more sensitive and serious film than their usual horror, blood and thunder I would be considered. So a meeting was arranged with Joan Fontaine when she was on a brief visit to London and we got on like a house on fire. She was happy with me and I was enchanted with her, and I got the job... I was pleased with the majority of the suspense aspect and working with Joan. I did a play with her later." While shooting, Frankel was asked by producer Monty Berman to become the establishing director of his new series,

The Champions. Frankel's television career continued with instalments of *The Avengers*, *Department S*, *UFO* and *Hammer House of Mystery and Suspense*.

Not all of Kneale's screenplay was to Frankel's satisfaction. "They went a little potty by writing a semi-orgy scene at the end which I was not quite happy with," he says. Kneale, on the other hand, had a complaint of his own: "There's nothing as funny as people imagining they're witches. It's naturally comic. I think a cleverer director would have faced that possibility of it all turning into laughs and he would have managed to make it really horrible, creepy and threatening."

While original producer John Temple-Smith prepared Boudicca-on-a-budget *The Viking Queen*, Anthony Nelson Keys oversaw production of *The Devil's Own* at Bray Studios (ABPC Elstree having been fully booked) and on location in Hambleden. Like Bette Davis before her, Joan Fontaine was granted a higher-than-usual salary and a percentage of the producers' profits.

Hammer's post-production difficulties began on 22 June when it was noted that its new title for the film, *The Witches*, would clash with a United Artists picture of the same name being distributed in America. It was decided to revert to *The Devil's Own* for American distribution and retain *The Witches* in Britain. On 28 July, Hammer's company directors were dismayed to learn that the BBFC had provisionally granted the film an A certificate — the kiss of death for a horror subject. By the time *The Witches* was delivered to British distributors ABC in October, its certification had been massaged up to the required X.

Following a première at the London Pavilion on 21 November 1966, *The Witches* went on general release (supported by *Death is a Woman*) on 9 December. *Kinematograph Weekly* was impressed with the scenery, if little else: "The film opens with an exciting African sequence prior to the credits, but is then content to amble along in the quite pleasing atmosphere of village life... A well-made picture in many ways,

which fails to make the grade." An aggressive publicity campaign by ABC failed to stimulate a public whose taste in Hammer films had been desensitised by the more lurid offerings exhibited during 1966. Joan Fontaine was reportedly devastated by the disappointing box-office results. *The Witches* effectively brought her long film career to an end.

Unsettling, though compromised by an hysterical climax, *The Witches*' effective exploitation of its picturesque location predates both *The Prisoner* and *The Wicker Man*. When *The Witches* strikes the right balance it succeeds as an engrossing thriller, even if it ultimately disappoints as Hammer horror.

Previous page: "Give me a skin for dancing in..." Stephanie (Kay Walsh) covets the virgin Linda (Ingrid Brett).
Top: The ceremony reaches its fevered conclusion.
Above: The fragile Gwen Mayfield (Joan Fontaine) is plagued by memories of African voodoo.
Left: Gwen spills her own blood, with arresting consequences.

FRANKENSTEIN CREATED WOMAN

**Principal photography 4 July to
12 August 1966
Released 18 May 1967
Certificate X
Duration 86 mins
Colour
Director Terence Fisher**

Newly-arrived in a small mittel-*European town, Baron Frankenstein (Peter Cushing) is engaged in a series of experiments to determine whether or not the soul departs the body at the point of physical death. He is assisted by an alcoholic doctor, Hertz (Thorley Walters), and a simple-minded dogsbody Hans (Robert Morris). In a local tavern, three feckless, well-to-do young bloods taunt Hans' disfigured sweetheart, Christina (Susan Denberg) and are forcibly expelled by Hans and landlord Kleve (Alan MacNaughtan). The bloods return later that night and bludgeon Kleve to death. Hans, the son of a convicted murderer, is unjustly accused of the crime, and is later executed. Distraught, Christina drowns herself. Months pass, and the Baron succeeds in placing Hans' soul in Christina's reconstructed body. Now a radiantly beautiful but amnesiac young woman, the revived Christina — urged on by that part of herself possessed by Hans — is driven to seek out the three young men responsible for Kleve's murder, and slay them one-by-one...*

nd God Created Woman, Roger Vadim's notorious Brigitte Bardot vehicle of 1957, had inspired Anthony Hinds to suggest the spoof title *And Then Frankenstein Created Woman* in 1958 as a possible follow-up to *The Revenge of Frankenstein* (an instalment proposed around this time for possible inclusion in the later abandoned *Tales of Frankenstein* television series featured a bewitching but murderous female Creature, too). The notion became sidelined and instead *The Evil of Frankenstein* went into development in mid-1962, performing well in America upon release. Its sequel was initially announced as *Fear of Frankenstein*, but abandoned when Hinds' earlier suggestion was revived and its title "enthusiastically endorsed" by Darryl Zanuck of partners Twentieth Century-Fox.

Intended to be mounted at ABPC Elstree, the film switched to the smaller Bray facility when the former was found to be booked solid. Several revisions were made to the script prior to shooting over the high summer of 1966: scenes showing the Chief

NOW HAMMER HAVE CREATED THE ULTIMATE IN EVIL!

PETER CUSHING · SUSAN DENBERG · THORLEY WALTERS

FRANKENSTEIN CREATED WOMAN

Gaoler gloating over Hans' imminent execution, Christina and Hans' joint funerals, and Anton's bloody demise were trimmed or excised altogether. Hinds' script, also, would have had Christina stabbing herself to death at the climax: ultimately, she drowns herself once more. Playing the film's two tragic, star-crossed lovers were Hammer newcomers Robert Morris (who would play a British Rocket Group scientist in *Quatermass and the Pit*, shot the following year), and Susan Denberg, whom Morris recalls as "very sweet, very friendly. I liked her very much. She was very mixed up with that rather fast Polanski crowd, and also very much into the drug scene. She'd often arrive on set in the mornings somewhat the worse for wear..."Alan MacNaughtan, playing Christina's grumpy father, Kleve, adopted a

Previous page: *Bodysnatchers Frankenstein (Peter Cushing) and Hertz (Thorley Walters) prepare for a long haul.*
Far left: *Bray, 2 August 1966. Cushing helps leading lady Susan Denberg celebrate her twenty-second birthday.*
Left: *Cushing and Walters on Bernard Robinson's laboratory set.*
Below left: *It's alive. And it's beautiful...*

SUSAN DENBERG: CHRISTINA

faux European accent to better match Denberg's natural Austrian vowels. Denberg, however, was later dubbed into a more natural English and MacNaughtan was obliged to revoice himself in consequence! Throughout shooting, the film's leading lady threw herself at the mercy of the company's publicity machine. Denberg was featured in several photocalls and personal appearances around the time, including an on-set photo shoot to mark her twenty-second birthday, and presenting prizes at a go-kart Grand Prix in Battersea Park.

Initially planned as support for the film was Hammer's *Prehistoric Women* (later *Slave Girls*), which was delayed. Instead, *The Mummy's Shroud* took second billing upon its 1967 release. *Films and Filming* drew an analogy between the Baron and Sherlock Holmes, with Hertz as his "Dr Watsonish assistant", and *Variety* noted that "[Peter] Cushing could walk through the Frankenstein part blindfold by now but still treats it as seriously as though he were playing Hamlet."

Frankenstein Created Woman is a grim fairy tale with undertones of both a theological and psychological bent. Acclaimed American director Martin Scorsese selected it as part of a National Film Theatre season of his favourite films in January 1987. "If I single this one out," he remarked, "it's because here they actually isolate the soul, a bright blue shining translucent ball. The implied metaphysics is close to something sublime."

Born Dietlinde Ortrun Zechner on 2 August 1944, model/actress Denberg was brought up in Klagenfurt, an Austrian resort. At eighteen, she left for London, where she worked briefly as an au pair before auditioning for the renowned Bluebell Girls troupe. Touring in America, she signed with Warner Brothers to play a randy German chambermaid in the film *An American Dream*, and featured in an early *Star Trek* episode, 'Mudd's Women'. *Playboy* magazine selected her as its centrefold of August 1966 and soon after she was chosen as Hammer's Christina. Post-*Frankenstein*, however, she became plagued by mental health problems elicited by drug abuse. Recovered, she sold her story to Britain's *News of the World* in November 1969, apparently in anticipation of a comeback that wasn't to be.

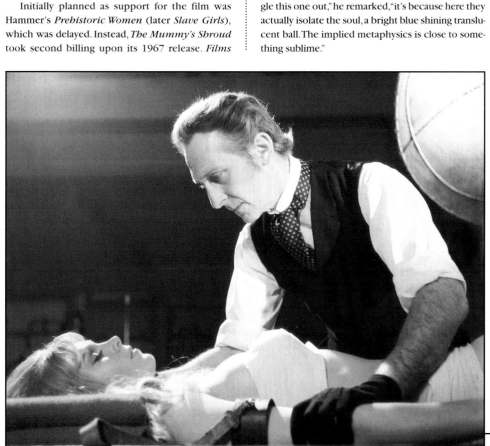

Throughout the fifties and sixties, Exclusive/Hammer successfully exploited actresses ranging from Hy Hazell (in *The Lady Craved Excitement*) and Joan Rice (in the girls in gaol movie *Women Without Men*) through to sexual icons such as Ursula Andress and Raquel Welch. (Even Billie Whitelaw's lingerie was lewdly exposed in posters for the otherwise worthy *Hell is a City*.) The host of graduates from Hammer's very own charm school include names both obscure — and *very* familiar...

DIANA DORS

Proclaiming herself "the only sex symbol Britain has produced since Lady Godiva", Swindon siren Diana Dors — born Diana Fluck — was a RADA-trained Rank protégée. She appeared in two Exclusive/Hammer thrillers: *The Last Page*, playing blackmailing bookshop clerk Ruby Bruce, and *The Saint's Return*, in which, billed as "guest star", she was employed during filming to spice up one scene wearing a strategically-placed bath towel. Diana reversed the trend whereby Hammer backer Robert Lippert shipped his artistes to Britain when she signed a contract with the American impresario and was briefly exported Stateside. In 1955, her role as a condemned killer in *Yield to the Night*

HAMMER GLAMOUR

cemented her status as the 'British Monroe'. Come the seventies, she cropped up in *Nothing But the Night* and the inspired Vincent Price black comedy *Theatre of Blood*. Later a newspaper agony aunt, she died in 1984.

DIANE CILENTO

Fledgling New Guinea-born artiste Diane Cilento made her film début, aged nineteen, as Jeanette in the 1952 Exclusive/Hammer production *Wings of Danger*. Eight years later, having acquired star status via *The Admirable Crichton*, she took the leading role of newly-wed Denise in Hammer's suspenseful 1960 melodrama *The Full Treatment* (aka *Stop Me Before I Kill!*). Shot on location in Cannes, the film concerns the honeymooning Colebys. Following a car crash, husband Alan (Ronald Lewis) develops an impulse to murder his radiant young bride. Oscar-nominated for her performance in *Tom Jones*, Diane played prim schoolteacher Miss Rose opposite Christopher Lee in 1973's *The Wicker Man*, was married to Sean Connery for over ten years, and is the mother of acting son Jason.

SHIRLEY EATON

Likewise, blonde Shirley Eaton is still best known for her Connery connection; in 1964, plastered in gold paint to play the luckless Jill Masterson, she fell victim to Bond villain Auric Goldfinger. Shirley, a former child star who was a seemingly ubiquitous light comedy player throughout the fifties, was third-billed as Jane in Hammer's 1958 all-at-sea burlesque *Further Up the Creek*. She played a still larger part in 1961's *A Weekend With Lulu*. As Deirdre, vivacious girlfriend to roguish Tim (Leslie Phillips), she suffers when mother Irene Handl joins the pair on holiday to prevent any hanky-panky aboard Lulu, an ice-cream van borrowed from Tim's chum (Bob Monkhouse). Noteworthy also for her role in the seminal comedy thriller *What a Carve Up*, Shirley retired from acting shortly after headlining the Fu Manchu spin-off *Sumuru*.

MARIE DEVEREUX

Referring to busty *Stranglers of Bombay* starlet Marie Devereux, Gallic critic "M. Caine" drooled: "[her] stunningly exposed bosom is of quite

demential sumptuousness... [she] contemplates the atrocities with a pleasure so intense (and so evidently erotic) that she glistens with sweat. I am astonished by the presence of this proud figurehead of female sadoscophilia who can have escaped from the scissors of Auntie Censorship only by some miracle..." Surrey model Devereux, Spanish on her mother's side, came to Hammer's attention after appearing briefly in Laverstock Productions' *The Scamp*. She was a harem girl in *I Only Arsked*, the aforementioned torturess in *The Stranglers of Bombay*, a vampirised village girl (albeit with her name incorrectly spelled on the credits) in *The Brides of Dracula*, a Lulubelle in *A Weekend With Lulu* and Maggie in *The Pirates of Blood River*. *Solo* number eight, a fifties glamour magazine devoted entirely to Marie, is, understandably, highly collectable.

STEFANIE POWERS

American Stefania Zofia Federkiewicz, better known as Stefanie Powers, came to attention with her role in *McLintock!*, prior to shooting Hammer's *Fanatic* alongside Hollywood legend Tallulah Bankhead in 1964. Stefanie played Pat, who was imprisoned by Bankhead's matronly religious maniac Mrs Trefoile for daring to become engaged to a man other than Trefoile's deceased son. Throughout 1966, Stefanie appeared on American network television as the eponymous *The Girl From U.N.C.L.E.*, a failed spin-off from the noted spy series. In 1968, she headlined the *Journey to the Unknown* episode 'Jane Brown's Body', in which she gave an impressive performance as a nameless girl who, brought back from the dead following her suicide, relearns her entire identity from absolute scratch. The following year, she virtually reprised her *Fanatic* role in Hammer's *Crescendo*. 1979 saw Powers cast as one of the two husband and wife crimebusters in *Hart to Hart*, the TV series for which she's now best known.

**Principal photography 12 September to
21 October 1966
Released 18 May 1967
Certificate X
Duration 84 mins
Colour
Director John Gilling**

Mezzera, Egypt, 1920: an expedition in search of the fabled tomb of the boy Pharaoh Kab-to-Bey is miss-ing in the desert. Financed by pompous, self-aggrandising nabob Stanley Preston (John Phillips), the party includes archaeologist Sir Basil Walden (André Morell), Preston's son Paul (David Buck) and lin-guist Claire de Sangre (Maggie Kimberley). The team discover an inscription which leads them to the buried sepulchre. However, in underground caverns, their progress is stalled by Hasmid Ali (Roger Delgado), self-proclaimed keeper of the tomb, who warns them entry to the tomb will lead to their deaths. They are joined by a search party led by Preston himself. Inside the tomb, they discover the Pharaoh's remains covered by a sacred shroud upon which are written arcane words of life and death. Back in Mezzera, Sir Basil falls ill. He is confined to an asylum, but escapes into the city streets, where he seeks refuge in the salon of the raddled mystic Haiti (Catherine Lacey). The clairvoyant foresees his doom. Haiti's son, Hasmid, breaks into a temporary museum housing artefacts recovered from the tomb and reads the words of life from the shroud, reanimating the terrible mummified form of Prem (Eddie Powell), Kab-to-Bey's devoted slave. Hasmid sends it out to execute Sir Basil...

he *Mummy's Shroud* was the final feature to be mounted by Hammer at Bray Studios, their home of sixteen years. It featured actress Elizabeth Sellars in a principal role; coincidentally, 1951's *Cloudburst*, Hammer's first Bray feature, was the only other picture made by the company in which Sellars appeared!

This, the third of the company's Egyptology-derived pictures, was scripted by director John Gilling from an outline supplied by executive producer Anthony Hinds. One day was spent on location at a local sandpit, with the remainder of the film being shot at Bray during the autumn of 1966. *She*'s John Richardson was originally cast as Paul Preston, *The Mummy's Shroud*'s heroic young male lead, but late in the day his role passed to David Buck. (Buck also appeared in 'Jane Brown's Body', a *Journey to the Unknown* episode.) Co-star Maggie Kimberley had featured in Gilling's previous picture, *Where the Bullets Fly*. Dickie Owen, the titular fiend in the earlier

Beware the beat of the cloth-wrapped feet!

THE MUMMY'S SHROUD

STARRING ANDRE MORELL · JOHN PHILLIPS · DAVID BUCK and ELIZABETH SELLARS · also starring CATHERINE LACEY · MAGGIE KIMBERLEY
Screenplay by JOHN GILLING · From an original story by JOHN ELDER · Produced by ANTHONY NELSON KEYS · Directed by JOHN GILLING · TECHNICOLOR · RELEASED THROUGH WARNER-PATHÉ

The Curse of the Mummy's Tomb, played the living Prem in flashback, while Hammer stunt man Eddie Powell played Prem's reanimated self — and, in cos-tume, participated in a proposed promotional tie-in for the Milk Marketing Board. Photographs survive detailing the grisly make-up applied to actor Andre Morell to reveal the true extent of Prem's pulping of Sir Basil's head. The gore is missing from the finished print, where Sir Basil's demise is indicated by close-cutting and the judicious application of gruesome sound effects.

The mummy itself was described in Gilling's script not as the wrinkled prune seen in the film but, icono-clastically, as "the perfect semblance of a human face and body. Skin, hair, etc is intact yet so opaque in appearance that one might suspect it could crumble if breathed upon." In the event, the mummy's costume was based on a genuine relic resident in the British Museum's Egypt Rooms of a later, Roman-era body. (It

DANS
LES GRIFFES
DE LA MOMIE

can still be seen today, in room sixty.) Its impressive demise, wherein the creature claws away at its own disintegrating head, was filmed at Les Bowie's Slough studio. It was assistant Ian Scoones' gloved hands that crumbled a dummy wax head filled with fuller's earth, paint dust and a prop skeleton. The effect took weeks of experimentation to achieve. With the completion of the film's final scenes on Friday 21 October 1966, an era came to an end. Hammer realised their long-planned intention to vacate Bray Studios shortly after and, bar special effects photography for *When Dinosaurs Ruled the Earth* and *Moon Zero Two*, no further Hammer product was shot at the facility.

Like *Frankenstein Created Woman*, to which it played as support, *The Mummy's Shroud* premièred in America on 15 March 1967, opening at London's New Victoria on 18 May. Reviews were largely scathing, although several singled out Michael Ripper's Longbarrow as a particularly fine character study.

An accomplished second feature, *The Mummy's Shroud* is pacy enough to sustain its nicely characterised, albeit formulaic, storyline. The well-staged murders perpetrated by Prem are, however, too infrequent a highlight. Unusually for Hammer, the token blonde, Claire, is granted a proper narrative function to perform (her ability to read the "words of death") rather than to be merely lusted after/menaced by the latest nasty. Tellingly, in on-set publicity stills, actress Maggie Kimberley was pictured falling out of her bra while the mummy loomed over her. *Plus ça change...*

Both Hammer's long-term stunt man and Christopher Lee's regular double, ex-despatch rider Eddie Powell's break into films came when, post-demob, he joined Jock Easton's Soho-based Stunt Agency. Later, Roy Ashton noted Powell's physical likeness to Lee and suggested the jobbing stunt man as a suitable double for the company's saturnine star. Thereafter, Powell performed many of Lee's most hazardous sequences: Kharis' drowning in *The Mummy*, the Count's icy immersion in *Dracula Prince of Darkness*. In addition to supervising all action work on films such as *The Devil Rides Out*, Powell also played acting roles for the company: a swarthy Arab no-good in *She*, the Horned Beast itself in *The Devil Rides Out*, The Inquisitor in *The Lost Continent*. His largest role, however, was as revitalised mummy Prem in *The Mummy's Shroud*. During the scene wherein photographic chemicals are hurled at the revenant, Powell came a cropper when he gagged on acid fumes. Married to the company's stalwart wardrobe mistress Rosemary Burrows, Powell's last Hammer feature was *To the Devil a Daughter* in which, set fully alight, he realised Anthony Valentine's brimstone-fuelled demise.

Previous page (left): *André Morell recovers from Sir Basil's bloody, but unseen, demise.*
Previous page (right): *Maggie Kimberley undresses for a revealing publicity shot.*
Below left: *Stanley Preston (John Phillips) dictates his dubious memoirs to put-upon secretary Longbarrow (Michael Ripper).*

**Principal photography 27 February to
25 April 1967
Released 7 November 1967
Certificate X
Duration 97 mins
Colour
Director Roy Ward Baker**

Redevelopment work at Hobbs End underground station is halted by the discovery of unusual skeletal remains. Palaeontologist Dr Matthew Roney (James Donald) believes the bones and skulls prove that humans walked the Earth as long ago as 5,000,000 years. Professor Quatermass (Andrew Keir) is intrigued by the discovery of a giant 'unexploded bomb' alongside the fossils. Working with Roney's assistant, Barbara Judd (Barbara Shelley), Quatermass traces a history of paranormal disturbance in the area back to Roman times. The attempts of Colonel Breen (Julian Glover) to drill through the impenetrable casing of the 'bomb' trigger a disorientating cacophony. Soon after, a segment of the casing melts away to reveal its long-dead alien occupants — the 'imps and demons' of local legend. The decomposing aliens are removed, but the disturbances surrounding the capsule grow in intensity each time it absorbs energy. Evidence of a Martian 'race memory' leads Quatermass to an astonishing conclusion: the skeletons found at Hobbs End belonged to genetically altered apes, released by Martians establishing a colony-by-proxy on Earth. Amid mounting chaos, the glowing capsule drives those with the inherited Martian instincts into a murderous frenzy...

he BBC's version of *Quatermass and the Pit*, starring André Morell as the Professor alongside Anthony Bushell and Michael Ripper, was originally transmitted as a six-part serial between December 1958 and January 1959. The BBC estimated that nearly one in three British adults watched the final episode — confirmation, were any needed, of author Nigel Kneale's profound effect on fifties' television.

Hammer optioned the subject from Kneale in April 1961, but soon encountered difficulties in arousing American co-production interest. Columbia, already unhappy with Hammer's delivery of domestic-appeal subjects like *The Ugly Duckling* and *A Weekend With Lulu* (which in the States carried 'American' sub-titles), declined to add an expensive adaptation of a BBC science fiction serial to the list.

Hammer had already anticipated American confusion by abbreviating the story title to simply *The Pit*, and in September 1961 Nigel Kneale and Anthony Hinds simplified things further by reducing the

£180,000 budget in an attempt to make Columbia reconsider. Kneale's screenplay (entitled *Quatermass and 'The Pit'*, a compromise between his original title and that favoured by Hammer) was finally completed on 26 March 1964 and shifted the original story's action from a building site to a London Underground station. Despite later reservations from Brian Lawrence that the story's ending was "a little complicated", this, along with other essential elements from the BBC teleplay, survived. By now, however, Hammer's relationship with Columbia had cooled and the project was postponed.

JAMES DONALD · ANDREW KEIR · BARBARA SHELLEY · JULIAN GLOVER
QUATERMASS AND THE PIT

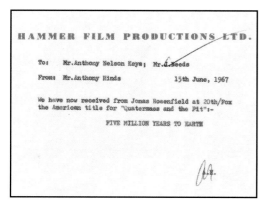
In July 1966, *Quatermass and the Pit* (*The Pit* had been dropped as a title when Hammer were alerted to a short film bearing the same name) was added to the roster of films to be co-produced by Seven Arts and distributed by Twentieth Century-Fox in the States. Hammer had already assured Nigel Kneale that Brian Donlevy would not be asked to play Quatermass again, but had some difficulty in choosing a replacement. James Carreras discussed American actor Van Heflin, while Brian Lawrence favoured Peter Finch. Over the coming months, Kenneth More, Jack Hawkins, Trevor Howard, Harry Andrews, Anthony Quayle and André Morell were all discussed.

Anthony Hinds found choosing a director more straightforward, offering Roy Ward Baker the chance to resume his film career following a lengthy sojourn in television. The cast included Duncan Lamont, who had played Carroon in the BBC's *Quatermass Experiment*, and Julian Glover, who had previously impressed Baker in his 1965 *The Avengers* episode 'Two's a Crowd'. James Donald, who had appeared in *The Bridge on the River Kwai* and *The Great Escape*, was top-billed as Roney. An American in his first two Hammer appearances, the head of the British Experimental Rocket Group became Scottish when Andrew Keir was cast as Quatermass.

Denied space at the busy ABPC Elstree, producer Anthony Nelson Keys took *Quatermass and the Pit* across the road to the MGM Borehamwood studios. A vacant backlot and improved facilities gave the finished film an extra polish, while helping to keep final costs below the £275,000 budget. The adage that 'the investment was on the screen' was especially true here: British distributors ABPC were represented by the ABC television cameras covering the events at Hobbs End, while the underground station set was decorated with posters advertising Hammer's *Dracula Prince of Darkness* and *The Witches*.

Following a special screening and luncheon for distribution executives, held at the Warner Theatre in Leicester Square on 26 September, *Quatermass and the Pit* premièred on 9 November 1967. ABC general release began on 19 November, with *Circus of Fear* as support. In the United States, Twentieth Century-Fox released the film in March 1968 with the thoughtful new title *Five Million Years to Earth*. Less could be said of the American trailer, which promised that "women will be defiled by the invaders from outer space!"

"I was very happy with Andrew Keir and very happy with the film," says Nigel Kneale. "There are, however, a few things that bother me…The special effects in Hammer films were always diabolical." Following *Quatermass and the Pit*, Anthony Hinds approached Kneale for a new instalment in the saga. The fourth story was later developed by the BBC in the early seventies and ultimately produced as *Quatermass* by Euston Films/Thames Television in 1979. John Mills played the Professor. Andrew Keir reprised his portrayal for Kneale's reflective BBC radio serial *The Quatermass Memoirs* in 1996.

Nigel Kneale's philosophical treatise on the duality of Man survives with its ingenuity and Cold War topicality intact. Roy Ward Baker's vigorous direction enriches a challenging storyline, while a fine cast are more than deserving of Kneale's typically detailed character observations. Some variable effects work aside, *Quatermass and the Pit* is a thought-provoking highlight of British exploitation cinema.

BARBARA SHELLEY: BARBARA JUDD

Barbara Shelley made her seventh and final Hammer appearance in *Quatermass and the Pit*. Born in London in 1933, she embarked upon a modelling career in 1951, thereafter making several films in Italy before her English language début in the title role of Alfred Shaughnessy's 1957 chiller *Cat Girl*. Her first Hammer film, the wartime exploitation picture *The Camp on Blood Island*, was produced the same year (she reappeared, albeit in a different role, in the sequel *The Secret of Blood Island* some years later). Shelley fell victim to a preternatural feline once more in *The Shadow of the Cat* and, playing the icy Carla Hoffmann, was possessed by the spirit of *The Gorgon*, working alongside both Peter Cushing and Christopher Lee for the first time. She was enthralled — and enthralling — as the doomed Vanessa in *Rasputin the Mad Monk*, shot immediately after *Dracula Prince of Darkness*. Subsequent to *Quatermass and the Pit*, she turned largely to the stage.

Previous page: Quatermass (Andrew Keir, far right) witnesses the mesmerising power of the alien capsule first hand.
Far left: Quatermass examines one of the decomposing creatures.
Left: Roney (James Donald) prepares to confront the monstrous apparition. A night sky background was matte-ed in 'behind' the crane.

Principal photography 1 May to
10 May 1967, 15 May to 12 July 1967
Released 11 January 1968
Certificate X
Duration 95 mins
Colour
Director Roy Ward Baker

Every year, the one-eyed Mrs Taggart (Bette Davis) gathers her family to celebrate the anniversary of her marriage. The late Mr Taggart is honoured by his sons Henry (James Cossins), Terry (Jack Hedley) and Tom (Christian Roberts), while their waspish mother uses the 'celebration' as an opportunity to nurture their crippling dependence on her. Terry's wife Karen (Sheila Hancock) and Tom's new fiancée Shirley (Elaine Taylor) put up the greatest resistance to Mrs Taggart's vicious psychological warfare, but they are left similarly undermined. Timid bachelor Henry watches from the sidelines, until a shocking discovery by Shirley reveals the compulsive transvestism that keeps him under his mother's thumb. Her other sons have secrets of their own: Terry and Karen are emigrating to Canada, and Tom has made Shirley pregnant. That evening, Henry leaves the house in Terry's car to steal clothing from washing lines. After a bungled getaway, the police find the empty car with a sari, a suspender belt and two pairs of panties on the front seat. As Mrs Taggart threatens to blackmail the innocent Terry into staying in England, a vengeful Tom plans to have sex with Shirley in his mother's bed. Mrs Taggart, however, has anticipated everything...

After *The Nanny*, Jimmy Sangster's wife warned him that if he ever made another Bette Davis picture she would leave the country. Unfortunately, upon completing the script of *The Anniversary*, he discovered that no one else was interested in producing it. "Right on cue, my wife left the country," remembers Sangster. "I got on with the job in hand."

By spring 1966, Twentieth Century-Fox's cut of the gross from *The Nanny* had hit $2,250,000. Seven Arts, Hammer's other American co-production partners during this period, had also fostered an appreciation of Bette Davis: her daughter, Bea, had married into the family of president Eliot Hyman.

Hammer's search for a follow-up to *The Nanny* took them to the West End. Bill MacIlwraith's hit comedy *The Anniversary* was felt to be an obvious vehicle for Bette Davis in Mona Washbourne's role as the manipulative Mrs Taggart. Hammer purchased the film rights in August 1966, and Jimmy Sangster volunteered to write the screenplay the following month. He would ultimately collaborate with an

I Spy
with my little eye
Something
beginning with
SEX...
and I mean to put
a stop to it.

BETTE DAVIS in
THE ANNIVERSARY

Also starring SHEILA HANCOCK JACK HEDLEY JAMES COSSINS and CHRISTIAN ROBERTS and ELAINE TAYLOR

unaccredited Anthony Hinds. Seth Holt was contracted elsewhere, so Sangster approached American Daniel Petrie to direct the film. Petrie had remade Davis' *Dark Victory* as the Susan Hayward vehicle *The Stolen Hours*, relocating the action to contemporary England. His inventive handling of the confined *A Raisin in the Sun* also suggested his experience may be suited to broadening a stage play for the big screen. Unfortunately, Petrie's stipulations didn't meet with Sangster's approval, so he never even got near the great lady. Acclaimed television director Alvin Rakoff was recommended to Sangster, who flew him to Los Angeles for an audition with Bette Davis. Following an initial meeting, Sangster spent two hours with his dubious star, ultimately swaying her by promising that another director could be found if she changed her mind. On 16

February 1967, Sangster telephoned Hammer House with the following message: "Miss Davis has approved Alvin Rakoff... not altogether plain sailing."

On 25 April, Bette Davis arrived in England with companion Violla Rubber. Davis was domiciled in Elstree's The Chantry, a large house near the ABPC studios where filming commenced on 3 May. The cast did not take well to Davis, and the adulation she demanded particularly riled Sheila Hancock. (Their relationship had already been soured by Davis' declaration that she would have preferred *The Nanny*'s Jill Bennett to have played Karen.) A more serious rift soon developed when Davis protested over the television-style techniques employed by Rakoff, who rigidly blocked and marked his actors' moves in advance. On the evening of Monday 8 May, Davis summoned Sangster to her dressing room. Her comments were noted: "If I continue with Rakoff my nerves will not stand it," she said. "I'll be a basket case within a week." Davis demanded that Sangster take over direction of the film. When he declined, Davis refused to continue. The following day, Rakoff shot around Davis' absence while executive producer Anthony Hinds accompanied Sangster on a visit to The Chantry. Davis refused to budge, and at lunchtime on 10 May filming ground to a halt.

Sangster was left reeling from Davis' misinterpretation of his original offer to replace the film's director ("nobody could assume I was talking about a time when we were twenty-five per cent into the picture"), while Anthony Hinds cabled Seven Arts with an anguished "What a life." They nevertheless moved quickly to minimise the dormant film's overspend. Rakoff was paid in full and Roy Ward Baker was recruited to replace him, mere days after completing *Quatermass and the Pit*. Baker immediately

decided to remount the film from scratch. As a safeguard against future controversy over the extent of his contribution to the picture (not to mention Hammer's notorious cost-cutting reputation), he ordered that the wooden staircase dominating ABPC's stage four be re-constructed in a different shape, thus rendering the existing footage incongruous. The crew, meanwhile, were put to work shooting 'artistes tests' for *The Vengeance of She*. *The Anniversary* resumed filming on 15 May, and proceeded uncomfortably until 12 July. Location work took place inside the florist's on Borehamwood's Shenley Road, and outside The Chantry, which doubled as the exterior of Mrs Taggart's house. By the time the film opened at London's Rialto on Thursday 11 January 1968, the coffers of BD Productions had been swelled by Bette Davis' hefty salary of £71,429 (plus expenses).

The Anniversary commenced a highly successful circuit release on 18 February, supported by *The Night Caller*, a low budget science fiction thriller directed by Hammer regular John Gilling. *The Anniversary* was released on 7 February in America, where it received a mixed reception. "It all reminds one of a love scene in a funeral parlour," claimed *Variety*. The harshest critic of all was Alvin Rakoff, who later dismissed *The Anniversary* as "a mess of a film built around Davis' foolish, overbaked posturings and camera-hoggings."

Bette Davis' eminent bankability convinced both Sangster and Hammer that it would be worth enduring a third collaboration, but costs proved prohibitive. Perhaps it was just as well: *The Anniversary* is an exhausting affair, Davis' dynamic central performance failing to lift the film above its all-too-obvious origins.

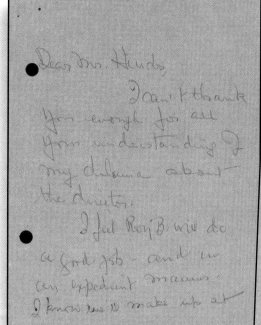

Previous page: *Mrs Taggart (Bette Davis) toasts her late husband. Shirley (Elaine Taylor), Tom (Christian Roberts), Terry (Jack Hedley), and Karen (Sheila Hancock) endure the ritual.*
Above: *'Roy B' was an old acquaintance of 'Bette D', and the star readily agreed to his appointment as stand-in director. The above note must have come as a relief to executive producer Anthony Hinds.*
Left: *The strained atmosphere was briefly lifted by Bette Davis' Independence Day celebrations on 4 July 1967. Roy Ward Baker admires another great performance.*

**Principal photography 7 August to
29 September 1967
Released 7 July 1968
Certificate X
Duration 95 mins
Colour
Director Terence Fisher**

Rural England: the Duc de Richleau (Christopher Lee) and Rex Van Ryn (Leon Greene) visit their protégé Simon (Patrick Mower) to discover he is about to host a meeting of his thirteen-member astronomical society. The Duc discovers that the society is a cover for a Devil-worshipping sect presided over by the powerful Mocata (Charles Gray). The Duc takes Simon back to his house in a bid to free him of Mocata's influence. Simon is compelled to escape and, together with another novice, Tanith (Niké Arrighi), falls back into Mocata's clutches. Simon and Tanith attend a woodland Black Mass and are prepared for their re-baptism into evil. Mocata summons the Goat of Mendes — the Devil himself — before Rex and the Duc sabotage the ceremony, taking Simon and Tanith to a house owned by Richard and Marie Eaton (Paul Eddington and Sarah Lawson). Nowhere, however, is safe from Mocata's omnipresent magic. Inside the house, the Duc draws a holy circle on the floor to repel the terrifying apparitions conjured to overwhelm them. A giant tarantula, and then the Angel of Death, threaten the circle's boundaries. During the battle of nerves, Tanith is killed and Peggy (Rosalyn Landor), the Eatons' young daughter, is taken to be sacrificed by Mocata's Satanists...

ince September 1963, the film rights to three of Dennis Wheatley's bestsellers — *The Devil Rides Out*, *The Satanist* and *To the Devil a Daughter* — had been with the production services company Michael Stainer-Hutchins and Peter Daw Ltd. In February 1964, Peter Daw told *Kinematograph Weekly*: "We formed our company recently to explore the field of options on neglected properties and finding financial backing for them, and also to be associated with the productions ourselves." In November 1963, Daw and Stainer-Hutchins became associated with Hammer when James Carreras acted on Christopher Lee's advice and optioned all three properties. A persuasive story outline had already been prepared: "We see Satanists at work in the City of London... a midnight orgy on the plains of Salisbury... a ceremony of purification among the ruins of the oldest temple in Britain, the fabulous Stonehenge... and meet the infamous 'Beast' in his luxurious Temple of the Obscene,

deep in the slums of dockland."

Despite reservations about the "very boring" books of Dennis Wheatley, Anthony Hinds commissioned American writer John Hunter (whose association with Hinds dated back to the Exclusive/Hammer thriller *The Rossiter Case*, produced in 1950) to adapt *The Devil Rides Out*. Hunter was contracted on 26 January 1964 but, ironically, Hinds rejected his first draft on the grounds that it was "far too English." Like many of Hammer's projects of the time, *The Devil Rides Out* was offered to Universal for first refusal and therefore it had to appeal to the American market. In September 1964, Richard Matheson was commissioned to follow up *Fanatic* with a new take on *The Devil Rides Out*.

Concerns over the Satanism highlighted by the story may have delayed the film's development. In assessing Nigel Kneale's script of *The Devil's Own* (aka *The Witches*) in 1965, the BBFC's John Trevelyan had warned that "we would not be willing to accept any misuse of Christian emblems or any parodies of Christian prayer." *The Witches* ultimately gave the BBFC little cause for concern (on those grounds, at least), but in *The Devil Rides Out* Hammer were exploring new, more explicit, territory.

By summer 1966, Seven Arts, Twentieth Century-Fox and ABPC had been convinced and pre-production began in earnest. As repayment for the role he'd played in bringing *The Devil Rides Out* to the screen, Dennis Wheatley urged Hammer to cast Christopher Lee against type as the Duc de Richleau. After initially considering *Goldfinger* villain Gert Frobe for the role of Mocata, Hinds opted for Charles Gray, who himself was between Bond appearances in *You Only Live Twice* and *Diamonds are Forever*. Fresh from appearing as Little John in Hammer's *A Challenge for Robin Hood*, Leon Greene joined the cast as Rex. He would be dubbed by Patrick Allen in the finished print.

Following *Quatermass and the Pit*, producer Anthony Nelson Keys favoured returning to MGM Borehamwood for *The Devil Rides Out*. Hammer, however, were contractually obliged to use ABPC Elstree, where Terence Fisher began shooting on stages eight and nine during August. On 15 September, a delighted Mr and Mrs Wheatley were shown around the sets of *The Devil Rides Out* and *The Lost Continent*, a large-scale fantasy based on another Wheatley novel, *Uncharted Seas*.

When it was all over, an exhausted Christopher Lee reported back to his fan club members: "I finished *The Devil Rides Out* about two weeks ago, after five extremely unpleasant nights in the rain and damp in the woods near Pinewood Studios...I have high hopes

for this film, and it will prove, once and for all, that I can be accepted in a completely normal role."

Michael Stainer-Hutchins and Peter Daw remained attached to *The Devil Rides Out* as unaccredited associate producers. Stainer-Hutchins also supervised the lengthy special effects photography, which caused considerable headaches for Anthony Hinds. Other problems became apparent on viewing the first rough cut: "It was terrible!" remembers Hinds. "However, with a bit of revoicing, some minor editing and a good meaty score, it really turned out to be quite good."

Across the Atlantic, Hammer's partners were less enthusiastic. The opinions of Joseph Sugar, the executive vice-president of Warner Bros-Seven Arts (Eliot Hyman had, by now, bought out Jack Warner), counted for a lot and he was deeply concerned about Hammer's latest offering. "Joe... seems to think that *The Devil Rides Out* is a Western," read the news, "and he thinks the budget of £285,000 is too much for a Western."

Upon its July 1968 release, *The Devil Rides Out* was hailed as a return to form by impressed critics. In the United States, however, disappointment with *The Devil's Bride* (as the 'Western' had been retitled) and *The Lost Continent* precipitated Fox's withdrawal from future co-productions. Although Warner Bros-Seven Arts were growing similarly uneasy, Kenneth Hyman stayed loyal to James Carreras and Hammer's last link with an American major stayed open for a while longer.

As a finely crafted Hammer horror, redolent of Terence Fisher's Gothics from the late fifties, *The Devil Rides Out* seems little-compromised by concessions made to appease the BBFC. While perhaps too dated to appeal to American audiences of the time, the film is now regarded as a milestone in the careers of Terence Fisher and Christopher Lee.

Previous page: *Marie Eaton (Sarah Lawson), the Duc de Richleau (Christopher Lee) and Richard Eaton (Paul Eddington) watch as Mocata prepares to sacrice Peggy's soul to the "king of death"...*
Above left: *The hypnotic Mocata (Charles Gray).*
Above right: *Marie, Richard, the Duc and Simon (Patrick Mower) defend themselves from Mocata's dark forces.*
Below: *The cover of Hammer's original story outline, prepared in 1963.*

DRACULA HAS RISEN FROM THE GRAVE

**Principal photography 22 April to
4 June 1968
Released 7 November 1968
Certificate X
Duration 92 mins
Colour
Director Freddie Francis**

All is not well in a tiny village in the European province of Keinenburg. A year after Dracula — the vampiric malefactor who'd killed a girl in the local church — is destroyed, Catholic Monsignor Ernst Muller (Rupert Davies) visits the hamlet to discover that its peasant folk will no longer go to Mass, for the shadow of Dracula's castle touches the church in the evenings. Alongside the village's craven Priest (Ewan Hooper), the Monsignor hikes to Dracula's mountainside castle, where he performs an exorcism, sealing the castle doors with a huge and ornate Holy cross. A storm breaks, however, and the Priest tumbles down a rocky outcrop, cracking both his head and the surface of a frozen river. Beneath the ice lies the body of Count Dracula (Christopher Lee), and blood from the Priest's wound drips onto the vampire's lips, reviving him. Having enslaved the Priest to his will, Dracula follows the Monsignor's trail home to the town of Keinenburg, where Muller lives with both his sister (Marion Mathie) and his daughter-in-law, Maria (Veronica Carlson). The pretty Maria is beloved to atheist Paul (Barry Andrews), who works at the Café Johann. Dracula attacks the Café's brassy barmaid Zena (Barbara Ewing) and, with her in his thrall, has his coffin installed in the bar's dingy cellars — the closer to Maria, upon whom the vampire will feed, thus revenging the Monsignor's sanctification of his evil house...

With Twentieth Century-Fox now out of the picture, Hammer's new co-production deal with Warner Bros-Seven Arts was launched with *Dracula Has Risen From the Grave*. A pre-sales brochure had been prepared by August 1967 — before writer Anthony Hinds had even completed a plot synopsis! — and the film announced to the trade press in mid-February 1968.

Hammer's second *Dracula* sequel proper was being readied to shoot for six weeks from 18 March 1968 when scheduled director Terence Fisher was knocked down in a road accident. His leg broken, Fisher deferred to Freddie Francis, fresh from shooting Amicus' *Torture Garden* at Bray. Francis found himself plunged into a series of negotiations with Christopher Lee, upon whose appearance the film had been pre-sold to the American distributor. Lee, however, had made no such commitment. After Lee had shared "a great deal of slightly hysterical and acrimonious discussions", he allowed himself to be

persuaded by James Carreras.

Although wary of Zena's apparently sexual infatuation with the Count, the BBFC objected only to scenes of the Priest chopping up Zena's body with an axe, which were amended to have her corpse simply burned in the bakery ovens. Early scripts had named Maria as 'Gisela', and the name was eventually given to the hapless girl found suspended in the church bell at the outset and later exhumed by the Priest. Peter Noble, London correspondent for *The Hollywood Reporter*, noted twenty-three year-old Veronica Carlson's casting as Maria in rabid style: "Veronica, like Hammer's previous discoveries, Ursula Andress and Olinka Berova, is blonde, photogenic and stacked...And under contract to Hammer...

(And engaged!)." Bit-part actress Carlson's bikini-clad appearance in a tabloid newspaper had drawn her to the company's attention; she went on to make two further Hammer horrors. Carrie Baker, playing the later-exhumed 'Dead Girl in Bell', was paid £25 per day — bar those spent in the coffin, for which her rate was reduced to a mere £15.

On 22 April, one month later than planned, *Dracula Has Risen From the Grave* went before the cameras at Pinewood Studios. Location work was completed towards the end of May at both Black Park and on the slopes of Box Hill, Surrey (in post-production, the Box Hill exteriors were considerably enhanced by the addition of Dracula's towering castle courtesy of Shepperton-based matte artist Peter Melrose). Unusually, Francis and director of photography Arthur Grant elected to use amber filters to colour Dracula's appearances in nightmarish hues.

The film wrapped on 4 June, two days over schedule and only a few thousand pounds over budget, and premièred at the New Victoria in early November. Actor Ewan Hooper was astonished to discover that his voice had been overdubbed throughout. The 30 November edition of *Kinematograph Weekly* noted that the picture had broken the ABC chain's record Sunday take. ABC chief executive Robert Clark announced that very week that Hammer had another Dracula in pre-production.

A minor triumph of style over content, *Dracula Has Risen From the Grave* succeeds by virtue of Francis' adventurous direction, the director extracting from John Elder's formulaic screenplay a number of subtextual ironies around religious themes (Paul's Act Three conversion, Dracula impaled on a giant cross). Most remarkable, however, is the scene where the atheist Paul's staking of the vampire fails due to his lack of faith. Lee was appalled by this uncharacteristically daring act of iconoclasm, but it remains the film's most striking scene.

In April 1968, it was announced that Hammer Film Productions had become one of eighty-five companies to be garlanded with the Queen's Award to Industry for that year, since over the three years previous, the company's films had earned just under £3 million in overseas markets. James Carreras had noted Hammer's export achievements when applying for the Award in October 1967. "This company has made a very real and substantial contribution to the United Kingdom's balance of payments," he'd urged. At Hammer House, telegrams of congratulation were received from, among others, Earl Mountbatten, Peter Cushing, cameraman/scriptwriter Peter Bryan, Exclusive staffer Henry Halsted, Charlie Drake, and the BBFC's John Trevelyan. The Award was formally presented to the company on Wednesday 29 May on the Pinewood sets of *Dracula Has Risen From the Grave* by Brigadier Sir Henry Floyd, Lord Lieutenant of the County of Buckingham. It was received by long-standing construction manager Arthur Banks on behalf of the assembled Hammer representatives, including Cushing, the *Dracula* cast and crew, and most of the company's executive Wardour Street staff. Shot that morning was Dracula's demise and, having witnessed a gored-up Lee writhing around with a huge prop cross apparently harpooned through his torso, the Lord Lieutenant began his pre-prepared speech thus: "I know that you have had great success with what are termed 'horror films', but I was glad to learn from your Chairman that the word 'horror' does not include scenes of actual personal violence..."

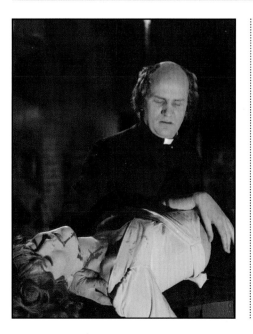

Previous page: *The infamous staking scene –* "I thought it was quite wrong," *says Christopher Lee, who concedes that* "the audience at the time thought it was stunning."

Previous page: *The poster image by artist Tom Chantrell was, incredibly, a customised self-portrait.*

Above: *James Carreras, Arthur Banks, Peter Cushing, Christopher Lee and Anthony Hinds at Pinewood Studios.*

Above left: *For whom the bell tolls – the hapless Carrie Baker.*

Left: *The Priest (Ewan Hooper) carries Zena (Barbara Ewing) to a less than conventional cremation.*

JOURNEY TO THE UNKNOWN

On Tuesday 2 April 1968, at London's Dorchester Hotel, James Carreras hosted a press reception to announce a deal concluded between Hammer, Twentieth Century-Fox and America's ABC TV. Having spent years trying to break into the small screen, Hammer was to produce its first television series.

a "possible TV series based on horror product" had been discussed at a company meeting of 3 May 1967. James Carreras was due to visit New York with the notion of hiring out Bray Studios to Fox for both feature production and a television series based on *One Million Years B.C.*. By 8 June, the "possible fifty-two minute series of horror-type product" bore a provisional title: *Fright Hour*. Come 14 February 1968, prior to securing the necessary support from an American network, Fox had amended both the series format and provisional title (now *Tales of the Unknown*).

The powerful ABC network eventually agreed to take the series. Fox appointed Joan Harrison its executive producer (she fulfilled this function on all bar three of the seventeen episodes). The formidable Harrison had started her career as a screenwriter and was formerly assistant to Alfred Hitchcock, her credits including *Jamaica Inn*, *Rebecca* and *Foreign Correspondent*. Between 1955 and 1963, she'd produced the acclaimed anthology series *Alfred Hitchcock Presents*. Her pedigree, therefore, was undeniable, as was that of *Alfred Hitchcock Presents/Psycho* writer Robert Bloch, who'd supply two scripts for *Journey*

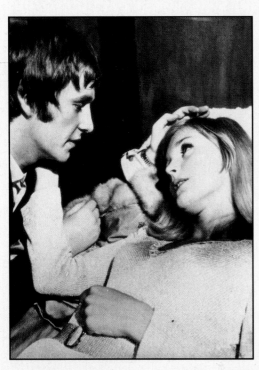

to the Unknown, as the series was known by the time of its press launch. A reluctant Hinds was appointed as line producer, and Hammer stalwarts James Needs and Philip Martell the series' supervising editor and musical supervisor respectively. Such was the draw of Hammer and Harrison that, late in June, it was announced that British regional broadcaster London Weekend Television had bought all seventeen episodes of Fox's "collection of psychological suspense dramas" sight unseen.

Journey to the Unknown was largely produced by two units of technicians, units A and B, working on alternate episodes between 24 May and 27 November 1968 at the MGM studios in Borehamwood. A third unit, C, was added later — and one episode, 'The Madison Equation', was shot in association with Intertel, a television facilities rental company established by entrepreneur Michael Style. Together with his production partner Harry Fine, Style would become further entangled with Hammer, as would a number of other *Journey to the Unknown* contributors: directors Alan Gibson and Peter Sasdy; composer Harry Robinson; plus actors Anthony Corlan, Barbara Jefford, Damian Thomas and Dennis Waterman. Certain episodes also employed a number of Hammer alumni: directors Roy Ward Baker and Don Chaffey; writer Richard Matheson; director of photography Moray Grant; and actors Patrick Allen, Jane Asher, Ann Bell, David Buck, Adrienne Corri, Allan Cuthbertson, Michael Gough, Catherine Lacey, Suzanna Leigh, Alan MacNaughtan, Marne Maitland, Stefanie Powers, Michael Ripper and Melissa Stribling. (Unsurprisingly, most episodes headlined artistes more familiar to American audiences: Barbara Bel Geddes, Joseph Cotten, Roddy McDowall and Vera Miles.) Each instalment was shot over roughly two weeks and, in total, the series cost £1,305,855 to produce.

Journey to the Unknown premièred on ABC on Thursday 26 September 1968 with 'Eve', in which a lovelorn store assistant, Albert (Dennis Waterman), fantasises that a wax shop-window mannequin he's named Eve (Carol Lynley) comes to life and falls in love with him. The obsessed Albert murders his boss, Mr Royal (Michael Gough), when the latter threatens to have Eve melted down to make way for new models — and Albert and Eve go on the run... The episode's bizarre open ending was to prove typical: Albert, set upon by two bikers, is dying and the camera cuts to the again immobile Eve, a tear trickling down its cheek. The *New York Daily News* noted 'Eve' to be "an engrossing fantasy with subtle overtones."

In Britain, *Journey to the Unknown* was deprioritised by many ITV regions, none of which had a vested interest in the independently-produced show. First broadcast by LWT beginning in November, it aired patchily around the country over the next few years, and in no coherent order.

The series exacted a heavy toll on Hammer. Not only would its arduous post-production process lead long-term supervising editor James Needs to quit (he'd only cut occasional films for the company thereafter), it was also a contributory factor in Anthony Hinds' later decision to resign his directorship. "I wasn't anti-television, but I thought I was a bit old for starting again," he said, in an interview with Tony Earnshaw. "They quite sensibly said they wanted an American producer, Joan Harrison — and in fact I found myself working as a production manager under her which, if you've been producing your own films for fifteen years, you don't enjoy very much."

Journey to the Unknown has much to commend it, and its eerie title sequence, set in a deserted fairground, is certainly memorable. Several instalments are especially noteworthy: 'The New People', in which an elite of sophisticates enjoy murderous pastimes; 'Somewhere in a Crowd', wherein a TV reporter becomes aware that the same five disparate individuals seem to be present at a series of unexpected catastrophes; 'Jane Brown's Body', in which the tragic past of a suicidal young woman is uncovered when she is brought back from the dead by an experimenting doctor; the demented 'The Last Visitor', set in a seaside boarding-house; Bloch's 'The Indian Spirit Guide', a spooky drama concerning ersatz clairvoyants; and 'Matakitas is Coming', a taut and worrying thriller set entirely in a library which, after closing hours, shifts backwards in time to ensure the reincarnation of a girl sacrificed to the Devil in 1927.

Journey to the Unknown forges a bond between the contemporary settings and stylings of Hammer's suspense thrillers and the Gothic themes of their horror work to often considerable effect. Although much overshadowed by the company's later, and more widely-seen, television efforts, the series merits greater attention than it is usually awarded.

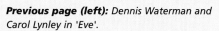

Previous page (left): Dennis Waterman and Carol Lynley in 'Eve'.
Previous page (right): Roddy McDowall as Rollo Verdew in the conspiracy thriller 'The Killing Bottle'.
Above: Tom Adams in director Roy Ward Baker's episode 'The Indian Spirit Guide'.
Left: Jane Asher, who had made a brief unaccredited appearance in The Quatermass Xperiment, starred in 'Somewhere in a Crowd'. The episode was directed by Alan Gibson.

FRANKENSTEIN MUST BE DESTROYED

Principal photography 13 January to
26 February 1969
Released 22 May 1969
Certificate X
Duration 97 mins
Colour
Director Terence Fisher

Evading arrest by Inspector Frisch (Thorley Walters) and his policemen, Baron Frankenstein (Peter Cushing) goes to ground at a boarding-house run by Anna Spengler (Veronica Carlson). Anna's mother is sick, and her escalating nursing fees are met by Karl (Simon Ward), a doctor at the local asylum. Karl raises the money on Anna's behalf by stealing drugs from the asylum and selling them on the black market. A discarded packet of cocaine incriminates the couple to Frankenstein, who blackmails them into assisting in his experiments. Karl reluctantly helps Frankenstein liberate the insane genius Dr Brandt (George Pravda) from his cell. Brandt developed a successful technique to 'freeze' human brains, thus preserving their knowledge beyond the body's death, just before he went mad. The Baron intends restoring Brandt's sanity and learning his secrets, but is frustrated to learn that the strain of the kidnap has left Brandt's life hanging by a thread. Frankenstein transplants Brandt's brain into the body of asylum surgeon Professor Richter (Freddie Jones). The distraught Karl and Anna try to escape Frankenstein's clutches, while Brandt's widow (Maxine Audley) joins the police investigations. Brandt awakes in Richter's body, and decides that Frankenstein must die for his crimes...

nthony Hinds began scripting *Frankenstein Must Be Destroyed* in October 1967, a mere four months after the release of *Frankenstein Created Woman*. When financial backing threatened to stall progress, Hinds suggested the film could be sandwiched between *Dracula Has Risen From the Grave* and suspense thriller *The Claw* in an economical back-to-back package produced by Anthony Nelson Keys. By February 1968, however, co-finance had been secured from Warner Bros-Seven Arts and Terence Fisher assigned to direct. The production now only awaited a script...

Frankenstein Must Be Destroyed came at a bad time for Hinds, whose duties were becoming increasingly dominated by *Journey to the Unknown*. Salvation was found in two unlikely sources: Anthony Nelson Keys and prolific Hammer assistant director Bert Batt collaborated on a new storyline. Their inventive pitch, which addressed topical concerns about drug abuse alongside the more familiar examination of transplant ethics, was

formally commissioned on 17 June. Batt completed the shooting script on 9 December, although he was also on hand throughout the filming of *Frankenstein Must Be Destroyed* (in his capacity as assistant director) to help with the considerable additions needed to the screenplay.

The production of *Frankenstein Must Be Destroyed* at ABPC Elstree marked the final engagement for supervising art director Bernard Robinson. The architects' drawings Frankenstein uses to plan Brandt's kidnap are typical of Robinson's attention to detail. Although never visible on screen, copy on the drawings credits: "Finkelberg & Haupstraum Architects... This building erected in the grounds of the manor of the Baskervilles of stone from the quarry at Frankheim before the fall of the previous family." Robinson died on 2 March 1970. He proved irreplaceable.

FRANKENSTEIN MUST BE DESTROYED!

THE SCREEN'S MOST FANTASTIC FIEND
...AND HAMMER SAY SO!

PETER CUSHING
SIMON WARD · VERONICA CARLSON · THORLEY WALTERS · FREDDIE JONES · MAXINE AUDLEY

Hammer continued to promote Veronica Carlson by casting her as Anna Spengler, whose lover, Karl, was played by fresh-faced RADA graduate Simon Ward in his first film. Terence Fisher was especially pleased with his choice of actor for Richter/Brandt: "Freddie Jones plays a man who has his brain transplanted to a new body by Frankenstein, and he goes to visit his wife who fails to recognise him and rejects him," he recalled for *Cinefantastique*. "I loved that subject, which I thought was a most difficult one to portray, and I thought about that film

more than any other I've done because of this element."

In late February, James Carreras made one of his rare studio visits and decided to throw his weight around. At his crude insistence, a hastily written sequence where Frankenstein apparently rapes Anna (while Karl is conveniently away at the asylum) was instigated. "They were trying to work out how to tear my night-gown off without exposing me, because there was no nudity in my contract," remembers Veronica Carlson. "Every alternative was more vulgar than the last, and it was just the most horrendous thing... Terry [Fisher] cut it short. He said, 'Cut! That's enough,' and he just turned away... Peter and I just stayed there and held on to each other." Ironically, the scene was excised from the American print.

Following a snowfall that threatened continuity problems during location shooting, *Frankenstein Must Be Destroyed* was completed slightly over budget at £186,331. After playing for two weeks at the Warner Theatre in the West End to only fair business, the film commenced ABC general release on 8 June.

Old meets new in this spiral of unrelenting despair — Thorley Walters' bumbling policeman is a trapping from fifties Hammer, and it seems almost cruel to pit him against the "scientist, surgeon, madman, murderer!" described in the film's trailer. Fisher expertly orchestrates such knife-edge highlights as the kidnap of Brandt, and the sequence where a burst water main expels a buried corpse. The film's most haunting element, however, is Freddie Jones' anguished performance as Brandt/Richter, surely the most sympathetic 'creature' in the entire series.

ANTHONY NELSON KEYS: PRODUCER/STORYLINE

Hammer publicity notes of 1964 describe Anthony Nelson Keys as "Quicksilverish, dapper, and a fellow of infinite jest... There isn't a job in film-making — from focus-pulling to sound recording — that he didn't learn the hard way: by actually doing it." Keys was the son of stage comedian Nelson Keys and belonged to a talented family. Two of his brothers, Basil Keys and John Paddy Carstairs, also worked for Hammer. *The Steel Bayonet*, produced in 1956, began Keys' regular association with Hammer. In 1959, he was appointed general manager of Bray Studios; in 1964, alongside executives from co-owners Columbia and ABPC, he represented Hammer on a three-man committee established to keep the facility busy. Later, Keys formed Charlemagne Productions with Christopher Lee and made *Nothing But the Night* for Rank in 1972. Following establishing work for Hammer on *To the Devil a Daughter*, Keys devoted his time to the Richmond and Twickenham Golf Club. He died, apparently during a round, in 1984. "They've all been satisfying," he reflected, when asked about his films in 1972. "I won't say I haven't been disappointed in some things, but there has been such variety."

Previous page: Camera operator Neil Binney captures Baron Frankenstein (Peter Cushing), scythe in hand.
Left: Ella Brandt (Maxine Audley) is confronted by her late husband (Freddie Jones).

M O O N   Z E R O   T W O

Principal photography 31 March to
10 June 1969
Released 26 October 1969
Certificate U
Duration 100 mins
Colour
Director Roy Ward Baker

In the year 2021, pioneering space pilot Bill Kemp (James Olson) and his engineer Karminski (Ori Levy) make a dangerous living salvaging damaged satellites in their dilapidated ferry ship, Moon 02. At Moon City, Bill meets Clementine Taplin (Catherina Von Schell), who asks him for help in finding her missing brother Wally. The sinister J.J. Hubbard (Warren Mitchell) interrupts a game of Moonopoly to tell Bill about a huge asteroid — 6,000 tons of gemstone sapphire — that is about to make its closest approach to the moon since 1998. He makes Bill an offer he can't refuse: a brand new space ferry in return for help in 'piloting' the sapphire to the far side of the moon. Such asteroid rustling is highly illegal, but Bill is tempted and the first part of the plan is carried out. At the Lazy 'B' Saloon, Hubbard's bodyguard Harry (Bernard Bresslaw) leans on Bill to dissuade him from helping Clementine find her brother. Bill forcefully resists the pressure. Sharing a Moon-Bug, Bill and Clementine make the arduous journey to Wally's last-known whereabouts, only to find him dead inside his sabotaged space suit. Escaping an ambush, Bill and Clementine discover that Wally was prospecting at the exact spot where Hubbard intends to crash-land the asteroid...

"We are in space. Against the stars drifts a communications satellite; about three feet in diameter, sprouting aerials, but silent. From behind and beyond appears a spaceship. A small one, some forty feet long and ten feet in diameter, with three engines — which can fire forwards or backwards — just ahead of its middle and three landing pads on widespread struts at its tail. But it is obviously an old ship: dented and battered, scratched and patched. Its registration letters are half flaked away but still readable: MOON 02."

So began a lengthy story outline by Gavin Lyall, Frank Hardman and Martin Davison dated 2 May 1967. Negotiations to buy the screen rights to *Moon Zero Two* continued throughout May – Hammer had joined the space race to capitalise on NASA's imminent moon landing, and planned to spend £500,000 to do it in style. Raising the American part of that budget was initially problematic, Twentieth Century-Fox showing James Carreras the door when he took the idea to New York. However, Kenneth Hyman of War-

ner Bros-Seven Arts was more accommodating. Jimmy Sangster was pencilled in to both produce and write the original screenplay early in 1968. In light of his technical abilities and *Quatermass* experience, Roy Ward Baker was nominated as director.

While other non-horror subjects like *Mistress of the Seas*, *The Bride of Newgate Jail* and *Black Beauty* fell by the wayside in the late sixties, interest in *Moon Zero Two* was maintained by mounting speculation over the approaching Apollo mission. Seemingly unfazed by the release of the groundbreaking *2001* in 1968, Hammer launched their own space odyssey with special effects photography at ABPC Elstree and Bray Studios early in 1968. Kubrick had taken three years to make *2001*; *Moon Zero Two* would take just over three months.

Aware that the unusually high budget would still

not satisfy the subject's demands, Roy Ward Baker had suggested shooting certain space sequences at an aircraft hangar in Cardington, Cambridgeshire. His request was denied. "It was hopeless," he remembers. "We tried to fly people on wires and all this kind of stuff, but you need elaborate technical apparatus which requires large, silent studios... It never got to work."

Today's Cinema's gossip girl Ronnie Cowan visited ABPC Elstree in April: "I had a 'ball'! The Hammer/Warner Bros-Seven Arts *Moon Zero Two* set is something else. The story deals with everyday life on the moon in the year 2021. The frontier days when moonmen were he-men and anyone could stake a claim if they didn't float off into space first. With producer Michael Carreras describing it as a Space Western, I suggested retitling it 'High Moon'. I got a dirty look, well it was only a thought!"

During post-production, Michael Carreras (who had ultimately written the final shooting script as well as producing the film) was buzzing with ideas.

He proposed that, if *Moon Zero Two* was a hit, then both a television series and a sequel should be prepared. He set to work on a follow-up in June, while in July his enthusiasm clearly caught on at Warner Bros-Seven Arts, who planned to issue an LP of Don Ellis' groovy score. The plug was pulled on all these plans when dismal box-office receipts indicated that the public took the moon rather more seriously than Hammer had anticipated. Michael's follow-up screenplay, rather unfortunately titled *Disaster in Space*, was never filmed.

Moon Zero Two's many highlights include Stokes Cartoons' brilliant title sequence, the no-gravity barroom brawl and dialogue like, "That monument there is where Neil Armstrong landed back in 1969." The whole tongue-in-cheek exercise uncannily predicts the kitsch psychedelia of Gerry Anderson's TV series *UFO* and *Space: 1999*, the latter also starring Catherina Von Schell. An absolute must for lava-lamp lovers everywhere, *Moon Zero Two* is so far out it's very nearly in.

Born in 1916, Roy Baker began his career at Gainsborough Studios before making his directorial début with the John Mills film *The October Man* in 1947. After working in Hollywood in the early fifties, during which time he directed Richard Widmark and Marilyn Monroe in *Don't Bother to Knock*, Baker made his best-remembered films at Rank: *The One That Got Away* and the *Titanic* drama *A Night to Remember*. From *Quatermass and the Pit* on, he was credited as Roy Ward Baker, since sound editor Roy Baker had recently moved into the same tax bracket, causing much confusion at the Inland Revenue. One of Hammer's most versatile talents, Baker directed such diverse pictures as *The Anniversary*, *Moon Zero Two* and *The Legend of the 7 Golden Vampires*. In the early seventies, he inherited Freddie Francis' mantle of Amicus' 'house director', making *Asylum*, *And Now the Screaming Starts!* and *Vault of Horror*. *The Monster Club*, which Baker directed for Amicus' Milton Subotsky, brought his association with the genre to an end in 1980.

TASTE THE BLOOD OF DRACULA

Principal photography 27 October to
5 December 1969
Released 7 May 1970
Certificate X
Duration 95 mins
Colour
Director Peter Sasdy

Every month, Hargood (Geoffrey Keen) leaves his wife and daughter, ostensibly to conduct charitable work in the East End. In reality, he joins fellow hedonists Paxton (Peter Sallis) and Secker (John Carson) in the pursuit of illicit thrills. At a brothel run by the effeminate Felix (Russell Hunter), Hargood has his whore taken from him by the contemptuous Lord Courtley (Ralph Bates), a felon known to dabble in black magic. Courtley takes the three men to visit antiques dealer Weller (Roy Kinnear), who sells them the clasp, the ring, the cloak and the powdered blood of Count Dracula. In a deconsecrated church, Courtley mixes his own blood with the powder in a ceremony intended to summon the Prince of Darkness. Hargood, Paxton and Secker refuse to join Courtley in drinking the concoction. As Courtley chokes on the blood, the three men beat him to death. During the night, Courtley's body is reborn as Count Dracula (Christopher Lee) and the vampire vows to destroy those who killed his servant. Later, a lecherous Hargood advances on his daughter, Alice (Linda Hayden), who escapes into the night. She falls under the mesmeric influence of Dracula and, like Paxton's daughter and Secker's son after her, is compelled to administer his revenge...

Among the unsolicited scripts arriving at Hammer House in spring 1969 was a ready-made follow-up to *Dracula Has Risen From the Grave. Dracula's Feast of Blood*, by Freddie Francis' son Kevin, picked up where the last instalment in the saga left off. After full consideration by Brian Lawrence and James Carreras, the script was formally rejected by Hammer on 19 May.

Christopher Lee had been persuaded to make *Dracula Has Risen From the Grave* against his better judgement and, in summer 1969, reacted badly to James Carreras' request that he star in *Taste the Blood of Dracula*. "I felt I had discharged any obligations I had to the company," says Lee, who asked for what he considered a fair salary. "By this time I had discovered just how successful Hammer films were in the United States, and how well-known I was. I told my agent to tell Hammer that if they really didn't have any money then they could pay me a percentage of the American distributor's gross."

This, it was decided, was out of the question. On

24 June 1969 it was agreed that Christopher Lee should be replaced, and a younger actor found to "create a new Dracula image." Hammer's "new boy", as James Carreras described him, was twenty-nine year-old Ralph Bates. Although Bates had never made a film before, he had made an impression playing the title role in the Caligula episode of Granada Television's *The Caesars* in autumn 1968. He was cast as similarly depraved aristo Lord Courtenay — a Baron Meinster for the seventies.

The news did not go down well in New York, and Warner Bros-Seven Arts reminded Hammer that they had agreed to co-finance the film on the condition that Christopher Lee played Dracula. Producer Aida Young was sent to negotiate with the recalcitrant star. "I was determined that we should have Christopher," she recalls, "and I took him to lunch at Le Caprice to discuss it. I think he'd liked *Dracula Has Risen From*

DRINK A PINT OF BLOOD A DAY

Warner Bros presents A Hammer Film Production

TASTE THE BLOOD OF DRACULA

TECHNICOLOR

CHRISTOPHER LEE   Screenplay by JOHN ELDER Produced by AIDA YOUNG
Directed by PETER SASDY Released through WARNER PATHE

the Grave, and he knew that I cared about the films. I'm glad he agreed to do it, because he was superb. And he loved it — I think he would have been so upset if somebody else had done it. Not that anybody else *could* have done it, of course."

"On November 3rd, I start what I hope will positively be my last film for Hammer," Lee told his fan club members. "The tasteful title is *Taste the Blood of Dracula*. As usual, words fail me, as indeed they will also do in the film." Lee's last-minute change of heart had left little time for John Elder to write him into his screenplay. Once Lord Courtley (as the character was ultimately named on screen) had 'tasted the blood' of the vampire Count, Elder simply transformed him into Dracula. Courtley's reduced role left Bates with only five days' work in the six week schedule, and allowed Lee to do little but linger in the wings, picking off Courtley's corrupt malefactors one by one.

Near the ABPC Elstree studios where interiors were shot from October onwards, locations were found at Scratchwood and Aldenham Park. North London location shooting took place at Highgate Cemetery and St Andrew's Church in Totteridge Lane, while a private house near Barnet doubled for the exterior of the Hargood household.

Hammer's problems with *Taste the Blood of Dracula* didn't end when filming wrapped on 5 December. Kevin Francis became alerted to the fact that *Taste the Blood of Dracula* featured a few familiar elements: "There was a scene of mine, and I can't remember what it was now, or there might have been two scenes, in *Taste the Blood of Dracula* which were lifted from *Dracula's Feast of Blood*," he said in an interview with Tony Earnshaw. "John Elder didn't put my two scenes in. It was actually somebody else on the film who had read my script and said, 'We can nick that and we can nick that'... they had to pay me a large sum of money before they could release *Taste the Blood of Dracula*."

Although the matter was resolved to everyone's satisfaction, it raised a new hypothetical spectre. Should an accusation of plagiarism ever be levelled at John Elder, then how could Anthony Hinds prove that, as a company director, he was unaware of the content of scripts submitted to Hammer? After years of mounting disenchantment over his role at Hammer, and the diminishing industry in general, the *Taste the Blood of*

Dracula wrangle was the final straw for Hinds. He readily accepted the company solicitor's suggestion that he relinquish his directorship. Anthony Hinds' resignation became effective on 19 May 1970, a year to the day after *Dracula's Feast of Blood* was rejected.

Taste the Blood of Dracula was double-billed with *Crescendo*. Following a New Victoria première, the two films commenced general release from 7 June 1970. The brutality of *Taste the Blood of Dracula* hinted at things to come, as did the bare breasts visible in both films. Although possibly influenced by the poster's absurd slogan, reviews for the film indicated that Hammer's traditional Gothic horrors were becoming perceived as ironic exercises: "A better-than-average Hammer horror which addicts will enjoy with a giggle and a shiver," claimed *The Sunday Express*.

Taste the Blood of Dracula skilfully unravels the fabric of Victorian society, exposing the hypocrisy within. In adopting a viewpoint sympathetic to the young cinema-goers of 1970, John Elder couched his latest *Dracula* in the progressive anti-establishment ethos of the times. Now distanced from the details of its turbulent production, and the era of its release, *Taste the Blood of Dracula* retains an impressive all-round quality that distinguishes Peter Sasdy's film début as the finest genuine *Dracula* sequel in the entire series.

Previous page: Hargood (Geoffrey Keen), Secker (John Carson) and Paxton (Peter Sallis) watch the audacious Lord Courtley (Ralph Bates) with mounting trepidation.
Top: Isla Blair shelters Christopher Lee from a downpour on location.
Above: Dracula (Christopher Lee) founders before the overwhelming power of faith.
Far left: "They drink his blood," warned the American poster, "and the horror begins."
Left: A publicity shot of Dracula and Alice (Linda Hayden). Hayden later appeared in the Hammer House of Horror episode 'Black Carrion'.

1969's new year's honours list rewarded James Carreras with a knighthood in recognition of his tireless fund-raising for the Variety Club. His day job, however, brought little cheer. In late 1969, a resilient Hammer had attempted to defy what *Kinematograph Weekly* called "the draining away of American finance" by entering into co-production with American International Productions. Just as he had for Kenneth Hyman two years before, Sir James hired a room at the Savoy to celebrate. Sam Arkoff and Jim Nicholson, AIP's chairman and president respectively, failed to attend. The first Hammer/AIP film, *The Vampire Lovers*, proved to be the last, and Hammer was once more cast adrift.

With the introduction of colour television now added to the threats facing the ailing British film industry, Hammer took advantage of relaxed censorship by introducing full-frontal nudity and lesbianism into its films in an attempt to buck a further decline in cinema attendance.

"I did not like the change that came after I left," observes Anthony Hinds, "when it was thought that the films would have increased audience appeal by making them soft-porn shows. I thought the originals were sexy enough by implication without having to resort to tired music hall tricks... Jim Carreras thought this was great. He was a showman. He told me, 'God, you can do anything now.' I thought, 'Well, I'm not sure that doing everything is what it's all about.'"

Following Hinds' 'retirement', the doors of Hammer House were thrown open to independent

producers and writers — anyone, it seems, who could provide Sir James with an idea for a poster or, more importantly, some co-production money.

The films from this period were largely financed by either ABPC (who fell under the control of Electrical Musical Industries in summer 1969) or Rank Film Distributors. Bernard Delfont, the chairman and chief executive of ABPC, was a close friend of Carreras', and continued a long tradition of the company's support for Hammer product. With American money now out of the equation, however, budgets added up to a great deal less than Hammer had been used to in the halcyon days of Fox/Seven Arts co-production. (ABPC's Elstree manager Bryan Forbes, a former actor who had appeared in *Quatermass 2*, would come to resent Hammer's domination of his studio with pictures far removed from the type he personally favoured.)

In May 1970, ABPC created Anglo-EMI Film Distributors from the merged Associated British-Pathé and Anglo-Amalgamated. Under chairman and chief executive Nat Cohen, another of Carreras' acquaintances, Anglo-EMI distributed much of Hammer's product in the early seventies. Cohen's production programme (which included Hammer's *On the Buses*) proved far more profitable than that instigated by Forbes; from March 1971 he added Forbes' respon-

sibilities to his own.

By the end of 1970, Rank had also begun co-financing/distributing Hammer films, but Sir James' relationship with managing directors Frank Poole and Fred Thomas would ultimately prove less fruitful.

Sir James Carreras had charmed EMI and Rank into securing his company's short-term future, but felt less comfortable about taking Anthony Hinds' place in

Previous page (below left): Tuesday 13 January 1970 — at the Savoy, Ingrid Pitt and Peter Cushing celebrate Hammer's co-production deal with AIP.
Previous page (above right): Christopher Lee and producer Aida Young at Elstree during production of Scars of Dracula *in 1970. The trade press proclaimed* Scars *and its co-feature* The Horror of Frankenstein *to be the first Hammer pictures made with entirely British finance.*
Previous page (below right): At Elstree, Reg Varney, Sir James Carreras, Doris Hare, Nat Cohen and Valerie Leon dine beneath the Queen's Award to Industry banner.
Left: Michael Carreras (pointing) and director Don Chaffey on location in Africa for Creatures the World Forgot *in 1970.*
Below: A still of American poster artwork prepared by Warner Bros for The Satanic Rites of Dracula *in 1973. Warner Bros never issued the film, and the poster is now a rarity.*
Bottom: Producer Roy Skeggs and director Terence Fisher at Elstree during production of Frankenstein and the Monster From Hell *in autumn 1972.*

overseeing production. Forced to find someone who could co-ordinate Hammer's now disparate talent, he turned to his son. In October 1970 Michael Carreras was called by his father, and offered a full-time position at Hammer as executive producer. Although Michael had enjoyed little success in carving out a career away from Hammer (Capricorn hadn't made a film since *What a Crazy World*), returning to the job he had walked away from seven years earlier held little appeal. Sir James came back with a new offer — would Michael return if made managing director? Under pressure from his mother, Michael eventually relented. On 8 December, Michael Carreras' appointment was formally agreed at Hammer House; he commenced office from 4 January 1971.

Alarmed at the jumble of projects initiated in Anthony Hinds' absence, Michael immediately appointed Roy Skeggs 'production supervisor' and gave him responsibility over the independent producers taking credit for many of Hammer's films. Under Skeggs, 'Little Hammer House' at MGM-EMI (formerly ABPC) Elstree became an autonomous production unit, with its own script and accounts departments.

Ten films were produced during 1971: six were co-financed by EMI, three by Rank and one, *Dracula A.D. 1972*, by Warner Bros, the result of a short-lived alliance between Sir James Carreras and Warner chairman Ted Ashley. But the market was shrinking fast. Low budget horror films, strictly costed to return their outlay without American distribution, flooded the market, diminishing the dwindling demand yet further. The emergence of violent American films, such as *Bonnie and Clyde*, *Night of the Living Dead* and *The Wild Bunch*, prompted unfavourable comparisons with Hammer's more old-fashioned fare, and attempts to re-invent Hammer horror with such films as *Dr Jekyll & Sister Hyde* and *Captain Kronos Vampire Hunter* fell flat.

Sir James' influence was seen through to its natural conclusion with *The Satanic Rites of Dracula*, the second and final modern day Dracula that he had part funded through Warner Bros. By the time filming wrapped on 3 January 1973, Carreras had run out of favours to call; major studio distribution for Hammer pictures in America was now a thing of the past, and even British finance/distribution was difficult to find for anything other than low budget television spin-offs. Soon, even that source of income would dry up.

Sir James, it seems, had long since seen the writing on the wall. Aware that a knighthood was on the cards and that the Hymans were out of the picture, he had offered EMI a seventy-five per cent interest in Hammer in June 1969. The deal, between Carreras and Bernard Delfont, was never concluded. In 1972, Carreras renewed his efforts to off-load the company, engineering a merger between Hammer and Studio Film Laboratories Ltd. When this, too, came to naught, Carreras opened negotiations with some of his fellow tenants at Hammer House.

On 1 January 1972, *Cinema TV Today* (the trade paper's changed title itself indicative of the crisis facing British film production) reported that "The Tigon Group and its entrepreneur founder Laurie Marsh are being welded together via a series of property deals that will transform Tigon into a mini ABC or Rank." Tigon, which now included former BBFC chief John Trevelyan amongst its company directors, was expanding rapidly; Carreras hoped Marsh would absorb Hammer as a production arm of the group, and offered the company for sale.

By this time, Sir James had promoted his son from managing director to chief executive, but communication between the two remained poor. Upon discovering his father's plans, Michael decided to outbid Laurie Marsh and keep Hammer in the family. On Brian Lawrence's suggestion, Michael approached Imperial Chemical Industries (ICI) for the necessary capital, which was loaned by the company's Pension Funds Securities (PFS) division. Michael borrowed an initial £400,000 to fund his purchase of the company

made for TV 'new' films. British TV companies have now started to produce films directly for TV and the UK circuits are beginning to show made for TV films in the cinemas.

"These last two policies are disaster for the producer of 'mid-priced' theatrical films who cannot compete with either the price or efficiency of TV production... It is essential that Hammer moves into new areas, and it is my current policy to concentrate on the following: TV series, movies for TV, and exploitation theatrical films via tape production."

Hammer produced only one film, an adaptation of the TV sit-com *Man About the House*, in 1974. With the heavy drop in production, and both capital and production loans interest payments to find, Hammer suffered near cash flow starvation. Following a round of redundancies, the company now employed only eleven people: Michael Carreras and Brian Lawrence's staff occupied the front half of the second floor of Hammer House, while Roy Skeggs and his staff continued to operate from 'Little Hammer House' at Elstree.

Carreras explored new avenues in his search for alternate means of finance: *Kali... Bride of Dracula*, from a script by Don Houghton, was initiated by Warner Bros as a means of employing the distributor's 'frozen' rupees; *The Experiment*, from a script by John Gould, would have been financed with Canadian 'tax shelter' money and pre-sales to various European countries; *The Impaler*, by Brian Hayles, would have told the story of the notorious Vlad Tepes with Rumanian or Hungarian co-finance; and *Chaka Zulu — The Black Napoleon*, an adaptation of Rider Haggard's *Nada the Lily*, was slated for production in co-operation with the South African government. None would see fruition. Carreras attempted to fund *To Kill a Stranger*, a thriller by Tudor Gates, and *The Savage Jackboot*, a war story by Don Houghton, via the traditional American means. There were no takers.

Carreras persisted, offering the retitled *Vlad the Impaler* to director Ken Russell in October 1974. Russell's response illustrated much about the company's dated approach to a genre it once commanded.

"Without a doubt, the year 1973 has been both a difficult and unusual one for Hammer," reported Michael Carreras at the company's annual general meeting on 5 June 1974. "In addition to the change of overall company structure and internal reorganisation, the British film industry as a whole has experienced severe regression from the almost total withdrawal of traditional American distributors' production finance, at a time when British distributors had already cut back severely... In the cinemas, the current trend is for the 'big star name' picture to attract audiences, and it has proved so successful that the major companies are continuing to follow this policy with a subsequent loss of interest (and shortage of finance for) the less expensive 'middle ground' picture.

"Sex, kung fu and horror have maintained their hold on the 'exploitation' audiences. TV has gained further strength by showing bigger and newer 'old' films, together with an endless supply of American

from his father.

Sir James, disappointed at Tigon's performance-related terms, accepted his son's offer, and tendered his resignation from the board of directors on 31 January 1973. It was accepted by Michael and Brian Lawrence the same day. When the inscrutable Sir James finally brought his illustrious film career to an end, even those who worked alongside him saw no indication of any disillusionment with the industry. "He was unhappy Michael had come back," says Roy Skeggs, "so he got out himself."

Michael Carreras' chairmanship of Hammer got off to a difficult start when Bernard Delfont rescinded on a programme of ongoing EMI finance informally agreed with Sir James. Michael found fresh funds in Hong Kong, but the £200,000 borrowed from PFS to finance Hammer's share of *The Legend of the 7 Golden Vampires* and *Shatter* would further cripple the struggling company.

SIR H. RIDER HAGGARD'S

CHAKA ZULU

THIS IS A HAMMER FILM

The Black Napoleon

Hammer's royalties through his own company, Tintern Productions Limited. Roy Skeggs took his place on the board of directors.

In 1975, Carreras finally secured finance for a new horror film. With funds sourced from, amongst others, Nat Cohen at EMI and Terra Filmkunst in Germany, *To the Devil a Daughter* went before the cameras on 1 September.

Michael's bold plans for the future of Hammer were at serious odds with its diminished capacity, influence and reputation. *The Legend of the 7 Golden Vampires*, *Shatter* and *To the Devil a Daughter* were expensive failures that fell some way short of revitalising the company's fortunes.

The seeds of Hammer's imminent collapse had already been sown.

"In your letter you say you feel it time the horror movie became respectable," wrote Russell. "In my opinion it always has been and to my mind *Vlad* is no exception. All the potentially sexy scenes are downright coy! What I have always felt is that most horror movies rely on gratuitous sadism instead of spine chilling invention. And once again *Vlad* backs up my theory: the blood bath at the end is as unnecessary as it is obnoxious. Blood, particularly movie blood, is not synonymous with horror. Thanks for thinking of me all the same, and please don't misunderstand me. I would like to make a horror film with you — a *real* one."

Ultimately, *Vlad the Impaler* proved impossible to finance anyway. "I was never able to find one company that would say, 'OK, we will take on the entire cost'," said Carreras. "It was always, 'If you can find a co-producer', or 'If you can find underwriting for the below-the-line costs.' At that point, it should have been given to somebody whose total time could have been concentrated on that one project. Unfortunately, I never had that time."

"It wasn't Michael's fault," says Roy Skeggs of Hammer's difficulties. "He was trying hard and it wouldn't happen. It was so easy before, but Jimmy was a man for his time. And Michael came at a bad time."

Although Anthony Hinds had declined Michael's offer to rejoin the company, he continued to originate ideas and rework scripts from Hammer's bottom drawer, often free of charge. His letters to Michael Carreras were full of encouragement and advice for his beleaguered friend. One letter, dated 8 April 1975, concerned a film that would sweep away much that had gone before: "Trying to work out why *Jaws* has been such a phenomenal success worldwide," he wrote. "It is excellent, of course, but not *that* excellent..."

Hammer limped on.

Towards the end of 1974, Brian Lawrence decided to call it a day. His resignation became effective on 31 December, after which he continued to collect

Principal photography 19 January to
4 March 1970
Released 3 September 1970
Certificate X
Duration 91 mins
Colour
Director Roy Ward Baker

In the province of Styria, an exotic Countess (Dawn Addams) leaves her daughter, Marcilla (Ingrid Pitt), in the charge of General Spielsdorf (Peter Cushing). While the Countess travels Europe, Marcilla befriends the General's niece, Laura (Pippa Steele). Plagued by nightmares of being attacked by a giant cat, Laura becomes ill. Marcilla devotes herself to Laura's care, but Laura wastes away and dies shortly after. Marcilla, now calling herself Carmilla, soon reappears in the household of Englishman Morton (George Cole), a neighbour of the General. Like Laura, Morton's daughter, Emma (Madeline Smith), is seduced by Carmilla. Meanwhile, the General, through his friend Baron Hartog (Douglas Wilmer), hears of the legend of the Karnstein dynasty — an ancient family of vampires. One in particular has eluded the hunter Hartog; her portrait bears an uncanny resemblance to Carmilla...

irst serialised in the magazine *The Dark Blue* between December 1871 and March 1872, Joseph Sheridan Le Fanu's dream-like novella *Carmilla* predated Stoker's *Dracula* by twenty-five years. *The Vampire Lovers*, the first of a trilogy of films loosely connected by the character Carmilla Karnstein, was proposed to Hammer in 1969 by Fantale Films Ltd — a partnership between producers Harry Fine and Michael Style, and writer Tudor Gates. Harry Fine had spotted the story's commercial potential and enlisted Gates, who "tarted up the storyline considerably." Gates' script exploited the anticipated raising of the X certificate's minimum age restriction from sixteen to eighteen; *The Vampire Lovers'* explicit blend of lesbianism and viscera would have been unthinkable before.

In December, Hammer secured $400,000 towards the film's budget from American International Productions, previously noted for Roger Corman's cycle of Edgar Allan Poe adaptations. AIP suggested a number of alterations to the draft script, including having the Man in Black's ultimate disintegration into a skeleton amended to pave the way for a possible sequel.

Casting the film proved difficult. Agent John Redway recommended Shirley Eaton for the role of Carmilla, but James Carreras was unenthusiastic. "Shirley Eaton... is about thirty-two and, I am afraid, too old," he wrote to Harry Fine on 4 December. Carreras instead recommended the younger Polish actress Ingrid Pitt, "who was in *Where Eagles Dare* and looked very good." Hammer later defended its casting to the Ministry of Labour, arguing that "this particular role of a female vampire requires special physical characteristics which Miss Pitt does possess and which we have not been able to find in the many British artistes we have considered." AIP was unhappy about co-financing a film with a relative unknown in the lead, and on 23 December told Harry Fine: "we would feel much more secure if we could also have a typical Hammer cast involved." To appease their American partners, Hammer/Fantale offered Peter Cushing a cameo role shortly before filming began. Alongside Cushing, Ingrid Pitt was introduced to the press at the Savoy Hotel on Tuesday 13 January 1970.

The BBFC's John Trevelyan was alarmed by the screenplay's "dangerous cocktail" of sex and horror. In a letter to Harry Fine dated 26 January 1970, he complained that Tudor Gates' script contained "a lot of material that we would be unhappy about even with an X at eighteen... I want you to take my comments seriously since if you do not we are likely to have on our hands a film that we cannot pass for

Beautiful temptress ...or Bloodthirsty monster ?

...She's the NEW HORROR FROM HAMMER!

THE VAMPIRE LOVERS

A HAMMER-AMERICAN INTERNATIONAL PRODUCTION

INGRID PITT · GEORGE COLE · KATE O'MARA and PETER CUSHING as the General

"THE VAMPIRE LOVERS"

Also Starring FERDY MAYNE · DOUGLAS WILMER and Guest Star DAWN ADDAMS Screenplay by TUDOR GATES Produced by HARRY FINE & MICHAEL STYLE Directed by ROY WARD BAKER · TECHNICOLOR · Released by MGM-EMI

VIVACIOUS Ingrid Pitt is being paid to make your flesh creep. Not in this lovely picture, of course, but in a moving one to be made by those experts in horror Hammer Films and American International. The title is promising . . . Vampire Lovers. The makers are convinced it will make a big star out of 25-year-old Ingrid. Picture: BEN JONES.

Sunday Mirror

84   January 11, 1970   No. 332

INGRID PITT: CARMILLA

Ingrid Pitt was offered the starring role in *The Vampire Lovers* soon after meeting James Carreras at the première party for *Alfred the Great* in 1969. The full-frontal nudity demanded by the script bothered her little: "I remember my first nude scene with Maddy Smith was coming up and, although neither of us particularly minded, at that time it wasn't an every-day event. Jimmy Carreras was okay about it but I was told that the other producers, Harry Fine and Michael Style, were a bit po-faced. I was walking to the stage when I met Fine and Style, looking very dejected, walking in the opposite direction. I felt so sorry for them. As I drew near I stopped and ripped open my dressing gown with all the *brio* of an experienced flasher on Hampstead Heath." The vivacious Pitt again bared all as *Countess Dracula*, and spoofed her reputation as the queen of early seventies horror in Amicus' *The House That Dripped Blood*. After a brief appearance in *The Wicker Man*, her career continued away from the genre roles that made her a cult figure. Her later film work includes *Who Dares Wins* and *Wild Geese II*. She made her best-known television appearances in *The Zoo Gang*, *The Comedy of Errors*, *Smiley's People* and *Doctor Who*. One of the most prominent, and popular, of all Hammer stars, Ingrid is now a successful author.

exhibition in this country." Certain scenes which he objected to — such as those depicting "punctured breasts" — would remain, but he warned against "a dream orgasm ending in a scream" ("I do not like this at all") and reminded Hammer to be cautious about their portrayal of lesbianism in light of the Board's "firm treatment" of Robert Aldrich's *The Killing of Sister George* in 1969. (Three days later, Trevelyan sent a confidential note to Sir James Carreras asking him to use his "personal influence" over Fine and Style to "keep this film within reasonable grounds.")

Director Roy Ward Baker (who also expressed reservations about the explicit lesbianism in the script) had already begun shooting interiors at ABPC Elstree's stages eight and nine by the time Trevelyan's report arrived at Hammer House. Filming continued on stage two and on location, including the clubhouse of the nearby Moor Park golf course. Unfortunately, the establishment's tennis courts can be glimpsed during one scene. A final cost of £165,227 reflected the belt-tightening Hammer was forced to endure since losing the support of major American distributors.

The Vampire Lovers opened at London's New Victoria on 3 September, double-billed with biker flick *Angels From Hell*. General release followed on

4 October. Audiences were enthusiastic, and by December the programme had taken £58,897 on the London circuits alone. At that time, AIP were confident that the film would gross over $1,000,000 in America. A sequel, *Lust For a Vampire*, was already complete.

Seen today, Ingrid Pitt's seductive performance and Roy Ward Baker's inventive direction conspire to make *The Vampire Lovers* a better film than it perhaps deserves to be. Brazenly exploitative, it set the tone for Hammer's increasingly explicit direction throughout the seventies.

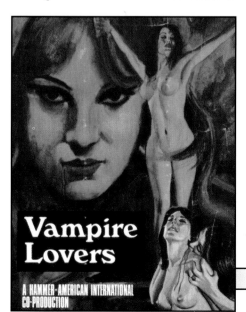

Vampire Lovers

A HAMMER-AMERICAN INTERNATIONAL CO-PRODUCTION

Previous page (above left): General Spielsdorf (Peter Cushing) and the Countess (Dawn Addams).
Previous page (above right): A beautifully decorated coffin — Carmilla (Ingrid Pitt), Emma (Madeline Smith), the Governess (Kate O'Mara), Laura (Pippa Steele) and 'First Vampire' (Kirsten Betts).
Above left: Baron Hartog (Douglas Wilmer) and Roger Morton (George Cole).
Far left: Pre-production artwork from Kinematograph Weekly, 24 January 1970. "For heaven's sake stop AIP from putting out the kind of publicity recently shown in the trade press!" implored John Trevelyan of Sir James Carreras shortly afterwards.
Left: Carmilla has an entrancing effect on Emma Morton.

Principal photography 16 March to
29 April 1970
Released 8 October 1970
Certificate X
Duration 95 mins
Colour
Director Jimmy Sangster

His smutty 'anatomy diagrams' confiscated, teenage prodigy Victor Frankenstein (Ralph Bates) evades the cane by exploiting his schoolmaster's hypochondria. Victor's friends — Henri (Jon Finch), Stephan, Maggie and Elizabeth (Veronica Carlson) — congratulate him. At the Frankenstein castle, Victor makes clear to his father (George Belbin) his intention to go to university in Vienna, but the Baron vetoes this. Coldly, Victor sabotages a shooting rifle, which later explodes in the Baron's face, killing him. Victor uses his inheritance to decamp to Vienna. Six years pass, and Victor leaves after getting the Dean's daughter pregnant. Returning home with fellow student Wilhelm (Graham James), he rescues Elizabeth and her father (Bernard Archard), an eminent professor, from two highwaymen. He kills one, and covertly beheads him. Hidden away from housekeeper and 'bedwarmer' Alys (Kate O'Mara), he and Wilhelm set about researching into the revival of dead tissue...

*i*n April 1967, Hammer lodged a successful objection to Tony Tenser Films' attempt to register the title *Horrors of Frankenstein* for future production. It had a certain ring to it, however...

A near-remake of *The Curse of Frankenstein*, the latest *Frankenstein* restarted the Baron's misdeeds from scratch, with Ralph Bates in the title role. (Anthony Hinds, casting his mind back thirteen years, warned against including any character or sequence that might infringe Universal's copyright.)

The script was derived from a story outline by actor and television writer Jeremy Burnham, who'd played Connelly in Hammer's *The Brigand of Kandahar*. Most of the eventual film's key details were in Burnham's outline, titled simply *Frankenstein*, although the conclusion was rather different. After the murder of Alys, the monster was to escape and run amok in a local village — "creating mayhem, knocking down every object which stands in its way" — before returning to the castle to menace "Elisabeth". She is rescued by Henri, who fires bullet after bullet into the creature. However, their escape is blocked by Victor, who, holding the pair at gunpoint,

instructs his monster to kill them. Elisabeth incinerates the creature with a burning torch, reducing it to ashes. Now "completely mad", Victor "gets down on his hands and knees, fawning over his dead 'baby'."

Hammer sent Burnham's version to Jimmy Sangster, then in Los Angeles, asking him to rewrite it. Uninspired, Sangster declined. They contacted him again, offering him the producership: "I still wasn't interested. Then I thought about it a bit and called them. I'd do it if they let me direct. They must have been pretty desperate by then because they said, 'yes'."

That August, a German film company were reported to have expressed an interest in financing the picture. Hammer, however, had been courting Bernard Delfont, both brother to entertainment magnate Lew Grade and a Variety Club associate of James Carreras. The British film industry was changing fast; in the summer, the powerful EMI conglomerate had acquired control of ABPC (and therefore ABPC Elstree Studios). Late in November, Delfont, chairman and chief executive of ABPC, agreed that ABPC would entirely finance *The Horrors of Frankenstein* [sic] and a second Hammer feature, *Scars of Dracula*, to the tune of

£200,000 apiece. There was a downside however as overseas distribution could not be set until the films had been shot.

The story had been rewritten in a blackly comic vein, Sangster amending the ending and giving the cold Victor a pronounced libido. "The 'Permissive' Society catches up with Frankenstein," claimed the press book. "You will see [Ralph Bates' Frankenstein] forsake test tubes and Bunsen burners for a romp in a fine four-poster with the delicious Kate O'Mara. And no man could be criticised for that!" Shot at MGM-EMI Elstree (formerly ABPC), Sangster's directorial début also featured Dave Prowse, a 6'7" one-time champion weightlifter, as the Monster. Prowse played a Strongman in the later *Vampire Circus*, and went on to embody a Frankenstein creation once more.

Misguidedly, *The Horror of Frankenstein* (as the film was ultimately titled) spares pathos not for creature nor creator, but for an array of supporting characters tangential to the plot: simple Stephan, lovelorn Elizabeth, the grave robber's wife (played by Joan Rice, star of Exclusive's *Women Without Men*). Its comic strokes are deft enough, but a novelty alone. *Frankenstein*, one concludes, just wasn't meant to be light-hearted.

HORROR OF FRANKENSTEIN

starring
RALPH BATES KATE O'MARA VERONICA CARLSON and **DENNIS PRICE**

Screenplay by JEREMY BURNHAM and JIMMY SANGSTER   Produced and directed by JIMMY SANGSTER

Castle Dracula: a chittering vampire bat dribbles blood over mouldering remains, thus reincarnating the Count (Christopher Lee). The inhabitants of a nearby village, alerted to the fiend's revival, march upon the castle and set fire to it, despite the misgivings of their priest (Michael Gwynn). Later, they discover that a swarm of bats has descended upon the church where their womenfolk have sought sanctuary, and their wives and children have been torn to shreds. Years pass; roguish Paul (Christopher Matthews) makes a hasty exit from the town of Kleinenburg pursued by officers of the Burgomaster, whose daughter he has seduced. He passes through the village, but is sent away by the local inn's surly landlord (Michael Ripper). Inadvertently hitching a ride in a carriage driven by Dracula's manservant, Klove (Patrick Troughton), he ends up at the castle, where he is bedded by Tania (Anouska Hempel), a vampire from whom the Count suckles. Dracula stabs Tania to death when she attempts to feed off Paul. Meanwhile, both Paul's elder brother Simon (Dennis Waterman) and the besotted Sarah (Jenny Hanley) arrive in search of him. They, too, become house guests of the urbane and evil Count...

**Principal photography 7 May to
23 June 1970
Released 8 October 1970
Certificate X
Duration 96 mins
Colour
Director Roy Ward Baker**

*O*ne of the company's bloodier films, *Scars of Dracula* broke the sequence begun with Hammer's 1958 original, as no attempt was made to link it to the conclusion of *Taste the Blood of Dracula*. Set once more in an east European neverwhere, it comes across as more in the style of a Universal picture. Its surprisingly verbose and chatty Count invokes not the snarling revenant of previous Hammer sequels, but Bela Lugosi at his most theatrical.

Developed as a companion piece to *The Horror of Frankenstein*, its first draft screenplay was deemed unsuitable, and "considerable re-writing" was requested on 25 February 1970. Roy Ward Baker was contracted to direct, and elected to go all out for gory shock effect. *Scars of Dracula*'s establishing sequence, wherein the villagers discover the (literally) eyeball-popping carnage perpetrated upon their womenfolk by Dracula's bats, was consciously constructed as such: "I was determined it was going to be horrible..." Baker's preparatory work drew him to read Bram Stoker's original, inspiring Baker to add in the shots of Dracula scaling his castle's walls — a scene

from the novel never previously attempted on film. "I had to fight like a tiger to get them to build a set to do it, and then it was pretty crappy, but I made my point," he recalls. "That was the only contribution I felt I had made to the Dracula cycle..."

Scars of Dracula was shot largely at Elstree in the early summer, with a small amount of location work shot in the Scratchwood area, just off the A1 Barnet by-pass. Via Gloria Lillibridge, Christopher Lee informed his fan club that he suspected the script lacked connection with previous Draculas so that the character could be more readily recast should he turn it down. *Journey to the Unknown* star Dennis Waterman and Jenny Hanley, later a presenter of children's magazine show *Magpie*, played John Elder's now-traditional chaste Hansel and Gretel types, Simon and Sarah. Patrick Troughton made his penultimate Hammer appearance, and supposedly hung a still of Klove being branded by Dracula in his toilet. Television starlet Anouska Hempel later married Sir Mark Weinberg, chairman of Allied Dunbar; now Lady Weinberg, she's allegedly one of the richest women in

Britain. Comic relief policeman David Leland became a noted writer/director of British films such as *Mona Lisa* and *Wish You Were Here*. Although only one filmed scene was removed at the insistence of the BBFC — Dracula bending over Tania's corpse, drinking gore from the stab wounds in her chest — other sequences were trimmed (the killings of Tania and the priest). The sounds of Klove dismembering Tania with a saw were toned down, too.

The *The Horror of Frankenstein/Scars of Dracula* double-bill performed relatively well on its London release, grossing a total of £55,385 in the capital. American Continental Films picked up the US rights (the deal was on favourable terms but American Continental lacked the distribution clout to make the bill a hit). Following the Count's cursory despatch in a rather inglorious blaze (once more courtesy of redoubtable stuntman Eddie Powell), Hammer realised the need to sharpen Dracula's bite. The arch-vampire, it seemed, was in need of fresh blood.

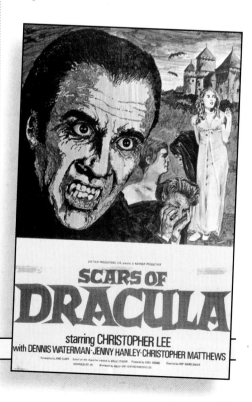

**SCARS OF
DRACULA**

starring CHRISTOPHER LEE
with DENNIS WATERMAN · JENNY HANLEY · CHRISTOPHER MATTHEWS

Come the seventies, a new, more liberal attitude to the baring of female flesh prevailed. Whereas several of the company's starlets would prosper — Kate O'Mara, Stephanie Beacham, Joanna Lumley — others would find continued exposure hard to maintain.

HAMMER GLAMOUR

OLINKA BEROVA

"Of all the hundreds of actresses I've worked with, she was the most beautiful," says Roy Skeggs when recalling Czech Olinka Berova, star of *The Vengeance of She*. In October 1964, even before the original *She* had been unleashed, Hammer had announced a sequel, *Ayesha — The Return of She*, but were undone when Ursula Andress proved unwilling to recreate the role. Although *Frankenstein Created Woman*'s Susan Denberg was briefly mooted as a possible replacement, producer Aida Young apparently scoured six European countries for a suitable girl to play Carol, Ayesha's latter-day reincarnation. She discovered twenty-one year-old Olinka, a 37-23-36 veteran of twelve pictures, including the obscure *Lemonade Joe*. Her casting was announced at a reception at the Savoy in June 1967. "She has a wonderful career ahead of her," enthused the producer...

VERONICA CARLSON

A smattering of judo expertise had led Veronica Carlson to her blink-and-you'll-miss-it début in *The Vengeance of She* director Cliff Owen's Morecambe and Wise comedy *The Magnificent Two*. In 1968, Hammer nominated Veronica as "Dracula's most beautiful victim!" when she was cast as corrupted Catholic Maria in *Dracula Has Risen From the Grave*. She'd been a schoolgirl fan of the company's films: "I saw Herbert Lom as the Phantom of the

Opera and I loved the lead vampire in *Brides of Dracula*. He was really dishy..." A gifted artist, her sketched-between-takes portrait of Christopher Lee featured in the film's press book. After fronting the company's Christmas card for 1968, Veronica fell victim to Peter Cushing's lecherous Baron as Anna Spengler in *Frankenstein Must Be Destroyed*. The fol-

lowing year, she played opposite another Baron, Ralph Bates, in the black *The Horror of Frankenstein*; to comic effect, however, this Victor shunned Veronica's virginal Elizabeth for Kate O'Mara's vampish Alys. She made a pretty foil for Cushing in Tyburn's *The Ghoul*, but altogether less impressive was the Freddie Francis-directed David Niven spoof, *Vampira*. A far better performer than her roles would ever allow, Veronica is fondly remembered for more than just her looks.

JULIE EGE

"A crack shot, an excellent skier, Norwegian beauty Julie Ege learned how to hurl a spear fifty feet at a moving target for her starring role in *Creatures the World Forgot*. Julie's instructor was a member of a local tribe inhabiting the Namib desert where the film was shot. Asked what he thought of his tall, blonde, blue-eyed 36-24-36 pupil, the native's praise was overwhelming: 'the lady can hunt for my tribe any day...' (or words to that effect)." Press book puff aside, Julie, a former Miss Norway, was a Golders Green *au pair* prior to her first major role — playing an *au pair* in the Marty Feldman comedy *Every Home Should Have One* (she'd already been one of Blofeld's 'angels of death' — alongside fellow Hammerettes Jenny Hanley, Anouska Hempel, Sylvianna Henriques, Joanna Lumley and Catherina Von Schell — in the Bond adventure *On Her Majesty's Secret*

Service). Following her monosyllabic part as Hammer cavegirl Nala, she helped spoof the company's product in *Go For a Take*, an uncanny little comedy which satirised low budget British film production of the time, wherein she was a cringing bimbo actress terrorised by Dennis Price's hammy vampire count. Julie's second and final Hammer role was as eventually-befanged Scandinavian widow Vanessa Buren in *The Legend of the 7 Golden Vampires*. Soon after, she returned to Norway, became a nurse and took a degree in history.

MADELINE SMITH

Sussex-born Madeline Smith — apparently discovered working in a London boutique — made a tiny appearance as the young Dolly, a fragile prostitute called upon to service Geoffrey Keen's debauched Hargood in *Taste the Blood of Dracula*'s bordello scenes. In 1970, playing petite, doe-eyed Emma Morton, she fell victim to Ingrid Pitt's equally depraved Carmilla in *The Vampire Lovers*. Her final Hammer appearance was in *Frankenstein and the Monster From Hell*, shot two years later, in which, as Sarah, mute daughter to the director of the asylum wherein the Baron perpetrates his bloody deeds, she was selected as the Monster's mate. Like Julie Ege, Madeline, aka Maddy, turned up in the feature version of *Up Pompeii* — and was a Bond girl, too, in *Live and Let Die* (Madeline being the first of OO7 Roger Moore's many conquests). Her CV also includes much television work, plus the horror comedy *Theatre of Blood*. She was married to the late *The Mummy's Shroud/Journey to the Unknown* actor David Buck.

CAROLINE MUNRO

Caroline Munro was signed up after being spotted on billboards as the exotic proponent of Lamb's Navy Rum. Her draft contract with the company, who initially intended to showcase her in the later-scuppered *The Day the Earth Cracked Open* (aka *When the Earth Cracked Open*), required her to "co-operate fully with... stills sessions designed to launch

her as 'the Hammer find of 1971'." She made her Hammer début in *Dracula A.D. 1972* instead, in which she played a teenager bloodied at the Black Mass which summons up the Count. Later, as gypsy girl Carla, she was besotted by *Captain Kronos Vampire Hunter*. She made many film appearances in the mid-to-late seventies — opposite Peter Cushing and Doug McClure in Amicus' *At the Earth's Core*, as a homicidal helicopter pilot in *The Spy Who Loved Me* — and was briefly a hostess on the television quiz show *3-2-1*. "The Hammer films always had a big impact in the States," she recalls. "It was really an invaluable calling card for any actress. Of course, I wasn't with the studio in its heyday, but the important thing is that I did do one of the Dracula films."

Previous page (above): "Love goddess! Priestess of passion! Eternal sex symbol!" Hammer's publicists gave Olinka Berova's character a lot to live up to in The Vengeance of She.

Previous page (bottom left): Veronica Carlson in a publicity shot taken around the time of Dracula Has Risen From the Grave.

Previous page (bottom right): Julie Ege as Nala in Creatures the World Forgot.

Above: Hammer starlet Madeline Smith was a familiar face on British television throughout the seventies and eighties.

Left: A provocative publicity shot of Caroline Munro, taken to promote Dracula A.D. 1972.

**Principal photography 6 July to
18 August 1970
Released 17 January 1971
Certificate X
Duration 95 mins
Colour
Director Jimmy Sangster**

Reincarnated via black magic, vampire Carmilla Karnstein (Yutte Stensgaard), posing as debutante Mircalla, is enrolled at an exclusive all-girls boarding-school by a woman claiming to be the Countess Herritzen (Barbara Jefford). Researching legends associated with the nearby Karnstein castle, Gothic storyteller Richard Lestrange (Michael Johnson) becomes infatuated with Mircalla, and tricks his way into a teaching post. Mircalla's bloody desires are temporarily satisfied by the murders of both a serving-girl and a fellow student. The latter killing is concealed by schoolmaster Giles Barton (Ralph Bates), an academic fascinated by the occult. He confronts Mircalla with his suspicions concerning her true identity; his theories are soon to be horribly confirmed...

arly in 1970, midway through production of *The Vampire Lovers*, Fantale sent Hammer its outline for a sequel, *To Love a Vampire*. On 25 February, Roy Skeggs suggested that, if shot during May and June, the film could be made at Bray, with nearby Oakley Court doubling for the girls' school crucial to its realisation. To Sir James Carreras' disappointment, *The Vampire Lovers* backers AIP passed on the chance to support the film. In June, it was made public that *To Love a Vampire* had been picked up by EMI, thus extending the association begun with

The Horror of Frankenstein and Scars of Dracula.

Dated 6 April, Tudor Gates' first draft script contained a number of continuity references to *The Vampire Lovers*, all of which were excised before principal photography commenced. One of Barton's books, titled *The Karnsteins. A History of Evil*, would be seen to be have been penned by Baron Von Hartog; in Lestrange's dream sequence, he would have imagined being smothered by Mircalla's *alter ego*, a cat. *To Love a Vampire* is an apt title for this script, less concerned with libido, more with matters of the heart. At one point, Lestrange near swoons when distracted from his lecture on the Romantic poets — "Wordsworth, Byron, Shelley, Keats" — by Mircalla's "tender, compassionate" gaze. When the pair first make love, Mircalla "weeps." (In this draft, Mircalla would take one final victim: ineffectual headmistress Miss Simpson.)

Gates wrote the role of perverse diabolist Barton for Peter Cushing, who was forced to drop out of the film at the eleventh hour when his wife Helen fell gravely ill. Almost simultaneously, scheduled director Terence Fisher became incapacitated and Hammer had Jimmy Sangster replace him. Less than a week prior to shooting on location and at MGM-EMI Elstree — the Bray plans having since been scotched — Ralph Bates signed up to play Barton "as a favour to Peter and Jimmy. I thought it was a tasteless film and I regret having anything to do with it."

Danish actress/model Yutte Stensgaard — who had featured in a number of *Carry Ons*, Amicus' *Scream and Scream Again* and Tigon's bizarre *Zeta One* — took the pivotal role of Mircalla. (Although she confessed to harbouring Oscar ambitions, her career extended little beyond a six-month stint as a hostess on the TV quiz *The Golden Shot*.) Mike Raven reprised John Forbes-Robertson's role as the Man in Black (the credit roller, however, names his character 'Count Karnstein'). Raven relished his horror film début, but was disappointed to be dubbed by Valentine Dyall.

The film's worthier pretensions long since sidelined, producers Fine and Style renamed it *Lust For a Vampire* and took the cutting out of its busy director's hands. A reel five scene wherein Mircalla would be seen to seduce — and then feed on —

naked schoolgirl Amanda (Judy Matheson) was entirely removed upon the instruction of the BBFC. Upon viewing the picture at a Hammersmith cinema, Sangster and Bates were astonished to hear a cheesy pop song, 'Strange Love' — lyrics by Frank Godwin, vocals by 'Tracy' — dubbed over the key Mircalla/Lestrange love scene. "I have never been so embarrassed in my life when that song came on!" grimaces Sangster. Raven, a rhythm and blues DJ on Radio One, was similarly appalled: "That horrified me more than anything in the entire film!"

Lust For a Vampire is pleasing enough — until one considers what Fisher, Cushing and Bray's craftsmen might have made of Gates' reasonably literate draft.

Imre Toth (Sandor Eles) is bequeathed the stables of Count Nadasdy, a former comrade-in-arms of his father's, to the disgust of Captain Dobi (Nigel Green), a loyal Nadasdy retainer. Nadasdy's aged and cruel widow, Elisabeth (Ingrid Pitt), née Bathory, is equally outraged to learn that she must share his estate with absent daughter Ilona (Lesley-Anne Down). Later, the Countess' chambermaid, Teri (Susan Brodrick), is accidentally cut, spattering Elisabeth's face with her blood. Elisabeth, astounded, summons maid Julie (Patience Collier), discovering that where the girl's blood fell, her skin has become rejuvenated. The next morning, Teri has disappeared and a radiant, youthful Elisabeth is introduced to the castle staff as 'Ilona', returned from abroad. Dobi, Elisabeth's lover of many years, has been let in on his mistress' secret and has arranged for the real Ilona to be abducted. To Dobi's chagrin, 'Ilona' seduces the handsome Imre, and when her appearance fades she has Julie procure another victim. But, shortly after becoming engaged to Imre, her features fail again. She becomes ever more hideous, and the blood of a whore does not have the same effect. Learned Master Fabio (Maurice Denham) discovers why: she must bathe only in the blood of virgins to retain her preternatural looks...

**Principal photography 27 July to
4 September 1970**
Released 31 January 1971
Certificate X
Duration 93 mins
Colour
Director Peter Sasdy

Thanks again to Sir James Carreras' connections, *Countess Dracula* was the first of an eventual four features to be underwritten by Rank Film Distributors, which was originally announced as a three-film deal comprising *Countess Dracula*, *Dr Jekyll & Sister Hyde* and *Village of the Vampires*.

Filmed at Pinewood, *Countess Dracula* recycled sets first seen in *Anne of the Thousand Days*, Universal's 1969 Richard Burton/Geneviève Bujold Henry VIII biopic. Ingrid Pitt, retained from *The Vampire Lovers*, revelled in the lead role, but came to express reservations over the film's rather watered-down approach to the Bathory legend: "I don't think it was cruel enough, horrifying enough. It needed more cruelty, throat slashing, blood hounds, blood!" (Rank later expressed similar sentiments.) Nigel Green, a South African-born actor whose star was in the ascendant post-*Zulu*, made only two further pictures; he died from an accidental overdose of sleeping pills on 15 May 1972.

Pitt was appalled to find her natural East European inflections overdubbed in the finished print. (Despite this, she remains a fervent, and much-loved,

Hammer advocate.)

The lush and richly-designed *Countess Dracula* is shot through with startling camerawork (slow-motion, tilted angles, glittering filters, a jarring dissolve to red) and some clever storytelling (the Countess' first reversal to her natural age), but its distinctly anaemic blood-lettings fail to lift a rather tiresome tale of court intrigue.

Were it not for the curiosity of a Jesuit priest living in Budapest in 1729, *Countess Dracula* might never have been made. He unearthed documents dated 2 January 1611, which had been suppressed by the Catholic Church for over a century. The documents recorded the cross-examination of four servants called as witnesses before the court that tried Hungarian noblewoman Erzsebet Bathory, aka 'the Beast of Csejthe'. The Countess, once married to Ferenc Nadasdy, was walled up inside her own castle, having been found guilty of the murders of over 300 women. Her atrocities were manifold: she froze girls alive, jabbed hot needles beneath their fingernails, "cut their flesh and made them grill it." She was most noted, however, for bathing in the blood of peasant girls, believing it might keep her young.

Hammer's 1970 production drew solely on the latter trait (infused, perhaps, with a touch of *The Picture of Dorian Gray*). Inspired by Gabriel Ronay, a Bathory scholar whose academic *The Truth About Dracula* would be published in 1972, the film was co-produced by independent Alexander Paal, previously part-responsible for Exclusive's fifties thrillers *Mantrap* and *Four Sided Triangle*. Hungarian Peter Sasdy was hired to direct this fanciful redressing of a monster from his native land, and the film's titles showed details from a painting of Bathory's exploits by nineteenth-century Hungarian artist Istvan Cook.

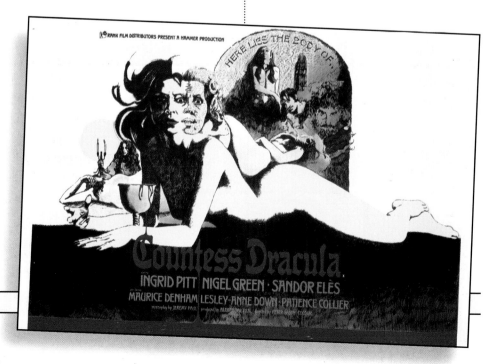

BLOOD FROM THE MUMMY'S TOMB

Principal photography 11 January to February 1971
Released 7 October 1971
Certificate X
Duration 94 mins
Colour
Director Seth Holt (and Michael Carreras, unaccredited)

London, the present day: a young woman, Margaret (Valerie Leon), suffers a recurring nightmare in which she sees an ancient Egyptian queen, to whom she bears an uncanny resemblance, sealed up in a sarcophagus. The priests who entomb her first chop off her hand, but, after throwing the member to the jackals, are killed by a mysterious and powerful force that lacerates their throats. The day before her birthday, Margaret's father, archaeologist Professor Fuchs (Andrew Keir), gives her a ruby ring. It transpires that the ring was discovered when, twenty years before, Fuchs and four others — Corbeck (James Villiers), Dandridge (Hugh Burden), Berigan (George Coulouris), and Helen Dickerson (Rosalie Crutchley) — broke into the tomb of Queen Tera and found the ring on her disembodied hand. Her perfectly preserved body lay in a golden coffin beside it, with the stump of her arm leaking blood. At that moment, thousands of miles away, Margaret's mother died giving birth to her. Margaret, it seems, is a vessel for Tera's magic. Soon, when a certain celestial conjunction is complete and three key artefacts assembled beside Tera's corpse, this evil sorceress will be born anew...

*d*racula author Bram Stoker's 1903 novel *The Jewel of the Seven Stars*, a mystical thriller concerning a Great Experiment to reincarnate the dead according to arcane science, had been noted by prospective film producer Howard Brandy. In 1970, a chance meeting with Christopher Wicking, a screenwriter for *Vampire Lovers* backers AIP, led Brandy to propose a version of Stoker's Egyptological opus, based on a treatment by the pair, to James Carreras. Sir James took on the film only after the title was changed to the rather more lurid *Blood From the Mummy's Tomb*.

Wicking, whose work alongside writer/producer Gordon Hessler included *Scream and Scream Again* and *Murders in the Rue Morgue*, delivered a first draft markedly more explicit than the eventual film. Helen Dickerson, for example, perishes after she and a coven of fellow Tera-worshippers, performing black magic rites in the buff, are denoun-

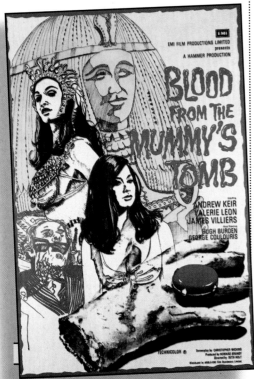

ced by the spirit of the cat who will tear them to pieces: "She says you've worshipped other deities," snarls Margaret, "have called and called for the Christian Devil — who you should know doesn't exist..." Then, amidst the coven's naked and bloodied bodies — "we can't tell the living from the dead" — Margaret makes love to her "slave", the villainous Corbeck. Hessler was one of three mooted directors (the others being Peter Duffell, then best known for Amicus' *The House That Dripped Blood*, and Claude Watham). Ultimately, the job went to Seth Holt, who'd last worked for Hammer on *The Nanny*. Holt engaged Valerie Leon, a stunning 5' 11" actress whose mainstream exposure had been limited to a

handful of *Carry On* movies and a series of ads for Hai Karate aftershave, to double up as Margaret/Tera. (He'd first used her as a stand-in for Julie Newmar, best known as Catwoman in the *Batman* TV series, on *Monsieur Lecoq*.) Leon acquited herself with credit; twice a Bond girl, she regularly appeared on television throughout the seventies. Peter Cushing took the part of her father, the scheming Julian Fuchs.

Meanwhile, Sir James, in dire need of an experienced individual to oversee Hammer's diverse production schedule, invited his son back into the corporate fold and Michael became Hammer's managing director on 4 January 1971. One week later, and

funded by EMI, *Blood From the Mummy's Tomb* went before the Elstree cameras. At the end of the first day, Cushing was informed that his beloved wife Helen had been rushed to Canterbury Hospital. His scenes were hurriedly rescheduled. Helen died of emphysema on the Thursday. Cushing would never recover from her loss.

Former Professor Quatermass Andrew Keir took Cushing's place on the 18th. Production continued apace. And then, on 14 February, at the end of the fifth of a six-week schedule, Holt suffered a sudden, terminal, heart attack. While cast and crew grieved, Michael Carreras attempted to assess the amount of work needed to complete the film, and discovered that Holt, an experienced editor, had left behind a mish-mash of baffling footage. "Seth hadn't shot any entrances or departures," he recalled. "He had only

shot the main action. Perhaps he had planned to use dissolves, perhaps not... There were some very strange, incomplete sequences, and a lot of missing material." Although Carreras did briefly entertain the notion of hiring another director, possibly Don Sharp, to restart the film from scratch, he elected to complete the outstanding scenes himself, unaccredited, and approximating Holt's style as best he could (the largest remaining sequence featured the asylum-bound Berigan). Holt's funeral took place during the last few days of shooting. It was a remarkable send-off, according to actor James Villiers: "Hammer lent us one of the original hearses from one of their many films, with the plumed horses and the fine carriage with the black drapings and silver trappings, used in every single Dracula film ever made, and we followed along behind this marvellous hearse and buried the old bean..."

Blood From the Mummy's Tomb premièred at the National Film Theatre on 7 October as part of a retrospective of the company's films, and was favourably, perhaps kindly, reviewed when released later in the month as the lower half of a bill headlining *Dr Jekyll & Sister Hyde*. Although it undoubtedly contains some of the strongest set pieces in any of Hammer's latter-day *oeuvre*, it would be wrong to pass off its disjointed and sometimes incomprehensible narrative as befitting an otherworldly ambience strived for by its director. Equally, it would be prosaic to claim that this unhappy film, beset by tragedy, was cursed from the start.

ANDREW KEIR: PROFESSOR FUCHS

Andrew Keir, a regular member of Hammer's informal repertory company, was called upon to deputise for Peter Cushing on *Blood From the Mummy's Tomb*: "Michael Carreras rang me one Friday night to say that they were in trouble. Peter Cushing's wife had died. Could I help them out, come in and do it? I told them to leave the script at the gate and I'd come down. I was living in Wales, so I travelled overnight, learned the script and started on Monday..." Born in 1926, Scottish Keir, briefly a coal miner, started his career at Glasgow's Citizens Theatre. He appeared in Exclusive/Hammer's *The Lady Craved Excitement* alongside Hy Hazell and Sid James and, over a decade later, tied his mast to Hammer swashbucklers *The Pirates of Blood River* and *The Devil-Ship Pirates*, before donning the habit of fiery friar Father Sandor for *Dracula Prince of Darkness*. Next he was Octavian in *The Viking Queen*. One year later came his largest Hammer role, that of Nigel Kneale's ever-questioning hero in *Quatermass and the Pit*.

Previous page: *Valerie Leon and Sunbronze Danny Boy, pet 'puddy' of on-screen boyfriend Tod Browning.*
Above left: *11 January 1971 — a rare still of Leon with Peter Cushing during the latter's single day's work on the film.*
Left: *"Valerie was chosen from hundreds of contenders for the part," claimed a Blood From the Mummy's Tomb publicity brochure, "and now she blazes the same Hammer trail that took such beauties as Raquel Welch, Ursula Andress and Olinka Berova to international screen star status."*

Principal photography 25 January to
5 March 1971
Released 3 October 1971
Certificate X
Duration 85 mins
Colour
Director Peter Sasdy

Jack the Ripper returns to his home in Berner Street, Whitechapel, and murders his wife while their young daughter, Anna, watches from her cot. Anna (Angharad Rees) grows up with fake medium Mrs Golding (Dora Bryan), who forces her into prostitution. Anna's first client, MP Dysart (Derek Godfrey), makes her a gift of a jewelled brooch. She seems transfixed when it catches the light, and summons incredible strength to skewer Mrs Golding with a poker. John Pritchard (Eric Porter), a doctor intrigued by the new technique of psychoanalysis, takes Anna into his care. When Pritchard's maid, Dolly (Marjie Lawrence), places a jewelled necklace around Anna's neck she is once again transfixed. She slashes Dolly's throat with a broken mirror, impaling a shard in her neck. Anna returns to Berner Street, and is taken in by lesbian whore Long Liz (Lynda Baron). Anna is once again induced to kill, stabbing Liz in the eye with a clutch of hat pins. During a visit to a genuine medium, Madame Bullard (Margaret Rawlings), Anna relives her childhood trauma and unwittingly reveals that the violent spirit of Jack the Ripper lives on. Pritchard is on the verge of identifying Anna's psychotic trigger when, once more possessed, she turns on him with a sword...

ammer had not revisited the infamous White-chapel murders since *Room To Let* in 1949. The company soon made up for lost time, producing *Hands of the Ripper* and *Dr Jekyll & Sister Hyde* almost concurrently. *Hands of the Ripper* was script-ed by Lew Davidson, one of a number of writers commissioned by Sir James Carreras between Anthony Hinds' departure from Hammer House and Michael Carreras' return. Principally financed by Rank, and therefore produced at the distributor's Pinewood Studios, *Hands of the Ripper* was the support feature to *Twins of Evil* and cost almost exactly as much to make.

Director Peter Sasdy and Aida Young, both working on their final Hammer film, recruited an experienced television star to headline the picture. "Eric Porter was not a Hammer actor," Sasdy remembers. "They said,

HANDS OF THE RIPPER

Eric Porter · Jane Merrow · Dora Bryan

Angharad Rees · Derek Godfrey

'You can't get him!'... I had the arrogance of a young man then and I couldn't care less. Why not try to get to the top?" Porter had previously made *The Lost Continent* for Hammer, but by 1970 was primarily known for his portrayal of Soames in the popular BBC drama *The Forsyte Saga*. Aida Young cast twenty-three year-old Angharad Rees as Anna after spotting her in the television play *Why We Are Fled*. For her film début, the actress sought advice from her father, a professor of psychology at St Bartholomew's Hospital. "I consulted him on a number of technical points and he was very understanding," she told *Films Illustrated*. "I saw Anna as a straight, innocent girl who had been through hard times. She is totally normal to all outward appearances and to herself, and that was what made her all the more horribly sad

for me... From an actress' point of view, the part offered total scope."

The most demanding sequences in the film were those set in St Paul's Cathedral at the climax: the blind Laura (Jane Merrow) is trapped in the Whispering Gallery with a psychotic Anna. The dying Pritchard, having finally grasped the nature of Anna's schizo-phrenia, pleads with her from the ground. "I asked for permission to shoot in St Paul's Cathedral, but they wouldn't have us," remembers Aida Young. "I went to St Paul's anyway, and we took a dozen stills which the special effects people used to trick the final shots. We built the Whispering Gallery in the studio, and cut to the stills of St Paul's. It looked wonderful."

The graphic violence in *Hands of the Ripper* was the most nauseating yet seen in a Hammer film. In America, the MPAA insisted on trimming the murders of both Dolly and Long Liz, and the film was distrib-

Evening Standard

THE RIPPER STRIKES AGAIN?

There is violence in this girl. It's still there now—something horribly violent. Her father—well-dressed, well-spoken, a nobleman . . . years ago. There's blood on his clothes. The man has murdered the mother of his child.

That child . . . is Anna. The man . . . is the Ripper.

uted by Universal only after sixteen seconds of footage had been censored.

When *Hands of the Ripper* was released with *Twins of Evil* in October 1971, its quality was recognised by *Variety*: "Well-directed by Peter Sasdy, the tension is skilfully developed. Murders are particularly gruesome and there are shocks that will have the most hardened film-goer sitting up... Angharad Rees makes the pretty killer entirely credible."

The cracks in *Hands of the Ripper* are papered over admirably. Kenneth Talbot's soft-focused photography, and Christopher Gunning's wistful theme, help establish an almost tranquil atmosphere for Peter Sasdy to fracture at carefully paced intervals. *Hands of the Ripper* expertly mixes the sophistication expected of Hammer's films with the gore its new audiences demanded.

PETER SASDY: DIRECTOR

Hungarian director Peter Sasdy came to prominence with *The Caves of Steel*, a popular Isaac Asimov adaptation in BBC2's *Story Parade* series. The play, which starred Peter Cushing and John Carson, was first transmitted by the fledgling channel in June 1964. Sasdy had already proved himself on *Journey to the Unknown* by the time Aida Young invited him to direct *Taste the Blood of Dracula*. "Basically, I'm still catering for the three types of built-in Hammer audiences," he told *Kinematograph Weekly* in 1970. "One: the large number of people who go to the films to be frightened and consider that reality can be more frightening than fiction; two: those who go there for a certain kind of laugh, the laugh that comes out of nervous tension; and three: the type of audience that goes for sexual thrills. I wanted to avoid the third group, but one has to believe that the three groups exist. They are the people who go to the box office, pay ten shillings and go to see a Hammer film." In the early eighties, Sasdy became a key director of *Hammer House of Horror* and *Hammer House of Mystery and Suspense*. His television work continues to enjoy acclaim, although the path of his career has not always been smooth. "He's a perfectionist," says admirer Aida Young, "and directors like that have a hard time."

HANDS OF THE RIPPER
ERIC PORTER   JANE MERROW
ANGHARAD REES   DEREK GODFREY
DORA BRYAN

Previous page: *Bleeding to death, Pritchard (Eric Porter) tries to save the threatened Laura (Jane Merrow).*
Above left: *This single-sheet 'newspaper' was offered to London cinema managers as a promotional gimmick. Rather less inspired was Rank's suggestion that "The theme of hand care is a 'natural' for* Hands of the Ripper, *enabling you to tie up with stockists of hand creams, lotions, oil, gloves and nail varnish for the care and protection of hands."*
Above right: *From left to right, Eric Porter, Derek Godfrey and Peter Sasdy at Pinewood Studios.*
Left: *Mrs Golding (Dora Bryan) protects Anna (Angharad Rees) from the lecherous Dysart (Derek Godfrey).*

**Principal photography 22 February to
30 March 1971
Released 17 October 1971
Certificate X
Duration 97 minutes
Colour
Director Roy Ward Baker**

Victorian London: Professor Robertson (Gerald Sim) grows concerned about his young friend, Dr Jekyll (Ralph Bates), whose obsessive quest for the elixir of life takes precedence over everything. That includes the doting Susan (Susan Brodrick), who shares the flat above Jekyll's with her brother Howard (Lewis Fiander). Jekyll needs female hormones to continue his research, and necrophiliac mortuary attendant Byker (Philip Madoc) turns a blind eye while Jekyll takes the glands he needs from dead girls. When Byker's supply is exhausted, he turns to grave robbers Burke (Ivor Dean) and Hare (Tony Calvin). They begin murdering girls to meet Jekyll's demands, and his experimentation continues. Jekyll drinks his elixir, which transforms him into a beautiful woman (Martine Beswick). Jekyll later tells an inquisitive Susan that the woman is his sister, the widowed Mrs Hyde. When an angry mob turns on Burke and Hare, Jekyll begins murdering Whitechapel prostitutes himself, removing their glands with surgical precision. Professor Robertson becomes suspicious of his friend, but is seduced and murdered by the increasingly powerful Hyde. She next seduces Howard, before realising that by killing Susan she may be free of Jekyll's influence forever...

*i*n the late sixties, Hammer films shared studio space at Elstree with a number of other productions, including ABC Television's *The Avengers*. Following the cancellation of *The Avengers* in 1969, co-producer Brian Clemens decided to resume his film career: "I came up with an idea: *Dr Jekyll & Sister Hyde*. I couldn't believe nobody had ever done that. I mentioned it to Jimmy [Carreras] and he said, 'Come up and see me in two days at Hammer House.' When I arrived for the appointment he'd already had the poster made. So I knew I had a deal."

The pre-production artwork was inspired by an idea that Clemens had originally outlined to Carreras on the back of an envelope. "A free and FRESH adaptation of the original classic," began Clemens' notes. "A story to fit any Period. Or modern day... Jekyll changes from a powerful man — into a slim, beautiful, full-breasted woman! And yet he retains his male mind. And his male drives. And his male strength... [Jekyll]

uses Sister Hyde as the perfect disguise — he roams the streets like Jack the Ripper — seeking out his victims... and they are easy to find, because why should they fear a woman like themselves?... murdering them, and pillaging their bodies for their experiments."

Clemens next prepared a treatment that firmly established the setting as the gaslit Whitechapel of the 1880s. The seventeen-page document was punctuated by brief snatches of dialogue: "This is what I am going to do," resolves a furious Hyde. "I am going to kill that fancy faced little bitch Susan. Kill her and have Mark for myself. And then Doctor Jekyll will be blamed... but he won't be anywhere to be found." Clemens' screenplay, which opened with a "grateful acknowledgement to Robert Louis Stevenson", would re-christen the improbably named Mark Spencer as Howard.

Along with his partner from *The Avengers*, Albert

Fennell, Clemens was contracted to produce his screenplay in October 1970. Originally intended for Rank, the film's co-finance was ultimately shouldered by EMI. To direct the picture, Hammer considered Jimmy Sangster, Peter Sasdy, Alan Gibson and Gordon Hessler (who had united Vincent Price, Christopher Lee and Peter Cushing for the previous year's *Scream and Scream Again*). By December, the job had been given to the reliable Roy Ward Baker, who had worked with Clemens and Fennell on *The Avengers*. While casting the film, Baker had some help from Hammer House. "Sir James Carreras suggested Martine Beswick," he remembers. "He said, 'She's the girl for this,' and he was absolutely right... You put her and Ralph Bates together and they looked exactly alike." Since starring in *Slave Girls*, Beswick had concentrated her career on American television. In 1971, she lived in West London with her photographer hus-

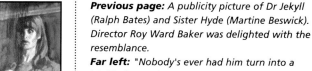

Previous page: A publicity picture of Dr Jekyll (Ralph Bates) and Sister Hyde (Martine Beswick). Director Roy Ward Baker was delighted with the resemblance.
Far left: "Nobody's ever had him turn into a bird before," claimed the press book.
Left: Pre-production artwork inspired by Brian Clemens' original story outline.
Below left: Burke (Ivor Dean, centre) and Hare (Tony Calvin, right) deliver a cadaver to Dr Jekyll.

RALPH BATES: DR JEKYLL

Born in 1940, Ralph Bates was already a busy stage and television actor by the time he made his film début in *Taste the Blood of Dracula*. In 1970, publicity photos were taken of Peter Cushing 'handing over' his most famous role to the younger actor — Bates later insisted that *The Horror of Frankenstein* was never intended to be anything other than a one-off 'flashback' to the Baron's licentious youth. Bates stood in for Cushing on *Lust For a Vampire* but gave his most memorable Hammer performance in *Dr Jekyll & Sister Hyde*. Virginia Wetherell, the actress who played Betsy in the film, became his wife in 1973. "She was the first lady I killed," Bates later joked, "and the relationship has been going steadily downhill ever since." Bates' final Hammer film was *Fear in the Night*, a suspense thriller in which he starred alongside Peter Cushing and Joan Collins. He went on to appear in Tyburn's *Persecution*, and was reunited with Collins for *I Don't Want to Be Born*. Latterly, Bates' career was dominated by television and he became well-known for roles in *Poldark*, *Penmarric* and, most notably, the sit-com *Dear John*. He died of pancreatic cancer in 1991.

band, former Hammer leading man John Richardson. Interviewed in the *Dr Jekyll & Sister Hyde* press book, she offered her thoughts on the role: "Sister Hyde is incredibly, blatantly sexy; loves men, revels in being a woman. That's how we all dream of being. Every woman's fantasy is to be a wife in the kitchen and a whore in the bedroom. Any girl who denies that is lying."

The shooting of *Dr Jekyll & Sister Hyde* was entirely confined to stages three and four of EMI-MGM-EMI Elstree, and began on 22 February 1971. From March onwards, Hammer's *On the Buses* began shooting on stages one and six at the facility. The respective performances of both films illustrates the changing landscape of British cinema attendance in the early seventies. *On the Buses* broke eighty-eight all-time house records during its first week of general release in August 1971, grossing £2,500,000 by March 1973. The *Dr Jekyll & Sister Hyde/Blood From the Mummy's Tomb* double-bill managed a mere £2,376 in its opening week at London's New Victoria. The general release receipts told a similar story of diminishing interest in Hammer's horror product.

As Hammer's search for new ideas became increasingly desperate, Brian Clemens came to the rescue with irony. Roy Ward Baker's sympathy with the arch screenplay ensures that the laughs are all intentional. Cinema audiences of the day clearly thought the joke had been taken too far — in retrospect, they just had no sense of humour.

Hammer's early seventies box-office fortunes were transformed not by homicidal she-males, nor kinky vampiresses with Sapphic proclivities — but, oddly enough, by Stan and Jack, two lecherous buffoons from the Luxton Town and District Bus Company. Television spin-off *On the Buses* was a box-office phenomenon in 1971, and its astounding success led Hammer to wring more from the same comedic vein.

The company was, of course, no stranger to the notion of exploiting formats successful in other media. Back in the fifties and early sixties, the spin-off adventures of Dick Barton, Richard Greene's Robin Hood and Professor Bernard Quatermass had all made a sizeable impact — as had the cinema version of *Life With the Lyons*, a domestic sit-com revolving around the misadventures of the hapless Lyon family. Derived from a BBC radio series that transferred to television in 1955, *Life With the Lyons* starred husband and wife Ben Lyon and Bebe Daniels, plus cleaner-than-clean children Barbara and Richard, and concerned the Lyons' efforts to avoid eviction. Released in May 1954, it was followed just seven months later by a sequel, *The Lyons in Paris*; both pictures were written and directed by Val Guest. Rather more earthy was *I Only Arsked*, a 1958 effort drawn from *The Army Game*, Granada Television's hugely popular National Service comedy of the late fifties and early sixties (via *The Ugly Duckling*, Hammer attempted to make a big-screen star of *I Only Arsked*'s Bernard Bresslaw). A little later, originals *Don't Panic Chaps!* and *Watch It Sailor!* tried to repeat the humour-in-uniform formula instigated by both *I Only Arsked* and the naval comedy *Up the Creek*. The latter, its complement comprising

an array of British comic talent — David Tomlinson, Peter Sellers, Lionel Jeffries and Wilfrid Hyde White — had already spawned the sequel *Further Up the Creek*. *Sands of the Desert* and *A Weekend With Lulu* were, respectively, vehicles for comedians Charlie Drake (catchphrase: "Hello my darlings!") and Leslie Phillips (catchphrase: "I say…").

Due largely to American investors' unwillingness to back subjects with only domestic, ergo British, appeal, Hammer had not produced a comedy picture since the 1962 fiasco that was *The Old Dark House* when, in 1971, it was announced that the company was to make *On the Buses*, drawn from the LWT sit-com of the same name, for British conglomerate EMI. Recalls Roy Skeggs, Hammer production supervisor turned producer: "Jimmy [Carreras] called me into his office and said, 'This film is being made for pennies, so I want you to produce it.' I said, 'Do you mind if I don't? I can't stand the thing on television.' He said, 'Produce it or go', and pointed to the door. So I produced it. We made it for £97,000 and it took £1.4 million in its first six weeks in Britain and Australia alone. And it's still making money…"

On the Buses tampered little with the formula that had made the series a hit from 1969 on: our heroes, roguish bus company employees Stan Butler (Reg Varney) and Jack (Bob Grant), devise a series of witless endeavours designed to undo the liberated *femme* drivers hoisted upon the service by Stephen Lewis' pop-eyed and Führer-esque inspector Blakey (catchphrase: "I'll get you, Butler!"). Domestic disharmony *chez* Stan, meanwhile, revolves around sister

Olive (Anna Karen), mother (Doris Hare) and good-for-nothing brother-in-law Arthur (Michael Robbins). Two sequels followed in rapid succession: *Mutiny On the Buses* temporarily expanded Stan's route via Windsor Safari Park, and *Holiday On the Buses* relocated its sacked principals to a down-at-heel Welsh holiday camp.

Unsurprisingly, given the impressive results achieved by *On the Buses*, Hammer was busy signing up as many small screen stars as possible. In March 1972, barely six months after *On the Buses*' release, treatments — all ultimately unused — were being prepared for Benny Hill, The Two Ronnies and Terry Scott (a project tantalisingly titled *The Scott Report on Sex, Wife-swapping and the Permissive Society*). The next Hammer comedy to be released was *That's Your Funeral*, drawn from a short-lived 1971 BBC1 series. It proved a not-so-glorious undertaking. A would-be black farce concerning the misadventures of the partnership that runs the Holroyd Funeral Home (Raymond Huntley, David Battley and Bill Fraser), it contained cameos by *On the Buses*' Michael Robbins, *Taste the Blood of Dracula*'s Roy Kinnear — plus producers Michael Carreras and Roy Skeggs, seen as mourners during the opening credits. The film's gallows humour was not confined to those sharing lines on screen. "We had a chap playing a dead body in a wheelchair," remembers Skeggs, "and half way through filming he died. It was rumoured on the set that Roy Skeggs had rung his family and asked if he could finish the picture for half his fee!" Indeed, Rank was reluctant to release the film, so distasteful did

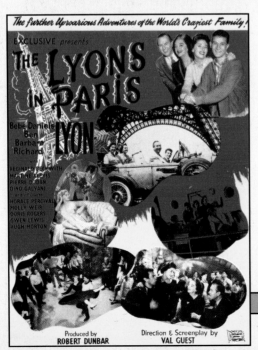

The further Uproarious Adventures of the World's Craziest Family!

EXCLUSIVE presents
THE LYONS IN PARIS
Bebe Daniels
Ben
Barbara
Richard
LYON

REGINALD BECKWITH WITH
MARTINE ALEXIS
PIERRE DUDAN
DINO GALVANI
AND
HORACE PERCIVAL
MOLLY WEIR
DORIS ROGERS
GWEN LEWIS
HUGH MORTON

Produced by
ROBERT DUNBAR

Direction & Screenplay by
VAL GUEST

Previous page (top): On the Buses regulars Arthur (Michael Robbins), Jack (Bob Grant), Mum (Doris Hare), Stan (Reg Varney), Olive (Anna Karen) and Blake (Stephen Lewis). Films and Filming nominated the first film in the series as British "box office champion" of 1971.
Left: Navy larks with Jane (Shirley Eaton) and Lieutenant Commander Fairweather (David Tomlinson) in Further Up the Creek.
Below: The press book promoting Hammer's final comedy, the saucy Man About the House.
Bottom: When a bereaved family complained to Rank about a Hammer film crew, the release of That's Your Funeral was brought into doubt. Bill Fraser starred as irreverent undertaker Basil Bulstrode.

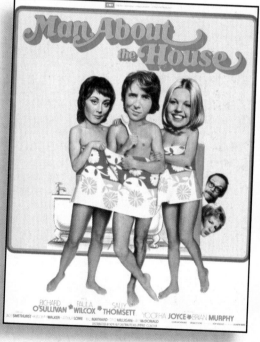

they find the subject matter.

Nearest and Dearest, from the Granada series of 1968 to 1973, came next. Concerning sibling rivalry amongst North Country pickle-bottlers Hylda Baker and Jimmy Jewel, it was deemed a box-office failure and a projected sequel went unmade (as did another Baker vehicle, Mafioso spoof *The Godmother*). *Love Thy Neighbour*, however, was very much a product of its unenlightened times, its premise being the hilarious comic consequences resulting from a racist bigot's loathing for his Jamaican next-door-neighbour. Featuring Jack Smethurst and Rudolph Walker as the constantly-at-loggerheads pair, it was adapted from Thames TV's popular series of 1972 to 1976. Anticipated sequel *Love Thy Neighbour Again* never materialised. Other series which failed to make their mooted transition included *My Wife Next Door*, a short-lived BBC1 sit-com co-devised by Brian Clemens and starring John Alderton and Hannah Gordon as neighbouring former marrieds, and *The Rag Trade*, *On the Buses*' creators Ronald Chesney and Ronald Wolfe's early sixties series (which was revived in the seventies) set in a dressmakers' and featuring *The Anniversary*'s Sheila Hancock (this projected follow-on would have borne the title *The Rag Trade Goes Mod*).

Others jumped on the bandwagon set rolling by *On the Buses*, as a host of comedies were transferred to the big screen via other production companies during this period (*Steptoe and Son*, *Dad's Army* et al). The last Hammer comedy was *Man About the House*, which top-billed Richard O'Sullivan as laddish Robin Tripp, condemned to flatshare with two gorgeous albeit scatty young women, Chrissy and Jo (Paula Wilcox and Sally Thomsett). Replete with a bizarre, almost post-modern climax played out in a television studio — which featured not only Spike Milligan as himself, but also *Love Thy Neighbour*'s Smethurst and Walker chummily playing a symbolic game of chess — *Man About the House* was released in Christmas week, 1974. The film was a sizeable hit, taking £90,000 in the London area alone. After Brian Lawrence and Roy Skeggs left Hammer, their Cinema Arts company produced the film version of *Man About the House* spin-off, *George and Mildred*. An adaptation of the Leonard Rossiter sit-com *Rising Damp*, also produced by Cinema Arts, concluded the last successful cycle of pictures initiated by Hammer. By the time the film was released in 1980, Skeggs and Lawrence had turned their attention to the more serious business of re-establishing the House of Horror.

Principal photography 22 March to
30 April 1971
Released 3 October 1971
Certificate X
Duration 87 mins
Colour
Director John Hough

The village of Karnstein: the witch-hunting Brotherhood, led by zealous puritan Gustav Weil (Peter Cushing), seek out a woodman's daughter (Judy Matheson) whom they believe to be a servant of the Devil — and burn her at the stake. Recently orphaned, Weil's nieces, identical twins Frieda and Maria Gellhorn (Madelaine Collinson, Mary Collinson) arrive in Karnstein, where their inappropriate dress immediately earns them their uncle's approbation. The Brotherhood harass rakish libertine Count Karnstein (Damien Thomas), who lives in a castle above the village. The Count, however, has the protection of the Emperor, and Weil is unable to execute the Count as he would dearly wish. For his amusement, the Count arranges a black magic ceremony, invoking Satan and sacrificing a girl on the castle altar. Blood drips through a crack in the sarcophagus onto a shrouded corpse within — that of the Count's ancestor, Mircalla (Katya Wyeth), whose spectral form appears and makes him one of the Undead. The wild Frieda becomes entranced by the Count, and is vampirised by him. She is later caught, blood on her lips, by the Brotherhood. Gustav decrees that Frieda will be burned, but the Count breaks her out of her prison cell, and exchanges Frieda for her prim and virtuous sister...

wins of Evil, the last in Fantale's vampire trilogy, focused not on the gorgeous Mircalla but on her decadent descendant, the young Count Karnstein (Fantale's bloodsucking nymphet made a token appearance, however). Supported by Rank, Hammer finalised a deal with Fantale to produce the film on 5 January 1971. In place of the rejected *The Vampire Virgins* (aka *Village of the Vampires*), which would have seen Peter Cushing as a vengeful Count Karnstein, Tudor Gates' *Twins of Evil* cast a posse of cruel witchfinders as the true villains of the piece. "One was able to inflect, in the seventies, the intolerance of the Puritans," claims Gates. "The climate at the time was more sympathetic."

Twenty-nine year-old Hammer newcomer John Hough was signed to direct, having made his mark on episodes of television's *The Avengers* and *The Saint*. In 1969, he'd made an iconoclastic TV pilot, *Wolfshead: The Legend of Robin Hood*, for Bill Anderson Productions. Rejected by London Weekend Television, rights in *Wolfshead* were later purchased by Hammer. The company hoped to develop the fifty-

four minute film as a TV series, but to no avail; it was eventually released as support to Cliff Richard's final film *Take Me High* in 1973. Meanwhile, Hough directed his first feature, *Eye Witness*, on location in Malta. According to later publicity notes, he then penned an article in the trade press which was highly critical of contemporary horror film production ("I said what was wrong with horror films and how it should be put right"). The feature was noted by Fantale's Harry Fine, and led Hough to *Twins of Evil*. Hough filled the cast list with a number of *Wolfshead* alumni — David Warbeck, Kathleen Byron, Peter Stephens, Roy Boyd, Inigo Jackson and Sheelah Wilcox — and Peter Cushing returned to the Hammer fold just two months after the death of wife Helen. Gustav Weil was

his coldest, harshest characterisation to date.

Maltese-born Madelaine and Mary Collinson, both eighteen, were duly cast as the titular twins, having been spotted by the producers between the leaves of the October 1970 edition of *Playboy* magazine. Modelling assignments "all over Britain and continental Europe" had led the siblings to the studio of legendary gentleman smutbroker Harrison Marks, for whom they'd featured in a short, punningly titled *The Halfway Inn*. Minor roles in features — *Come Back Peter*, *The Love Machine* — led them to Fine and Style's door. (A publicity hound's dream, their casting begat several features headed "Which is witch?", or permutations thereof.) *Twins of Evil* was shot at Pinewood and on location in Black Park in the spring of 1971, and cost £205,067 overall. During filming, twenty-eight year-old Damien Thomas, the company's most promising Dracula substitute since Ralph Bates, managed to break one of his 'fangs' on Madelaine's neck.

Early in October, billed above co-feature *Hands of the Ripper*, *Twins of Evil* premièred at London's New Victoria. The Collinson sisters were on hand, as were Cushing, Katya Wyeth, Michael Carreras, Rank Film Distributors' managing director Frank Poole, plus *Hands of the Ripper* folk Peter Sasdy, Eric Porter and Angharad Rees. The bill took a respectable £4,379 in its first week, but played to only average takings on general release from 17 October on. Meanwhile, overseas distributor CIC was delighted by the film. CIC's Arthur Abeles had a suggestion to make when, on 17 September, he wrote to Sir James Carreras: "Dear Jim, Baby... We have just seen *Twins of Evil* and are still shaking. This is really the stuff that the horror fans are looking for... However, in view of all the blood-sucking and the fact that the word Dracula is almost as big as the word Hammer in connection with a film of this type, is there any reason why we can't call it 'Twins of Dracula', or some other title in which Dracula appears?" "You're a genius!" wrote back Carreras. "Shall we make new title or you? (You pay!)." Thus *Twins of Evil*'s American title came into being...

However, the film did not survive its transatlantic crossing intact. The MPAA had fired a warning shot over Hammer's corporate bow after reading the script in March, noting that "reasonable discretion" would have to be taken while shooting some of the more gruesome vignettes. "We caution you against any exploitation of nudity," added reader Eugene G. Dougherty. Evidently, the MPAA did not feel that their warnings had been heeded. On 28 February 1972, thirty-four separate cuts — totalling five minutes and thirty-six seconds — were made, by Hammer, according to the MPAA's prescription.

Bar a couple of rather crude and out-of-place exposures, *Twins of Evil* substitutes the exploitation of flesh for the exploitation of violence, albeit with good reason. A tightly plotted tragedy, with characters painted in shades of grey (as opposed to, say, John Elder's black and white) and heavily influenced by pictures such as *Matthew Hopkins Witchfinder General*, it has an intensity and sense of purpose rare in horror.

Previous page: *A revealing publicity shot. From the top: Katya Wyeth, the Collinsons, plus Maggie Wright (left) and Luan Peters (right).*
Above left: *Puritan Gustav Weil (Peter Cushing) lays down the law to lovestruck schoolteacher Anton Hoffer (David Warbeck).*
Above right: *Racy pre-production artwork.*
Below: *Via blood sacrifice, Count Karnstein (Damien Thomas) invokes the spirit of vampiric ancestor Mircalla.*

V A M P I R E   C I R C U S

**Principal photography 9 August to
21 September 1971
Released 30 April 1972
Certificate X
Duration 87 mins
Colour
Director Robert Young**

Schtettel, mittel-*Europe: schoolteacher's wife Anna Mueller (Domini Blythe) leads a young girl to the castle of her lover, Count Mitterhouse (Robert Tayman), where the vampire Count murders the girl. Professor Mueller (Laurence Payne) gathers together a horde of villagers and, at the castle, they overcome the demon. Impaled upon a sharpened stake, he curses them all: "Your children will die to give me back my life!" The villagers blow up the castle, but Anna hauls her dying lover's body to the crypt. He instructs her to seek out his cousin. Fifteen years pass. Disease runs rife and the village is quarantined, but a convoy led by a gypsy woman (Adrienne Corri) manages to cross the blockade. This is the Circus of Nights, and Schtettel's children thrill to the performers' antics. The gypsy woman — actually Anna — has the castle crypt uncovered; feline acrobat Emil (Anthony Corlan), it transpires, is the Count's kinsman. They have come to fulfil Mitterhouse's bloody vow...*

ir James Carreras was distinctly cool to the film treatment which crossed his desk on 24 May 1971. "Very, very bloody," he wrote in a memo to son Michael. "I suppose OK for the rest of the world, but I dread to think what will happen in the USA."

The subject was *The Vampire Circus*; a treatment by George Baxt, whose association with the company went back as far as *The Revenge of Frankenstein*, had been purchased by Hammer on 29 March. The film was scripted by Judson Kinberg and produced by independent Wilbur Stark. Michael Carreras was receptive to the possibilities that *Vampire Circus* offered in terms of extending Hammer's horror vocabulary — notions which Nadja Regin, a former Bond girl who'd appeared in *Don't Panic Chaps!* and now worked as a script reader for the company, had picked out from the screenplay, too. "*Vampire Circus* introduces an element of beauty, colour, magic and excitement into an ambience of sickness, fear and death," she remarked in a memo dated 25 July, and proceeded to suggest a host of arresting additions. The

young Hauser brothers, she proposed, might be enticed to pass through the circus' Mirror of Life rather differently: "Why not attract them with a fairy tale vision... An ice palace, for instance, to which they are taken in a deer-driven sleigh, or a giant dragon kite, which can fly them towards the castle... magic oblivion in which they reach the Count's crypt — and their death." Regin was, however, baffled by the script's "almost pathological obsession with children victims", and lobbied to have events in the opening sequence — in which Anna lures a young girl to her death at the hand of her vampiric lover, whereupon the pair have sex ("One lust feeds the other...") — reordered on the grounds that it was "strongly reminiscent of the Moors murder."

That same day Sir James, mindful of the tough reputation already accrued by newly-appointed BBFC secretary Stephen Murphy, predicted that: "if shot as scripted 50% will end up on the cutting room floor." He added: "What's happened to the great vampire/ Dracula subjects we used to make without all this

unnecessary gore and sick-making material?"

The film was shot at Pinewood over the high summer. On set, Hammer reliables mixed with an array of genuine circus performers (a number of whom, not being British nationals, had to apply for special permits under the terms of the Aliens Order of 1953 to appear). Anton Rodgers had been cast to portray Mueller, but was taken ill with stomach pains on Sunday 8 August, one day before photography commenced. Laurence Payne substituted for him. The piece was directed by Hammer newcomer Robert Young, who was very much in tune with the surreal take Michael Carreras sought. However, Young fell behind schedule and Hammer was unable to go beyond Rank's allotted six weeks. A number of scenes remained unshot, and Young was forced to cut around the missing material. (He later directed 'Charlie Boy', an episode of the *Hammer House of Horror* TV series.)

True to one of Sir James' pronouncements, *Vampire Circus* did indeed run into trouble in America, where roughly three minutes' footage was cut. An elegant and visually absorbing revenge tragedy — only two of the many principal characters survive its gory unfolding — the film succeeds admirably on all levels; its pell-mell prologue is almost lengthy enough to function as a featurette in itself.

D E M O N S   O F   T H E   M I N D

Tortured Elizabeth Zorn (Gillian Hills), having escaped her Aunt Hilda (Yvonne Mitchell), takes up with medical student Carl Richter (Paul Jones). Recaptured, she is taken back to the estate of her father, Baron Zorn (Robert Hardy). Believing she and her brother Emil (Shane Briant) to be tainted by hereditary madness, Zorn keeps them under lock and key, but at night he releases Emil, who murders local women. Discredited psychiatrist Falkenberg (Patrick Magee) attempts to unravel the family history and it transpires that the children witnessed their mother cut her own throat. It is apparent that Emil nurses incestuous desire for his sister. Falkenberg has prostitute Inge (Virginia Wetherell) dressed in Elizabeth's clothes in an attempt to cure this, but Emil strangles her. Carl has followed Elizabeth's trail, and falls in with local villagers who, egged on by a manic priest (Michael Hordern), identify Zorn as the 'demon' responsible for the killings of their daughters. Too late, Falkenberg deduces that Emil is the unwilling instrument of Zorn's unacted desires — but Emil, now utterly deranged, kills Hilda and goes on the run with Elizabeth. Zorn shoots Falkenberg, and pursues his children. Blood, he vows, will have blood...

Principal photography 16 August to September 1971
Released 5 November 1972
Certificate X
Duration 89 mins
Colour
Director Peter Sykes

Still titled *Blood Will Have Blood*, the film shot during the late summer at MGM-EMI Elstree and on location both at Wykehurst Park, a turreted Sussex folly designed by renowned nineteenth-century architect Augustus Pugin, and a lakeside on the Aldenham Estate. (Press notes made the extravagant and entirely false claim that the film was part-shot in Bavaria.) The mechanisms employed by Patrick Magee's Falkenberg were adapted by designer Michael Stringer's team from devices used by Austrian Franz Mesmer, hypnotism's heretical pioneer.

Distributors EMI did not release the (retitled) film for over a year, and then only as support to Harry Allan Towers' trashy *Tower of Evil*. Oblique, difficult, ambitious and suffused with an air of primal dread, *Demons of the Mind* deserved better. The Zorns, a repressed and lunatic Addams Family in period garb, were plainly not the kind of people that Hammer's audience wished to have move in next door.

S omething of a curate's egg, the cod-Freudian *Demons of the Mind* continued to foster the artier side to Hammer's seventies roster. It was not always so; in an earlier draft, submitted in the late summer of 1970 by independent producer Frank Godwin, the dysfunctional Zorns' neuroses stemmed from the curse of lycanthropy. Oddly, Hammer would only consider the story for future production after it was "rewritten, cutting out the werewolf sequences."

Under the working title *Blood Will Have Blood* — a phrase swiped from *Macbeth* by screenwriter Christopher Wicking — the film was announced for EMI production starting 28 June 1971, but was delayed when casting uncertainties developed. In the director's chair was thirty-two year-old Australian *emigré* Peter Sykes, whose *Venom*, an independently produced British thriller filmed in Germany, had caught Michael Carreras' eye. Sykes suggested the distinguished Paul Scofield for the role of Zorn, having worked with him in the theatre. However, Scofield

shunned his offer, as did James Mason. Until very late in the day, Elizabeth was intended for pop icon Marianne Faithfull. (Once wild for kicks in the Adam Faith vehicle *Beat Girl*, the elfin Gillian Hills, ex-of Antonioni's *Blow Up* and Kubrick's *A Clockwork Orange*, stood in.) Sykes did, however, mine the late sixties R'n' B scene in casting Paul Jones, formerly the lead singer/harmonica player in Manfred Mann, who had earlier appeared solo in Sykes' *The Committee*.

Most notably, *Demons of the Mind* introduced to Hammer the boyish Shane Briant, a twenty-five year-old who made three further appearances for the company (as a babyish killer in *Straight On Till Morning*, the arrogant Durward heir in *Captain Kronos Vampire Hunter* and as the Baron's assistant in *Frankenstein and the Monster From Hell*). Briant, a former law student, had managed Dublin's Trinity College Theatre during his final year, where his Hamlet set him on his acting career. The damaged Emil secured him a substantial film début.

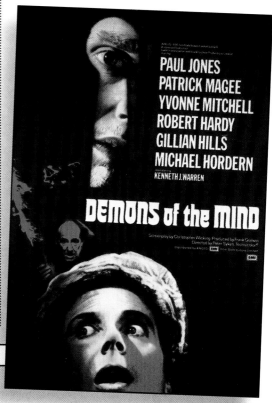

PAUL JONES
PATRICK MAGEE
YVONNE MITCHELL
ROBERT HARDY
GILLIAN HILLS
MICHAEL HORDERN
KENNETH J. WARREN

DEMONS of the MIND

Screenplay by Christopher Wicking. Produced by Frank Godwin
Directed by Peter Sykes. Technicolor®

Distributed by ANGLO EMI Film Distributors Limited

D R A C U L A   A . D .   1 9 7 2

**Principal photography 27 September to
5 November 1971
Released 28 September 1972
Certificate X
Duration 95 mins
Colour
Director Alan Gibson**

Hyde Park, 1872: for Lawrence Van Helsing (Peter Cushing), the strain of destroying Count Dracula (Christopher Lee) proves too much, and he dies alongside his adversary. Van Helsing is buried in the churchyard of St Bartolph's. During the funeral, one of Dracula's disciples (Christopher Neame) buries his master's ashes nearby. Chelsea, 1972: at the Cavern bar, Johnny Alucard (Christopher Neame) offers his gang of thrill-seeking hippies a date with the Devil. The location is to be the desanctified St Bartolph's. Jessica Van Helsing (Stephanie Beacham) resists the casual sex and hard drugs enjoyed by the other gang-members, but reluctantly agrees to go along with Johnny's Black Mass. Most of the gang flee in terror before the ceremony reaches its conclusion — the resurrection of Count Dracula. Dracula claims gang-member Laura (Caroline Munro) as his first victim in a series of gruesome murders. Baffled police inspector Murray (Michael Coles) seeks advice from occult expert Lorrimer Van Helsing (Peter Cushing), Jessica's grandfather. Dracula has returned to purge the house of Van Helsing, and Lorrimer must face his grandfather's immortal foe...

nthony Hinds drew the line at a modern-day Dracula picture, so the job went to television scribe Don Houghton, whose *When the Earth Cracked Open* had already been added to Hammer's 'forthcoming productions' schedule in 1970. Houghton's *Dracula — Chelsea* storyline impressed Sir James Carreras, who contracted the writer in October. The story became *Dracula/Chelsea 1972*, before evolving into a shooting script entitled *Dracula Today*.

Distributors Warner Bros (now under the control of the Kinney National Service Corporation) had noted the success of AIP's *Count Yorga — Vampire*, in which Robert Quarry prowled present-day Los Angeles. Don Houghton's *Dracula Today*, however, was irretrievably undermined by a perspective on youth culture that seemed a good decade behind the times. The kids drink cola in the Cavern bar, fight over tickets for the "jazz spectacular" at the Albert Hall, and say things like, "she has a new batch of discs for the stereo. Some way-out stuff just come in from

Copenhagen."

The film's music, which took on a new significance in this bell-bottomed Dracula, caused special problems. Houghton had scripted a party appearance by Rod Stewart's group The Faces, and a contract was prepared in September 1971. Weeks later, they made way for Kinney-contracted band Stoneground, an obscure San Francisco act led by Sal Valentino. It was, perhaps, an unfortunate decision, as The Faces' best-selling breakthrough album, *A Nod's as Good as a Wink... To a Blind Horse*, hit the charts in December. The incidental music was supplied by ex Manfred Mann guitarist Michael Vickers, whose score was part re-recorded by Don Banks (composer on such films as *Captain Clegg, The Evil of Frankenstein* and *Rasputin the Mad Monk*) and supplemented by library tracks.

For Warner Bros' benefit, Hammer reunited Peter

Cushing's Van Helsing with Christopher Lee's Dracula. Although he had initial reservations about the contemporary setting, Cushing was delighted to appear in *Dracula Today* ("So long as these pictures make money... I will always do them," he said during filming). Lee was appalled when he read the script, and Sir James Carreras had to pull out all the stops to make it worth the actor's while. Lee finally consented, but would veto many of the lines intended to reinvent the character as no less than Satan himself: "I was always here," Dracula would have told Johnny, when his disciple demanded the reward of immortality. "Always... Since the dawn of time. Since the rebel angels descended into Hell. Since darkness followed light... I am Dracula, Lord of Darkness, Master of the Walking Dead! I am the Curse, the Apollyon, Angel of the Destroying Furies! I am the Apocalypse!"

The King's Road kids were headed up by Christopher Neame as Johnny Alucard and Stephanie Beacham as Jessica. "The obligatory altar dress caused me the most problems," recalls the buxom actress. "One couldn't wear any underwear, so when I was lying down it was less convincingly rounded." The sticky tape applied to keep everything in place

"caused enormous problems for the sound people." Neame and Beacham would be reunited in the 1988 season of American soap opera *Dynasty*.

Dracula Today was directed by Canadian Alan Gibson, who, following his initiation on *Journey to the Unknown*, made his feature film début with *Crescendo* in 1969. Josephine Douglas (the former producer/co-presenter of the BBC's pioneering pop show *6.5 Special*) was invited to produce the picture by her friend Sir James Carreras. Gibson and Douglas failed to see eye-to-eye, and their relationship was fraught during shooting.

Dracula Today was released as *Dracula A.D. 1972*, alongside Freddie Francis' indescribable *Trog*, in September 1972. A promotional film trumpeting the film's release followed Alan Gibson's crew on location and at Elstree, in addition to interviewing Christopher Lee in his London home. "I can assure every one of you watching that Vlad V. Tepes Dracula *did* exist," he insisted, from beneath a bushy moustache. In the United States, Warner Bros premièred the film with a Broadway gala, and distributed the feature with a three-minute preface called *Horror Ritual*. During the support film, audience members were invited to join the Dracula Society and put through the 'oath'. Warner's new owners were clearly less sympathetic towards Hammer's product than the Hyman family had been before them.

"The trendies vampirised by the resuscitated Count... are patently phony," commented *Monthly Film Bulletin*, "and the attempt to reconcile Transylvania with SW3 merely sends the script haywire." Such criticism was largely representative of the slating *Dracula A.D. 1972* received on its original release, and the film has long-suffered a reputation as Hammer's most monumental misjudgement. Considering that any remaining elements of the studio's visual identity were largely discarded by Alan Gibson's gimmicky direction, any comparison with previous entries in the series seems fairly redundant. *Dracula A.D. 1972* gets more entertaining with the passing of time, and is perhaps best enjoyed as an endearing, if naïve, picture of an era that never was.

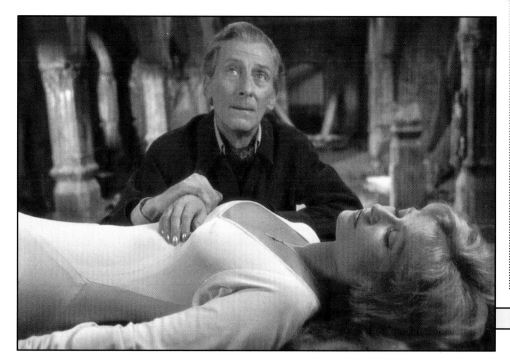

Previous page: In the Cavern, Johnny Alucard (Christopher Neame) attempts to convince his sceptical friends, including Gaynor (Marsha Hunt, left) and Anna (Janet Key, right), that the traumatic Black Mass had been a stunt.
Above left: A nonchalant Christopher Lee poses for a publicity picture with (from left to right) Caroline Munro, Stephanie Beacham, Marsha Hunt and Janet Key.
Above right: Contact sheet pictures showing Peter Cushing, Christopher Lee and Christopher Neame during filming on the impressive St Bartolph's set.
Left: A concerned Van Helsing (Peter Cushing) feels for a pulse from granddaughter Jessica (Stephanie Beacham).

CAPTAIN KRONOS VAMPIRE HUNTER

**Principal photography 10 April to
27 May 1972
Released 7 April 1974
Certificate AA
Duration 91 mins
Colour
Director Brian Clemens**

When a young girl in the village of Durward is found emaciated, drained of all youth, Dr Marcus (John Carson) summons former comrade-in-arms Captain Kronos (Horst Janson), who arrives with hunch-backed assistant Professor Grost (John Cater) in tow. Cast out from her clan for dancing on a Sunday, gypsy Carla (Caroline Munro) has hitched a ride with the pair, whom she discovers to be vampire hunters. Vampires exist in many forms, and a spate of attacks indicates that Durward is cursed by such a presence. Marcus, meanwhile, has cause to suspect that the rich Durward family are involved. At their grand estate, he questions heirs Paul and Sara (Shane Briant and Lois Daine). Their bed-bound mother (Wanda Ventham) blames Marcus for the death of husband Lord Hagen, a plague victim. The doctor is later assaulted by the mystery vampire. Upon his instruction, Kronos and Grost experiment on Marcus to find the one method that will negate this particular vampiric strain. Successful, his friend destroyed, Kronos devises a plan to expose the fiend — by using Carla, now his lover, as bait...

"There are as many species of vampire as there are beasts of prey," Professor Grost helpfully informs Dr Marcus during the course of *Captain Kronos Vampire Hunter*. "Their method and motive for attack can vary in a hundred different ways... The traditional stake through the heart does not always hold good, you know. Some can only be destroyed by hanging or decapitation — or fire, or water, or by other means... The cross can only protect those who firmly believe."

Brian Clemens' second Hammer screenplay proved every bit as joyfully iconoclastic as his first, *Doctor Jekyll & Sister Hyde.* "They said, 'We'd like a vampire movie from you.' I'm not a vampire fan, but I ran all the Peter Cushing and Christopher Lee films and the thing that occurred to me was that the hero was really the vampire... it was very predictable that Van Helsing would end up putting a stake through him and that would be that. There was no tension in these films for me, so I created a whole new vam-

pire lore and a superhero — a bit like a Marvel Comics hero, really." In *Captain Kronos Vampire Hunter*, a dead toad, buried in a box, will spring to life if a vampire walks across it, and flowers will wilt in a vampire's wake. The film continued Hammer's seventies quest to revitalise genre mythologies. (And, possibly, their own: at one point, vampire Lady Durward claims, "I'm a Karstein by birth — and the Karsteins are blessed with many dark secrets..." Is it possible that she's distantly related to Carmilla's Karnstein clan?)

Clemens made his directorial début on the film, again co-produced by long-term associate Albert Fennell. The casting of *Dracula A.D. 1972*'s Caroline Munro was suggested by the company, keen to further exploit their newest discovery. Finding a suitable artiste to play Clemens' swashbuckling hero proved more problematic — "we wanted someone who looked good, could act... was good on a horse

and was good with a sword" — and Clemens had to search beyond Britain for an actor who could fulfil such a brief. He found his star in German Horst Janson. (Despite Janson's perfect English, Hammer insisted that he be dubbed by *Carry On* actor Julian Holloway.) The director called up a number of *Avengers* alumni, too: composer Laurie Johnson, actors John Cater, John Carson and the late Ian Hendry as mercenary Kerro. Hendry, according to Clemens, "needed the work because he was a piss artist. It was only a three-day part, but a very important part. I spoke to him and said, 'Ian, you will be good, won't you?' He said, 'I'll lay off the booze totally.' When I went into make-up the next day at 7.30 in the morning he had a lager in his hand. I said, 'I thought you were going to lay off.' He said, 'This isn't booze, this is lager...'"

Shot on location and at Elstree's MGM-EMI studios in the early summer of 1972, *Captain Kronos*

Vampire Hunter's modest budget couldn't quite accommodate some of Clemens' wilder notions — a golden coach containing a golden coffin for Kronos to sleep in, for example — and pressures of time ensured that Kronos' showdown swordfight with the revenant Hagen would not be realised to the director's satisfaction, either. Nevertheless, after Kronos had ridden off into the sunset — heading "Anywhere. Everywhere. Wherever there is evil to be fought" — Clemens hoped that his hero's adventures would continue, having devised him with one eye to a string of sequels: "I deliberately called him Kronos, which is Greek for 'time', because he could've moved through time." No explanation would ever have been given for Kronos' time travels. As per Clint Eastwood's Man With No Name series, each film would have opened with him simply there. "He could've appeared in the twentieth century — he was a pretty anachronistic hero because he smoked pot and meditated... The Kronos stories weren't all going to be about vampires. They'd have been about inexplicable events really, leaning towards the supernatural or legend... He could have easily come up against Frankenstein's monster."

It wasn't to be. *Captain Kronos* was mostly funded via a returnable loan from the National Film Finance Corporation. With no assured distribution, it was barely released in Britain, and then only almost two years after it wrapped. "It didn't have any publicity at all. Nothing," Munro told *Fangoria*. "In fact, we weren't even told it was coming out. It just crept out in Hammersmith... me and my family went to see it one evening. And that was it. We never heard another word about it." The good Captain's adventures did continue, albeit briefly, in the first

three issues of *The House of Hammer* magazine, wherein he did battle with toothsome vampire overlord Count Balderstein, but it was woeful distribution that put paid to his screen career. Rapier-witted, clever and occasionally shocking — Marcus' protracted 'execution', for example — the film deserved to reach a far wider audience. Television screenings alone have ensured its now considerable reputation. Perhaps, given its 'teaser' scene, Kronos' personal 'K' logo and its galumphing theme music, a television series is exactly what it always should have been.

Previous page: Kronos (Horst Janson, right) swashes his buckle versus reinvigorated swordsman Hagen (William Hobbs, left), while his vampirised widow (Wanda Ventham) and gypsy Carla (Caroline Munro) look on.
Top: Kronos shields himself from the no-longer-hideous Lady Durward (Wanda Ventham).
Above: Grost (John Cater), for whom 'toad in the hole' is a professional duty, not merely a repast.
Left: "What I liked about it was its old fashioned appeal," said Horst Janson in the Captain Kronos Vampire Hunter *press book*. "It is a backlash from all the sex and violence in modern films."

FRANKENSTEIN AND THE MONSTER FROM HELL

Principal photography 18 September to 27 October 1972
Released 2 May 1974
Certificate X
Duration 99 mins
Colour
Director Terence Fisher

A bodysnatcher (Patrick Troughton) is spotted exhuming a corpse for young surgeon Dr Simon Helder (Shane Briant). Helder's experiments are terminated when he is arrested for sorcery, and sentenced to five years imprisonment in an asylum for the criminally insane near Carlsbad. The asylum is ostensibly run by a corrupt director (John Stratton), but his strings are being pulled by the blackmailing Dr Karl Victor (Peter Cushing). Victor is assisted in his duties as resident medical practitioner by the beautiful Sarah (Madeline Smith), a mute girl the inmates call Angel. Victor admits his true identity to Helder — he is Baron Victor Frankenstein, pursuing his depraved research safe in the knowledge that all bar a few members of the asylum staff believe him to be dead. Helder becomes Frankenstein's apprentice, and discovers that the Baron is using the body of hulking inmate Schneider as the basis for his latest experiment. The Monster (Dave Prowse) is given new eyes, the hands of a craftsman and the brain of brilliant suicide victim Professor Durendel (Charles Lloyd Pack). The tormented Monster initially shows promise, but the violent personality of Herr Schneider soon begins to re-assert itself. Frankenstein decrees that the Monster must be reborn, unblemished, and selects Sarah as its mate...

Although entries in Hammer's Frankenstein series had become less frequent than Dracula sequels (the Frankenstein films took longer to recoup their costs), the Baron remained an integral part of Hammer's portfolio.

When Rank turned *Frankenstein and the Monster From Hell* down, Michael Carreras secured the lion's share of finance from Paramount in spring 1972. In return for its slice of the budget, Paramount received distribution rights to all territories bar Britain. After the false start of *The Horror of Frankenstein*, a film pre-sold to an American distributor could ill-afford to repeat an experimental approach and a relatively unknown star. *Frankenstein and the Monster From Hell* restored Peter Cushing as the Baron, taking the series back to its Gothic horror roots.

Frankenstein and the Monster from Hell was the latest in Peter Cushing's prolific string of films since the death of his wife in January 1971. "It is the answer to my prayers," he said, when asked about his tireless schedule. The loss of Helen had a devastating effect on

Cushing, and the dramatic change in his facial appearance did not go unnoticed by John Elder. The shooting script's description of the Baron observed that: "He looks a little older and shows signs of strain." Cushing's preparation was as meticulous as ever. On 31 August he wrote to Roy Skeggs with the details of his new hairpiece (he later lamented that it "made me look rather like Helen Hayes") and wrote again the following day to specify the Baron's surgical implements. Shane Briant co-starred as Simon Helder, the Baron's latest protégé, while starlet Madeline Smith was given her most prominent Hammer role as the tragic Sarah. (Producer Skeggs had originally wanted Caroline Munro for the part. The idea was nixed by Michael Carreras when *Captain Kronos Vampire Hunter* was packaged with the film for American distribution.)

Whereas the Dracula sequels had been handled by

JOSEPH E. LEVINE PRESENTS AN AVCO EMBASSY PICTURE
A HAMMER FILM PRODUCTION · A TERENCE FISHER FILM

FRANKENSTEIN
AND THE MONSTER FROM HELL X
STARRING PETER CUSHING / SHANE BRIANT / MADELINE SMITH
WRITTEN BY JOHN ELDER · PRODUCED BY ROY SKEGGS · DIRECTED BY TERENCE FISHER · TECHNICOLOR®
AN AVCO EMBASSY RELEASE

various directors in recent years, first refusal on Hammer's Frankenstein films was always given to Terence Fisher. "We met in a pub and I talked him into doing *Monster From Hell*," remembers Skeggs. "He'd lost a lot of confidence after his two road accidents, but I eventually persuaded him to come back. I'm very glad I did." Together with Skeggs, Fisher revised John Elder's script, most notably removing a scene where Dr Helder feeds scraps of human flesh to some stray cats. ("Terry does not like this scene, to say nothing of working with cats," Skeggs explained in a memo to Michael Carreras.)

Economy dictated that Scott MacGregor's prevailing asylum sets were all squeezed onto stage four at MGM-EMI Elstree, ready for filming in September. Fisher made the most of his lean resources, creating a stifling, claustrophobic atmosphere with the help of Brian Probyn's subdued lighting. "I didn't sleep at all the night before I started directing this film: wondering if I was going to make a good job of it," Fisher told *Liverpool Echo* reporter Tom Hutchinson during filming. "I think any creator feels the same way." The film was completed in October, Skeggs' careful budgeting ensuring a final cost of just £137,200.

The film was granted an X certificate by the BBFC in November 1972, only after the asylum director's murder and the scene where the inmates "tear gobbets of flesh out of [the Monster], eat them, paddle in his blood, etc" were trimmed. The search for a British distributor then began. *Frankenstein and the Monster From Hell* was picked up by Joe Levine's Avco-Embassy in early 1973, and eventually released in May 1974. Box-office receipts of just £1,774 for the first week at the London Astoria told their own story

On 24 October 1972 Peter Cushing performed his final scene as Frankenstein — the closing shot of the film, where the obviously insane Baron resolves to begin again. But there would be no more sequels. Terence Fisher's haunting, melancholy swansong would be an epitaph for Hammer horror itself.

TERENCE FISHER: DIRECTOR

Terence Fisher was born in 1904, and began his career in the film industry as an editor for Gainsborough Studios in 1936. His 1950 Rank/Gainsborough production *So Long at the Fair* brought him to the attention of Anthony Hinds, who invited him to direct Hammer's first Robert Lippert co-production the following year. After *The Last Page*, Fisher made a further twenty-eight films for Hammer. The most significant among these were undoubtedly *The Curse of Frankenstein* and *Dracula*, which reinvented the genre and established a lasting commercial foundation for the company. Perhaps out of frustration over his resulting 'typecasting', Fisher amplified the romantic sub-texts in his Hammer films, refusing throughout to label them as anything other than "macabre". By the time he was asked to direct *Frankenstein and the Monster From Hell*, his health was poor and his relaxed style dated. "The future frightens me," he revealed during filming. "It's a tough business is the film business and I wonder if I'll get any work after this picture." Sadly, his fears proved justified. When Hammer's Frankenstein series ended, so did the career of its most celebrated director. Terence Fisher died in June 1980.

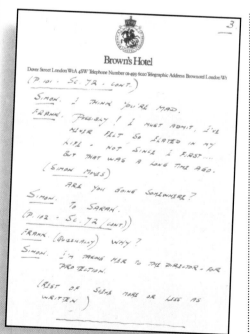

Previous page: Simon (Shane Briant) and Sarah (Madeline Smith) pity Frankenstein's tormented Monster (Dave Prowse).

Above: Terence Fisher, at work on Scott MacGregor's laboratory set. "In *Frankenstein and the Monster From Hell* the Baron verbalises his ideal when he calls himself the creator of man," said Fisher in 1975. "You've had so many monsters by then that at last you say where this monster has come from. He comes from Hell, from Evil, from Frankenstein's mistaken belief that he is the creator of man, which of course he isn't, and will never succeed in being."

Far left: On the very edge of insanity, the gaunt Baron Frankenstein (Peter Cushing) conducts his final experiment.

Left: On 6 September 1972, Cushing wrote to Roy Skeggs with some amendments to scene seventy-two, in which the Baron suggests mating his Monster with Sarah. "Do hope this will be helpful."

THE SATANIC RITES OF DRACULA

Principal photography 13 November 1972 to
3 January 1973
Released 13 January 1974
Certificate X
Duration 88 mins
Colour
Director Alan Gibson

London, now: government agent Hanson (Maurice O'Connell) infiltrates Pelham House — headquarters of Psychical Examination and Research Group PERGE — where he sees four prominent individuals, including his security services minister, participate in a Satanic ritual. Mortally wounded, Hanson reports his discoveries to his SI7 seniors. Baffled, they call upon Special Branch officer Murray (Michael Coles), who has experience of such matters. In turn, Murray calls upon Lorrimer Van Helsing (Peter Cushing), who identifies one of the four men involved as Nobel prize-winning Professor Keeley (Freddie Jones), a former associate whom he discovers to have developed a new and lethal strain of bubonic plague. Meanwhile, SI7's Jane (Valerie Van Ost) has been kidnapped. She awakes in Pelham House, where Count Dracula (Christopher Lee) takes her blood. Murray, SI7's Torrence (William Franklyn) and Van Helsing's grand-daughter Jessica (Joanna Lumley) investigate the house, and Jessica discovers a cellarful of chained-up vampire women, including Jane. Van Helsing connects the original four suspects to property speculator D. D. Denham and concludes that the reclusive Denham is Dracula, whom he speculates wishes to destroy all life on earth via the plague, thus terminating his own wretched existence. Carrying a gun loaded with one silver bullet in his pocket, Van Helsing visits Denham's penthouse, casting himself as the vampire's assassin...

Christopher Lee's dissatisfaction with Hammer's Dracula series had, by late 1972, reached boiling point. Asked about the then titled *Dracula is Dead and Well and Living in London* just prior to shooting, he responded frankly: "I'm doing the next one under protest. I think it's fatuous. I can think of twenty adjectives... fatuous, pointless, absurd. It's not a comedy... [but] it's a comic title. I don't see the point. I don't see what they hope to achieve... I just hope they [the audience] realise that I am struggling against insuperable odds on occasion to remain true to the author's original character."

The direct sequel to *Dracula A.D. 1972* was well into pre-production long before the latter was released; by 16 March 1972, Jimmy Sangster was reported to be preparing a treatment, *Dracula is Dead... But Alive... and Well... and Living in London* [sic], for Warner Bros. (It's unknown how much, if any, of Sangster's storyline survived in Don Houghton's script.) The new film maintained direct continuity to its predecessor, referring to St Bartolph's church, for

example (although the method of Dracula's resurrection, via disciple Chin Yang, merited but a fleeting mention). Lee's efforts to preserve Dracula's integrity were genuine. Joanna Lumley, the former Bond girl who replaced Stephanie Beacham in the role of Jessica Van Helsing, recalls him having the source novel to hand at all times on set. (As in *Dracula A.D. 1972*, he'd squeeze in a line paraphrased from Stoker's: "'My revenge is just begun! I spread it over centuries, and time is on my side...'") Peter Cushing was no less fastidious. He thoroughly overhauled Van Helsing's spiel concerning methods of vampire disposal and, in the margins of his script, quite rightly questioned the Count's "mortal dread of silver": "This bothers me because of the silver ring 'Dracula' wears." (The ring remains extant in the picture, prominent in the closing moments wherein Van Helsing apprises himself of it — prompting, as writer Denis Meikle has remarked, speculation as to

EVIL BEGETS EVIL ON THE SABBATH OF THE UNDEAD!

The Satanic Rites of DRACULA

CHRISTOPHER LEE · PETER CUSHING · MICHAEL COLES · WILLIAM FRANKLYN · FREDDIE JONES · JOANNA LUMLEY

The Satanic Rites of Dracula has been unfairly maligned, not least by its star, for it actually gives the Count something to do other than skulk in crypts and pounce on Sir James Carreras' latest nubile protégé, which is no bad thing. Here Dracula assumes the persona of a comic strip supervillain (although his desire to destroy all life on Earth, and thus himself, does seem a touch *outré*). It has almost precisely the ambience of a feature-length *Avengers* episode, too, casting Cushing as Steed and Lumley as his gorgeous sidekick. (Indeed, substitute Coles/Murray for Gareth Hunt's Mike Gambit, and the prescience of the analogy becomes truly uncanny.)

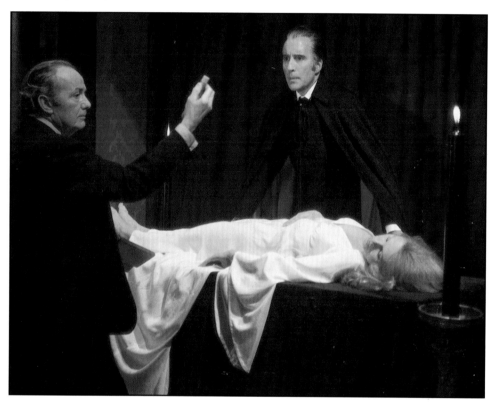

"what Houghton might have come up with had this line of inquiry been allowed to develop.")

Also from the *Dracula A.D. 1972* ensemble were director Alan Gibson and actor Michael Coles. Costing a then-substantial £223,450, the picture was filmed on location and at MGM-EMI Elstree as 1972 became 1973. Lumley's autobiography records the mechanism by which effects supervisor Les Bowie achieved the graphic despatch of Valerie Van Ost's vampirised Jane: "A metal brace encircled her chest, with an indentation in front in which was inserted one end of the stake. The stake was telescopic like a stage dagger; as it drove in a blood bag filled with Kensington Gore burst and she howled like a wolf. A visitor to the set had to be helped away, it looked so realistic." (This notorious shot, in which Van Ost's breast slips free, was cut from later video releases.)

Distributor Warner Bros expressed little enthusiasm for the finished print, despite its title being changed in post-production to the less remarkable (albeit more accurate) *The Satanic Rites of Dracula*. Supported by *Blacula*, it opened at the London Rialto to little fanfare early in 1974. *Time Out*'s Dave [sic] Pirie commented: "The beguiling message underlying Hammer's latest modern-dress Dracula movie is that the real vampires of modern London are property speculators. The idea is amazing (after all Dracula started off as a subversive myth) but inevitably it tends to get lost... still a vast improvement on the last in the series." Despite holding a New York press screening in autumn 1976 (alongside Amicus' *From Beyond the Grave*), Warner Bros decided against releasing the film in America, where it didn't see light of day until independent distributor Dynamite issued it under the flaccid title *Count Dracula and His Vampire Bride* late in 1978.

The film lost Hammer its only true Dracula for good. In 1974 Lee firmly stated: "I will *not* play that character anymore. I no longer *wish* to do it, I no longer *have* to do it and I no longer *intend* to do it. It is now part of my professional past, just one of the roles I have played in a total of 124 films." He has remained true to his word.

THE LEGEND OF THE 7 GOLDEN VAMPIRES

**Principal photography 22 October to
11 December 1973
Released 29 August 1974
Certificate X
Duration 89 mins
Colour/Panavision
Director Roy Ward Baker (and Chang Cheh,
unaccredited)**

Transylvania, 1804: Eastern occultist Kah (Chan Shen) travels to the castle of Count Dracula (John Forbes-Robertson), where the vampire takes Kah's shape. A century later, lecturing at China's Chung King university, Professor Van Helsing (Peter Cushing) relates to a class of students a certain oriental legend. It is said that, each year, come the seventh moon, seven vampires in golden masks descend upon a remote village. Once, a farmer named Hsi Tien-En destroyed one of the creatures, seizing the bat medallion containing its life force. The students react with disdain. However, one student, Hsi Ching (David Chiang), later tells Van Helsing that Hsi Tien-En was his grandfather, and the village his ancestral home, Ping Kuei. He begs Van Helsing's assistance. The expedition to Ping Kuei is to be financed by widowed thrill-seeker Vanessa Buren (Julie Ege), whom Van Helsing's son, Leyland (Robin Stewart), has met. They travel with Hsi Ching's five brothers and sister, Mai Kwei (Shih Szu), all martial arts experts. On the road, Mai Kwei falls for Leyland, and Hsi Ching for Vanessa. At Ping Kuei, they build a barricade and prepare for the vampires' night-time assault. Vanessa, however, is vampirised in the attack. Hsi Ching, forced to destroy her, kills himself. And Mai Kwei is carried off by the last remaining vampire to their temple, where their foul overlord awaits...

By 1973, Hammer was finding it increasingly difficult to initiate genre projects. British distributors seemed willing only to support cheap comedies, but there were signs that even that market was starting to deflate. Doors always open to the clubbable Sir James Carreras would be closed to son Michael; no one appeared willing to support the humble Hammer horror. A new approach was desperately needed. Michael discovered both an as yet untapped genre ripe for exploitation and a co-production partner in the East.

In the early seventies, a slew of martial arts movies had achieved unprecedented success in the West. The first to cross over, *King Boxer*, was followed by a string of high-kicking kung fu pictures. Hong Kong's hottest export, Bruce Lee, achieved international fame following the release of his final completed film, *Enter the Dragon*, in 1973. By happy coincidence, Don Houghton's father-in-law was a personal friend of Run Run Shaw, a leading light in the Kowloon-based Shaw Brothers company, the producers of *King Boxer*. Thus Houghton's script, *The Legend of the 7 Golden Vamp-*

ires — touted as "The First Kung Fu Horror Spectacular!" — was born.

On 21 February 1973, Houghton, who would be asked to produce the film for Hammer, was chauffeur-driven to a meeting with Run Run at the Shaw Brothers Studios on Clear Water Bay Road, Hong Kong, where they discussed a co-production deal for three-and-a-half hours. The following day, Houghton met Run Run's nephew, Vee King Shaw, the man in charge of production and distribution. A deal was struck whereby Hammer and the Shaws would share production costs on two pictures (the other being *Shatter*, a contemporary thriller). The pictures would be shot entirely in Hong Kong and a start date of 3 September was envisaged.

Shooting didn't actually commence until late in October and last-minute wrangling between the two sides over the precise costs each company would

shoulder almost scuppered the films altogether. Hammer cast only Peter Cushing, Nordic bombshell Julie Ege, Robin Stewart and *The Vampire Lovers'* Man in Black John Forbes-Robertson. The remainder, including contract players David Chiang and Shih Szu, were paid for by the Shaws. Upon his arrival in Hong Kong, veteran director Roy Ward Baker encountered numerous difficulties. The stages were not sound-proofed (all Shaw films were later dubbed, due to the variety of dialects they would be released in); suitably barren and undeveloped locations proved near-impossible to find; and several of the few English crew members would not attempt to co-operate civilly with their Chinese co-workers. In addition, on 31 October, Run Run viewed the first rough cut kung fu sequence and declared it unsatisfactory, demanding that the remaining action scenes be shot by one of the company's own directors. (A second unit was duly formed under Chang Cheh who, in addition, shot extra martial arts scenes for a 110-minute Far East release, giving rise to a so-called 'uncut' version.)

The Legend of the 7 Golden Vampires went well over budget. Following its completion, the cost to the Shaw Brothers' in-house facilities was revised upwards from the original estimate to the tune of $HK800,000. This would have a significant effect on Hammer, who had already taken out a substantial loan to pay its contribution to the two pictures. And the company's Hong Kong nightmare was not yet over. The indifferent *Shatter*, Cushing's last Hammer feature, proved, if anything, even more problematic. Houghton, shanghaied against his wishes to produce, was summarily dismissed by Carreras when accused of going native. Likewise, director Monte Hellman took an early bath when creative differences arose between Carreras and himself.

Nevertheless, eventual distributor Warner Bros was delighted with *The Legend of the 7 Golden Vampires*, and went on record as anticipating excellent returns, while a British première was set for the Warner Rendezvous on Thursday 29 August. That month, it was confirmed that the film had opened to "very big business" in Singapore. (Critically, despite fine British results, Warners decided not to distribute the film in America. The film was sold on and sneaked out as *The Seven Brothers Meet Dracula* five years later.) Seven

small cuts were made to the British print by the BBFC. Carreras was overjoyed by *Melody Maker*'s review of the film, which he kept on file. Complimenting its "trash aesthetic", critic Charles Shaar Murray wrote: "*The Legend of the 7 Golden Vampires* is perhaps the worst film I've ever seen...The part of Christopher Lee is played by a gent named John Forbes-Robertson, who is not over-endowed with either presence or charisma and looks like an old queen whose make-up has run... The part of Peter Cushing is played, rather reluctantly and without much enthusiasm, by Peter Cushing...The part of a pair of big tits with a Swedish accent is played by Julie Ege." He concluded: "why do otherwise intelligent people pay money to see this garbage? I don't know. That's why I'm going to see it again next week."

Like *The Stranglers of Bombay*, *The Legend of the 7 Golden Vampires* is, structurally, more a Western than anything else. Enormous fun, it has a slightly quaint air of derring-do about it. As Van Helsing, Cushing narrated the film's soundtrack LP in the style of a *Boys' Own* adventure; it fitted. Sadly, it was this fine actor's last portrayal of the character.

Previous page: Dracula (John Forbes-Robertson) continues his bloodline through disciple Kah (Chan Shen).
Left: Peter Cushing as Professor Van Helsing.
Below: Van Helsing strikes camp with the Seven Brothers.
Bottom: Producers Michael Carreras and Vee King Shaw with stars Peter Cushing and Stuart Whitman, in Hong Kong for Shatter. *"In my opinion this film is a mess and I am very despondent about it,"* Michael wrote to Brian Lawrence in London on 3 March 1974. *"It seems to lack any point of interest, the action sequences lack excitement, the dialogue scenes are dull and Hong Kong looks like a slum. I just don't know how to salvage it... I doubt if I will ever be able to convey to you the frustrations that have occurred here — it is an episode of my life that I wish to forget as soon as possible. I never want to produce or direct another picture again — it's been that bad."*

Principal photography 1 September to
24 October 1975
Released 19 February 1976
Certificate X
Duration 93 minutes
Colour
Director Peter Sykes

Bavaria, the present day: seventeen year-old nun Catherine Beddows (Nastassja Kinski) leaves the care of Father Michael Rayner (Christopher Lee) to visit her father in London. An anxious Henry Beddows (Denholm Elliott) asks John Verney (Richard Widmark) to take care of his daughter on his behalf. In Bavaria, Father Michael injects a woman with a lethal dose of morphine after she gives birth to an unseen child. During the woman's agonised labour, Catherine suffers simultaneous convulsions in London. On Catherine's eighteenth birthday, she opens up a present from Father Michael — an inverted crucifix bearing an effigy of the god Astaroth. John leaves Catherine in the care of his friends David (Anthony Valentine) and Anna (Honor Blackman). A Bishop (Derek Francis) tells John that Father Michael was ex-communicated for trying to create an avatar, the personification of a god that was to "renew the vital spirit of the world". John returns to find that a possessed Catherine has stabbed Anna through the face and escaped. She has been delivered to Father Michael, who prepares to rebaptise the girl to the Devil. Lying on an altar with her legs apart, Catherine dreams that a hideous, demonic baby is forcing its way into her womb...

o the Devil a Daughter was originally slated to comprise part of a television anthology of Dennis Wheatley's stories, *The Devil and All His Works*, proposed in 1973. Like so many projects during this period, the idea got little further than Hammer House.

Brian Lawrence arranged for EMI production chief Nat Cohen to attend a screening of *The Exorcist* on 11 March 1974, ahead of its British release, and Cohen agreed to support Hammer's development of *To the Devil a Daughter* as a feature film shortly after. Hammer had been granted a 'free run' on the novel by then option-holders Charlemagne, the production company owned by Christopher Lee and Anthony Nelson Keys. John Peacock was contracted to write a script in March 1974, and upon completion, discussions began with potential producer Keys.

Progress was delayed by Cohen, who was slow in formally committing to EMI's half of the budget. The cash-starved Hammer was dependent on Cohen's finance; funds were already so low that Anthony Nelson Keys' services had proved beyond the comp-

The evil power of black magic has fascinated millions of cinema-goers. First... "Rosemary's Baby." Then... "The Exorcist." And now a motion picture that probes further into the mysteries of the occult than any has dared before!

Dennis Wheatley's
"TO THE DEVIL...A DAUGHTER"

RICHARD WIDMARK · CHRISTOPHER LEE "TO THE DEVIL...A DAUGHTER" HONOR BLACKMAN · DENHOLM ELLIOTT · NASTASSJA KINSKI · ANTHONY VALENTINE EMI

any's reach. Michael Carreras asked Roy Skeggs to step in and simplify the script when Cohen baulked at the film's £430,000 budget and eight-week shooting schedule. The schedule proved impossible to reduce, but Skeggs recommended enough cuts to ultimately scale the budget down to £360,000.

Carreras attempted to interest AIP in co-financing the film, but their comments on the script illustrated its shortcomings all too clearly: "This has all the visual horrors, apparitions, nightmares, hallucinations and special effects to appeal to those who are into seeing occultism and exorcism conjured up. However, the story is written in a confusing style. While the central characters are good, interesting types, their inter-relationships are never satisfactorily explained which accounts for much of the confusion thereby leaving big holes in the overall plot... This needs a tremendous

morning and told me he was getting the first flight to Los Angeles. I managed to get to him by 6am, sat on the end of his bed and persuaded him to stay. He did the same the next week, and I went to him again. When it happened again I ignored him."

While Michael Carreras was in America, trying to raise the finance for Hammer's next planned project, *Vampirella*, filming in England grew increasingly fraught. "I didn't see Michael on the set for one moment during that picture," says Skeggs. "I was shooting round the script, I had the unions on my back... it was an absolute nightmare."

The greatest controversy, however, was aroused by the closing sacrificial scenes, shot on location in High Wycombe. Christopher Lee was especially unhappy with the film's bizarre climax: "Richard Widmark arrives, and I'm just about to sacrifice Kinski when he knocks me out by throwing a rock at me. He rescues her and you never see me again. But that was only part of what we actually shot. In the ending we originally shot, I regained consciousness, and saw him [Widmark] carrying the girl out. I picked up a knife and, forgetting the penalty, charged after them. The moment my foot touched the circle of blood there was divine intervention. There was a terrific flash of lightning that enveloped me from head to foot and I was thrown onto the ground in a crucified position."

"We couldn't get the end sequence," concurs Skeggs. "Everything we'd tried before had been rejected." It has been suggested that the original ending's passing similarity to the Count's demise in *Scars of Dracula* led to the unhappy compromise that closed the film with a strangely muted scuffle. On his return, Michael Carreras expressed dissatisfaction with the scene, but Nat Cohen denied him the extra funds to shoot something new.

To the Devil a Daughter premièred in Birmingham and Nottingham on 19 February, opening in London on 4 March. Its first week at the Leicester Square Odeon earned £9,807, and the film commenced an initially successful general release one day later. Plans to shoot Wheatley's *The Satanist*, starring Christopher Lee and Britt Ekland, never saw fruition.

A generation of film-making sensibilities separates *To the Devil a Daughter* from every single Hammer film that came before it. The avant-garde camera work and sound design now seem anachronistic, but Peter Sykes' fragmented narrative is arresting right up to the surreal (anti)climax. An unequivocal dismissal of all that had gone before, *To the Devil a Daughter* was a brave, if misguided, exercise. Michael Carreras' next throw of the dice would prove to be his last.

amount of work." In October, Christopher Wicking was commissioned to redraft Peacock's script.

Early in 1975, original director Don Sharp backed out and was replaced by Peter Sykes. The search for leading players was similarly problematic: Stacy Keach and Michael Sarrazin proved too expensive, while John Phillip Law and Anthony Perkins were rejected by Cohen. Richard Widmark was eventually signed to play John Verney, but not before he was granted script approval. Christopher Lee was cast as Father Michael, and improvised a performance of chilling intensity that stands as one of the finest characterisations of his career. Catherine Beddows was played by the fifteen year-old Nastassja Kinski, her casting a stipulation of a co-production deal finalised with German partners Terra Filmkunst in June.

The tortuous pre-production process only gave way to more serious difficulties when shooting finally commenced. "We just couldn't get the script right," remembers Roy Skeggs, who worked alongside Peter Sykes and unaccredited writer Gerry Hughes on the finished screenplay. "After each day's filming we would sit up until midnight, working on the next day's script. Richard Widmark would be given his script in make-up every morning — he called us Mickey Mouse Productions. I don't blame him in a way. In the second week of shooting he called me at 4am one

---

30th June, 1975.

Michael Carreras, Esq.,
Hammer Film Productions Ltd.,
Hammer House,
113/117 Wardour Street,
London W1V 4HN.

Dear Michael,

Many thanks for sending me the latest script which is supposed to be based upon my book, TO THE DEVIL A DAUGHTER.

In fact, it has no relation whatever to my novel and is a hopeless mess, the ending of which could not possibly be more unsatisfactory.

You will recall that when you made the film of THE DEVIL RIDES OUT you stuck to the story, and I do not have to tell you what an admirable success that film has proved. Why, in this case, should you get some scriptwriter to do a completely different story which cannot possibly bring you in anything like the money that would a story by myself? As evidence of my point it may interest you to know that a fortnight ago the first paperback edition of my novel, THE IRISH WITCH, was published by Arrow and the trade subscribed 295,000 copies at 65p.

My name is of very considerable value and I can see no reason why it should be abused; but in this particular case I do not actually own the rights, they are owned by Messrs. Brook-Richleau Ltd., a subsidiary of Booker McConnell, and I have sent the script on to them so that we may have their reactions to this appalling travesty which has been made of my story.

With kindest thoughts,

Yours ever,

Dennis

Previous page: Anna Fountain (Honor Blackman) is murdered by the possessed Catherine.

Above left: Catherine Beddows (Nastassja Kinski), wearing the inverted crucifix given her by Father Michael.

Above right: Dennis Wheatley's initial enthusiasm turned to bitterness. "He was appalled," says Christopher Lee. "I said, 'Dennis, I promise you this had nothing to do with me. I didn't know they were going to shoot it like this.' He told me he would never allow Hammer to film another one of his books."

Below: The original, unseen, conclusion of Hammer's final horror film, captured by photographer Ray Hearne. The shooting script had suggested a more ambitious demise still for Christopher Lee's Satanist: "Father Michael is killed by metamorphosis. He undergoes rapid magical transformation from creature to creature, becoming, in turn, a bear, a lizard, an ant, a maggot and finally, in death, himself again."

*d*uring the late seventies, Michael Carreras struggled to sustain Hammer in a British film industry that was really no longer any industry at all. "Jimmy Carreras used to say to me, 'You make the comedy, I'll make the horror'," remembers *Carry On...* producer Peter Rogers. By the late seventies, however, neither Rogers nor Carreras Junior could find the finance to make very much of either. Pinewood, Elstree and Shepperton ground to a standstill — at the beginning of 1975, not one single film was in production in any British studio. Even Tigon, who at one point seemed ambitious and powerful enough to swallow Hammer, had ceased production to see out the remainder of the decade as a minor distribution concern.

Without funds to develop new projects, and deals to realise them, Michael Carreras was left with little more than a brand name. And even that needed reinventing to remain viable. In November 1975, Carreras stretched his company's meagre resources to bring actress Barbara Leigh and an uncomfortable Peter Cushing to the 'Monstercon' convention in New York. Carreras was in town to stir up some hype, and raise some finance, for Hammer's most ambitious project yet: *Vampirella*. Based on the adventures of Warren Publishing's scantily clad supervixen, *Vampirella* would have been an irreverent excursion into *Rocky Horror* territory directed by Gordon Hessler. Originally outlined by Jimmy Sangster, and later developed by John Starr, Lew Davidson and Christopher Wicking, *Vampirella* was a decadent tongue-in-cheek romp. "She... is definitely female," reveal Michael Carreras' staccato notes on the story, "in her mid-twenties... attractive... intelligent, a swinger in the Chelsea late-night disco set — she has a bachelor pad that is... 'out of this world'... For a living she works as the 'sexy' half of a top class mind reading act. The other half is her 'father figure' known simply as Pendragon... They work only the plush living rooms of the very rich... the very influential... their West End homes, their country mansions, their yachts and occasionally, at special invitation, the top casinos of the world... their act is 'mind blowing'... for the illusions Pendragon creates are real magic — because Vampirella herself is 'out of this world'..."

Vampirella, Carreras explained, was a vampire who escaped from the planet Drakulon to Earth. Between gigs as Pendragon's glamorous assistant (the ability to transform into a bat came in handy during certain routines), Vampirella worked for the Space Operatives for Defence and Security, known affectionately to those few involved as 'SODS'.

Based in a subterranean Harley Street HQ, SODS (commanded by none less than Sir John Gielgud had Carreras had his way) defended the planet from the Akrons, an alien race who came to Earth via a "magnetic tear in the curtain of time".

Although inspired by a comic book, *Vampirella* was certainly not children's entertainment: "We watch with interest as her Phillipino [sic] houseboy fixes her a 'blood plasma' highball... she steps from her 'costume' and her body is oiled by her twin Burmese body servants... This is followed — if you can still bear to watch — by a quick 'karate-kung fu-judo' work-out with the Japanese chauffeur bodyguard... her varied body positions are almost 'mind blowing'... whatever else is blown is your own business."

Set in such curiously diverse locations as the Bermuda Triangle and Cheltenham Ladies' College, *Vampirella* plugged everything from steamy sex to martial arts massacres into its meandering storyline. Sub-plots from actual comic book stories were littered across the way. "In a nutshell," wrote Carreras, "Vampirella is a gallectic [sic] 'Modesty Blaize' [sic], an inter-stellar '007' and much... much... more... In fact... our only protector against unfriendly forces whether they come from crypt or coffin, graveyard or sorcerer's spell, inner or outer space... anywhere that is 'out of this world'..."

"It was really going to be geared for the college kids and young marrieds and have all the tongue-in-cheek you could get away with," remembered Carreras. "They were the people who would've been in tune with what we were trying to do anyway; it would've been marvellous and been playing everywhere forever." Over a year of development saw *Vampirella* passed over by AIP and Columbia before the rights reverted to copyright holder James Warren. Following the phenomenal success of *Star Wars* in 1977, Carreras attempted to persuade Warren to enter into partnership with Hammer to produce the film; nothing came of the suggestion, and *Vampirella* was added to a growing list of frustrations and regrets.

Vampirella's development drained yet more finance away from Hammer. Shortly after Carreras' return from Monstercon, co-director and company secretary Roy Skeggs quit after less than a year on the board. Skeggs' resignation was formally noted by a despondent Carreras at a meeting held on Wednesday 17 December 1975. "Michael wrote me a very sweet letter when I said I wanted to leave," says Skeggs. "He said I was one of the few professionals he had worked with. I think he must have been very upset at what was happening around him but it never came through in conversation." Skeggs

joined Lawrence in managing Hammer's film library and collecting royalties on the company's behalf. The two men had already formed their own production company, Cinema Arts International, with ousted Hammer writer/producer Don Houghton.

To take Skeggs' place on the board, the increasingly edgy PFS insisted on a recognised producer with a reputation that would hopefully attract some business in the company's direction. Carreras rubber-stamped the appointment of fellow creditor Euan Lloyd, who added his name to Hammer's headed paper from 1 January 1976. (Lloyd continued to pursue a successful career in tandem with his Hammer directorship, most notably producing the 1978 film *The Wild Geese*.) Tom Sachs, a former Hammer production manager, handled "nuts and bolts" duties, while Christopher Wicking continued to generate ideas in his semi-official capacity as Hammer's 'script department'.

Together with Lloyd, Carreras devised *Nessie — Monster From the Past*, a lavish effects picture to lift Hammer from stormy waters. By August 1977, this *Jaws/King Kong* hybrid had been offered to Toho, Columbia, ABC TV, Rank and Vee King Shaw in the search for co-finance. By March 1978, Carreras had secured tacit agreements with David Frost's Paradine Productions and Toho in Japan for a $7,000,000 co-production. Christopher Wicking's

Previous page: *Michael Carreras (right) looks on while Peter Cushing inspects a brochure promoting the proposed* Vampirella *film at the 'Monstercon' in New York, November 1975.*
Below left: *A page from Michael Carreras' typed* Vampirella *synopsis. "The fact that it didn't get made is still my greatest disappointment," claimed Carreras towards the end of his life.*
Below right: *Bryan Forbes' revised 'shooting script' for* Nessie, *dated March 1978, features illustrations such as this, detailing the ancient sunken city in the Indian Ocean.*

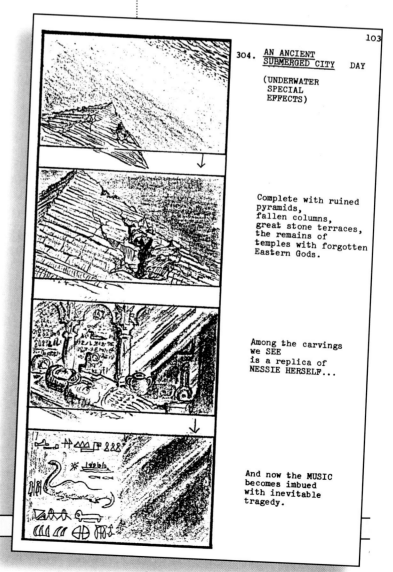

screenplay, written from a treatment by John Starr, was then replaced by a 'shooting script' by Bryan Forbes. Michael Anderson, responsible for 1977's *Orca — Killer Whale*, was slated to direct.

In Forbes' ambitious *Nessie*, a truck containing the dangerous chemical Mutane 4 crashed into Loch Ness, stirring the dormant creature within. A television film unit trailed the monster as she journeyed from the Loch through the North Sea, through the English channel, past Gibraltar, around Cape Horn and through the Indian Ocean, spectacularly destroying an oil rig and a hovercraft in her path. The monster was finally killed in the Sunda Straits, off Java.

The creature didn't emerge until scene 220, almost two-thirds into the script, in which a hapless swimmer came face to face with the huge beast: "Shock cut — enormous close up (special effects) as the scaly lid of an eye opens close to Candy. Candy is turned away from it, and now as she moves slightly she turns to face it." In scene 223, the effects workshops at Toho would have been called upon to finally reveal the awesome beast: "Nessie moves (special effects) and it is as if the whole ocean bed is in upheaval. The ridge trembles and then disintegrates as her bulk lumbers into arcane life." When the potential backers at Columbia moved on, and delays over financing instilled disinterest in Toho,

the project was placed in what Carreras termed "dry dock". He was putting on a brave face — *Nessie* was but another dashed hope.

In summer 1977, the cash crisis forced Carreras and Sachs out of Hammer House itself and into more modest offices at Pinewood Studios. It was while at Pinewood that Carreras finally got the green light he had been searching for since 1975. *The Lady Vanishes*, a remake of Alfred Hitchcock's 1938 comedy-thriller, had first appeared on Hammer's schedule in 1973 as a proposed 'Movie of the Week' produced on video for American television. *Vlad the Impaler* author Brian Hayles prepared a screenplay in 1974, and Carreras later persuaded the ABC network to promise half the finance for a package that included director John Moxey and stars Candice Bergen, Michael Douglas and Hermione Gingold. By 1977, Carreras had persuaded AIP and Rank (who owned the film's remake rights) to co-finance *The Lady Vanishes*, from a new script by George Axelrod (the American writer responsible for *Breakfast at Tiffany's* and *The Manchurian Candidate*, amongst others). The 'casting by committee' process familiar from *To the Devil a Daughter* was in full swing by November 1977, as Carreras sought lead actors acceptable to both his partners. George Segal had been lined up to play Robert Condon, but Diane Keaton, Candice Bergen and Jacqueline Bisset had already turned the role of Amanda Kelly down by the time AIP rejected Goldie Hawn, Cybill Shepherd, Diana Rigg and Lauren Hutton.

When AIP lost interest in the project altogether, Carreras made up the missing half of the $4,000,000 budget with money from Columbia — by the beginning of 1978, *The Lady Vanishes* was set to go with stars George Segal, Ali MacGraw, Herbert Lom and Angela Lansbury, and director Mike Newell. Disaster struck once more when Columbia dropped out. By now funding Hammer entirely from his own pocket, and facing long-standing debts to Barclays Bank and the Bank of America, Carreras hoped he could hang on long enough for the profit flow that would save the company. He eventually persuaded Rank to finance *The Lady Vanishes* themselves, but was dealt a further blow before filming even began. Its patience wearing thin, PFS froze the Hammer Film Productions account in August 1978, diverting all incoming monies towards offsetting the company's debt. No longer free to function as Hammer Film Productions, Carreras revived a dormant Hammer subsidiary, Jackdaw, and renamed it Hammer Films Limited. It was under this new identity that Carreras oversaw shooting on *The Lady Vanishes*, which finally began on 11 December 1978, with Elliott Gould and Cybill Shepherd in the lead roles. Angela Lansbury, as Miss Froy, and Herbert Lom, as Dr Hartz, survived. Director Anthony Page, fresh from the Richard Burton film *Absolution*, had been hired just six weeks before.

After a month on location in Austria, *The Lady Vanishes* returned to Pinewood Studios and further location work in London. As filming progressed, the budget spiralled way beyond that originally agreed. Carreras was removed, and Rank completed the

film, forfeiting Hammer's rights in the process. *The Lady Vanishes* premièred in London on 5 May 1979, but by this time the film's relative merits and performance were of little consequence to anyone other than Rank. Its patience finally exhausted, PFS had called time on a debt now in excess of £800,000. Michael Carreras was told to step down from the company his family had headed since 1935.

On 22 February 1979, Carreras broke the news to the company's accountant Bill Croft: "There has been a dramatic turn of events in PFS attitude towards the Hammer Group which in essence means no more trading after 31 March," he wrote. "The new company — Hammer Films Limited — will shut up shop, pass over to Hammer Film Productions Limited its assets and quietly fade away. Tintern will continue to collect the Hammer residuals and I will cease to be an officer of any of the companies."

Only after the facts had been relayed did Carreras allow himself a note of poignancy: "It is the end of an era."

Carreras was a broken man, exhausted by the struggle to keep Hammer afloat and disillusioned by the machinations of an industry that had dealt his dream blow after blow. He would never make another film.

"I wasn't a ruthless enough businessman," he reflected, in an interview with Steve Swires. "I was really trapped by my own desire to hold on to something that was sinking into a financial swamp. Obviously, I had always wanted Hammer to survive. I didn't want to see a company which had been in my family's hands for so long wrested away. Many harsher people with better sense would have cut their losses at least two years before, and wouldn't have dribbled everything away trying to save a company that was really dead from the neck upwards."

In a single sentence note typed from Hammer's Elstree office, Carreras resigned his directorship on 30 April 1979. On 2 May, Euan Lloyd followed suit, and Hammer fell under the control of the Official Receiver.

ICI clearly had no use for a film production company or library, and invited Brian Lawrence and Roy Skeggs to continue collecting Hammer royalties on its behalf. On 8 October 1979, it went one step further and sanctioned the appointment of Lawrence and Skeggs to replace Carreras and Lloyd on the Hammer board. Lawrence, who had been content to stay in the background during his long association with Hammer, and Skeggs, his similarly publicity-shy Cinema Arts partner, found themselves with a stricken company they could barely afford to exploit. Following a meeting with financiers Charles Denton, Jack Gill and Lew Grade, the solution was at hand. "We had one big lunch," remembers Skeggs, "and we got the Hammer television series and the film of [sit-com] *Rising Damp*." Acting as Cinema Arts, Lawrence and Skeggs licensed the name Hammer from ICI for a collection of television horror stories under the title *The House of Hammer*. The revenue from the series, produced in 1980 and transmitted under the title *Hammer House of*

Horror, essentially funded Lawrence and Skeggs' purchase of Hammer from a relieved ICI. The company changed hands for just £100,000. "It was a good investment," admits Skeggs.

A second season of *Hammer House of Horror* was scuppered when backers ITC sank with its ill-fated attempt to *Raise the Titanic* in 1980, but Lawrence and Skeggs, now free to trade as Hammer Film Productions Limited, secured co-finance from Twentieth Century-Fox for a series of feature-length TV movies produced between 1983 and 1984. The series, transmitted in America as *Fox Mystery Theatre* [sic] and in Britain as *Hammer House of Mystery and Suspense*, was Lawrence's final Hammer production. Already in semi-retirement, he brought his forty year association with the company to an end on 31 May 1985. Roy Skeggs gained full equity in the company from thereon.

'Tennis Court', the final episode of *Hammer House of Mystery and Suspense*, had wrapped at 5.20pm on 28 June 1984. Since that day, Hammer has been frustrated in its attempts to launch new projects by many of the same hurdles that beset Michael Carreras in the early seventies. The silence from Borehamwood has been punctuated only by television co-productions *The World of Hammer*, a 1990 series of highlights from Hammer films, and *Flesh and Blood*, a 1994 documentary narrated by Christopher Lee and Peter Cushing, just months before the latter's death.

With each passing year, the talents that gave Hammer its very identity are diminished in number. And with each passing year, the expectancy of Hammer's loyal enthusiasts grows. Roy and his son Graham, now a co-director, are faced with a significant challenge in their efforts to resume production. There is, however, perhaps a greater challenge still — that of ensuring any such production stays true to Hammer's rich legacy.

Previous page (above): *Another poster, another lost opportunity.*
Previous page (below): *A weary Michael Carreras with actor Arthur Lowe, on location at Marylebone Station for* The Lady Vanishes *in 1979.*
Above: *Cinema Arts converted Hampden House to use as a location, studio and production base for the* Hammer House of Horror *television series in 1980.*
Below: *From left to right, David McCallum, Roy Skeggs and Brian Lawrence during production of 'The Corvini Inheritance' episode of* Hammer House of Mystery and Suspense.

The demise of Michael Carreras' Hammer afforded a fresh opportunity to the company's new directors. Embracing the themes and subjects largely shunned by their predecessor, Brian Lawrence and Roy Skeggs would reunite many familiar talents for a collection of quintessential excursions into Hammer horror.

*L*awrence and Skeggs were picking up where Michael Carreras had left off, in more ways than one. *The Hammer House of Horror Mystery and Suspense* had been devised in 1973 as a videotaped anthology intended to capitalise on Hammer's reputation, while diminishing its dependence on the increasingly dicey practice of film production. The idea was one of many unsuccessfully floated by Carreras during the mid-seventies. On 8 April 1976 he had advised Anthony Hinds to, "Stand by — there is a possibility of a new ninety minute series for video." On 9 August, he requested "classic Gothic horrors" to go towards thirteen programmes featuring the company's best-known characters, including Dracula, Frankenstein, the Mummy and the Werewolf. The project was scuppered not so much by growing cynicism over Hammer's pulling power, but more by the ready abundance of classic Hammer films already available for screening at a fraction of the cost. The series was forgotten in the pursuit of more ambitious projects.

In 1979, Lawrence and Skeggs initiated *The House of Hammer* under the auspices of their production company Cinema Arts International (although direc-

tors of Hammer Film Productions by October 1979, they had yet to gain control of the company). The name Hammer was licensed from ICI, and funding principally sourced from Lew Grade's Incorporated Television Company Limited (ITC). By early 1980, it became clear that Cinema Arts had inherited little more than the idea of a horror anthology from Hammer's previous management. *The House of Hammer* would feature contemporary stories with new characters, albeit in a style more reminiscent of Hammer's sixties productions than the progressive variations of the seventies. "It was like making the old Hammer horrors," remembers Skeggs, "except we had the joy of letting the baddies win."

To oversee the series' scripting, Lawrence and Skeggs hired story editor Anthony Read, a writer best known for producing the popular seventies dramas *The Troubleshooters* and *The Lotus Eaters* for the BBC. Under a prevailing "tits and blood" ethos, Read commissioned relatively explicit and gory screenplays centred around traditional genre themes — werewolves, hauntings and even cannibalism were all stirred into a heady brew. The end result was a sometimes uncomfortable marriage of nostalgia with exploitation-style nudity and gore that was brave for prime time television.

By the time Anthony Read joined the production in April 1980, the first script was already in place: John Elder had sent Hammer's new owners 'Visitor From the Other Side' on spec, and it was commis-

sioned in February. One of the series' less conspicuous instalments, the retitled 'Visitor From the Grave' was shunted towards the back of the schedule.

Along with the rest of the crew, Read was based at Hampden House in Great Hampden, Buckinghamshire. In the best Hammer tradition, Cinema Arts had leased the former girls' school for use as a 'house studio'. All thirteen episodes would be shot in or around the building, which featured prominently under the series' opening credits. Producer Roy Skeggs lived in the stable, and used the former headmaster's oak-panelled study as his office; the science labs were converted into editing rooms and a preview theatre. Filming began on 9 July with 'Witching Time', Read's tale of a time-jumping witch (Patricia Quinn) who claims a musician (Jon Finch) as her first twentieth century victim. Outstanding among the remaining episodes was 'Rude Awakening', a near-surreal recurring nightmare story by former BBC head of drama Gerald Savory. Starring as bewildered estate agent Norman Shenley, Denholm Elliott invested the episode with a nervous intensity that recalled his scene-stealing performance as Henry Beddows in *To the Devil a Daughter*. The most fondly remembered instalment, however, is undoubtedly 'The Silent Scream', for which Skeggs persuaded Peter Cushing to play a sadistic pet shop owner who torments a former convict (Brian Cox). The episode was a distinguished conclusion to Cushing's association with Hammer.

Special effects were supervised by the late Les Bowie's former assistant Ian Scoones, who would describe his six months on the series as the happiest of his career. *The Sunday Times* visited Scoones in the Hampden House workshop he dubbed "The Little Dungeon". Reporter Martin Plimmer seemed to find the experience disconcerting: "Dressed entirely in black except for a blood red shirt, he talks in a cultured drawl worthy of Boris Karloff, through a permanent veil of cigarette smoke. His sinister elegance upstages the lumpy human shape straining through the body bag behind him." Scoones claimed to get through five gallons of (fake) blood a week on the series. "Oh yes, I have nightmares," he added, "about butterflies and daffodils and things."

Lawrence and Skeggs' claim to the series' title was more than legitimised by the impressive roll call of old hands: in addition to Peter Cushing, Denholm Elliott and Jon Finch, stars such as Diana Dors, Rosalyn Landor and Anthony Valentine made return appearances. Behind the lens, Alan Gibson, Peter Sasdy, Don Sharp and Robert Young numbered among those invited to direct. "Roy Skeggs rang me up," remembers Don Sharp, "and said, 'We've got this series going and we're going to use as many of the old Hammer directors as possible. Are you interested?' He sent me a story of Devil worship — 'Guardian of the Abyss' — and after a few rewrites away we went. It was a bit more ambitious than making your regular television episode and was like making a mini-Hammer feature. It was a joy to do."

"Every ten days two hour-long television frighteners are being churned out to spearhead ITV's anxious efforts in the autumn ratings battle," wrote the *Evening Mail*'s Stafford Hildred on 4 September. "Hammer Films — those champion chillers of the fifties and sixties — have been revived by a draft of £2,000,000 of Lord Grade's money, and a new generation of screen nightmares is taking shape." Peter Sasdy, interviewed by *Camera Angle* magazine, claimed that efficient team-work ensured that deadlines were met. "Schedules are tight, homework is formidable and the discipline is strict," he said. "Discipline isn't imposed — it's accepted as quite natural by everyone."

Under the title *Hammer House of Horror*, the series began its ITV network transmission at 9.15pm on 13 September 1980. 'Witching Time', the first episode to go into production, was also the first televised. "This Hammer revival is going to shake up the TV scene," Skeggs told Stafford Hildred. "Programmes

have been becoming very bland but there's nothing lukewarm about our approach. People have always gone for good old-fashioned horror films and that's what we're going to give them. We've got strong stories and some super casts — people like Julia Foster, Marius Goring, Prunella Gee, and it's marvellous to have Peter Cushing back from the old Hammer days. We're doing this thirteen and another series next year... Hammer is definitely back."

The series' revenue provided Lawrence and Skeggs with the means to buy Hammer Film Productions back from ICI, although a deal for a second season of episodes was lost with the demise of ITC. Although sometimes overlooked by purists, Anthony Hinds included, the show remains highly regarded by many. And in its most successful instalments, *Hammer House of Horror* is worthy of comparison with some of the better films from its namesake's canon.

Previous page (above): Norman Shenley (Denholm Elliott) and his seductive secretary Lolly Fellowes (Lucy Gutteridge) in 'Rude Awakening'. Their affair is less a dream, more a nightmare without end...
Previous page (below): The ruthless Martin Blueck (Peter Cushing) in 'The Silent Scream': "Lay the right bait and almost any animal will walk in of its own accord."
Below: Actor Ray Lonnen is 'stabbed' with a spring-loaded dagger in 'Guardian of the Abyss'. Effects supervisor Ian Scoones (right) prepares the Kensington Gore.
Bottom: Producer Roy Skeggs (beside the camera lens) and his crew-members in the hall at Hampden House.

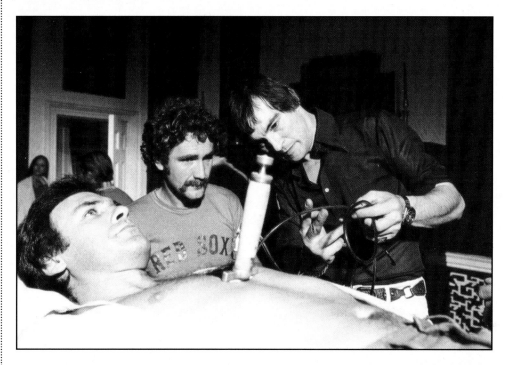

The company's third fully-fledged television venture, a series of thirteen thrillers with a macabre or extraordinary twist, shared its lead — and its backing — not with bloodier antecedent *Hammer House of Horror*, but with its long-forgotten sixties cousin *Journey to the Unknown*.

Late in 1982, a publicity brochure was issued by Hammer Film Productions Limited detailing a baker's dozen of ninety-minute TV movies that would comprise a forthcoming anthology series, *The Hammer House of Mystery and Suspense* (soon to be stripped of its definite article). These thirteen punningly titled instalments — 'Half a Pound of Tuppenny Cyanide', 'Diary of a Country Killer', 'The Lady is For Burning', 'Saraband For Sara', 'Scream and Scream Again' (no relation to the 1969 film of the same name), 'Deadly Night Maid', 'Give Me Back My Body', 'By the Light of the Blood Red Moon', 'Death's Pretty Children', 'The Evil That Men Do', 'He Who Shrieks Loudest', 'Gallow Bait' and 'Death Wrapped For Christmas' — erred from the full-blooded *Hammer House of Horror* mix, favouring serial killer sagas, locked room poisoning enigmas and that old company standby, the insanity-themed thriller. (To wit, 'Death Wrapped For Christmas' was outlined as: "The freshly fallen snow lies outside, a large log fire burns bright in the hearth, the Christmas tree has been decorated with tinsel, the mistletoe hangs from the main oak beam...but so does the lady of the house.")

None of these made their way into the finished series, production of which was planned to precede an anticipated but ultimately unmade second series of *Hammer House of Horror* proper. Producers Brian Lawrence and Roy Skeggs secured finance from Twentieth Century-Fox Television, co-producers of *Journey to the Unknown* nearly fifteen years before, who would air the shows in America under the catch-all title *Fox Mystery Theatre* [sic]. Fox's backing came with two significant provisos: first, and not according to Skeggs' preference, that the programmes would be made for the one-and-a-half hour broadcast slots favoured by Fox's marketing executives; and second, that they would contain little graphic horror content, a notable dilution of the grisly *Hammer House of Horror* approach. "We had to give them all the Hammer content minus the blood and gore," said Skeggs, towards the conclusion of principal photography. "It is as near Hammer as possible without going all the way."

The thirteen projected tales earlier assembled under the aegis of story editor Don Houghton were written off; a subsequent open invitation, via literary agents, to established authors garnered Hammer and Fox nearly 250 substantive storylines to mull over. Several of those selected came from former Hammer screenwriters — Jeremy Burnham (*The Horror of*

Frankenstein), Brian Clemens (*Dr Jekyll & Sister Hyde*, *Captain Kronos Vampire Hunter*), Houghton himself, plus *Hammer House of Horror* writer David Fisher and *Journey to the Unknown* scribe Michael J. Bird. Others — Dennis Spooner, Martin Worth — were old television hands, and at least one script, 'The

Haunted Tennis Court', had been earlier intended for feature production (its title had been whittled down to 'Tennis Court' by the time of broadcast).

Hammer House of Mystery and Suspense employed a crew of forty-four over thirty-six weeks of filming, with each episode being shot over ten to thirteen days. Over-runs were outlawed, Hammer being keen to stay within the total $3-4,000,000 budget plan that had impressed Fox. Despite Hammer's production base remaining at Elstree, only one episode ('The Late Nancy Irving') included any footage shot at the studios themselves; actual interiors, deemed more cost-effective, were found in places such as the grand Knebworth House, Elstree's Edgwarebury Hotel, EMI's Abbey Road recording studios and even, for 'The Corvini Inheritance', former company haunt Hampden House, its tenancy since taken by an insurance firm. Skewed spy thriller 'Czech Mate', the first of the series to go before the cameras (on 31 October 1983, oddly enough), featured Viennese locations. Over the following nine months, the *Hammer House of Mystery and Suspense* ventured as far afield as Yugoslavia, Cornwall and Dover's white cliffs.

As had been the case during Hammer's earlier collaboration, Fox insisted on the casting of here-today American television players in every film. That didn't, of course, prevent the placement of some familiar Hammer names throughout: Tom Adams, Isla Blair, Sandor Eles, Linda Hayden, Carol Lynley and even Oscar Quitak (seen in *The Revenge of Frankenstein* a good quarter-century before). Likewise, much-used behind-the-scenes talent was well-represented: directors Cyril Frankel, Val Guest, John Hough and Peter Sasdy were all on hand, as were a number of other technical alumni — much to the amusement of one-time Jessica Van Helsing Stephanie Beacham. "It was lovely to work with all the people from Hammer again," she recalled, following production of the time-jumping Cornish chiller 'A Distant Scream'. "It was real 'blast from the past' time because all the technicians were the same people with slightly more crows' feet and pot bellies. A lot of fat tummies on that unit I can't remember from when I worked on *Dracula A.D. 1972*..." It was hoped that roles might be found

for both Peter Cushing and Christopher Lee, but nothing suitable was written for the former, and the latter was reluctant to make the trip from America.

Not long before filming 'Tennis Court', the final segment, *Starburst* magazine asked Skeggs whether or not he'd enjoyed working on the series. "Not really, to be perfectly frank," he replied. "It used to be good fun, but it isn't so much on this... But if you care, you get like this and, let's face it, I have set myself a high target on anybody's terms."

Just like *Journey to the Unknown* before it, the series fell victim to audience indifference in America and staggered region-by-region airing in Britain when broadcast from September 1984 on, but it still managed to conjure up something of Hammer's old voodoo here and there: in 'The Late Nancy Irving', a tale of neo-vampiric blood transfusion; in 'Mark of the Devil', Clemens' saga of a supernatural tattoo; in 'Black Carrion', a wry Houghton-scripted instalment set in and around a shady manor house inhabited by two fraternal sixties pop sensations; in the truly bizarre 'Child's Play', wherein a family entombed in their home become aware that they are but the inhabitants of a doll's house; in 'And the Wall Came Tumbling Down', a witchcraft-inflected thriller spanning four centuries; and in the awesome 'Tennis Court', which rose way above its outlandish premise.

Hammer House of Mystery and Suspense may not provide the most satisfying full stop to the story of Britain's most successful independent film company — by rights, the Hammer saga ought to end bloody, a disarranged young couple emerging from a blazing rural mansion with the most terrible sounds ringing fresh in their ears — but this *House* was built over the foundations of another establishment entirely: a house buried in time and shrouded in shadow, a house that casts a stranger spell...

A house with ghosts. An old dark house indeed.

Previous page (above): Mike Preston (Nicholas Clay) discovers that normal service has been interrupted in 'Child's Play'.
Previous page (below): Vicky Duncan (Susan George) behind asylum bars in 'Czech Mate'.
Above: Hammer veteran Val Guest directing 'In Possession' with Carol Lynley.
Below left: Maggie Dowl (Hannah Gordon) and John Bray (Peter Graves) in 'Tennis Court'.
Below right: Michael Harris (David Carradine) and Rosemary Richardson (Stephanie Beacham) in 'A Distant Scream', directed by John Hough.

This A-Z index to the output of the Exclusive Films Limited/Hammer Film Productions Limited group of companies between 1935 and 1979 is the most complete of its kind ever published. It documents all short films and features produced by the company and its many subsidiaries. Controversy surrounds the status of many of the short films released by Exclusive in the forties and fifties. Although the actual production of such films was often undertaken by outside companies, Exclusive/Hammer actively participated in all such films included here. A further appendix lists television productions.

The films are noted thus: British title; year of first British public exhibition; approximate duration of British exhibition print; original British censor's certificate; film stock/screen ratio. A brief synopsis or outline is then followed by credits for: leading players [Lp]; screenplay [Scrp]; producer [Prod]; and director [Dir]. Where any of these are missing, the information is either inapplicable — there are rarely leading players in a travelogue, for example — or, sadly, unavailable.

In addition, full cast plus extended credits listings are supplied for those films given individual entries in the main text. Principal cast members and character names are listed as given on screen, and in on-screen order. (It should be noted, however, that several films do not caption character names. In this instance, names have been listed either as given in press books or other release documentation, as scripted, or as noted in the artistes' original contracts.) Following the word 'and', additional cast credits, not given on screen, are indicated. Before the late seventies, it was common practice for actors in minor roles to go unaccredited; using original artistes' contracts, press books and so on, we have attempted to correct this. It should be recognised that these are not 'extras', but individually contracted members of the actors' union Equity (including, in some cases, professional dancers and the like).

Selected technical/production credits follow. Abbreviations used, and in this order, are: M [music composer]; M sup [musical supervisor]; Dp [director of photography]; Prod des [production designer]; Art dir [art director]; Sup ed [supervising editor]; Ed [editor]; Make-up [make-up supervisor]; Spfx [special effects]; Scrp [screenplay]; Exec prod [executive producer]; Assoc prod [associate producer]; Prod [producer]; Dir [director]. Credits are only those given on screen, and their precise designation may be simplified for the sake of convenience. Unique or otherwise noteworthy credits — choreographers, for example — are sometimes given; these are written out in full.

THE ABOMINABLE SNOWMAN

(see pages 26-27)

Cast: Forrest Tucker (Tom Friend), Peter Cushing (Dr Rollason), Maureen Connell (Helen Rollason), Richard Wattis (Peter Fox), Robert Brown (Ed Shelley), Michael Brill (McNee), Wolfe Morris (Kusang), Arnold Marle (Lhama), Anthony Chin (Majordomo).

Selected credits: M: Humphrey Searle. M sup: John Hollingsworth. Dp: Arthur Grant. Prod des: Bernard Robinson. Art dir: Ted Marshall. Ed: Bill Lenny. Make-up: Phil Leakey. Scrp: Nigel Kneale. Exec prod: Michael Carreras. Assoc prod: Anthony Nelson-Keys. Prod: Aubrey Baring. Dir: Val Guest.

THE ADVENTURES OF PC 49

1949 67m cert U bw

PC 49 tracks down a gang of thieves who have shot a nightwatchman in a raid.

Lp: Hugh Latimer, Patricia Cutts, John Penrose.

Scrp: Alan Stranks, Vernon Harris. Prod: Anthony Hinds. Dir: Godfrey Grayson.

THE ANNIVERSARY

(see pages 118-119)

Cast: Bette Davis (Mrs Taggart), Sheila Hancock (Karen Taggart), Jack Hedley (Terry Taggart), James Cossins (Henry Taggart), Elaine Taylor (Shirley Blair), Christian Roberts (Tom Taggart), Timothy Bateson (Mr Bird), Arnold Diamond (Head Waiter), Sally-Jane Spencer (Florist), Albert Shepherd, Ralph Watson (Workmen).

Selected credits: M sup: Philip Martell. Title music played by The New Vaudeville Band. Dp: Harry Waxman BSC. Prod des: Reece Pemberton. Sup ed: James Needs GBFE. Ed: Peter Weatherley GBFE. Make-up: George Partleton. Scrp: Jimmy Sangster. Prod: Jimmy Sangster. Dir: Roy Ward Baker.

THE BANK MESSENGER MYSTERY

1937 56m cert U bw

A former bank clerk encounters a group of thieves.

Lp: George Mozart, Francesca Bahrie, Paul Neville.

Prod: Lawrence Huntington. Dir: Will Hammer.

THE BLACK WIDOW

1951 62m cert A bw

Mark Sherwin is attacked on a lonely road, but his assailant dies in a car crash. The trail leads back to Sherwin's wife.

Lp: Robert Ayres, Christine Norden, Anthony Forwood.

Scrp: Allan MacKinnon. Prod: Anthony Hinds. Dir: Vernon Sewell.

BLOOD FROM THE MUMMY'S TOMB

(see pages 144-145)

Cast: Andrew Keir (Fuchs), Valerie Leon (Margaret/Tera), James Villiers (Corbeck), Hugh Burden (Dandridge), George Coulouris (Berigan), Mark Edwards (Tod Browning), Rosalie Crutchley (Helen Dickerson), Aubrey Morris (Doctor Putnam), David Markham (Doctor Burgess), Joan Young (Mrs Caporal), James Cossins (Older Male Nurse), David Jackson (Younger Male Nurse), Jonathan Burn (Saturnine Young Man), Graham James

Above: Break in the Circle.

(Youth in Museum), Tamara Ustinov (Veronica), Penelope Holt, Angela Ginders (Nurses), Tex Fuller (Patient), Madina Luis, Omar Amoodi, Abdul Kader, Oscar Charles, Ahmed Osman, Soltan Lalani, Saad Ghazi (Priests), Sunbronze Danny Boy (Tod's Cat) and Sarah Mathiesen (Double and Stand In for Valerie Leon).

Selected credits: M: Tristram Cary. M sup: Philip Martell. Dp: Arthur Grant. Des: Scott MacGregor. Ed: Peter Weatherley GBFE. Make-up: Eddie Knight. Spfx: Michael Collins. Scrp: Christopher Wicking. Prod sup: Roy Skeggs. Prod: Howard Brandy. Dir: Seth Holt [and Michael Carreras, unaccredited].

BLOOD ORANGE

1953 76m cert A bw

A model wearing a new 'blood orange' dress is murdered. An ex-FBI agent investigates the fashion house concerned.

Lp: Tom Conway, Mila Parely, Naomi Chance.

Scrp: Jan Read. Prod: Michael Carreras. Dir: Terence Fisher.

BREAK IN THE CIRCLE

1955 91m cert U colour

A financier and an adventurer double-cross one another as they try to smuggle a scientist out of East Germany.

Lp: Forrest Tucker, Eva Bartok, Marius Goring.

Scrp: Val Guest. Prod: Michael Carreras. Dir: Val Guest.

BRED TO STAY

1947 36m cert U bw

Why French horses have been winning races.

Scrp: A. A. Houset. Prod: A. A. Houset. Dir: A. A. Houset.

THE BRIDES OF DRACULA

(see pages 50-51)

Cast: Peter Cushing (Doctor Van Helsing), Martita Hunt

(Baroness Meinster), Yvonne Monlaur (Marianne), Freda Jackson (Greta), David Peel (Baron Meinster), Miles Malleson (Dr Tobler), Henry Oscar (Herr Lang), Mona Washbourne (Frau Lang), Andree Melly (Gina), Victor Brooks (Hans), Fred Johnson (Cure), Michael Ripper (Coachman), Norman Pierce (Landlord), Vera Cook (Landlord's Wife), Marie Deveruex [sic] (Village Girl) and Susan Castle (Maid), Michael Mulcaster (Latour), Harry Pringle (Jacques), Harold Scott (Severin).
Selected credits: M: Malcolm Williamson. M sup: John Hollingsworth. Dp: Jack Asher BSC. Prod des: Bernard Robinson. Sup ed: James Needs. Ed: Alfred Cox. Make-up: Roy Ashton. Spfx: Sydney Pearson. Scrp: Jimmy Sangster, Peter Bryan, Edward Percy. Exec prod: Michael Carreras. Assoc prod: Anthony Nelson-Keys. Prod: Anthony Hinds. Dir: Terence Fisher.

THE BRIGAND OF KANDAHAR
(see pages 78–79)
1965 81m cert U colour/scope
A half-caste officer in the Bengal Lancers is unjustly accused of deserting a colleague. Disgraced, he turns traitor.
Lp: Ronald Lewis, Oliver Reed, Duncan Lamont, Yvonne Romain.
Scrp: John Gilling. Prod: Anthony Nelson Keys. Dir: John Gilling.

THE CAMP ON BLOOD ISLAND
(see pages 28–29)
1958 82m cert X bw/scope
Fearing a massacre, prisoners in an isolated Japanese POW camp struggle to prevent their cruel captors learning that the war has ended.
Lp: André Morell, Carl Mohner, Edward Underdown, Barbara Shelley.
Scrp: Jon Manchip White, Val Guest. Prod: Anthony Hinds. Dir: Val Guest.

CANDY'S CALENDAR
1946 36m cert U bw
Candy, a cat, calculates his lifespan not in years but by his contacts with people, animals and birds. Narrated by Bruce Belfrage.
Dir: Horace Shepherd.

CAPTAIN CLEGG
(see pages 70–71)
Cast: Peter Cushing (Dr Blyss), Yvonne Romain (Imogene), Patrick Allen (Captain Collier), Oliver Reed (Harry), Michael Ripper (Mipps), Martin Benson (Rash), David Lodge (Bosun), Derek Francis (Squire), Daphne Anderson (Mrs Rash), Milton Reid (Mulatto), Jack MacGowran (Frightened Man), Peter Halliday (1st Sailor), Terry Scully (2nd Sailor), Sydney Bromley (Tom Ketch), Rupert Osborn (Gerry), Gordon Rollings (Wurzel), Bob Head (Peg-Leg), Colin Douglas (Pirate Bosun) and Gerry Crampton (Tattooed Sailor), Harold Gee (Fiddler).
Selected credits: M: Don Banks. M sup: Philip Martell. Dp: Arthur Grant BSC. Sup ed: James Needs. Ed: Eric Boyd-Perkins. Art dir: Don Mingaye. Make-up: Roy Ashton. Spfx: Les Bowie. Fight sequences supervisor: Bob Simmons. Scrp: John Elder. Additional dialogue: Barbara S. Harper. Prod: John Temple-Smith. Dir: Peter Graham Scott.

CAPTAIN KRONOS VAMPIRE HUNTER
(see pages 158–159)
Cast: Horst Janson (Kronos), John Carson (Dr Marcus), Shane Briant (Paul Durward), Caroline Munro (Carla), John Cater (Grost), Lois Daine (Sara), Ian Hendry (Kerro), Wanda Ventham (Lady Durward), William Hobbs (Hagen), Brian Tully (George Sorell), Robert James (Pointer), Perry

Soblosky (Barlow), Paul Greenwood (Giles), Lisa Collings (Vanda Sorell), John Hollis (Barman), Susanna East (Isabella Sorell), Stafford Gordon (Barton Sorell), Elizabeth Dear (Ann Sorell), Joanna Ross (Myra), Neil Seiler (Priest), Olgar Anthony (Lilian), Gigi Gurpinar (Blind Girl), Peter Davidson (Big Man), Terence Sewards (Tom), Trevor Lawrence (Deke), Jacqui Cook (Barmaid), Penny Price (Whore) and Linda Cunningham (Jane), Caroline Villiers (Petra), B.H. Barry, Michael Buchanan, Steve James, Ian McKay, Barry Smith, Roger Williams (Villagers).
Selected credits: M: Laurie Johnson. M sup: Philip Martell. Dp: Ian Wilson. Designer: Robert Jones. Ed: James Needs. Make-up: Jim Evans. Scrp: Brian Clemens. Prod sup: Roy Skeggs. Prod: Albert Fennell, Brian Clemens. Dir: Brian Clemens.

A CASE FOR PC 49
1951 81m cert U bw
PC 49 investigates when the model he has been guarding becomes implicated in the murder of a millionaire.
Lp: Brian Reece, Joy Shelton, Christine Norden.
Scrp: Alan Stranks, Vernon Harris. Prod: Anthony Hinds. Dir: Francis Searle.

CASH ON DEMAND
(see pages 68-69)
1963 66m cert A bw
An anguished bank manager witnesses a devious thief emptying his vault, but is powerless to prevent him.
Lp: Peter Cushing, André Morell, Richard Vernon.
Scrp: David T. Chantler, Lewis Greifer. Prod: Michael Carreras. Dir: Quentin Lawrence.

CELIA
1949 67m cert A bw
A young actress helps a friend to solve 'the sinister affair of poor Aunt Nora'.
Lp: Hy Hazell, Bruce Lester, John Bailey, Elsie Wagstaff, Ferdy Mayne.
Scrp: A.R. Rawlinson, Edward J. Mason, Francis Searle. Prod: Anthony Hinds. Dir: Francis Searle.

A CHALLENGE FOR ROBIN HOOD
(see pages 78–79)
1967 96m cert U colour
A legend is born when a Norman noble flees to the forest of Nottingham, and a band of Saxons adopt him as their leader.
Lp: Barrie Ingham, James Hayter, Leon Greene, Gay Hamilton.
Scrp: Peter Bryan. Prod: Clifford Parkes. Dir: C. M. Pennington-Richards.

CHASE ME, CHARLIE
1951 46m cert U bw
A collection of clips from Charlie Chaplin's Essanay films, with new narration by Michael Howard.

CLEAN SWEEP
1958 29m cert U bw
George Watson's domestic bliss is shattered when his wife discovers he has broken a promise never to gamble again.
Lp: Eric Barker, Thora Hird, Vera Day.
Scrp: Patrick Brawn. Prod: Anthony Hinds. Dir: Maclean Rogers.

CLOUDBURST
1951 92m cert A bw
A Foreign Office codebreaker seeks revenge for the murder of his wife.
Lp: Robert Preston, Elizabeth Sellars, Colin Tapley.

Above: Countess Dracula.

Scrp: Francis Searle, Leo Marks. Prod: Anthony Hinds. Dir: Francis Searle.

COPENHAGEN
1956 16m cert U colour/scope
A travelogue featuring Michael Carreras and his son Christopher. Narrated by Tom Conway.
Prod: Michael Carreras. Dir: Michael Carreras.

CORNISH HOLIDAY
1946 cert U bw
A visit to the countryside and workshops of Cornwall.
Dir: Harry Long.

COUNTESS DRACULA
(see page 143)
Cast: Ingrid Pitt (Countess Elisabeth), Nigel Green (Captain Dobi), Sandor Eles (Imre Toth), Maurice Denham (Master Fabio), Patience Collier (Julie), Peter Jeffrey (Captain Balogh), Lesley-Anne Down (Ilona), Leon Lissek (Sergeant of Bailiffs), Jessie Evans (Rosa), Andrea Lawrence (Ziza), Susan Brodrick (Teri), Ian Trigger (Clown), Niké Arrighi (Gypsy Girl), Peter May (Janco), John Moore (Priest), Joan Haythorne (Second Cook), Marianne Stone (Kitchen Maid), Charles Farrell (The Seller), Sally Adcock (Bertha), Anne Stallybrass (Pregnant Woman), Paddy Ryan (Man), Michael Cadman (Young Man), Hulya Babus (Belly Dancer), Lesley Anderson, Biddy Hearne, Diana Sawday (Gypsy Dancers), Gary Rich (1st Boy), Andrew Burleigh (2nd Boy), Albert Wilkinson, Ismed Hassan (Midgets).
Selected credits: M: Harry Robinson. M sup: Philip Martell. Dp: Ken Talbot BSC. Art dir: Philip Harrison. Ed: Henry Richardson. Make-up: Tom Smith. Spfx: Bert Luxford. Choreography: Mia Nardi. Scrp: Jeremy Paul. Story: Alexander Paal, Peter Sasdy, based on an idea by Gabriel Ronay. Prod: Alexander Paal. Dir: Peter Sasdy.

CREATURES THE WORLD FORGOT

(see pages 106-107)

1971 95m cert X colour

Twin brothers battle for the leadership of a Stone Age tribe.

Lp: Julie Ege, Brian O'Shaugnessy, Tony Bonner.

Scrp: Michael Carreras. Prod: Michael Carreras. Dir: Don Chaffey.

CRESCENDO

(see pages 62-65)

1970 95m cert X colour

A young music student visits the widow of an acclaimed composer and uncovers a dark secret.

Lp: Stefanie Powers, Margaretha Scott, James Olson, Jane Lapotaire.

Scrp: Alfred Shaughnessy, Jimmy Sangster. Prod: Michael Carreras. Dir: Alan Gibson.

CRIME REPORTER

1947 36m cert A bw

A crime reporter discovers that the killer of a taxi driver leads to a gang of Soho black marketeers.

Lp: John Blythe, George Dewhurst, Stan Paskin.

Scrp: Jimmy Corbett. Prod: Hal Wilson. Dir: Ben R. Hart.

THE CURSE OF FRANKENSTEIN

(see pages 22-24)

Cast: Peter Cushing (Victor Frankenstein), Hazel Court (Elizabeth), Robert Urquhart (Paul Krempe), Christopher Lee (Creature), Melvyn Hayes (Young Victor), Valerie Gaunt (Justine), Paul Hardtmuth (Professor Bernstein), Noel Hood (Aunt), Fred Johnson (Grandpa), Claude Kingston (Little Boy), Alex Gallier (Priest), Michael Mulcaster (Warder), Andrew Leigh (Burgomaster), Ann Blake (Wife), Sally Walsh (Young Elizabeth), Middleton Woods (Lecturer), Raymond Ray (Uncle), Ernest Jay (Undertaker).

Selected credits: M: James Bernard. M sup: John Hollingsworth. Dp: Jack Asher BSC. Prod des: Bernard Robinson. Art dir: Ted Marshall. Ed: James Needs. Assistant ed: Roy Norman. Make-up: Phil Leakey. Scrp: Jimmy Sangster. Exec prod: Michael Carreras. Assoc prod: Anthony Nelson-Keys. Prod: Anthony Hinds. Dir: Terence Fisher.

THE CURSE OF THE MUMMY'S TOMB

(see pages 84-85)

Cast: Terence Morgan (Adam Beauchamp), Ronald Howard (John Bray), Fred Clark (Alexander King), Jeanne Roland (Annette Dubois), George Pastell (Hashmi Bey), Jack Gwillim (Sir Giles Dalrymple), John Paul (Inspector Mackenzie), Dickie Owen (The Mummy), Jill Mai Meredith (Jenny), Michael Ripper (Nightwatchman), Harold Goodwin (Fred), Jimmy Gardner (Bert), Vernon Smythe (Jessop), Marianne Stone (Landlady) and Olga Dickie (Housekeeper), Michael McStay (Ra), Bernard Rebel (Professor Dubois).

Selected credits: M: Carlo Martelli. M sup: Philip Martell. Dp: Otto Heller BSC. Prod des: Bernard Robinson. Sup ed: James Needs. Ed: Eric Boyd Perkins. Make-up: Roy Ashton. Scrp: Henry Younger. Assoc prod: Bill Hill. Prod: Michael Carreras. Dir: Michael Carreras.

THE CURSE OF THE WEREWOLF

(see pages 56-57)

Cast: Clifford Evans (Alfredo), Oliver Reed (Leon), Yvonne Romain (Servant Girl), Catherine Feller (Cristina), Anthony Dawson (The Marques Siniestro), Josephine Llewellyn (The Marquesa), Richard Wordsworth (The Beggar), Hira Talfrey (Teresa), Justin Walters (Young Leon), John Gabriel (The Priest), Warren Mitchell (Pepe Valiente), Anne Blake (Rosa Valiente), George Woodbridge (Dominique), Michael Ripper (Old Soak), Ewen Solon (Don Fernando), Peter Sallis (Don Enrique), Martin Matthews (Jose), David Conville (Rico Gomez), Denis Shaw (Gaoler), Charles Lamb (Chef), Serafina Di Leo (Senora Zumara), Sheila Brennan (Vera), Joy Webster (Isabel), Renny Lister (Yvonne) and Kitty Attwood (Midwife), John Bennett (Policeman), Hamlyn Benson (Landlord), Ray Browne (Official), Loraine Caruana (Servant Girl [as child]), Michael Lewis (Page), Frank Sieman (Gardener), Desmond Llewelyn, Gordon Whiting (Footmen), Howard Lang, Stephen W. Scott, Max Butterfield, Michael Peake (Farmers), Rodney Burke, Alan Page, Richard Golding (Customers).

Selected credits: M: Benjamin Frankel. Dp: Arthur Grant BSC. Prod des: Bernard Robinson. Art dir: Don Mingaye. Sup ed: James Needs. Ed: Alfred Cox. Make-up: Roy Ashton. Spfx: Les Bowie. Scrp: John Elder. Exec prod: Michael Carreras. Assoc prod: Anthony Nelson Keys. Prod: Anthony Hinds. Dir: Terence Fisher.

CYRIL STAPLETON AND THE SHOW BAND

1955 29m cert U colour/scope

Cyril Stapleton's band in concert, featuring Lita Roza, Ray Burns and Bill McGuffie.

Prod: Michael Carreras. Dir: Michael Carreras.

THE DAMNED

(see pages 66-67)

Cast: MacDonald Carey (Simon Wells), Shirley Ann Field (Joan), Viveca Lindfors (Freya), Alexander Knox (Bernard), Oliver Reed (King), Walter Gotell (Major Holland), James Villiers (Captain Gregory), Thomas Kempinski (Ted), Kenneth Cope (Sid), Brian Oulton (Mr Dingle), Barbara Everest (Miss Lamont), Alan McClelland (Mr Stuart), James Maxwell (Mr Talbot), Rachel Clay (Victoria), Caroline Sheldon (Elizabeth), Rebecca Dignam (Anne), Siobhan Taylor (Mary), Nicholas Clay (Richard), Kit Williams (Henry), Christopher Witty (William), David Palmer (George), John Thompson (Charles), with David Gregory, Anthony Valentine, Larry Martyn, Leon Garcia, Jeremy Phillips (Teddy Boys), Fiona Duncan (Control Room Guard), Edward Harvey (Doctor), Neil Wilson (Guard).

Selected credits: M: James Bernard. M sup: John Hollingsworth. Dp: Arthur Grant BSC. Prod des: Bernard Robinson. Art dir: Don Mingaye. Sup ed: James Needs. Ed: Reginald Mills. Make-up: Roy Ashton. Sculpture: Elisabeth Frink. Scrp: Evan Jones. Exec prod: Michael Carreras. Assoc prod: Anthony Nelson Keys. Prod: Anthony Hinds. Dir: Joseph Losey.

DANGER LIST

1957 22m cert A bw

Three hospital patients are mistakenly prescribed a dangerous drug. Can they all be traced in time?

Lp: Philip Friend, Honor Blackman, Mervyn Johns.

Scrp: J.D. Scott. Prod: Anthony Hinds. Dir: Leslie Arliss.

THE DARK LIGHT

1951 66m cert A bw

Three unfriendly lighthouse keepers rescue three people who turn out to be thieves.

Lp: Albert Lieven, David Greene, Norman MacOwen.

Scrp: Vernon Sewell. Prod: Michael Carreras. Dir: Vernon Sewell.

THE DARK ROAD

1948 72m cert A bw

A writer tells the story of a young boy's descent into the criminal underworld.

Lp: Charles Stuart, Joyce Linden, Mackenzie Ward.

Prod: Henry Halsted. Dir: Alfred Goulding.

DAY OF GRACE

1959 27m cert U colour/scope

When a young boy's sheep dog is threatened, a kindly farmer provides a reprieve.

Lp: Vincent Winter, John Lawrie [sic], Grace Arnold, George Woodbridge.

Scrp: Jon Manchip White, Francis Searle. Prod: Francis Searle. Dir: Francis Searle.

DEATH IN HIGH HEELS

1947 47m cert A bw

Detective Inspector Charlesworth investigates a poisoning at a Bond Street dress shop.

Lp: Don Stannard, Elsa Tee, Veronica Rose.

Scrp: Christianna Brand. Prod: Henry Halsted. Dir: Lionel Tomlinson.

DEATH OF AN ANGEL

1952 64m cert A bw

Christopher Boswell takes up practice with Dr Welling, a sick man whose wife is murdered. Boswell uncovers the killer.

Lp: Patrick Barr, Jane Baxter, Raymond Young.

Scrp: Reginald Long. Prod: Anthony Hinds. Dir: Charles Saunders.

DELAYED FLIGHT

produced 1964 bw

Little is known about this short feature, produced back-to-back with *The Runaway*.

Lp: Helen Cherry, Hugh McDermott, Paul Williamson.

Prod: Bill Luckwell. Dir: Tony Young.

DEMONS OF THE MIND

(see page 155)

Cast: Robert Hardy (Zorn), Shane Briant (Emil), Gillian Hills (Elizabeth), Yvonne Mitchell (Hilda), Paul Jones (Carl), Patrick Magee (Falkenberg), Kenneth J. Warren (Klaus), Michael Hordern (Priest), Robert Brown (Fischinger), Virginia Wetherell (Inge), Deirdre Costello (Magda), Barry Stanton (Ernst), Sidonie Bond (Zorn's Wife), Thomas

Below: The Devil-Ship Pirates.

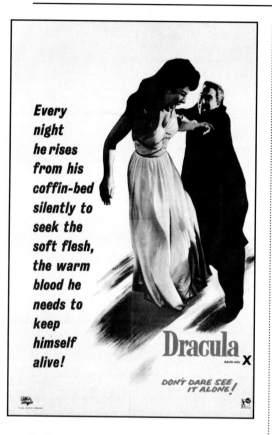

Every night he rises from his coffin-bed silently to seek the soft flesh, the warm blood he needs to keep himself alive!

Dracula X
Adults only

DON'T DARE SEE IT ALONE!

Heathcote (Coachman), John Atkinson (1st Villager), George Cormack (2nd Villager), Mary Hignett (Matronly Woman), Sheila Raynor (Old Crone), Jan Adair (1st Girl), Jane Cardew (2nd Girl).
Selected credits: M: Harry Robinson. M sup: Philip Martell. Dp: Arthur Grant. Des: Michael Stringer. Ed: Chris Barnes. Make-up: Trevor Crole-Rees. Scrp: Christopher Wicking, from an original story by Christopher Wicking, Frank Godwin. Prod sup: Roy Skeggs. Prod: Frank Godwin. Dir: Peter Sykes.

THE DEVIL RIDES OUT
(see pages 120–121)
Cast: Christopher Lee (Duc de Richleau), Charles Gray (Mocata), Niké Arrighi (Tanith), Leon Greene (Rex), Patrick Mower (Simon), Gwen Ffrangcon-Davies (Countess), Sarah Lawson (Marie), Paul Eddington (Richard), Rosalyn Landor (Peggy), Russell Waters (Malin) and Yemi Ajibade (African), John Bown (Receptionist), Richard Huggett (Financier), Ahmed Khalil (Indian), Willie Payne (Servant), Keith Pyott (Max), Mohan Singh (Mocata's Servant), Zoe Starr (Indian Girl), Peter Swanwick (Teuton), John Falconer, Liane Aukin, Bert Vivian, Anne Godley (Satanists).
Selected credits: M: James Bernard. M sup: Philip Martell. Dp: Arthur Grant BSC. Prod des: Bernard Robinson. Sup ed: James Needs. Ed: Spencer Reeve. Make-up: Eddie Knight. Spfx: Michael Stainer-Hutchins. Choreographer: David Toguri. Scrp: Richard Matheson. Prod: Anthony Nelson Keys. Dir: Terence Fisher.

THE DEVIL-SHIP PIRATES
(see pages 78–79)
1964 86m cert U colour/scope
The crew of a damaged pirate ship terrorise a Cornish village.
Lp: Christopher Lee, John Cairney, Barry Warren.
Scrp: Jimmy Sangster. Prod: Anthony Nelson Keys. Dir: Don Sharp.

DICK BARTON AT BAY
1950 68m cert U bw
A British scientist and his daughter are kidnapped by a foreign agent. Dick Barton tracks them to Beachy Head lighthouse.
Lp: Don Stannard, Tamara Desni, George Ford.
Scrp: Ambrose Grayson, J.C. Budd, E. Trechmann. Prod: Henry Halsted. Dir: Godfrey Grayson.

DICK BARTON SPECIAL AGENT
1948 70m cert U bw
Dick Barton tangles with a villainous doctor who plans to destroy England with germ bombs.
Lp: Don Stannard, George Ford, Jack Shaw.
Scrp: Alan Stranks, Alfred Goulding. Prod: Henry Halsted. Dir: Alfred Goulding.

DICK BARTON STRIKES BACK
1949 73m cert U bw
A band of criminals threaten mass destruction with a deadly vibrating ray. Dick Barton foils their plans atop the Blackpool Tower.
Lp: Don Stannard, Sebastian Cabot, Jean Lodge.
Scrp: Ambrose Grayson. Prod: Anthony Hinds. Dir: Godfrey Grayson.

DICK TURPIN — HIGHWAYMAN
1957 22m cert U colour/scope
Dick Turpin steals a gold dowry, but ultimately proves there is honour amongst thieves.
Lp: Philip Friend, Diane Hart, Allan Cuthbertson.
Scrp: Joel Murcott. Prod: Michael Carreras. Dir: David Paltenghi.

DON'T PANIC CHAPS!
(see pages 28–29 & 150–151)
1959 85m cert U bw
During wartime, a glamorous Italian castaway upsets British and German troops stationed in the Adriatic.
Lp: Dennis Price, George Cole, Thorley Walters, Harry Fowler, Nadja Regin.
Scrp: Jack Davies. Prod: Teddy Baird. Dir: George Pollock.

DRACULA
(see pages 30–32)
Cast: Peter Cushing (Van Helsing), Christopher Lee (Count Dracula), Michael Gough (Arthur Holmwood), Melissa Stribling (Mina Holmwood), Carol Marsh (Lucy Holmwood), John Van Eyssen (Jonathan Harker), Olga Dickie (Gerda), Valerie Gaunt (Vampire Woman), Janina Faye (Tania), Barbara Archer (Inga), Charles Lloyd Pack (Doctor Seward), George Merritt (Policeman), George Woodbridge (Landlord), George Benson (Frontier Official), Miles Malleson (J. Marx, the Undertaker), Geoffrey Bayldon (Porter), Paul Cole (Lad), Guy Mills (Coach Driver), Dick Morgan (Driver's Companion), John Mossmann (Hearse Driver).
Selected credits: M: James Bernard. M sup: John Hollingsworth. Dp: Jack Asher BSC. Prod des: Bernard Robinson. Sup ed: James Needs. Ed: Bill Lenny. Make-up: Phil Leakey. Spfx: Sidney Pearson. Scrp: Jimmy Sangster. Exec prod: Michael Carreras. Assoc prod: Anthony Nelson-Keys. Prod: Anthony Hinds. Dir: Terence Fisher.

DRACULA A.D. 1972
(see pages 156–157)
Cast: Christopher Lee (Count Dracula), Peter Cushing (Professor Van Helsing), Stephanie Beacham (Jessica Van Helsing), Christopher Neame (Johnny Alucard), Michael Coles (Inspector), Marsha Hunt (Gaynor), Caroline Munro (Laura), Janet Key (Anna), William Ellis (Joe Mitcham),

Philip Miller (Bob), Michael Kitchen (Greg), David Andrews (Detective Sergeant), Lally Bowers (Marion), Constance Luttrell (Mrs Donnelly), Michael Daly (Charles), Artro Morris (Police Sergeant), Jo Richardson (Crying Matron), Penny Brahms (Hippy Girl), Brian John Smith (Hippy Guy), Stoneground [Tim Barnes, John Blakeley, Brian Godula, Lynne Hughes, Deirdre La Porte, Corey Lerios, Lydia Mareno, Steve Price, Annie Sampson, Sal Valentino] (Rockgroup) and Jane Anthony ('Debby' Girl), Flanagan (Go-Go Girl), John Franklyn-Robbins (Minister).
Selected credits: M: Michael Vickers. M sup: Philip Martell. Dp: Dick Bush. Designer: Don Mingaye. Ed: James Needs. Make-up: Jill Carpenter. Spfx: Les Bowie. Scrp: Don Houghton. Prod: Josephine Douglas. Dir: Alan Gibson.

DRACULA HAS RISEN FROM THE GRAVE
(see pages 122–123)
Cast: Christopher Lee (Dracula), Rupert Davies (Monsignor), Veronica Carlson (Maria), Barbara Ewing (Zena), Barry Andrews (Paul), Ewan Hooper (Priest), Marion Mathie (Anna), Michael Ripper (Max), John D. Collins (Student), George A. Cooper (Landlord), Chris Cunningham (Farmer), Norman Bacon (Boy) and Carrie Baker (Dead girl in bell).
Selected credits: M: James Bernard. M sup: Philip Martell. Dp: Arthur Grant BSC. Supervising art dir: Bernard Robinson. Sup ed: James Needs. Ed: Spencer Reeve. Make-up: Heather Nurse, Rosemary McDonald-Peattie. Spfx: Frank George. Scrp: John Elder. Prod: Aida Young. Dir: Freddie Francis.

DRACULA PRINCE OF DARKNESS
(see pages 96–97)
Cast: Christopher Lee (Dracula), Barbara Shelley (Helen), Andrew Keir (Father Sandor), Francis Matthews (Charles), Suzan Farmer (Diana), Charles Tingwell (Alan), Thorley Walters (Ludwig), Philip Latham (Klove), Walter Brown (Brother Mark), George Woodbridge (Landlord), Jack Lambert (Brother Peter), Philip Ray (Priest), Joyce Hemson (Mother), John Maxim (Coach Driver).
Selected credits: M: James Bernard. M sup: Philip Martell. Dp: Michael Reed. Prod des: Bernard Robinson. Art dir: Don Mingaye. Sup ed: James Needs. Ed: Chris Barnes. Make-up: Roy Ashton. Spfx: Bowie Films Ltd. Scrp: John Sansom. Prod: Anthony Nelson Keys. Dir: Terence Fisher.

DR JEKYLL & SISTER HYDE
(see pages 148–149)
Cast: Ralph Bates (Dr Jekyll), Martine Beswicke (Sister Hyde), Gerald Sim (Professor Robertson), Lewis Fiander (Howard), Dorothy Alison (Mrs Spencer), Neil Wilson (Older Policeman), Ivor Dean (Burke), Paul Whitsun-Jones (Sgt Danvers), Philip Madoc (Byker), Tony Calvin (Hare), Susan Brodrick (Susan), Dan Meaden (Town Crier), Virginia Wetherell (Betsy), Geoffrey Kenion (1st Policeman), Irene Bradshaw (Yvonne), Anna Brett (Julie), Jackie Poole (Margie), Rosemary Lord (Marie), Petula Portell (Petra), Pat Brackenbury (Helen), Liz Romanoff (Emma), Will Stampe (Mine Host), Roy Evans (Knife Grinder), Derek Steen (1st Sailor), John Lyons (2nd Sailor), Jeanette Wild (Jill), Bobby Parr (Young Apprentice), Julia Wright (Street Singer).
Selected credits: M: David Whitaker. M sup: Philip Martell. 'He'll Be There', words and music by Brian Clemens. Dp: Norman Warwick BSC. Designer: Robert Jones. Ed: James Needs GBFE. Make-up: Trevor Crole-Rees. Spfx: Michael Collins. Scrp: Brians Clemens. Prod: Albert Fennell, Brian Clemens. Dir: Roy Ward Baker.

DR MORELLE — THE CASE OF THE MISSING HEIRESS
1949 73m cert A bw

Morelle's assistant tries to solve the the mystery of the murder of her friend, and the famous hypnotist helps her avoid a similar fate.
Lp: Valentine Dyall, Julia Lang, Philip Leaver
Scrp: Roy Plomley, Ambrose Grayson. Prod: Anthony Hinds. Dir: Godfrey Grayson.

THE EDMUNDO ROS HALF-HOUR
1959 30m cert U colour/scope
Latin American sounds from Edmundo Ros, Morton Frazer's Harmonica Gang and others.
Prod: Michael Carreras. Dir: Michael Carreras.

ENCHANTED ISLAND
1958 13m cert U colour/scope
A travelogue about the South Sea Islands, including a scene where two boys catch an octopus by hand. Narrated by Simon Lack.
Photography: Carl Kaiser, Martin Curtis.

THE ERIC WINSTONE BANDSHOW
1955 29m cert U colour/scope
Eric Winstone conducts his band, with solo spots from Alma Cogan, Kenny Baker and The George Mitchell Singers.
Prod: Michael Carreras. Dir: Michael Carreras.

ERIC WINSTONE'S STAGECOACH
1956 30m cert U colour/scope
The bandleader's guests include: Michael Carreras. Alma Cogan and the Ray Ellington Quartet.
Prod: Michael Carreras. Dir: Michael Carreras.

THE EVIL OF FRANKENSTEIN
(see pages 80–81)
Cast: Peter Cushing (Frankenstein), Peter Woodthorpe (Zoltan), Duncan Lamont (Chief of Police), Sandor Eles (Hans), Katy Wild (Beggar Girl), David Hutcheson (Burgomaster), James Maxwell (Priest), Howard Goorney (Drunk), Anthony Blackshaw, David Conville (Policemen), Caron Gardner (Burgomaster's Wife), Kiwi Kingston (The Creature) and Tony Arpino (Body Snatcher), Frank Forsyth (Manservant), Robert Flynn, Derek Martin (Roustabouts).
Selected credits: M: Don Banks. M sup: Philip Martell. Dp: John Wilcox BSC. Art dir: Don Mingaye. Sup ed: James Needs. Make-up: Roy Ashton. Spfx: Les Bowie. Scrp: John Elder. Prod: Anthony Hinds. Dir: Freddie Francis.

FACE THE MUSIC
1954 84m cert A bw
A famous trumpet player is suspected of having murdered a nightclub singer, and sets out to clear his name.
Lp: Alex Nicol, Eleanor Summerfield, John Salew, Paul Carpenter, Geoffrey Keen.
Scrp: Ernest Bornemann. Prod: Michael Carreras. Dir: Terence Fisher.

FANATIC
(see pages 62–65)
1965 96m cert X colour
A religious maniac imprisons her dead son's one-time fiancée.
Lp: Tallulah Bankhead, Stefanie Powers, Peter Vaughan.
Scrp: Richard Matheson. Prod: Anthony Hinds. Dir: Silvio Narrizano.

FEAR IN THE NIGHT
(see pages 62–65)
1972 86m cert X colour
Recovering from a nervous breakdown, a newly-wed is haunted by the spectre of a terrifying one-armed assailant.
Lp: Judy Geeson, Joan Collins, Ralph Bates, Peter Cushing.

Scrp: Jimmy Sangster, Michael Syson. Prod: Jimmy Sangster.
Dir: Jimmy Sangster.

FIVE DAYS
1954 72m cert A bw
A bankrupt pays a friend to kill him, so that his wife may collect his life insurance. He reneges, but the murder attempts don't stop.
Lp: Dane Clark, Paul Carpenter, Thea Gregory.
Scrp: Paul Tabori. Prod: Anthony Hinds. Dir: Montgomery Tully.

THE FLANAGAN BOY
1953 81m cert A bw
Promoter Guiseppe Vechi backs boxer Johnny Flanagan, who falls for Vechi's wife. She persuades him to kill Vechi.
Lp: Barbara Payton, Frederick Valk, John Slater, Sidney James.
Scrp: Guy Elmes, Richard Landau. Prod: Anthony Hinds. Dir: Reginald Le Borg.

FOUR SIDED TRIANGLE
1953 81m cert A bw
Graduates Bill and Robin devise a duplicating machine which Bill uses to make an identical copy of Robin's wife.
Lp: Barbara Payton, James Hayter, Stephen Murray, John Van Eyssen.
Scrp: Paul Tabori, Terence Fisher. Prod: Michael Carreras, Alexander Paal. Dir: Terence Fisher.

FRANKENSTEIN AND THE MONSTER FROM HELL
(see pages 160–161)
Cast: Peter Cushing (Baron Frankenstein), Shane Briant (Simon), Madeline Smith (Sarah), Dave Prowse (Monster), John Stratton (Asylum Director), Michael Ward (Transvest), Elsie Wagstaff (Wild One), Norman Mitchell (Police Sergeant), Clifford Mollison (Judge), Patrick Troughton (Bodysnatcher), Philip Voss (Ernst), Chris Cunningham (Hans), Charles Lloyd-Pack [sic] (Professor Durendel), Lucy Griffiths (Old Hag), Bernard Lee (Tarmut), Sydney Bromley (Muller), Andrea Lawrence (Brassy Girl), Jerold Wells (Landlord), Sheila D'Union (Gerda), Mischa De La Motte (Twitch), Norman Atkyns (Smiler), Victor Woolf (Letch), Winifred Sabine (Mouse), Janet Hargreaves (Chatter), Peter Madden (Coach Driver) and Gordon Richardson (Aggressive), Nicholas Smith (Death Wish), Hugh Cecil, Ron Eagleton, Lianne Gilmore, Beatrice Greek, Toni Harris, Peter Macpherson (Inmates).
Selected credits: M: James Bernard. M sup: Philip Martell. Dp: Brian Probyn BSC. Art dir: Scott MacGregor. Ed: James Needs. Make-up: Eddie Knight. Scrp: John Elder. Prod: Roy Skeggs. Dir: Terence Fisher.

FRANKENSTEIN CREATED WOMAN
(see pages 110–111)
Cast: Peter Cushing (Baron Frankenstein), Susan Denberg (Christina), Thorley Walters (Doctor Hertz), Robert Morris (Hans), Duncan Lamont (The Prisoner), Peter Blythe (Anton), Barry Warren (Karl), Derek Fowlds (Johann), Alan MacNaughtan (Kleve), Peter Madden (Chief of Police), Philip Ray (Mayor), Ivan Beavis (Landlord), Colin Jeavons (Priest), Bartlett Mullins (Bystander), Alec Mango (Spokesman) and Kevin Flood (Chief Gaoler), Lizbeth Kent (First Lady), John Maxim (Sergeant), Stuart Middleton (Young Hans), Anthony Viccars (Spokesman No 2), Patrick Carter, Howard Lang (Guards).
Selected credits: M: James Bernard. M sup: Philip Martell. Dp: Arthur Grant BSC. Prod des: Bernard Robinson. Art dir: Don Mingaye. Sup ed: James Needs. Ed: Spencer Reeve. Make-up: George Partleton. Spfx: Les Bowie. Scrp:

John Elder. Exec prod: Anthony Hinds. Prod: Anthony Nelson Keys. Dir: Terence Fisher.

FRANKENSTEIN MUST BE DESTROYED
(see pages 126–127)
Cast: Peter Cushing (Baron Frankenstein), Veronica Carlson (Anna), Freddie Jones (Professor Richter), Simon Ward (Karl), Thorley Walters (Inspector Frisch), Maxine Audley (Ella Brandt), George Pravda (Doctor Brandt), Geoffrey Bayldon (Police Doctor), Colette O'Neil (Mad Woman), Frank Middlemass, George Belbin, Norman Shelley, Michael Gover (Guests), Peter Copley (Principal), Jim Collier (Dr Heidecke), Allan Surtees, Windsor Davies (Police Sergeants) and Timothy Davies (Policeman), Robert Davis (Official), Caron Gardner (Passer-by), Robert Gillespie (Mortuary attendant), Michael Goldie (Warder), Edward Higgins (Workman), Elizabeth Morgan (Ella's friend), Dorothy Smith (Neighbour), Meadows White (Nightwatchman).
Selected credits: M: James Bernard. M sup: Philip Martell. Dp: Arthur Grant BSC. Supervising art director: Bernard Robinson. Ed: Gordon Hales. Make-up: Eddie Knight. Spfx: Studio Locations Limited. Scrp: Bert Batt, from an original story by Anthony Nelson Keys and Bert Batt. Prod: Anthony Nelson Keys. Dir: Terence Fisher.

THE FULL TREATMENT
1961 109m cert X bw/scope
On honeymoon in the south of France, a racing driver struggles to contain an unaccountable urge to murder his wife.
Lp: Claude Dauphin, Diane Cilento, Ronald Lewis, Francoise Rosay, Bernard Braden.
Scrp: Val Guest, Ronald Scott Thorn. Prod: Val Guest. Dir: Val Guest.

FURTHER UP THE CREEK
(see pages 150–151)
1958 91m cert U bw/scope
A ship sets sail for revolutionary Algerroca with a complement of holiday-makers who are said to be diplomats.
Lp: David Tomlinson, Frankie Howerd, Shirley Eaton, Thora Hird, Lionel Jeffries.
Scrp: John Warren, Len Heath, Val Guest. Prod: Henry Halsted. Dir: Val Guest.

THE GAMBLER AND THE LADY
1953 74m cert A bw
An American gangster running London gambling clubs becomes involved with a society lady.
Lp: Dane Clark, Kathleen Byron, Naomi Chance.
Prod: Anthony Hinds. Dir: Sam Newfield, Patrick Jenkins.

THE GLASS CAGE
1955 59m cert A bw
In a fairground, world champion starving man Sapoli, staging a fast behind glass, glimpses a killer.
Lp: John Ireland, Honor Blackman, Geoffrey Keen, Eric Pohlmann, Sidney James.
Scrp: Richard H. Landau. Prod: Anthony Hinds. Dir: Montgomery Tully.

THE GORGON
(see pages 82–83)
Cast: Peter Cushing (Doctor Namaroff), Christopher Lee (Professor Meister), Richard Pasco (Paul Heitz), Barbara Shelley (Carla Hoffmann), Michael Goodliffe (Professor Heitz), Patrick Troughton (Inspector Kanof), Joseph O'Conor (Coroner), Prudence Hyman (The Gorgon [credited 'Chatelaine']), Jack Watson (Ratoff), Redmond Phillips (Hans), Jeremy Longhurst (Bruno Heitz), Toni

Gilpin (Sascha Cass), Joyce Hemson (Martha), Alister Williamson (Janus Cass), Michael Peake (Policeman) and Sally Nesbit (Nurse).
Selected credits: M: James Bernard. M sup: Marcus Dods. Dp: Michael Reed. Prod des: Bernard Robinson. Art dir: Don Mingaye. Sup ed: James Needs. Make-up: Roy Ashton. Spfx: Syd Pearson. Scrp: John Gilling, from an original story by J. Llewellyn Devine. Prod: Anthony Nelson Keys. Dir: Terence Fisher.

HANDS OF THE RIPPER
(see pages 146-147)
Cast: Eric Porter (Pritchard), Angharad Rees (Anna), Jane Merrow (Laura), Keith Bell (Michael), Derek Godfrey (Dysart), Dora Bryan (Mrs Golding), Marjorie Rhodes (Mrs Bryant), Lynda Baron (Long Liz), Marjie Lawrence (Dolly), Norman Bird (Police Inspector), Margaret Rawlings (Madame Bullard), Elizabeth Maclennan (Mrs Wilson), Barry Lowe (Mr Wilson), A.J. Brown (Rev Anderson), April Wilding (Catherine), Anne Clune (1st Cell Whore), Vicki Woolf (2nd Cell Whore), Katya Wyeth (1st Pub Whore), Beulah Hughes (2nd Pub Whore), Tallulah Miller (3rd Pub Whore), Peter Munt (Pleasants), Philip Ryan (Police Constable), Molly Weir (Maid), Charles Lamb (Guard) and Ann Way (Seamstress).
Selected credits: M: Christopher Gunning. M sup: Philip Martell. Dp: Kenneth Talbot BSC. Art dir: Roy Stannard. Ed: Chris Barnes. Make-up: Bunty Phillips. Spfx: Cliff Culley. Scrp: L.W. Davidson, from an original story by Edward Spencer Shew. Prod: Aida Young. Dir: Peter Sasdy.

HELL IS A CITY
(see pages 68-69)
1960 98m cert A bw/scope
Inspector Martineau hunts a desperate fugitive through

Right: The Horror of Frankenstein.
Below: Hell is a City.

Manchester's mean streets.
Lp: Stanley Baker, John Crawford, Donald Pleasence, Maxine Audley, Billie Whitelaw.
Scrp: Val Guest. Prod: Michael Carreras. Dir: Val Guest.

HIGHWAY HOLIDAY
1961 25m cert U colour
Featurette sponsored by Total Oil. Britons go on an informal motor rally across Europe.
Prod: Ian Lewis. Dir: Ian Lewis.

HOLIDAY ON THE BUSES
(see pages 150-151)
1973 85m cert A colour
Sacked from the bus depot, Stan and Jack find jobs at a Welsh holiday camp.
Lp: Reg Varney, Stephen Lewis, Doris Hare, Michael Robbins, Anna Karen, Bob Grant.
Scrp/prod: Ronald Wolfe, Ronald Chesney. Dir: Brian Izzard.

THE HORROR OF FRANKENSTEIN
(see page 138)
Cast: Ralph Bates (Victor Frankenstein), Kate O'Mara (Alys), Veronica Carlson (Elizabeth), Dennis Price (Grave Robber), Jon Finch (Henri), Bernard Archard (The Professor), Graham James (Wilhelm), James Hayter (Bailiff), Joan Rice (His Wife [Grave Robber's wife]), Stephen Turner (Stephan), Neil Wilson (Schoolmaster), James Cossins (Dean), Glenys O'Brien (Maggie), Geoffrey Lumsden (Instructor), C. Lethbridge Baker (Priest), Terry Duggan (First Bandit), George Belbin (Baron), Hal Jeayes (Woodsman), Carol Jeayes (Little Girl), Michael Goldie (Workman), Dave Prowse (The Monster) and Sue Hammer (Maid).
Selected credits: M: Malcolm Williamson. M sup: Philip Martell. Dp: Moray Grant. Art dir: Scott MacGregor. Ed: Chris Barnes. Make-up: Tom Smith. Scrp: Jeremy Burnham, Jimmy Sangster. Prod: Jimmy Sangster. Dir: Jimmy Sangster.

THE HOUND OF THE BASKERVILLES
(see pages 38-39)
Cast: Peter Cushing (Sherlock Holmes), André Morell (Doctor Watson), Christopher Lee (Sir Henry), Marla Landi (Cecile), David Oxley (Sir Hugo), Francis De Wolff (Doctor Mortimer), Miles Malleson (Bishop), Ewen Solon (Stapleton), John Le Mesurier (Barrymore), Helen Goss (Mrs Barrymore), Sam Kydd (Perkins), Michael Hawkins (Lord Caphill), Judi Moyens (Servant Girl), Michael Mulcaster (Convict) and David Birks (Servant), Elizabeth Dott (Mrs Goodlippe), Ian Hewitson (Lord Kingsblood).
Selected credits: M: James Bernard. M sup: John Hollingsworth. Dp: Jack Asher BSC. Prod des: Bernard Robinson. Sup ed: James Needs. Ed: Alfred Cox. Make-up: Roy Ashton. Spfx: Sid Pearson. Scrp: Peter Bryan. Exec prod: Michael Carreras. Assoc prod: Anthony Nelson Keys. Prod: Anthony Hinds. Dir: Terence Fisher.

THE HOUSE ACROSS THE LAKE
1954 68m cert A bw
A writer is seduced by a wealthy woman, who then murders her husband on their yacht; only to discover she is two-timing him.
Lp: Alex Nicol, Hillary Brooke, Susan Stephen, Sidney James.
Scrp: Ken Hughes. Prod: Anthony Hinds. Dir: Ken Hughes.

HYSTERIA
(see pages 62-65)
1965 85m cert X bw
An amnesiac American suffers murderous hallucinations.
Lp: Robert Webber, Lelia Goldoni, Anthony Newlands.
Scrp: Jimmy Sangster. Prod: Jimmy Sangster. Dir: Freddie Francis.

I ONLY ARSKED
(see pages 28-29 & 150-151)
1959 82m cert U bw
A regiment of buffoons are entrusted with saving Britain's Middle Eastern oil supply.
Lp: Bernard Bresslaw, Michael Medwin, Alfie Bass, Geoffrey Sumner, Charles Hawtrey.
Scrp: Sid Colin, Jack Davies. Prod: Anthony Hinds. Dir: Montgomery Tully.

IT'S A DOG'S LIFE
1949 36m cert U bw
The breeding and training of racing greyhounds.
Dir: Leslie Lawrence.

THE JACK OF DIAMONDS
1949 73m cert U bw
A couple agree to take an adventurer on their yacht to locate a treasure chest lost off the French coast. He tries to double-cross them.
Lp: Nigel Patrick, Cyril Raymond, Joan Carol.
Scrp: Nigel Patrick, Cyril Raymond. Prod: Vernon Sewell. Dir: Vernon Sewell.

JUST FOR YOU
1956 30m cert U colour/scope
Cyril Stapleton and his Show Band, with guests Joan Regan and Ronnie Harris.
Prod: Michael Carreras. Dir: Michael Carreras.

KEEP FIT WITH YOGA
1951 30m cert U bw
Featurette.

THE KISS OF THE VAMPIRE
(see pages 76-77)
Cast: Clifford Evans (Professor Zimmer), Noel Willman (Ravna), Edward de Souza (Gerald Harcourt), Jennifer

Daniel (Marianne), Barry Warren (Carl), Jacquie Wallis (Sabena), Isobel Black (Tania), Peter Madden (Bruno), Vera Cook (Anna), Noel Howlett (Father Xavier), Brian Oulton (First Disciple), John Harvey (Police Sergeant), Stan Simmons (Servant), Olga Dickie (First Woman at Graveyard), Margaret Read (First Girl Disciple), Elizabeth Valentine (Second Girl Disciple).
Selected credits: M: James Bernard. M sup: John Hollingsworth. Dp: Alan Hume. Prod des: Bernard Robinson. Sup ed: James Needs. Art dir: Don Mingaye. Make-up: Roy Ashton. Spfx: Les Bowie. Scrp: John Elder. Prod: Anthony Hinds. Dir: Don Sharp.

THE LADY CRAVED EXCITEMENT
1950 69m cert A bw
Cabaret artistes Pat and Johnny anger an escaped lunatic at their club, then fall in with art smugglers.
Lp: Hy Hazell, Michael Medwin, Sidney James, Andrew Keir. Scrp: John Gilling, Edward J. Mason, Francis Searle. Prod: Anthony Hinds. Dir: Godfrey Grayson.

LADY IN THE FOG
1952 82m cert A bw
An American reporter investigates a murder in the London fog, eventually tracking the killers to an empty film studio.
Lp: Cesar Romero, Lois Maxwell, Bernadette O'Farrell, Geoffrey Keen.
Scrp: Orville H. Hampton. Prod: Anthony Hinds. Dir: Sam Newfield.

THE LADY VANISHES
1979 97m cert A colour/scope
On a train out of Nazi Germany, one of the passengers inexplicably disappears. But was she ever there?
Lp: Elliott Gould, Cybill Shepherd, Angela Lansbury, Herbert Lom.
Scrp: George Axelrod. Prod: Tom Sachs. Dir: Anthony Page.

LAND OF THE LEPRECHAUNS
1962 15m cert U colour
Featurette.

THE LAST PAGE
1952 84m cert A bw
In London, an American bookshop owner is blackmailed by his assistant and her boyfriend after becoming entangled in a homicide.
Lp: George Brent, Marguerite Chapman, Raymond Huntley. Scrp: Frederick Knott. Prod: Anthony Hinds. Dir: Terence Fisher.

THE LEGEND OF THE 7 GOLDEN VAMPIRES
(see pages 164–165)
Cast: Peter Cushing (Professor Van Helsing), David Chiang (Hsi Ching), Julie Ege (Vanessa Buren), Robin Stewart (Leyland Van Helsing), Shih Szu (Mai Kwei), John Forbes-Robertson (Dracula), Robert Hanna (British Consul), Chan Shen (Kah), James Ma (Hsi Ta), Liu Chia Yung (Hsi Kwei), Feng Ko An (Hsi Sung), Chen Tien Loong (Hsi San), Wong Han Chan (Leung Hon).
Selected credits: M: James Bernard. M sup: Philip Martell. Dp: John Wilcox BSC, Roy Ford. Art dir: Johnson Tsau. Ed: Chris Barnes. Make-up: Wiu Hsu Ching. Spfx: Les Bowie. Martial arts sequences staged by: Tang Chia, Liu Chia-Liang. Scrp: Don Houghton. Prod: Don Houghton, Vee King Shaw. Dir: Roy Ward Baker [and Chang Cheh, unaccredited].

LIFE WITH THE LYONS
(see pages 150–151)
1954 81m cert U bw
The hapless Lyon family fail to impress their new landlord, who refuses to sign their lease. They try to win back his favour.
Lp: Ben Lyon, Bebe Daniels, Barbara Lyon, Richard Lyon. Scrp: Val Guest. Prod: Michael Carreras. Dir: Val Guest.

THE LOST CONTINENT
(see pages 106–107)
1968 98m cert X colour
Crossing uncharted seas, the *SS Corta* is dragged to a long-forgotten island.
Lp: Eric Porter, Hildegard Knef, Suzanna Leigh, Tony

Beckley, Nigel Stock.
Scrp: Michael Nash. Prod: Michael Carreras. Dir: Michael Carreras.

LOVE THY NEIGHBOUR
(see pages 150–151)
1973 85m cert U colour
An Afro-Caribbean couple move next door to an Anglo-Saxon bigot.
Lp: Jack Smethurst, Rudolph Walker, Nina Baden-Semper, Kate Williams.
Scrp: Vince Powell, Harry Driver. Prod: Roy Skeggs. Dir: John Robins.

LUST FOR A VAMPIRE
(see page 142)
Cast: Barbara Jefford (Countess Herritzen), Ralph Bates (Giles Barton), Suzanna Leigh (Janet Playfair), Yutte Stensgaard (Mircalla), Michael Johnson (Richard Lestrange), Helen Christie (Miss Simpson), Mike Raven (Count Karnstein), Christopher Cunningham (Coachman), Harvey Hall (Inspector Heinrich), Michael Brennan (Landlord), Pippa Steel (Susan Pelley), Judy Matheson (Amanda), Caryl Little (Isabel), David Healy (Raymond Pelley), Jonathan Cecil (Biggs), Eric Chitty (Proffessor [sic] Herz), Jack Melford (Bishop), Christopher Neame (Hans), Kirsten Lindholm (Peasant Girl), Luan Peters (Trudi), Nick Brimble (First Villager), David Richardson (Second Villager), Vivienne Chandler, Erica Beale, Melinda Churcher, Melita Clarke, Jackie Leapman, Sue Longhurst, Patricia Warner (Schoolgirls) and Christine Smith (Schoolgirl).
Selected credits: M: Harry Robinson. M sup: Philip Martell. 'Strange Love' sung by: Tracy. Lyrics: Frank Godwin. Dp: David Muir. Art dir: Don Mingaye. Ed: Spencer Reeve. Make-up: George Blackler. Choreographer: Babbie McManus. Scrp: Tudor Gates. Prod: Harry Fine, Michael Style. Dir: Jimmy Sangster.

THE LYONS IN PARIS
(see pages 150–151)
1955 81m cert U bw
The Lyons celebrate their anniversary in Paris, but get involved with cabaret artiste Fifi Le Fleur and her jealous husband.
Lp: Ben Lyon, Bebe Daniels, Barbara Lyon, Richard Lyon, Horace Percival, Molly Weir.
Scrp: Val Guest. Prod: Robert Dunbar. Dir: Val Guest.

MAN ABOUT THE HOUSE
(see pages 150–151)
1974 90m cert A colour
A flatsharing trio attempt to avoid eviction.
Lp: Richard O'Sullivan, Paula Wilcox, Sally Thomsett, Brian Murphy, Yootha Joyce.
Scrp: Johnnie Mortimer, Brian Cooke. Prod: Roy Skeggs. Dir: John Robins.

MAN AT THE TOP
1973 87m cert X colour/scope
The ruthless Joe Lampton is appointed MD of a pharmaceutical company, and exploits the fact that his predecessor committed suicide.
Lp: Kenneth Haigh, Nanette Newman, Harry Andrews, John Quentin.
Scrp: Hugh Whitemore, John Junkin. Prod: Peter Charlesworth, Jock Jacobsen. Dir: Mike Vardy.

MANIAC
(see pages 62–65)
1963 87m cert X bw/scope
In France, an American becomes involved in a plot to free a

blowtorch-wielding killer from an asylum.
Lp: Kerwin Mathews, Nadia Gray, Donald Houston.
Scrp: Jimmy Sangster. Prod: Jimmy Sangster. Dir: Michael Carreras.

THE MAN IN BLACK

1950 75m cert A bw

The mysterious 'man in black' tells a tale of two murderesses.

Lp: Betty Ann Davies, Sheila Burrell, Sidney James, Anthony Forwood, Hazel Penwarden, Valentine Dyall.

Scrp: John Gilling. Prod: Anthony Hinds. Dir: Francis Searle.

A MAN ON THE BEACH

1956 29m cert U colour/scope

When a thief is wounded murdering his accomplice, he is given sanctuary by a benevolent stranger.

Lp: Donald Wolfit, Michael Medwin, Michael Ripper.

Scrp: Jimmy Sangster. Prod: Anthony Hinds. Dir: Joseph Losey.

MANTRAP

1953 79m cert A bw

A man found guilty of murder escapes an asylum; the private detective assigned to his wife discovers him to be innocent.

Lp: Paul Henreid, Lois Maxwell, Keiron Moore, Hugh Sinclair.

Scrp: Paul Tabori, Terence Fisher. Prod: Michael Carreras. Dir: Terence Fisher.

THE MAN WHO COULD CHEAT DEATH

(see pages 40-41)

Cast: Anton Diffring (Georges), Hazel Court (Janine), Christopher Lee (Pierre), Arnold Marle (Dr Ludwig Weiss), Delphi Lawrence (Margo), Francis De Wolff (Legris) and Marie Burke (Woman), John Harrison (Servant), Ian Hewitson (Roget), Gerda Larsen (Street girl), Charles Lloyd Pack (Man), Frederick Rawlings (Footman), Denis Shaw (Tavern customer), Middleton Woods (Little man), Lockwood West, Ronald Adam, Barry Shawzin (Doctors).

Selected credits: M: Richard Bennett. M sup: John

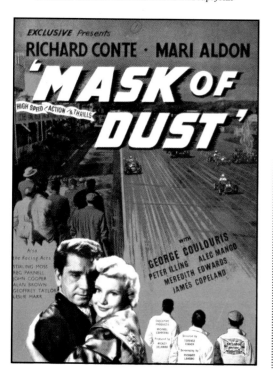

Hollingsworth. Dp: Jack Asher BSC. Prod des: Bernard Robinson. Sup ed: James Needs. Make-up: Roy Ashton. Scrp: Jimmy Sangster. Exec prod: Michael Carreras. Assoc prod: Anthony Nelson-Keys. Prod: Anthony Hinds. Dir: Terence Fisher.

MAN WITH A DOG

1957 20m cert U bw

An ailing war veteran relies on the kindness of others during his hour of need.

Lp: Maurice Denham, Sarah Lawson, Clifford Evans, John Van Eyssen.

Scrp: Jon Manchip White. Prod: Anthony Hinds. Dir: Leslie Arliss.

MASK OF DUST

1954 79m cert U bw

Against his wife's wishes, Pete Wells pursues his career as a racing driver through terrible circumstances.

Lp: Richard Conte, Mari Aldon, George Coulouris.

Scrp: Richard H. Landau. Prod: Mickey Delamar. Dir: Terence Fisher.

MEET SIMON CHERRY

1950 67m cert A bw

The Reverend Simon Cherry lodges at remote Harling Manor, where the owner's daughter is found dead.

Lp: Hugh Moxey, Jeanette Tregarthen, Anthony Forwood, Ernest Butcher, Zena Marshall.

Scrp: A.R. Rawlinson, Godfrey Grayson. Prod: Anthony Hinds. Dir: Godfrey Grayson.

MEN OF SHERWOOD FOREST

(see pages 78-79)

1954 77m cert U colour

The plans to free Richard the Lionheart from a German prison are stolen. Robin Hood and his men are entrusted to find them.

Lp: Don Taylor, Reginald Beckwith, Eileen Moore, David King Wood, Douglas Wilmer.

Scrp: Allan MacKinnon. Prod: Michael Carreras. Dir: Val Guest.

MODERN IRELAND

1953 15m cert U bw

Travelogue narrated by Robert Beatty.

Photography: Eric Lindeman. Dir: Eric Lindeman.

MONKEY MANNERS

1950 27m cert U bw

Behind the scenes at a monkey house in a zoo.

MOON ZERO TWO

(see pages 128-129)

Cast: James Olson (Kemp), Catherina Von Schell (Clem), Warren Mitchell (Hubbard), Adrienne Corri (Liz), Ori Levy (Karminski), Dudley Forster (Whitsun), Bernard Bresslaw (Harry), Neil McCallum (Space Captain), Joby Blanshard (Smith), Michael Ripper (1st Card Player), Robert Tayman (2nd Card Player), Sam Kydd (Barman), Keith Bonnard (Junior Customs Officer), Leo Britt (Senior Customs Officer), Carol Cleveland (Hostess), Roy Evans (Workman), Tom Kempinski (2nd Officer), Lew Luton (Immigrations Officer), Claire Shenstone (Female Hotel Clerk), Chrissie Shrimpton (Boutique Attendant), Amber Dean Smith, Simone Silvera (Hubbard's Girlfriends) with The GoJos [Michelle Barry, Sue Baumann, Jane Cunningham, Irene Gorst, Sally Graham, Brenda Krippen] (Hilton Bar Dancing Girls) and Athol Coats (Mercer), Tim Condron (Yellow Man), Freddie Earlle (Little Man), Martin Grace (Red Man), Robert Lee (Hotel Employee), Bill Weston (Green Man).

Above: The Phantom of the Opera.

Selected credits: M: Don Ellis. M sup: Philip Martell. Dp: Paul Beeson BSC. Art dir: Scott MacGregor. Ed: Spencer Reeve. Make-up: Ernest Taylor. Spfx: Les Bowie. Special effects photography: Kit West, Nick Allder. Titles: Stokes Cartoons Ltd. Choreographer: Jo Cook. Scrp: Michael Carreras, from an original story by Gavin Lyall, Frank Hardman and Martin Davison. Prod: Michael Carreras. Dir: Roy Ward Baker.

THE MUMMY

(see pages 42-43)

Cast: Peter Cushing (John Banning), Christopher Lee (The Mummy/Kharis), Yvonne Furneaux (Isobel/Ananka), Eddie Byrne (Inspector Mulrooney), Felix Aylmer (Stephen Banning), Raymond Huntley (Joseph Whemple), George Pastell (Mehemet Bey), Michael Ripper (Poacher), George Woodbridge (Police Constable), Harold Goodwin (Pat), Denis Shaw (Mike), Gerald Lawson (Irish Customer), Willoughby Gray (Dr Reilly), John Stuart (Coroner), David Browning (Police Sergeant), Frank Sieman (Bill), Stanley Meadows (Attendant), Frank Singuineau (Head Porter).

Selected credits: M: Franz Reizenstein. M sup: John Hollingsworth. Dp: Jack Asher BSC. Prod des: Bernard Robinson. Sup ed: James Needs. Ed: Alfred Cox. Make-up: Roy Ashton. Spfx: Bill Warrington. Technical advisor: Andrew Low. Scrp: Jimmy Sangster. Assoc prod: Anthony Nelson-Keys. Prod: Michael Carreras. Dir: Terence Fisher.

THE MUMMY'S SHROUD

(see pages 114-115)

Cast: André Morell (Sir Basil Walden), John Phillips (Stanley Preston), David Buck (Paul Preston), Elizabeth Sellars (Barbara Preston), Maggie Kimberley (Claire), Michael Ripper (Longbarrow), Tim Barrett (Harry), Richard Warner (Inspector Barrani), Roger Delgado (Hasmid), Catherine Lacey (Haiti), Dickie Owen (Prem), Bruno Barnabe (Pharaoh), Toni Gilpin (Pharaoh's Wife), Toolsie Persaud (Kah-to-Bey), Eddie Powell (The Mummy), Andreas Malandrinos (The Curator) and John Garrie (Arab Cleaner), Darroll Richards (Sage), George Zenios (Arab Reporter), Michael Rothwell, Terence Sewards, Roy Stephens (Reporters).

Selected credits: M: Don Banks. M sup: Philip Martell. Dp: Arthur Grant BSC. Art dir: Don Mingaye. Sup ed: James

Needs. Ed: Chris Barnes. Make-up: George Partleton. Spfx: Bowie Films Ltd. Story: John Elder. Scrp: John Gilling. Prod: Anthony Nelson Keys. Dir: John Gilling.

MURDER BY PROXY

1955 87m cert A bw
A hard-up American is paid to marry an heiress, but gets caught up in the murder of a wealthy financier.
Lp: Dane Clark, Belinda Lee, Betty Ann Davies.
Scrp: Richard Landau. Prod: Michael Carreras. Dir: Terence Fisher.

MUTINY ON THE BUSES

(see pages 150-151)
1972 89m cert U colour
Bus driver Stan blackmails his way into a cushy new route — through Windsor Safari Park.
Lp: Reg Varney, Doris Hare, Anna Karen, Michael Robbins, Bob Grant, Stephen Lewis.
Scrp/prod: Ronald Wolfe, Ronald Chesney. Dir: Harry Booth.

THE MYSTERY OF THE MARY CELESTE

1936 80m cert A bw
A ship is found floating in the Atlantic with its sails aloft, but no crew on board.
Lp: Bela Lugosi, Shirley Grey, Arthur Margaretson, Edmund Willard, George Mozart.
Scrp: Charles Larkworthy, Denison Clift. Prod: Henry Fraser Passmore. Dir: Denison Clift.

THE NANNY

(see pages 92-93)
Cast: Bette Davis (Nanny), Wendy Craig (Virgie Fane), Jill Bennett (Penelope), James Villiers (Bill Fane), William Dix (Joey), Pamela Franklin (Bobby), Jack Watling (Dr Medman), Maurice Denham (Dr Beamaster), Alfred Burke (Dr Wills), Harry Fowler (Milkman), Angharad Aubrey (Susy), Nora Gordon (Mrs Griggs), Sandra Power (Sarah).
Selected credits: M: Richard Rodney Bennett. M sup: Philip Martell. Dp: Harry Waxman BSC. Prod des: Edward Carrick. Sup ed: James Needs. Ed: Tom Simpson. Make-up: Tom Smith. Scrp: Jimmy Sangster. Prod: Jimmy Sangster. Dir: Seth Holt.

NATIONAL SPORTING CLUB

1961 14m colour
Featurette.

NEAREST AND DEAREST

(see pages 150-151)
1973 86m cert A colour
Sibling rivalry at a northern pickle-bottlers.
Lp: Hylda Baker, Jimmy Jewel, Eddie Malin, Madge Hindle.
Scrp: Tom Brennard, Roy Bottomley. Prod: Michael Carreras. Dir: John Robins.

NEVER LOOK BACK

1952 73m cert A bw
A barrister's reputation is jeopardised when she is implicated in a murder case.
Lp: Rosamund John, Hugh Sinclair, Guy Middleton.
Scrp: John Hunter, Guy Morgan, Francis Searle. Prod: Michael Carreras. Dir: Francis Searle.

NEVER TAKE SWEETS FROM A STRANGER

(see pages 68-69)
1960 81m cert X bw/scope
Tragic consequences result when Canadian courts fail two sexually abused children.
Lp: Gwen Watford, Patrick Allen, Felix Aylmer.
Scrp: John Hunter. Prod: Anthony Hinds. Dir: Cyril Frankel.

NIGHTMARE

(see pages 62-65)
1964 82m cert X bw/scope
A young woman, haunted by her mother's insanity, is manipulated to a malign end.
Lp: David Knight, Moira Redmond, Brenda Bruce, Jennie Linden, George A. Cooper.
Scrp: Jimmy Sangster. Prod: Jimmy Sangster. Dir: Freddie Francis.

O'HARA'S HOLIDAY

1960 21m colour
Featurette.
Prod: Peter Bryan. Dir: Peter Bryan.

THE OLD DARK HOUSE

(see pages 74-75)
Cast: Tom Poston (Tom Penderel), Robert Morley (Roderick Femm), Janette Scott (Cecily Femm), Joyce Grenfell (Agatha Femm), Mervyn Johns (Potiphar Femm), Fenella Fielding (Morgana Femm), Peter Bull (Casper & Jasper Femm), Danny Green (Morgan Femm), John Harvey (Club receptionist) and Amy Dalby (Woman Gambler).
Selected credits: M/m sup: Benjamin Frankel. Dp: Arthur Grant BSC. Prod des: Bernard Robinson. Sup ed: James Needs. Make-up: Roy Ashton. Spfx: Les Bowie. Titles: Chas Addams. Scrp: Robert Dillon. Assoc prods: Basil Keys, Donna Holloway. Prods: William Castle, Anthony Hinds. Dir: William Castle.

OLD FATHER THAMES

1946 cert U bw
The Thames passes through quaint villages, historic towns and the docklands of London, before flowing into the sea.
Dir: Hal Wilson, Ben R. Hart.

ONE MILLION YEARS B.C.

(see pages 104-105)
Cast: Raquel Welch (Loana), John Richardson (Tumak), Percy Herbert (Sakana), Robert Brown (Akhoba), Martine Beswick (Nupondi), Jean Wladon (Ahot), Lisa Thomas (Sura), Malva Nappi (Tohana), Richard James (Young Rock Man), William Lyon Brown (Payto), Frank Hayden (1st Rock Man), Terence Maidment (1st Shell Man), Micky De Rauch (1st Shell Girl), Yvonne Horner (Ullah).
Selected credits: M/special musical effects: Mario Nascimbene. M sup: Philip Martell. Dp: Wilkie Cooper. Art

dir: Robert Jones. Sup ed: James Needs. Ed: Tom Simpson. Make-up: Wally Schneiderman. Spfx: George Blackwell. Special visual effects created by: Ray Harryhausen. Prologue designed by: Les Bowie. Scrp: Michael Carreras, adapted from an original screenplay by Michell Novak, George Baker, Joseph Frickert. Assoc prod: Aida Young. Prod: Michael Carreras. Dir: Don Chaffey.

ON THE BUSES

(see pages 150-151)
1971 88m cert A colour
Two laddish bus company employees resist the introduction of female conductors.
Lp: Reg Varney, Doris Hare, Michael Robbins, Anna Karen, Stephen Lewis, Bob Grant.
Scrp/prod: Ronald Wolfe, Ronald Chesney. Dir: Harry Booth.

OPERATION UNIVERSE

1959 28m cert U colour/scope
British scientists lead the way, using the methods and equipment of the 'atomic age'. Narrated by Robert Beatty.
Scrp: Peter Bryan. Prod: Peter Bryan. Dir: Peter Bryan.

PARADE OF THE BANDS

1956 30m cert U colour/scope
Toe-tapping variety show including turns from Johnny Dankworth, Cleo Laine and others.
Prod: Michael Carreras. Dir: Michael Carreras.

PARANOIAC

(see pages 62-65)
1964 80m cert X bw
A prodigal son returns home to a privileged family who have long thought him dead — or does he?
Lp: Janette Scott, Oliver Reed, Liliane Brousse, Alexander Davion.
Scrp: Jimmy Sangster. Prod: Anthony Hinds. Dir: Freddie Francis.

THE PHANTOM OF THE OPERA

(see pages 72-73)
Cast: Herbert Lom (The Phantom/Professor Petrie), Heather Sears (Christine), Edward de Souza (Harry), Thorley Walters (Lattimer), Michael Gough (Ambrose), Harold Goodwin (Bill), Martin Miller (Rossi), Liane Aukin (Maria), Sonya Cordeau (Yvonne), Marne Maitland (Xavier), Miriam Karlin (Charwoman), Patrick Troughton (Ratcatcher), Renee Houston (Mrs Tucker), Keith Pyott (Tucker), John Harvey (Sergeant Vickers), Michael Ripper (1st Cabby), Miles Malleson (2nd Cabby), Ian Wilson (The Dwarf) and Leila Forde (Teresa), Geoff L'Cise (Frenchman in Tavern).
Selected credits: M: Edwin Astley. Dp: Arthur Grant. Prod des: Bernard Robinson. Art dir: Don Mingaye. Sup ed: James Needs. Ed: Alfred Cox. Make-up: Roy Ashton. Opera scenes staged by Dennis Maunder. Scrp: John Elder. Assoc prod: Basil Keys. Prod: Anthony Hinds. Dir: Terence Fisher.

THE PIRATES OF BLOOD RIVER

(see pages 78-79)
1962 84m cert U colour
A disestablished Huguenot heir takes up with a band of pirates.
Lp: Kerwin Mathews, Glenn Corbett, Christopher Lee, Marla Landi, Oliver Reed, Andrew Keir.
Scrp: John Hunter, John Gilling. Prod: Anthony Nelson Keys. Dir: John Gilling.

THE PLAGUE OF THE ZOMBIES

(see pages 100-101)
Cast: André Morell (Sir James Forbes), Diane Clare

(Sylvia), Brook Williams (Dr Peter Tompson), Jacqueline Pearce (Alice), John Carson (Clive Hamilton), Alex Davion (Denver), Michael Ripper (Sergeant Swift), Marcus Hammond (Martinus), Dennis Chinnery (Constable Christian), Louis Mahoney (Coloured Servant), Roy Royston (Vicar), Ben Aris (John Martinus), Tim Condron, Bernard Egan, Norman Mann, Francis Willey (The Young Bloods) and Jolyon Booth (Coachman), Jerry Verno (Landlord).
Selected credits: M: James Bernard. M sup: Philip Martell. Dp: Arthur Grant BSC. Prod des: Bernard Robinson. Art dir: Don Mingaye. Sup ed: James Needs. Ed: Chris Barnes. Make-up: Roy Ashton. Spfx: Bowie Films Ltd. Scrp: Peter Bryan. Prod: Anthony Nelson Keys. Dir: John Gilling.

THE PUBLIC LIFE OF HENRY THE NINTH
1935 60m cert U bw
A man aims to introduce a breezy 'new spirit' into Londoners' lives.
Lp: Leonard Henry, Betty Frankiss, George Mozart, Wally Patch.
Dir: Bernard Mainwaring.

QUATERMASS AND THE PIT
(see pages 116–117)
Cast: James Donald (Doctor Roney), Andrew Keir (Quatermass), Barbara Shelley (Barbara Judd), Julian Glover (Colonel Breen), Duncan Lamont (Sladden), Bryan Marshall (Captain Kotter), Peter Copley (Howell), Edwin Richfield (Minister), Grant Taylor (Police Sergeant Ellis), Maurice Good (Sergeant Cleghorn), Robert Morris (Watson), Sheila Steafel (Journalist), Hugh Futcher (Sapper West), Hugh Morton (Elderly Journalist), Thomas Heathcote (Vicar), Noel Howlett (Abbey Librarian), Hugh Manning (Pub Customer), June Ellis (Blonde), Keith Marsh (Johnson), James Culliford (Corporal Gibson), Bee Duffell (Miss Dobson), Roger Avon (Electrician), Brian Peck (Technical Officer), John Graham (Inspector), Charles Lamb (Newsvendor) and Peter Bennett (LT Official), Peter Bourne (2nd Electrician), John Bown (TV Interviewer), Simon Brent (Orderly Officer), David Crane (Attendant), Mark Elwes (2nd Technician), Joseph Greig (Pub Customer), Walter Horsbrugh (Messenger), Alastair Hunter (Doorkeeper), Elroy Josephs (Coloured Workman), Michael Poole (Older Workman), John Rutland (2nd LT Official), Albert Shepherd (Loader), Gareth Thomas (Workman), Ian White (TV Announcer), William Ellis, Leslie Southwick, Brian Walton (Journalists).
Selected credits: M: Tristram Cary. M sup: Philip Martell. Dp: Arthur Grant BSC. Supervising art director: Bernard Robinson. Art dir: Ken Ryan. Ed: Spencer Reeve. Make-up: Michael Morris. Spfx: Bowie Films Ltd. Scrp: Nigel Kneale. Prod: Anthony Nelson Keys. Dir: Roy Ward Baker.

QUATERMASS 2
(see pages 20–21)
Cast: Brian Donlevy (Quatermass), John Longdon [sic] (Lomax), Sydney James (Jimmy Hall), Bryan Forbes (Marsh), William Franklyn (Brand), Vera Day (Sheila), Charles Lloyd Pack (Dawson), Tom Chatto (Broadhead), John Van Eyssen (The PRO), Percy Herbert (Gorman), Michael Ripper (Ernie), John Rae (McLeod), Marianne Stone (Secretary), Ronald Wilson (Young Man), Jane Aird (Miss McLeod), Betty Impey (Kelly), Lloyd Lamble (Inspector), John Stuart (Commissioner), Gilbert Davis (Banker), Joyce Adams (Woman MP), Edwin Richfield (Peterson), Howard Williams (Michaels), Philip Baird, Robert Raikes (Lab Assistants), John Fabian (Intern), George Merritt (Super), Arthur Blake (Constable), Michael Balfour (Harry) and Alastair Hunter (Labour MP), Barry Lowe (Chris), Henry Raynor (Drunk), Joan Schofield (Woman shopper), Vernon Greeves, Ronald Wilson (1st

and 2nd men).
Selected credits: M: James Bernard. M sup: John Hollingsworth. Dp: Gerald Gibbs. Ed: James Needs. Art dir: Bernard Robinson. Make-up: Phil Leakey. Spfx: Bill Warrington, Henry Harris, Frank George. Story: Nigel Kneale. Scrp: Nigel Kneale, Val Guest. Production supervisor: Anthony Nelson Keys. Exec prod: Michael Carreras. Prod: Anthony Hinds. Dir: Val Guest.

THE QUATERMASS XPERIMENT
(see pages 16–17)
Cast: Brian Donlevy (Quatermass), Jack Warner (Lomax), Margia Dean (Judith Carroon), Richard Wordsworth (Victor Carroon), Thora Hird (Rosie), Gordon Jackson (TV Producer), David King-Wood (Briscoe), Harold Lang (Christie), Lionel Jeffries (Blake), Sam Kydd (Station Sergeant) and Jane Aird (Mrs Lomax), Margaret Anderson (Maggie), Jane Asher (Girl), Harry Brunsing (Night Porter), Eric Corrie (Young Man), Edward Dane (Station Policeman), Gron Davies (Green), Basil Dignam (Sir Lionel Dean), James Drake (Sound Engineer), Molly Glessing (Mother at zoo), Michael Godfrey (Fireman), Arthur Gross (Floor Boy), Ernest Hare (Fire Chief), Betty Impey (First Nurse), Fred Johnson (Inspector), Maurice Kauffman (Marsh), John Kerr (Laboratory Assistant), Henry Longhurst (Maggie's Father), Arthur Lovegrove (Sergeant Bromley), Barry Lowe (Tucker), Mayne Lynton (Zoo Official), Bartlett Mullins (Zoo Keeper), Frank Phillips (BBC Announcer), George Roderick (Local Policeman), John Stirling (Major), Marianne Stone (Second Nurse), Toke Townley (Chemist), Stanley Van Beers (Reichenheim), John Wynn (Best).
Selected credits: M: James Bernard. M sup: John Hollingsworth. Dp: Walter Harvey BSC. Ed: James Needs. Art dir: J. Elder Wills. Make-up: Phil Leakey. Spfx: Les Bowie. Story: Nigel Kneale. Scrp: Richard Landau, Val Guest. Prod: Anthony Hinds. Dir: Val Guest.

QUEER FISH
1952 28m cert U bw
The exotic highlights of the Regent's Park Zoo aquarium.
Narrated by Ratcliffe-Holmes.
Photography: Robin Still.

RASPUTIN THE MAD MONK
(see pages 98–99)
Cast: Christopher Lee (Rasputin), Barbara Shelley (Sonia), Richard Pasco (Dr Zargo), Francis Matthews (Ivan), Suzan Farmer (Vanessa), Dinsdale Landen (Peter), Renée Asherson (Tsarina), Derek Francis (Innkeeper), Joss Ackland (The Bishop), Robert Duncan (Tsarevitch), Alan Tilvern (Patron), John Welsh (The Abbot), John Bailey (Court Physician) and Mary Barclay (Superior Lady), Michael Cadman (Son), Lucy Fleming (Wide Eyes), Michael Godfrey (Doctor), Fiona Hartford (Daughter), Prudence Hyman (Chatty Woman), Bryan Marshall (Young Tough), Bridget McConnel (Gossip), Bartlett Mullins (Waggoner), Veronica Nicholson (Young Girl), Mary Quinn (Innkeeper's Wife), Celia Ryder (Fat Lady), Cyril Shaps (Foxy Face), Leslie White (Cheeky Man), Brian Wilde (Burly Brute), Jeremy Young (Court Messenger), Helen Christie, Maggie Wright (Tarts), Jay McGrath, Robert McLennan (Dancers).
Selected credits: M: Don Banks. M sup: Philip Martell. Dp: Michael Reed. Prod des: Bernard Robinson. Art dir: Don Mingaye. Sup ed: James Needs. Ed: Roy Hyde. Make-up: Roy Ashton. Scrp: John Elder. Prod: Anthony Nelson Keys. Dir: Don Sharp.

THE REPTILE
(see pages 102–103)
Cast: Noel Willman (Dr Franklyn), Jennifer Daniel

Above: The Revenge of Frankenstein.

(Valerie), Ray Barrett (Harry), Jacqueline Pearce (Anna), Michael Ripper (Tom Bailey), John Laurie (Mad Peter), Marne Maitland (Malay), David Baron (Charles Spalding), Charles Lloyd Pack (Vicar), Harold Goldblatt (Solicitor), George Woodbridge (Old Garnsey).
Selected credits: M: Don Banks. M sup: Philip Martell. Dp: Arthur Grant BSC. Prod des: Bernard Robinson. Art dir: Don Mingaye. Sup ed: James Needs. Ed: Roy Hyde. Make-up: Roy Ashton. Spfx: Bowie Films Ltd. Scrp: John Elder. Prod: Anthony Nelson Keys. Dir: John Gilling.

THE REVENGE OF FRANKENSTEIN
(see pages 34–35)
Cast: Peter Cushing (Doctor Victor Stein), Francis Matthews (Doctor Hans Kleve), Eunice Gayson (Margaret), Michael Gwynn (Karl), John Welsh (Bergman), Lionel Jeffries (Fritz), Oscar Quitak (Dwarf), Richard Wordsworth (Up Patient), Charles Lloyd Pack (President), John Stuart (Inspector), Arnold Diamond (Molke), Margery Gresley (Countess Barscynska), Anna Walmsley (Vera Barscynska), George Woodbridge (Janitor), Michael Ripper (Kurt), Ian Whittaker (Boy), Avril Leslie (Girl) and John Gayford (Footman), George Hirste (Dirty Old Patient), Raymond Hodge (Official), Eugene Leahy (Klein), Michael Mulcaster (Tattooed Man), Gordon Needham (Male Nurse), Julia Nelson (Inga), Robert Brooks Turner (Groom), Gerald Lawson, Freddy Watts, Middleton Woods (Patients).
Selected credits: M: Leonard Salzedo. Dp: Jack Asher BSC. Prod des: Bernard Robinson. Sup ed: James Needs. Ed: Alfred Cox. Make-up: Phil Leakey. Scrp: Jimmy Sangster. Additional dialogue: Hurford Janes. Exec prod: Michael Carreras. Assoc prod: Anthony Nelson Keys. Prod: Anthony Hinds. Dir: Terence Fisher.

THE RIGHT PERSON
1955 30m cert U colour/scope
In Copenhagen, a former resistance fighter seeks the traitor responsible for betraying his colleagues during the war.
Lp: Margo Lorenz, Douglas Wilmer, David Markham.
Scrp: Philip Mackie. Prod: Michael Carreras. Dir: Peter Cotes.

RIVER PATROL

1948 46m cert A bw
A Customs secret agent tracks down a gang of nylon smugglers from the Continent.
Lp: John Blythe, Wally Patch, Stan Paskin, Lorna Dean.
Scrp: Jimmy Corbett. Prod: Hal Wilson. Dir: Ben R. Hart.

RIVER SHIPS

1953 24m cert U bw
The ships, boats and small craft that give the pulse of life to the Thames. Narrated by Bernard Miles.
Prod: Peter Bryan. Dir: Peter Bryan.

ROOM TO LET

1950 68m cert A bw
In Victorian London, an escaped lunatic lodges with a family — who have cause to suspect he may be 'Jack the Ripper'.
Lp: Jimmy Hanley, Valentine Dyall, Christine Silver, Merle Tottenham, Constance Smith, Charles Hawtrey.
Scrp: John Gilling, Godfrey Grayson. Prod: Anthony Hinds. Dir: Godfrey Grayson.

THE ROSSITER CASE

1951 75m cert A bw
Liz Rossiter, paralysed in a car accident, discovers her husband to be in love with her sister Honor.
Lp: Helen Shingler, Clement McCallin, Sheila Burrell, Frederick Leicester.
Scrp: John Hunter, Francis Searle. Prod: Anthony Hinds. Dir: Francis Searle.

THE RUNAWAY

1964 62m bw
A Polish industrial chemist becomes embroiled in spy intrigue.
Lp: Greta Gynt, Alex Gallier, Paul Williamson.
Scrp: John Perceval, John Gerrarde Sharp. Prod: Bill Luckwell. Dir: Tony Young.

THE SAINT'S RETURN

1953 73m cert U bw

Simon Templar helps a friend who is the victim of a car accident, but discovers him to be involved with racketeers.
Lp: Louis Hayward, Sydney Tafler, Naomi Chance, Charles Victor, Diana Dors.
Scrp: Allan MacKinnon. Prod: Anthony Hinds. Dir: Seymour Friedman.

SANDS OF THE DESERT

(see pages 150-151)
1960 92m cert U colour
Travel agent Charlie Sands is sent to the desert to oversee the construction of a sabotaged holiday camp.
Lp: Charlie Drake, Peter Arne, Sarah Branch, Raymond Huntley.
Scrp: John Paddy Carstairs, Charlie Drake. Prod: Gordon L.T. Scott. Dir: John Paddy Carstairs.

THE SATANIC RITES OF DRACULA

(see pages 162-163)
Cast: Christopher Lee (Count Dracula), Peter Cushing (Van Helsing), Michael Coles (Murray), William Franklyn (Torrence), Freddie Jones (Professor Keeley), Joanna Lumley (Jessica), Richard Vernon (Mathews), Barbara Yu Ling (Chin Yang), Patrick Barr (Lord Carradine), Richard Mathews (Porter), Lockwood West (Freeborne), Valerie Van Ost (Jane), Maurice O'Connell (Hanson), Peter Adair (Doctor), Maggie Fitzgerald, Pauline Peart, Finnuala O'Shannon, Mia Martin (Vampire Girls), Marc Zuber, Paul Weston, Ian Dewar, Graham Rees (Guards) and John Harvey (Commisionaire).
Selected credits: M: John Cacavas. M sup: Philip Martell. Dp: Brian Probyn BSC. Art dir: Lionel Couch. Ed: Chris Barnes. Make-up: George Blackler. Spfx: Les Bowie. Scrp: Don Houghton. Assoc prod: Don Houghton. Prod: Roy Skeggs. Dir: Alan Gibson.

THE SCARLET BLADE

(see pages 78-79)
1963 82m cert U colour/scope
During the English Civil War, the son of a Royalist aide executed by the Roundheads takes up arms against Cromwell's forces.
Lp: Lionel Jeffries, Oliver Reed, Jack Hedley.
Scrp: John Gilling. Prod: Anthony Nelson Keys. Dir: John Gilling.

SCARS OF DRACULA

(see page 139)
Cast: Christopher Lee (Dracula), Dennis Waterman (Simon), Jenny Hanley (Sarah), Christopher Matthews (Paul), Patrick Troughton (Klove), Michael Gwynn (Priest), Michael Ripper (Landlord), Wendy Hamilton (Julie), Anouska Hempel (Tania), Delia Lindsay (Alice), Bob Todd (Burgomaster), Toke Townley (Elderly Wagonner), David Leland (First Officer), Richard Durden (Second Officer), Morris Bush (Farmer), Margo Boht (Landlord's Wife), Clive Barrie (Fat Young Man) and Olga Anthony (Young Girl at party), Eddie Powell (Stunt Double).
Selected credits: M: James Bernard. M sup: Philip Martell. Dp: Moray Grant. Art dir: Scott MacGregor. Ed: James Needs. Make-up: Wally Schneiderman. Spfx: Roger Dicken. Scrp: John Elder. Prod: Aida Young. Dir: Roy Ward Baker.

THE SECRET OF BLOOD ISLAND

(see pages 28-29)
1965 84m cert X colour
When a female secret agent parachutes into occupied Malaya, British POWs hide her from their brutal Japanese captors.
Lp: Jack Hedley, Barbara Shelley, Patrick Wymark, Charles

Tingwell.
Scrp: John Gilling. Prod: Anthony Nelson Keys. Dir: Quentin Lawrence.

SEVEN WONDERS OF IRELAND

1958 23m cert U bw
Travelogue.
Prod: Peter Bryan. Dir: Peter Bryan.

THE SHADOW OF THE CAT

(see pages 58-59)
Cast: André Morell (Walter Venable), Barbara Shelley (Beth Venable), William Lucas (Jacob), Freda Jackson (Clara), Conrad Phillips (Michael Latimer), Richard Warner (Edgar), Vanda Godsell (Louise), Alan Wheatley (Inspector Rowles), Andrew Crawford (Andrew), Kynaston Reeves (Grandfather), Catherine Lacey (Ella) and Rodney Burke (Workman), Vera Cook (Mother), Angela Crow (Daughter), John Dearth (Constable Hamer), George Doonan (2nd Ambulance Man), Howard Knight (Boy), Charles Stanley (Dobbins), Fred Stone (1st Ambulance Man), Kevin Stoney (Father).
Selected credits: Cat trainer: John Holmes. M/m sup: Mikos Theodorakis. Dp: Arthur Grant BSC. Prod des: Bernard Robinson. Art dir: Don Mingaye. Sup ed: James Needs. Ed: John Pomeroy. Make-up: Roy Ashton. Spfx: Les Bowie. Scrp: George Baxt. Prod: Jon Penington. Dir: John Gilling.

SHATTER

1974 90m cert A colour
In Hong Kong, an assassin is manipulated by vicious members of a drug syndicate.
Lp: Stuart Whitman, Ti Lung, Lily Li, Peter Cushing, Anton Diffring.
Scrp: Don Houghton. Prod: Michael Carreras, Vee King Shaw. Dir: Michael Carreras [and Monty Hellman, unaccredited].

SHE

(see pages 90-91)
Cast: Ursula Andress (Ayesha), Peter Cushing (Holly),

Bernard Cribbins (Job), John Richardson (Leo), Rosenda Monteros (Ustane), Christopher Lee (Billali), André Morell (Haumeid), Soraya, Julie Mendez, Lisa Peake (Night Club Dancers), John Maxim (Guard Captain), Cherry Larman, Bula Coleman (Handmaidens), Oo-Bla-Da Dancers (Native Dancers).
Selected credits: M: James Bernard. M sup: Philip Martell. Dp: Harry Waxman BSC. Art dir: Robert Jones. Sup ed: James Needs. Ed: Eric Boyd-Perkins. Make-up: John O'Gorman. Spfx: George Blackwell. Special processes: Bowie Films Ltd. Special effects make-up: Roy Ashton. Choreographer: Christyne Lawson. Scrp: David T. Chantler. Assoc prod: Aida Young. Prod: Michael Carreras. Dir: Robert Day.

SKIFFY GOES TO SEA
1947 34m cert U bw
A Thames ferryman yearns to go to sea — but finds life on board ship tougher than he expects.
Scrp: Bill Currie. Dir: Harry May.

SKY TRADERS
1953 21m cert U bw
Britain's freight planes are 'tramps of the international skies'. Narrated by Robert Beatty.
Prod: Peter Bryan. Dir: Peter Bryan.

SLAVE GIRLS
(see pages 106-107)
1968 95m cert X colour/scope
A big game hunter is transported back to an age where a savage queen rules over a forgotten region of Africa.
Lp: Martine Beswick, Edina Ronay, Michael Latimer, Stephanie Randall, Carol White.
Scrp: Henry Younger. Prod: Michael Carreras. Dir: Michael Carreras.

THE SNORKEL
1958 90m cert A bw
On the Italian Riviera, a man devises a cunning plan to kill his wife.
Lp: Peter Van Eyck, Betta St John, Mandy Miller.
Scrp: Peter Myers, Jimmy Sangster. Prod: Michael Carreras. Dir: Guy Green.

SOMEONE AT THE DOOR
1950 65m cert U bw
A young reporter inherits a mansion, where he fakes his own sister's death for a news story — but encounters a real mystery.
Lp: Yvonne Owen, Michael Medwin, Hugh Latimer.
Scrp: A.R. Rawlinson. Prod: Anthony Hinds. Dir: Francis Searle.

THE SONG OF FREEDOM
1936 80m cert U bw
An African *émigré* becomes famous and convinces the people of his homeland that he is their true king.
Lp: Paul Robeson, Elisabeth Welch, Esme Percy, Robert Adams.
Scrp: Ingram D'Abbern, Fenn Sheri. Prod: Enrique Carreras, Will Hammer. Dir: J. Elder Wills.

SPACEWAYS
1953 76m cert U bw
A rocket fails to return to Earth; coincidentally, two scientists go missing. An investigator speculates that their bodies are on board.
Lp: Howard Duff, Eva Bartok, Andrew Osborn.
Scrp: Paul Tabori, Richard H. Landau. Prod: Michael Carreras. Dir: Terence Fisher.

SPORTING LOVE
1936 70m cert U bw
Two brothers plan to run a horse in the Derby and, with the winnings, recover their family fortune.
Lp: Stanley Lupino, Laddie Cliff, Henry Carlisle.
Scrp: Fenn Sherie, Ingram D'Abbern. Dir: J. Elder Wills.

SPORTSMAN'S PARADISE
1963 15m cert U colour
The attractions of Ireland for tourists and sportsmen — particularly anglers.
Prod: Peter Bryan. Dir: Peter Bryan.

THE STEEL BAYONET
(see pages 28-29)
1957 85m cert A bw/scope
Tunis, 1943: a beleaguered company of British troops attempt to keep at bay advancing German tanks.
Lp: Leo Genn, Keiron Moore, Michael Medwin, Robert Brown, Michael Ripper.
Scrp: Howard Clewes. Prod: Michael Carreras. Dir: Michael Carreras.

STOLEN FACE
1952 72m cert A bw
An obsessed plastic surgeon remodels the face of convict Lily to resemble that of another man's fiancée. He marries Lily, but her criminal tendencies resurface.
Lp: Paul Henreid, Lizabeth Scott, Mary Mackenzie, André Morell.
Scrp: Martin Berkeley, Richard H. Landau. Prod: Anthony Hinds. Dir: Terence Fisher.

STRAIGHT ON TILL MORNING
(see pages 62-65)
1972 96m cert X colour
In London's bedsitterland, a naïve young woman becomes involved with a childlike serial killer.
Lp: Rita Tushingham, Shane Briant, Tom Bell, Annie Ross, Katya Wyeth, James Bolam.
Scrp: Michael Peacock. Prod: Michael Carreras. Dir: Peter Collinson.

THE STRANGER CAME HOME
1954 80m cert A bw
A kidnapped financier develops amnesia. He returns home three years later, only to be suspected of murder.
Lp: William Sylvester, Paulette Goddard, Patrick Holt.
Scrp/prod: Michael Carreras. Dir: Terence Fisher.

THE STRANGLERS OF BOMBAY
(see page 47)
Cast: Guy Rolfe (Lewis), Allan Cuthbertson (Connaught-Smith), Andrew Cruickshank (Henderson), George Pastell (High Priest), Marne Maitland (Patel Shari), Jan Holden (Mary), Paul Stassino (Silver), Tutte Lemkow (Ram Das) and Roger Delgado (Bundar), Marie Devereux (Karim), Margaret Gordon (Mrs Flood), John Harvey (Burns), Jack MacNaughtan (Corporal Roberts), Michael Nightingale (Flood), Stephen Scott (Walters), Ewen Solon (Camel Vendor), David Spenser (Gopali).
Selected credits: M: James Bernard. M sup: John Hollingsworth. Dp: Arthur Grant BSC. Prod des: Bernard Robinson. Art dir: Don Mingaye. Sup ed: James Needs. Ed: Alfred Cox. Make-up: Roy Ashton. Scrp: David Z. Goodman. Exec prod: Michael Carreras. Assoc prod: Anthony Nelson-Keys. Prod: Anthony Hinds. Dir: Terence Fisher.

SUNSHINE HOLIDAY
1958 13m cert U colour
Travelogue.

Above: Straight On Till Morning.

SWORD OF SHERWOOD FOREST
(see pages 78-79)
1960 80m cert U colour/scope
Robin Hood pits his wits against the Earl of Newark, who plans to murder the Archbishop of Canterbury.
Lp: Richard Greene, Peter Cushing, Richard Pasco, Sarah Branch.
Scrp: Alan Hackney. Prod: Richard Greene. Dir: Terence Fisher.

TASTE OF FEAR
(see pages 60-61)
Cast: Susan Strasberg ('Penny Appleby'), Ronald Lewis (Bob), Ann Todd (Jane Appleby), Christopher Lee (Dr Gerrard), John Serret (Inspector Legrand), Leonard Sachs (Spratt), Anne Blake (Marie), Fred Johnson (Father) and Bernard Brown (Gendarme), Richard Klee (Plainclothes Sergeant), Mme Lobegue (Swissair Hostess), Fred Rawlings (Plainclothes Sergeant), Rodney Burke, Gordon Sterne (Uniformed men), Heinz Bernard, Brian Jackson, Frederick Schrecker (Plainclothes men).
Selected credits: M: Clifton Parker. M sup: John Hollingsworth. Dp: Douglas Slocombe. Prod des: Bernard Robinson. Sup ed: James Needs. Ed: Eric Boyd-Perkins. Make-up: Basil Newall. Scrp: Jimmy Sangster. Exec prod: Michael Carreras. Prod: Jimmy Sangster. Dir: Seth Holt.

TASTE THE BLOOD OF DRACULA
(see pages 130-131)
Cast: Christopher Lee (Dracula), Geoffrey Keen (William Hargood), Gwen Watford (Martha Hargood), Linda Hayden (Alice Hargood), Peter Sallis (Samuel Paxton), Anthony Corlan (Paul Paxton), Isla Blair (Lucy Paxton), John Carson (Jonathan Secker), Martin Jarvis (Jeremy Secker), Ralph Bates (Lord Courtley), Roy Kinnear (Weller), Michael Ripper (Cobb), Russell Hunter (Felix), Shirley Jaffe (Hargood's Maid), Keith Marsh (Father), Peter May (Son), Reginald Barratt (Vicar), Maddy Smith (Dolly), Lai Ling (Chinese Girl), Malaika Martin (Snake Girl) and Peter Brace (Stunt Double for Dracula), Lai Ling (Chinese Bordello Girl), June Palmer (Private Room Girl), Amber Blare, Vicky Gillespie (Bordello Girls).
Selected credits: M: James Bernard. M sup: Philip Martell. Dp: Arthur Grant BSC. Art dir: Scott MacGregor. Ed: Chris Barnes. Make-up: Gerry Fletcher. Spfx: Brian Johncock. Scrp: John Elder. Prod: Aida Young. Dir: Peter Sasdy.

TEN SECONDS TO HELL
(see pages 28-29)
1959 93m cert A bw
In the ruins of post-war Berlin, a bomb disposal team is

progressively decimated and two of the squad clash over a woman.
Lp: Jack Palance, Jeff Chandler, Martine Carol.
Scrp: Robert Aldrich, Teddi Sherman. Prod: Michael Carreras. Dir: Robert Aldrich.

THE TERROR OF THE TONGS
(see pages 54–55)
Cast: Christopher Lee (Chung King), Geoffrey Toone (Jackson), Yvonne Monlaur (Lee), Brian Worth (Harcourt), Richard Leech (Inspector Dean), Marne Maitland (Beggar), Tom Gill (Beamish), Barbara Brown (Helena), Marie Burke (Maya), Bandana Das Gupta (Anna), Burt Kwouk (Ming), Roger Delgado (Wang How), Milton Reed [sic] (Guardian), Charles Lloyd Pack (Doctor), Eric Young (Confucius), Michael Hawkins (Priest), Johnny Arlan (Executioner) and Andy Ho (Lee Chung), Arnold Lee (Spokesman), Ewen Solon (Tang How), Santos Wong (Sergeant), Julie Alexander, Harold Goodwin, Peter Gray, Ronald Ing, Jules Ki-Ki, Su Lin, Michael Peake, Walter Randall, Poing Ping Sam, Ann Scott, Steven Scott, Cyril Shaps, Vincent Wong (other roles), June Barry, Mary Rose Barry, Audrey Burton, Ruth Calvert, Marialla Capes, Katie Cashfield, Patty Dalton, Louise Dickson, Pauline Dukes, Hazel Gardner, Valerie Holman, Julie Shearing, Valerie Shevaloff, Barbara Smith (Tong Room Girls).
Selected credits: M: James Bernard. M sup: John Hollingsworth. Dp: Arthur Grant BSC. Prod des: Bernard Robinson. Art dir: Thomas Goswell. Sup ed: Jim Needs. Ed: Eric Boyd-Perkins. Make-up: Roy Ashton, Colin Garde. Scrp: Jimmy Sangster. Exec prod: Michael Carreras. Assoc prod: Anthony Nelson-Keys. Prod: Kenneth Hyman. Dir: Anthony Bushell.

THAT'S YOUR FUNERAL
(see pages 150–151)
1973 82m cert A colour
A firm of undertakers harbours a drug smuggling ring. Its rivals mount a counter-offensive.
Lp: Bill Fraser, Raymond Huntley, David Battley, John Ronane, Dennis Price.
Scrp: Peter Lewis. Prod: Michael Carreras. Dir: John Robins.

Below: Vampire Circus.

THIRD PARTY RISK
1955 70m cert A bw
In Spain, an American songwriter meets a wartime colleague who is involved with art thieves.
Lp: Lloyd Bridges, Finlay Currie, Maureen Swanson.
Scrp: Robert Dunbar, Daniel Birt. Prod: Robert Dunbar. Dir: Daniel Birt.

36 HOURS
1954 80m cert A bw
A USAF pilot has only thirty-six hours in England in which to solve the mystery of the disappearance of his wife.
Lp: Dan Duryea, Elsy Albiin, Ann Gudron, Eric Pohlmann.
Scrp: Steve Fisher. Prod: Anthony Hinds. Dir: Montgomery Tully.

TICKET TO HAPPINESS
1959 30m cert U
A rich industrialist is persuaded to help out a youth club to which he is at first opposed.
Prod: Peter Bryan. Dir: Peter Bryan.

TO HAVE AND TO HOLD
1951 63m cert A bw
Upon learning that he has only a short time to live, crippled Brian Harding gives up all he has for the sake of others' happiness.
Lp: Avis Scott, Patrick Barr, Robert Ayres, Harry Fine.
Scrp: Reginald Long. Prod: Anthony Hinds. Dir: Godfrey Grayson.

TO THE DEVIL A DAUGHTER
(see pages 166–167)
Cast: Richard Widmark (John Verney), Christopher Lee (Father Michael), Honor Blackman (Anna), Denholm Elliott (Henry Beddows), Michael Goodliffe (George de Grass), Nastassja Kinski (Catherine), Eva Maria Meineke (Eveline de Grass), Anthony Valentine (David), Derek Francis (Bishop), Isabella Telezynska (Margaret), Constantin De Goguel (Kollde), Anna Bentinck (Isabel), Irene Prador (German Matron), Brian Wilde (Black Room Attendant), Petra Peters (Sister Helle), William Ridoutt (Airport Porter), Howard Goorney (Critic), Frances De La Tour (Salvation Army Major), Zoe Hendry, Lindy Benson, Jo Peters, Bobby Sparrow (Girls) and Ed Devereaux (Reporter), Bill Horsley (Curator).
Selected credits: M: Paul Glass. M sup: Philip Martell. Dp: David Watkin. Designer: Don Picton. Ed: John Trumper. Make-up: Eric Allwright, George Blackler. Spfx: Les Bowie. Scrp: Chris Wicking. Adaptation by John Peacock. Prod: Roy Skeggs. Dir: Peter Sykes.

TWINS OF EVIL
(see pages 152–153)
Cast in order of appearance: Inigo Jackson (Woodman), Judy Matheson (Woodman's Daughter), Peter Cushing (Gustav Weil), Harvey Hall (Franz), Alex Scott (Hermann), Sheelah Wilcox (Lady in Coach), Madelaine Collinson (Frieda Gellhorn), Mary Collinson (Maria Gellhorn), Kathleen Byron (Katy Weil), Roy Stewart (Joachim), Luan Peters (Gerta), Damien Thomas (Count Karnstein), Dennis Price (Dietrich), Maggie Wright (Alexa), Katya Wyeth (Countess Mircalla), David Warbeck (Anton Hoffer), Isobel Black (Ingrid Hoffer), Kirsten Lindholm (Young Girl at Stake), Peter Thompson (Gaoler) and Roy Boyd (Man in Graveyard), George Claydon (The Midget), Cathy Howard (2nd Girl on Tomb), Garth Watkins (Chief Mock Priest), John Fahey, Kenneth Gilbert, Derek Glynne-Percy, Sebastian Graham-Jones, Jason James, Bill Sawyer (Puritans), Maxine Casson, Vivienne Chandler, Doreen Chanter, Irene Chanter, Jackie Leapman, Annette Roberts

(Schoolgirls).
Selected credits: M: Harry Robinson. M sup: Philip Martell. Dp: Dick Bush BSC. Art dir: Roy Stannard. Ed: Spencer Reeve. Make-up: George Blackler, John Webber. Spfx: Bert Luxford. Scrp: Tudor Gates. Prod: Harry Fine, Michael Style. Dir: John Hough.

THE TWO FACES OF DR JEKYLL
(see pages 48–49)
Cast: Paul Massie (Jekyll/Hyde), Dawn Addams (Kitty), Christopher Lee (Paul Allen), David Kossoff (Litauer), Norma Marla (Maria), Francis De Wolff (Inspector), Joy Webster (First Brass) and Maria Andippa (Gypsy Girl), Frank Atkinson (Groom), John Bonney (Renfrew), Percy Cartwright (Coroner), Dennis Cleary (Waiter), Janine Faye (Jane), Felix Felton (First Gambler), Helen Goss (Nannie), Walter Gotell (Second Gambler), Doreen Ismail (Second Sphinx Girl), Anthony Jacobs (Third Gambler), William Kendall (Clubman), Roberta Kirkwood (Second Brass), Arthur Lovegrove (Cabby), Magda Miller (Sphinx Girl), Oliver Reed (Tough), Douglas Robinson (Boxer), Joe Robinson (Corinthian), Denis Shaw (Tavern Customer), Pauline Shepherd (Tavern Girl), Donald Tandy (Plainclothes Man), Joan Tyrill (Major Domo), Joyce Wren (Nurse), Prudence Hyman, Lucy Griffiths (Tavern Women), Archie Baker, Ralph Broadbent, Alex Miller, Laurence Richardson (Singers), Anthony Pendrell, Fred Stone (Cabinet ministers [Sphinx Customers]), Glenn Beck, Alan Browning, Rodney Burke, Clifford Earl (Young bloods [Sphinx Customers]), Roy Denton, Kenneth Firth, George McGrath, Mackenzie Ward (Business men [Sphinx Customers]), John Moore, J. Trevor-Davis (Officers [Sphinx Customers]), Bandana Des Gupta, Pauline Dukes, Hazel Graeme, Carole Haynes, Josephine Jay, Jean Long, Marilyn Ridge, Gundel Sargent, Patricia Sayers, Shirli Scott-James, Moyna Sharwin (Sphinx Girls).
Selected credits: Music and songs: Monty Norman, David Heneker. M sup: John Hollingsworth. Dp: Jack Asher BSC. Sup ed: James Needs. Ed: Eric Boyd-Perkins. Prod des: Bernard Robinson. Art dir: Don Mingaye. Make-up: Roy Ashton. Scrp: Wolf Mankowitz. Assoc prod: Anthony Nelson Keys. Prod: Michael Carreras. Dir: Terence Fisher.

THE UGLY DUCKLING
(see page 46)
Cast: Bernard Bresslaw (Henry Jekyll/Teddy Hide), Reginald Beckwith (Reginald), Jon Pertwee (Victor Jekyll), Maudie Edwards (Henrietta Jekyll), Jean Muir (Snout), Richard Wattis (Barclay), David Lodge (Peewee), Elwyn Brook-Jones (Dandy), Michael Ripper (Fish), Harold Goodwin (Benny), Norma Marla (Angel), Keith Smith (Figures), Michael Ward (Pasco), John Harvey (Det Sgt Barnes), Jess Conrad (Bimbo), Mary Wilson (Lizzie), Geremy Phillips (Tiger), Vicky Marshall (Kitten), Alan Coleshill (Willie), Jill Carson (Yum Yum), Jean Driant (M. Blum), Nicholas Tanner (Commissionaire), Shelagh Dey (Miss Angers), Sheila Hammond (Receptionist), Verne Morgan (Barman), Ian Wilson (Small Man), Cyril Chamberlain (Police Sergeant), Ian Ainsley (Fraser), Reginald Marsh, Roger Avon, Richard Statman (Reporters), Robert Desmond (Dizzy), Alexander Dore (Chemist Shop Customer), Joe Loss and his Orchestra and Malka Alamont (Fifi), Heather Downham (Margo), Lucy Griffiths (Cellist), Aldine Harvey (Jane), Ann Mayhew (Lucienne), Jacqueline Perrin (Ursula), Helen Pohlman (Amanda), Helga Wahlrow (Rosemary), Jack Armstrong, Jamie Barnes, Richard Dake, Stella Kemball, Aileen Lewis, Peter Mander, Lola Morice, Alecia St Leger (Old-Time Dancers).
Selected credits: M: Douglas Gamley. Dp: Michael Reed. Art dir: Bernard Robinson. Sup ed: James Needs. Ed: John Dunsford. Make-up: Roy Ashton. Story: Sid Colin. Scrp: Sid

Colin, Jack Davies. Exec prod: Michael Carreras. Assoc prod: Tommy Lyndon-Haynes. Dir: Lance Comfort.

UP THE CREEK
(see pages 150-151)
1958 83m cert U bw/scope
The new captain of *HMS Berkeley* discovers that the bosun likes running things his own way.
Lp: David Tomlinson, Peter Sellers, Wilfrid Hyde White, Vera Day.
Scrp: Val Guest, John Warren, Len Heath. Prod: Henry Halsted. Dir: Val Guest.

VAMPIRE CIRCUS
(see page 154)
Cast: Adrienne Corri (Gypsy Woman), Thorley Walters (Burgermeister), Anthony Corlan (Emil), John Moulder-Brown (Anton), Laurence Payne (Mueller), Richard Owens (Dr Kersh), Lynne Frederick (Dora), Elizabeth Seal (Gerta Hauser), Robin Hunter (Hauser), Domini Blythe (Anna Mueller), Robert Tayman (Count Mitterhouse), John Bown (Schilt), Mary Wimbush (Elvira), Christina Paul (Rosa), Robin Sachs (Heinrich), Lalla Ward (Helga), Skip Martin (Michael), Dave Prowse (Strongman), Roderick Shaw (Jon), Barnaby Shaw (Gustav), Milovan and Serena (The Webers), Jane Darby (Jenny Schilt), Sibylla Kay (Mrs Schilt), Dorothy Frere (Grandma Schilt), Giles Phibbs (Sexton), Jason James (Foreman), Arnold Locke (Old villager) and Sean Hewitt (First soldier), Anna Bentinck, Nina Francis, Drina Pavlovic, Jenny Twigge (Schoolgirls).
Selected credits: M: David Whitaker. M sup: Philip Martell. Dp: Moray Grant BSC. Art dir: Scott MacGregor. Ed: Peter Musgrave. Make-up: Jill Carpenter. Spfx: Les Bowie. Animal adviser: Mary Chipperfield. Scrp: Judson Kinberg. Prod sup: Roy Skeggs. Prod: Wilbur Stark. Dir: Robert Young.

THE VAMPIRE LOVERS
(see pages 136-137)
Cast: Ingrid Pitt (Marcilla/Carmilla), Pippa Steele (Laura), Madeline Smith (Emma), Peter Cushing (The General), George Cole (Morton), Dawn Addams (Countess), Kate O'Mara (Governess), Douglas Wilmer (Baron Hartog), Jon Finch (Carl Ebhardt), Ferdy Mayne (Doctor), Kirsten Betts (First Vampire), John Forbes-Robertson (Man in Black), Shelagh Wilcocks (Housekeeper), Harvey Hall (Renton), Janet Key (Gretchin), Charles Farrell (Landlord), Graham James (First Young Man), Tom Browne (Second Young Man), Joanna Shelley (Woodman's Daughter), Olga James (Village Girl) and Jill Easter (Woodman's wife), Lindsay Kemp (Jester), Sion Probert (Young Man in Tavern), Vicki Woolf (Landlord's Daughter).
Selected credits: M: James Bernard. M sup: Philip Martell. Dp: Moray Grant. Ed: James Needs. Art dir: Scott MacGregor. Make-up: Tom Smith. Scrp: Tudor Gates. Prod: Harry Fine, Michael Style. Dir: Roy Ward Baker.

THE VENGEANCE OF SHE
(see pages 106-107)
1968 101m cert A colour
An amnesiac young woman, the reincarnation of the all-powerful Ayesha, is drawn towards a strange destiny.
Lp: John Richardson, Olinka Berova, Edward Judd, Colin Blakely.
Scrp: Peter O'Donnell. Prod: Aida Young. Dir: Cliff Owen.

THE VIKING QUEEN
(see pages 78-79)
1967 91m cert A colour
In Roman-occupied Britain, warrior Salina leads an uprising against the invaders.

Lp: Don Murray, Carita, Donald Houston, Andrew Keir, Adrienne Corri.
Scrp: Clarke Reynolds. Prod: John Temple-Smith. Dir: Don Chaffey.

VILLAGE OF BRAY
1951 11m cert U bw
A tour of the Thames-side village of Bray.

VISA TO CANTON
1960 75m cert U colour
His brother held hostage by communists, the owner of a Hong Kong travel agency travels to Canton to seek out information for the Reds.
Lp: Richard Basehart, Lisa Gastoni, Eric Pohlmann.
Scrp: Gordon Wellesley. Prod: Michael Carreras. Dir: Michael Carreras.

WATCH IT SAILOR!
(see pages 150-151)
1961 89m cert U bw
Just prior to his wedding, a sailor runs into trouble with both the law — and his fiancée's mother.
Lp: Dennis Price, Liz Fraser, Irene Handl, Graham Stark, Vera Day.
Scrp: Falkland Cary, Philip King. Prod: Maurice Cowan. Dir: Wolf Rilla.

WE DO BELIEVE IN GHOSTS
1947 36m cert A bw
Three infamous ghosts haunt historic houses.
Lp: John Latham, Arthur Dibbs, Valerie Cornish.
Prod: Walter West. Dir: Walter West.

A WEEKEND WITH LULU
(see pages 150-151)
1961 89m cert A bw
Holidaying in an ice-cream van, an unmarried couple's designs are thwarted by the intervention of an overprotective mother.
Lp: Shirley Eaton, Leslie Phillips, Bob Monkhouse, Alfred Marks, Irene Handl.
Scrp: Ted Lloyd. Prod: Ted Lloyd. Dir: John Paddy Carstairs.

WHAT THE BUTLER SAW
1950 61m cert U bw
A native princess arrives at an English country house. The butler is her lover; confusion and chaos ensue.
Lp: Edward Rigby, Henry Mollison, Mercy Haystead.
Scrp: A.R. Rawlinson, Edward J. Mason. Prod: Anthony Hinds. Dir: Godfrey Grayson.

WHEN DINOSAURS RULED THE EARTH
(see pages 106-107)
1970 100m cert A colour
Blamed for the first appearance of the moon in the sky, a fair-haired girl is cast into a dangerous prehistoric wilderness.
Lp: Victoria Vetri, Robin Hawdon, Patrick Allen.
Scrp: Val Guest. Prod: Aida Young. Dir: Val Guest.

WHISPERING SMITH HITS LONDON
1952 82m cert U bw
An American detective, holidaying in England, investigates a murder that the local police believe to be suicide.
Lp: Richard Carlson, Greta Gynt, Herbert Lom, Rona Anderson, Alan Wheatley, Dora Bryan.
Scrp: John Gilling. Prod: Anthony Hinds. Dir: Francis Searle.

WHO KILLED VAN LOON?
1948 48m cert A bw

A diamond cutter's daughter is framed for the murder of the cutter's partner.
Lp: Raymond Lovell, Kay Bannerman, Robert Wyndham.
Scrp: Peter Cresswell. Prod: Anthony Hinds. Dir: Lionel Tomlinson, Gordon Kyle.

WINGS OF DANGER
1952 73m cert U bw
A charter pilot discovers that a friend is being blackmailed to smuggle counterfeit currency to the Continent.
Lp: Zachary Scott, Robert Beatty, Kay Kendall, Naomi Chance.
Scrp: John Gilling. Prod: Anthony Hinds. Dir: Terence Fisher.

THE WITCHES
(see pages 108-109)
Cast: Joan Fontaine (Gwen Mayfield), Kay Walsh (Stephanie Bax), Alec McCowen (Alan Bax), Ann Bell (Sally), Ingrid Brett (Linda), John Collin (Dowsett), Michele Dotrice (Valerie), Gwen Ffrangcon-Davies (Granny Rigg), Duncan Lamont (Bob Curd), Leonard Rossiter (Dr Wallis), Martin Stephens (Ronnie Dowsett), Carmel McSharry (Mrs Dowsett), Viola Keats (Mrs Curd), Shelagh Fraser (Mrs Creek), Bryan Marshall (Tom) and Kitty Attwood (Mrs McDowall), John Barrett (Mr Glass), Catherine Finn (Nurse), Prudence Hyman (Stephanie's Maid), Lizbeth Kent (1st villager), Artro Morris (Porter), Willie Payne (Adam), Charles Rea (Police sergeant), Rudolph Walker (Mark), Roy Desmond, Ken Robson, Brian Todd, Don Vernon, Terry Williams (Dancers).
Selected credits: M: Richard Rodney Bennett. M sup: Philip Martell. Dp: Arthur Grant BSC. Prod des: Bernard Robinson. Art dir: Don Mingaye. Sup ed: James Needs. Ed: Chris Barnes. Make-up: George Partleton. Choreographer: Denys Palmer. Scrp: Nigel Kneale. Prod: Anthony Nelson Keys. Dir: Cyril Frankel.

WOMEN WITHOUT MEN
1956 cert A bw
When an American singer escapes from prison, her trail leads the police to her fiancé — a wanted murderer.
Lp: Beverly Michaels, Joan Rice, Thora Hird, Avril Angers.
Scrp: Val Guest, Richard Landau. Prod: Anthony Hinds. Dir: Elmo Williams.

X THE UNKNOWN
(see pages 18-19)
Cast: Dean Jagger (Dr Adam Royston), Edward Chapman (Elliot), Leo McKern (McGill), Anthony Newley (Pte 'Spider' Webb), Jameson Clark (Jack Harding), William Lucas (Peter Elliot), Peter Hammond (Lt Bannerman), Marianne Brauns (Zena), Ian McNaughton ('Haggis'), Michael Ripper (Sgt Grimsdyke), John Harvey (Major Cartwright), Edwin Richfield (Old Soldier), Jane Aird (Vi Harding), Norman Macowan (Old Tom), Neil Hallet (Unwin), Kenneth Cope (Private Lancing), Michael Brook (Willie Harding), Fraser Hines (Ian) and Max Brimmell (Hospital Dir), Robert Bruce (Dr Kelly), Brown Derby (Vicar), Archie Duncan (Police Sgt Yeardye), Lawrence James (Second Guard), Edward Judd (Second Soldier), Stella Kemball (Nurse), Stephenson Lang (First Reporter), Phillip Levene (Security Man), Brian Peck (First Soldier), Anthony Sager (Gateman), Barry Steel (Soldier in Trench), John Stirling (Police Car Driver), John Stone (Gerry), Frank Taylor (PC Williams), Shaw Taylor (Police Radio Op), Neil Wilson (Russel).
Selected credits: M: James Bernard. M sup: John Hollingsworth. Dp: Gerald Gibbs. Ed: James Needs. Make-up: Philip Leakey. Spfx: Bowie Margutti Ltd, Jack Curtis. Scrp: Jimmy Sangster. Exec prod: Michael Carreras. Prod: Anthony Hinds. Dir: Leslie Norman.

YESTERDAY'S ENEMY
(see pages 28-29)
1959 95m cert A bw/scope
In the Burmese jungle, a British officer orders the execution of two locals in order to force an informant to talk.
Lp: Stanley Baker, Guy Rolfe, Leo McKern, Gordon Jackson.
Scrp: Peter R. Newman. Prod: Michael Carreras. Dir: Val Guest.

YOGA AND THE AVERAGE MAN
1951 26m cert U bw
Featurette.

YOGA AND YOU
1950 26m cert U bw
Featurette.

TELEVISION

This section lists the Hammer co-productions *Tales of Frankenstein*, *Journey to the Unknown*, *Hammer House of Mystery and Suspense* and *The World of Hammer*, plus the Cinema Arts International co-production *Hammer House of Horror* and Heidelberg Films-Bosustow Media Group co-production *Flesh and Blood*, both made "in association" with Hammer. Of Hammer's three originated series, only *Journey to the Unknown* received a network screening in America (and even then, not every episode was televised), and only *Hammer House of Horror* received a network screening in Britain. Establishing a meaningful transmission order for episodes is therefore impossible. The simultaneous shooting of many episodes in these series makes determining an accurate production order similarly difficult. For these reasons, episodes are considered in alphabetical order.

FLESH AND BLOOD — THE HAMMER HERITAGE OF HORROR
A two-part documentary examining the company's history, compiled in 1994. Narrated by Christopher Lee and Peter Cushing. (These programmes featured excerpts from the noteworthy BBC2 documentary *Hammer — The Studio That Dripped Blood!*, compiled in 1987.)

Selected series credits: Scrp: Ted Newsom. Assoc prod: Joe Dante, Bill Kelley, Roy Skeggs. Prod: Tee Bosustow, Ted Newsom. Dir: Ted Newsom.

HAMMER HOUSE OF HORROR
(see pages 172-173)

Selected series credits: M sup: Philip Martell. Story editor: Anthony Read. Exec prod: Brian Lawrence, David Reid. Prod: Roy Skeggs.

Carpathian Eagle
A series of murders evoke the legend of a Carpathian countess whose pet eagle tore out her lovers' hearts.
Lp: Anthony Valentine, Suzanne Danielle, Siân Phillips, Barry Stanton.
Scrp: Bernie Cooper, Francis Megahy. Dir: Francis Megahy.

Charlie Boy
Budding film producer Graham Elder inherits 'Charlie Boy', a carved African fetish with destructive voodoo powers.
Lp: Leigh Lawson, Angela Bruce, Marius Goring, Frances Cuka.
Scrp: Bernie Cooper, Francis Megahy. Dir: Robert Young.

Children of the Full Moon
When a couple holidaying in the West Country lose control of their car, they are taken in by a woman who lives with numerous children in a remote area of the forest.
Lp: Christopher Cazenove, Celia Gregory, Diana Dors, Robert Urquhart.
Scrp: Murray Smith. Dir: Tom Clegg.

Growing Pains
A strange poem in an old exercise book unleashes a vengeful spirit from beyond the grave.
Lp: Barbara Kellermann, Gary Bond, Norman Beaton, Matthew Blakstad.
Scrp: Nicholas Palmer. Dir: Francis Megahy.

Guardian of the Abyss
When an antiques dealer purchases a mirror with mysterious powers, the consequences include human sacrifice.
Lp: Ray Lonnen, Rosalyn Landor, John Carson, Paul Darrow.
Scrp: David Fisher. Dir: Don Sharp.

The House that Bled to Death
To the horror of its new occupants, 42 Colman Road begins to relive its gruesome history.
Lp: Nicholas Ball, Rachel Davis, Brian Croucher, Pat Maynard.
Scrp: David Lloyd. Dir: Tom Clegg.

The Mark of Satan
Edwin is convinced that the forces of evil are conspiring against him — everywhere he sees threats, and the number 666...
Lp: Peter McEnery, Georgina Hale, Emrys James, Anthony Brown.
Scrp: Don Shaw. Dir: Don Leaver.

Rude Awakening
Estate agent Norman Shenley is trapped in a recurring nightmare. His only ally throughout is his attractive secretary Lolly — but is she all that she seems?
Lp: Denholm Elliott, James Laurenson, Pat Heywood, Lucy Gutteridge.
Scrp: Gerald Savory. Dir: Peter Sasdy.

The Silent Scream
A German pet shop owner befriends a released convict, and offers him a job. The rear of the shop, however, hides a sinister secret.
Lp: Peter Cushing, Brian Cox, Elaine Donnelly, Anthony Carrick.
Scrp: Francis Essex. Dir: Alan Gibson.

The Thirteenth Reunion
When a journalist is assigned to investigate a dubious slimming clinic, her boyfriend is killed in a freak accident. Then his body disappears...
Lp: Julia Foster, Dinah Sheridan, Richard Pearson, Norman Bird.
Scrp: Jeremy Burnham. Dir: Peter Sasdy.

The Two Faces of Evil
A holidaying family are faced with a terrifying threat — who is the strange hitch-hiker?
Lp: Anna Calder-Marshall, Gary Raymond, Pauline Delany, Philip Latham.
Scrp: Ranald Graham. Dir: Alan Gibson.

Visitor from the Grave
When an intruder terrorises a girl in a lonely cottage she kills him with a shotgun. Her boyfriend buries the body in the woods, but the ordeal has only just begun.

Lp: Kathryn Leigh Scott, Simon MacCorkindale, Gareth Thomas, Mia Nadasi.
Scrp: John Elder. Dir: Peter Sasdy.

Witching Time
A strange young woman is found hiding in a barn near an isolated farm house. Can she really be a seventeenth century witch?
Lp: Jon Finch, Patricia Quinn, Prunella Gee, Ian McCulloch.
Scrp: Anthony Read. Dir: Don Leaver.

HAMMER HOUSE OF MYSTERY AND SUSPENSE
(see pages 174-175)

Selected series credits: M sup: Philip Martell. Executive story editor: Don Houghton. Story editor [except 'Czech Mate', 'A Distant Scream', 'The Late Nancy Irving' and 'The Sweet Scent of Death']: John Peacock. Assoc prod ['Black Carrion', 'A Distant Scream' only]: John Hough. Exec prod: Brian Lawrence. Prod: Roy Skeggs.

And the Wall Came Tumbling Down
The demolition of the church of St. Peters uncovers a sealed alcove containing two skeletons and a painting with a diabolical history.
Lp: Barbi Benton, Gareth Hunt, Brian Deacon, Peter Wyngarde.
Scrp: Dennis Spooner, John Peacock. Dir: Paul Annett.

Black Carrion
Paul Chater and Cora Berlaine set out in search of elusive sixties pop stars the Verne Brothers — and follow their trail to the ghost village of Briars Frome.
Lp: Season Hubley, Leigh Lawson, Norman Bird, Allan Love, Julian Litman.
Scrp: Don Houghton. Dir: John Hough.

Child's Play
The Preston family awake one morning to find all their clocks stopped, their luxury home encased in metal — and the temperature rising...
Lp: Mary Crosby, Nicholas Clay, Debbie Chasen.
Scrp: Graham Wassell. Dir: Val Guest.

The Corvini Inheritance
To help out a terrorised neighbour, an auction room security man sets up a camera previously used to monitor jewellery with a dark history.
Lp: David McCallum, Jan Francis, Terence Alexander.
Scrp: David Fisher. Dir: Gabrielle Beaumont.

Czech Mate
Troubled couple Vicky and John Duncan attempt a reconciliation in Prague — but John vanishes, and Vicky discovers a corpse in their hotel room.
Lp: Susan George, Patrick Mower, Richard Heffer, Peter Vaughan.
Scrp: Jeremy Burnham. Dir: John Hough.

A Distant Scream
A man named Harris, imprisoned for years for the murder of a girl, is close to death — and will not die easy unless he knows the identity of her true killer.
Lp: David Carradine, Stephanie Beacham, Stephen Greif, Stephen Chase.
Scrp: Martin Worth. Dir: John Hough.

In Possession
Frank and Sylvia Daly suffer a series of bizarre and terrifying visions from another time.

Lp: Carol Lynley, Christopher Cazenove, David Healy, Judy Loe.
Scrp: Michael J. Bird. Dir: Val Guest.

Last Video and Testament

The young widow of an electronics magnate hopes for a new life with her lover, but her dead husband's videotaped will suggests otherwise.
Lp: Deborah Raffin, David Langton, Oliver Tobias, Christopher Scoular.
Scrp: Roy Russell. Dir: Peter Sasdy.

The Late Nancy Irving

A top woman golfer, forced off the road in her car, awakes in a remote hospital — and discovers that the outside world believes her to be dead.
Lp: Christina Raines, Marius Goring, Simon Williams, Tony Anholt.
Scrp: David Fisher. Dir: Peter Sasdy.

Mark of the Devil

Insolvent murderer Frank Rowlett is marked by the tattooist's needle of his victim, and a terrible mark spreads across his body.
Lp: Dirk Benedict, Jenny Seagrove, George Sewell, John Paul.
Scrp: Brian Clemens. Dir: Val Guest.

Paint Me a Murder

The last work of artist Luke Lorenz — a man drowning at sea — is presumed to mirror his own apparent demise…
Lp: Michelle Phillips, James Laurenson, David Robb, Alan Lake.
Scrp: Jesse Lasky Jnr, Pat Silver. Dir: Alan Cooke.

The Sweet Scent of Death

A young couple discover an English girl dying amidst a rose bush in New York's Central Park. The death will have consequences ten years on…
Lp: Dean Stockwell, Shirley Knight, Michael Gothard, Carmen Du Sautoy.
Scrp: Brian Clemens. Dir: Peter Sasdy.

Tennis Court

Maggie and Harry Dowl inherit an English house — and find its dilapidated tennis court to be possessed by a strange and murderous force.
Lp: Peter Graves, Hannah Gordon, Jonathan Newth, Cyril Shaps.
Scrp: Andrew Sinclair. Dir: Cyril Frankel.

JOURNEY TO THE UNKNOWN

(see pages 124–125)

Selected series credits: Main title theme: Harry Robinson. M sup: Philip Martell. Post-production consultant: Robert Mintz. Sup ed: James Needs GBFE. Story editor: John Gould. Executive consultant: Jack Fleishmann. Exec prod: Joan Harrison [except 'The Killing Bottle', 'The Madison Equation', 'Stranger in the Family': Norman Lloyd]. Prod: Anthony Hinds.

The Beckoning Fair One

Recovering from a breakdown, an artist becomes obsessed by the portrait of a woman killed at his house twenty-five years earlier.
Lp: Robert Lansing, Gabrielle Drake, John Fraser, Larry Noble.
Scrp: William Woods, John Gould. Dir: Don Chaffey.

Do Me a Favor and Kill Me

A fading actor asks a friend to kill him in return for ten per cent of his life insurance money, thus sparing him obscurity.
Lp: Joseph Cotten, Judy Parfitt, Douglas Wilmer, Kenneth Haigh.
Scrp: Stanley Miller. Dir: Gerry O'Hara.

Eve

A rejected fantasist falls in love with a shop window mannequin, whom he believes to be alive.
Lp: Dennis Waterman, Carol Lynley, Michael Gough, Angela Lovell.
Scrp: Michael Ashe, Paul Wheeler. Dir: Robert Stevens.

Girl of My Dreams

Unwilling precognitive Carrie Clark is exploited by an opportunist who has seen one of her predictions become horribly true.
Lp: Michael Callan, Zena Walker, Justine Lord, Jan Holden.
Scrp: Robert Bloch, Michael J. Bird. Dir: Peter Sasdy.

The Indian Spirit Guide

Unscrupulous private detective Jerry Crown is commissioned by a wealthy widow to root out false clairvoyants.
Lp: Julie Harris, Tom Adams, Tracy Reed, Catherine Lacey.
Scrp: Robert Bloch. Dir: Roy Ward Baker.

Jane Brown's Body

A young woman gasses herself, but is brought back to life by a doctor who uses an experimental drug on her.
Lp: Stefanie Powers, David Buck, Alan MacNaughtan, Sarah Lawson.
Scrp: Anthony Skene. Dir: Alan Gibson.

The Killing Bottle

Composer Jimmy Rintoul needs his inheritance to launch his career, but brother Randolph stands in his way.
Lp: Roddy McDowell, Ingrid Brett, Barry Evans, William Marlowe.
Scrp: Julian Bond. Dir: John Gibson.

The Last Visitor

Holidaying at Southcliff-on-Sea's Beach Hotel, Barbara King finds a strange figure in her room one night.
Lp: Patty Duke, Kay Walsh, Geoffrey Bayldon, Joan Newell.
Scrp: Alfred Shaughnessy. Dir: Don Chaffey.

The Madison Equation

Enraged by her affair, the husband of a brilliant computer scientist programs her Complex OB computer to electrocute her.
Lp: Barbara Bel Geddes, Allan Cuthbertson, Sue Lloyd, Paul Daneman.
Scrp: Michael J. Bird. Dir: Rex Firkin.

Matakitas is Coming

A journalist researches the 1927 death of a young girl in the very library where she was murdered, apparently pledged to the Devil by her killer.
Lp: Vera Miles, Leon Lissek, Gay Hamilton, Lyn Pinkney.
Scrp: Robert Heverley. Dir: Michael Lindsay-Hogg.

Miss Belle

Embittered Miss Belle Weston, whose sister married the man she loved, brings their orphaned son up as a girl.
Lp: George Maharis, Barbara Jefford, Kim Burfield, Adrienne Posta.
Scrp: Sarett Rudley. Dir: Robert Stevens.

The New People

Luther Ames plays Mephistopheles is his small circle of friends — and condemns to death anyone who breaks his 'laws'.
Lp: Robert Reed, Jennifer Hilary, Patrick Allen, Milo O'Shea.
Scrp: Oscar Millard, John Gould. Dir: Peter Sasdy.

One On an Island

Alec Worthing's sloop *Victoria* is wrecked and he is marooned on a desert island. Then a girl called Vicki walks out of the sea…
Lp: Brandon De Wilde, Suzanna Leigh, John Ronane, Victor Maddern.
Scrp: Oscar Millard. Dir: Noel Howard.

Paper Dolls

Young Rodney Blake compels a school bully to throw himself out of a window; he may be one of four identical quads influenced by the powerful Steven.
Lp: Michael Tolan, Nanette Newman, Barnaby Shaw, Roderick Shaw.
Scrp: Oscar Millard. Dir: James Hill.

Poor Butterfly

A man is invited to a party thrown by one Sir Robert Sawyer, of whom he's never heard — and is unaware that the party's venue burned down forty years before.
Lp: Chad Everett, Bernard Lee, Fay Compton, Edward Fox.
Scrp: Jeremy Paul. Dir: Alan Gibson.

Somewhere in a Crowd

A TV commentator sees five strangely familiar faces in a crowd watching a disastrous ship's launching. Other tragedies occur; they are always present.
Lp: David Hedison, Ann Bell, Jane Asher, Jeremy Longhurst.
Scrp: Michael J. Bird. Dir: Alan Gibson.

Stranger in the Family

Science and showbusiness attempt to exploit a mutant boy with strange mental powers.
Lp: Janice Rule, Maurice Kaufmann, Anthony Corlan, Phil Brown.
Scrp: David Campton. Dir: Peter Duffel.

TALES OF FRANKENSTEIN

(see pages 36–37)

Selected series credits: Assoc prod: Curt Siodmak. Prod: Michael Carreras.

The Face in the Tombstone Mirror

[pilot episode]
Baron Von Frankenstein places the brain of a man who once pleaded with him to relieve his terminal illness inside a new body.
Lp: Anton Diffring, Helen Westcott, Don Megowan.
Scrp: Catherine Kuttner, Henry Kuttner. Dir: Curt Siodmak.

THE WORLD OF HAMMER

A series of excerpts from Hammer films, compiled in 1990. Narrated by Oliver Reed.

Selected series credits: Title theme: Bruce Bennett. Scrp: Ashley Sidaway, Robert Sidaway. Ed: Ashley Sidaway. Exec prod: John Thompson. Prod: Robert Sidaway.

The series comprised:
Chiller; Costumers; The Curse of Frankenstein; Dracula & the Undead; Hammer; Hammer Stars: Peter Cushing; Hammer Stars: Christopher Lee; Lands Before Time; Mummies, Werewolves & the Living Dead; Sci-Fi; Trials of War, Vamp; Wicked Women.